2500

DESCARTES' MEDICAL PHILOSOPHY

René Descartes from Geometria, à Renato Des Cartes, Anno 1637 Gallicè edita;
postea autem. Unà cum Notis Florimondi De Beune . . . *(Amsterdam: Ludovico
and Daniel Elzevirios, 1659).*

DESCARTES'
Medical Philosophy

*The Organic Solution
to the Mind-Body Problem*

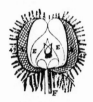

RICHARD B. CARTER

THE JOHNS HOPKINS UNIVERSITY PRESS
Baltimore and London

The Johns Hopkins University Press, Baltimore, Maryland 21218
The Johns Hopkins Press Ltd., London

Library of Congress Cataloging in Publication Data

Carter, Richard B. (Richard Burnett), 1931–
   Descartes' medical philosophy.

   Includes bibliographical references and index.
   1. Medicine—Philosophy. 2. Descartes, René,
1596–1650. 3. Medicine—Philosophy—History.
I. Title. [DNLM: 1. Philosophy, Medical—Biography.
WZ 100 C324d]
R723.C428   1983   128   82–14933
ISBN 0–8018–2894–5

Health is a state of complete physical, mental, and social well-being and not merely the absence of disease.
—Preamble to the Constitution of the World Health Organization

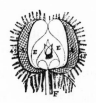

Contents

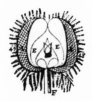

Acknowledgments

I TAKE GREAT PLEASURE in acknowledging my debt to those teachers and friends on whom I principally depended for the writing of this book.

Preeminate among my teachers was the late Jacob Klein, who manifested in his own work the best and clearest models for careful scholarship of which I am aware; furthermore, in his own work and life, Professor Klein provided the very model of what Philo has called νηφάλιος μεθή ("sober intoxication"). My debt to him as a teacher is endless, and I am grateful to have known and worked with him.

Outstanding among my more recent friends are James J. Lynch and his associates at the University of Maryland School of Medicine. Professor Lynch gave me help, untiring criticism and encouragement, and a privileged introduction to a host of his extremely helpful professional colleagues. Principal among these were Marshall Rennels, Professor of Anatomy and Director of Graduate Education in Anatomy and Professor of Neurology, and Ernest C. B. Hall-Craggs, Professor and Head, Division of Gross Anatomy. Dr. Rennels cheerfully and wittily offered me detailed directions for my scholarly journeys through the modern brain using Descartes' antique road map and Dr. Hall-Craggs did the same for the whole body. Without the detailed help of these two scholars of the human body I should have missed many points of central importance in Descartes' anatomical and physiological writings.

I am particularly grateful to Leon Wurmser, M.D., whose reading, critical remarks, and thousandfold encouragement were decisively important—and given at a time when his own business was most pressing and could have been expected to be totally preoccupying. Dr. Wurmser has always been a good friend when needed, and his help has been crucial to the timely completion of this book. Likewise, Christopher Kelly, Professor of Political Philosophy, read the manuscript very closely and discriminatingly and gave me all the help asked for, and more. George Balis, M.D., Professor of Psychiatry and Director of Medical Education in Psychiatry at the University of Maryland School of Medicine, took time out of his cruelly busy schedule to read the manuscript and to encourage me with his generous comments on it.

Elizabeth Bobrick Carter cheerfully saw me through the delivery of what would surely have been a very difficult birth had it not been for the infinitely resourceful exercise of her maieutic skills; her help and labor, precisely when it was least convenient for her to offer them, have shown her to be a friend indeed, in matters both great and small. My debt to Arthur Danto, Professor of Philosophy at Columbia University, is great; never obtrusive, Professor Danto was never too busy when called upon for help.

Mary Amster of Putney, Vermont, was the principal illustrator of this book. Her work speaks for itself, but its special appropriateness calls for my special thanks.

And next, there are two friends whose timely and gracious help in very difficult circumstances made leisure and quiet possible, without which the proper period for gestation would have been seriously shortened. Raymond S. Blake, C.L.U., and Anne C. Lewis, M.D., provided help so gracefully and quietly that anything like an accurate expression of my gratitude might seem to them an overstatement.

Finally, I take great pleasure in thanking William Sisler and the whole staff of the Johns Hopkins University Press for slapping my long-gestating conception into life. I am especially grateful to Maria Coughlin, who acted as the manuscript's pediatrician, making sure that the issue had the correct number of fingers and toes.

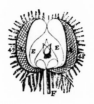

Author's Note

I WISH TO DRAW the reader's attention to several points that might give rise to unnecessary questions. The first of these is the matter of the differences of orthography in the French texts that I cite, and the second concerns my translations.

Concerning spelling, I have almost everywhere faithfully followed that found in my largest single source of Cartesian texts, the Adam and Tannery edition (12 volumes plus supplement; Paris: Leopold Cerf, Imprimeur-Editeur, 1897–1913). In that edition, the spelling of the holographs and first editions was exactly reproduced. Since several of Descartes' works were published in Holland and others in France, and, since the two countries followed a slightly different French "orthography," the reader will discover several different spellings of the same word, e.g., the word translated from French as "body" occurs both as *cors* and as *corps*. Again, the modern reader of French, i.e. of the Pleiade edition, need not be put off by the constant occurrence of *-oi-* in the place of the modern *-ai-* in the secondary endings of verbs. Also, in most places the reader will find that the use of the circumflexed vowel to indicate the absence of a silent 's' before a consonant is not used, e.g., *tête* will be spelled as *teste*. Several of these and other cases are never entirely normalized in the texts, and the reader will have to make the necessary adjustment in each occurrence.

The problem of Latin translations, especially, is a little more complicated. Descartes' Latin is often baroque and sometimes quite stilted; his style is often prolix—so much so, indeed, that the resulting ambiguities seem purposeful. In the translations that follow, I attempt not to interpret those ambiguities, but only to render them into English. They are thus often lacking in grace, but, given the Charybdis of "profound" interpretive translation and the Scylla of jagged accuracy, I have chosen Scylla.

DESCARTES' MEDICAL PHILOSOPHY

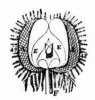

Introduction

There is nothing with which we can more fruitfully occupy
ourselves than to try to know ourselves. And the utility
which each of us has a right to hope for from that
knowledge not only concerns Ethics, as it appears to most
of us at first glance, but particularly Medicine, too. . . .
—Descartes, *The Description of the Human Body and*
All Its Functions

MEDICINE, ETHICS, AND THE MIND–BODY PROBLEM

And, although all these movements cease in the body when
it dies and the soul leaves it, no one should infer from this
that it is one and the same cause which brings it about
that the body is no longer proper to produce these motions,
and that the soul absents itself from that body.
—Descartes, *The Description of the Human Body and*
All Its Functions[1]

THE PHILOSOPHY of the present age is a philosophy that supports two individual and, at first sight, distinct, freedoms. One freedom is positive and the other is negative. The positive freedom is the freedom of each individual to pursue personal fulfillment as he may see that fulfillment. The other, negative freedom is freedom from limitations imposed by physical sickness and political restraints—from all tyranny or dictatorship. These two freedoms are obviously connected: We need freedom from restraint in order to have freedom to pursue personal fulfillment.

Today, most people believe that these two freedoms are rooted in nature and, in particular, are guaranteed by what is popularly known as the "first law of nature," *self-preservation*. According to this "law of laws," each and every definite entity in the universe, alive or not, is characterized by the fact that it acts in and reacts to its environment in a manner that maximizes its chances of survival. An unusually clear statement of this view is to be found in Lecture I of Pavlov's enormously influential book, *Conditioned Reflexes:*[2]

> It seems obvious that the whole activity of the organism should conform to definite laws. If the animal were not in exact correspondence with its environment, it would, sooner or later, cease to exist . . . The animal must respond to changes in the environment in such a manner that its responsive activity is directed towards the preservation of its existence. This conclusion holds also if we consider the living organism in terms of physical and chemical science. Every material system can exist as an entity only so long as its internal forces, attraction and cohesion, etc., balance the external forces acting upon it. This is true for an ordinary stone just as much as for the most complex chemical substances; and its truth should be recognized also for the animal organism. Being a definite circumscribed material system, it can only continue to exist as long as it is in continuous equlibrium with the forces external to it. . . .[3]

Pavlov sees that self-preservation also involves very highly complex processes that include what certainly appears to be conscious thought. He says:

> As another example of a reflex which is very much neglected, we may refer to what may be called the *investigatory reflex.* I call it the "What-is-it?" reflex. It is this reflex which brings about the immediate response in man and animals to the slightest changes in the world about them, so that they immediately orientate their appropriate receptor organ in accordance with the perceptible quality in the agent bringing about the change, making full investigation of it. The biological significance of this reflex is obvious: If the animal were not provided with such a reflex its life would hang by a thread. In man this reflex has been greatly developed with far-reaching results, being represented in its highest form by inquisitiveness—the parent of the scientific method through which we may hope one day to come to a true orientation in knowledge of the world around us.[4]

When we reflect that, in one time, a sense of wonder was thought to be the beginning of philosophy and science, and that now their beginning is the fear of death, we may well ask what happened, and who persuaded us that all vital endeavors are aimed at self-preservation.

Although Pavlov might not be expected to be very specific about the antecedents of his views, he is nevertheless entirely clear:

> The physiologist must take his own path, where a trail has already been blazed for him. Three hundred years ago Descartes evolved the idea of the reflex. Starting from the assumption that animals behaved simply as machines, he regarded every activity of the organism as a *necessary* reaction to some external stimulus, the connection

between the stimulus and the response being made through a definite nervous path: and this connection, he stated, was the fundamental purpose of the nervous structures in the animal body. This was the basis on which the study of the nervous system was firmly established . . . Descartes' conception of the reflex was constantly and fruitfully applied in these studies. . . .[5]

Thus, for Descartes, and for Pavlov 300 years later, the living organism is a self-preservative mechanism. Today, we tend to agree with our contemporary, John M. Reiner, a theoretical biologist, who titled one of his books *The Organism as an Adaptive Control System.*[6] In other words, we tend to consider something all but identical to the fear of death as the ultimate motive and rationale for all organic activity, and, according to Pavlov, again following Descartes, this applies for the *whole* of material existence, animate or inanimate.

Pavlov clearly grasps the relation between his own notion of reflex and the generally accepted notion of the *instinct* for self-preservation: he shows this when he establishes the link between neurological investigations and a theoretical concern with self-preservation. He says:

I shall now turn to the description of our material, first giving as a preliminary an account of the general conception of the reflex, of specific physiological reflexes, and of the so-called "instincts." Our starting-point has been Descartes' idea of the nervous reflex. This is a genuine scientific conception, since it implies necessity. It may be summed up as follows: An external or internal stimulus falls on some one or other nervous receptor and gives rise to a nervous impulse; this nervous impulse is transmitted along nerve fibres to the central nervous system, and here, on account of existing nervous connections, it gives rise to a fresh impulse which passes along outgoing nerve fibres to the active organ, where it excites a special activity of the cellular structures. Thus a stimulus appears to be connected of necessity with a definite response, as cause with effect. It seems obvious that the whole activity of the organism should conform to definite laws. If the animal were not in exact correspondence with its environment it would, sooner or later, cease to exist.[7]

As Pavlov certainly knew, humans in large measure conform to natural, definite laws, through their more or less rational search for those laws. How, then, is science possible, if human scientists live in a world of cause-and-effect instincts? At what point do we cease to be guided by our instincts and begin to be guided by our search for an adequate science? Such a search is the result of conscious choice; it is not a construct of instinct.

Descartes, whom Pavlov correctly identifies as the father of the mechanistic, deterministic, neurophysiological psychobiology of our age, faced the problem of freedom versus nature or instinct as no one since him has been able to do. This present book is concerned with his solution to the dilemma: How can we have a compound body, fabricated or programmed for maximal survival, and, at the same time, have the choice and the freedom to pursue the hypotheses of a science that provides us with the best means to survive as well as the best means to fulfill whatever potential we have beyond mere survival—if any?

Descartes used the science of medicine to construct a solution to that dilemma. For, the living body is a compound body formed of organ systems, and self-preservation is largely a matter of preserving all those organs and their interconnections intact.[8] Thus, if life is solely the motion compounded of the individual processes originating in the organs, then whatever it is that makes life both begin and continue once begun should be the same as what makes life worth living and of value to the healthy individual. This is how Descartes initially connected medicine, traditionally the healing art, with ethics, which traditionally contains precepts concerning the goals and ends of human life and action.[9]

To pursue this connection between medicine and ethics further: Cartesian physics is largely concerned with simple bodies, what we might today consider masses in motion. Once we deal with compound bodies, we leave the realm of physics, which deals with natural motions that can break up compound bodies, and thus destroy them, by resolving them back into the elements or components of which they were formed. After physics, which deals with simple bodies, we enter into the realm of medicine, which, after Descartes, becomes the study of organisms—defined as compound bodies or systems of simple bodies. In particular, medicine has become the study of organisms that are systems of simple bodies whose compound motion is life itself; the task of medicine is to teach humans how best to preserve the systems of organs intact. On the other hand, from medicine evolves Descartes' ethics, which deals with the relations among several of these (living, sentient) compound bodies, prescribing to all of them their mutual interrelations which permit them to act *as if* they were each organic parts of a larger group—society. Medicine thus secondarily becomes the study of how individuals living with other individuals effectively relate to each other in a way that parallels how the heart, liver, stomach, and spleen relate in order to keep the compound body alive and functioning.

In the 1840s and 1880s, the time of Karl Marx, a group of medically trained German radicals also connected medicine and political theory. They wrote and spoke about an ethical view of medicine, characterizing it as being essentially concerned with both the interrelations of the parts of the individual, compound human body and with the social interrelations to be found among the human individuals who comprise the parts of the state, or body politic. In the period just before and after the radical leftist revolution of 1848, a group of German physicians spoke very clearly and eloquently on this issue. The best-remembered of this group is the great Rudolf Virchow, whose book, *Cellular Pathology*, laid the groundwork for both clinical oncology and clinical pathology.

The notion of ethical, social medicine, as defined by the German group, is discussed extensively in George Rosen's *From Medical Police to Social Medicine*.[10] In the chapter "Health, History, and the Social Sciences," Rosen states that overcrowding due to poor city planning leads to sociopathic behavior, and that poor, overcrowded housing leads to pessimism, passivity, poor health, difficulty in household management, and child abuse (p. 37). In the chapter "What Is Social Medicine," under the subheading "Medicine—a Social Science. The idea of 1848," Rosen refers to the 1847 epidemic of typhus in Upper Silesia:

> Rudolf Virchow conceived of this outbreak as due to a complex of
> social and economic factors, and consequently expected little from
> any medical therapy. Instead, he proposed thoroughgoing social
> reform which in most general terms comprised "complete and
> unrestricted democracy, education, freedom and prosperity." [p. 61]

After manning a "red" barricade in Berlin on March 18, 1848, Virchow announced: ". . . my medical creed merges with my political and social creed" (p. 62). Virchow also showed his political sympathies by founding a weekly paper, *Die medicinische Reform (The Medical Reform)*. He said of his paper: "*The Medical Reform* comes into being at a time when the overthrow of our old political institutions is not yet completed, but when from all sides plans are being laid and steps taken toward a new political structure" (p. 62). Rosen continues, "This awareness of the relations of medicine to social problems Virchow formulated in the somewhat rhetorical but striking slogan:

> Medicine is a social science, and politics nothing but medicine on a
> grand scale.

(A major goal of this present work is to show what it means to say that social science and political science are both nothing but medicine.)

Virchow was not alone. In 1847, his associate, Salomon Neumann, wrote in *Die oeffentliche Gesundheitspflege und das Eigenthum (Public Health Care and Property)*: "medical science is intrinsically and essentially a *social* science, and as long as this is not recognized in practice we shall not be able to enjoy its benefits and shall have to be satisfied with an empty shell and a sham" (p. 64). Virchow's editorial assistant, Leubscher, stated that "medicine is purely social science" (p. 64). As if to explain that sentiment, Neumann stated:

If it is the duty of social man to combat and to help to endure the dangers which develop precisely because of social life, then it is equally clear that the state is obliged to combat and where possible destroy not only natural dangers, but those dangers to human life as well. [p. 64]

For, according to Neumann, "It is the duty of society, i.e., of the state, as a fundamental condition of all enjoyment and activity, to protect, and when endangered, to save, the lives and health of the citizens" (p. 64).

Virchow did not consider medicine to be some sort of charity or act of kindness of an enlightened government; for Virchow, the *definition* of democratic government is essentially tied up with the notion of health and the medical safeguards to health. He said:

The democratic state desires that all its citizens enjoy a state of well-being, for it recognizes that they all have equal rights. Since general equality of rights leads to self-government, the state also has the right to hope that everyone will know how through his own labor to achieve and to maintain a state of well-being within the limits of the laws set up by the people themselves. However, the conditions of well-being are health and education, so that it is the task of the state to provide on the broadest possible basis the means for maintaining and promoting health and education through public action . . . Thus it is not enough for the state to guarantee every citizen the basic necessities for existence, and to assist everyone whose labor does not suffice for him to acquire these necessities; the state must do more. It must assist everyone so far that he will have the conditions necessary for a healthy existence. [p. 64]

Rosen continues:

Virchow also developed a theory of epidemic disease as a manifestation of social and cultural maladjustment. Reasoning by analogy, he drew a parallel between the individual and the body politic [a pairing that provides the basic subject of this book]—"If disease is an expression of individual life under unfavorable conditions, then epidemics must be indicative of major disturbances of mass life." [pp. 65–66]

In sum, Virchow's argument allows that, *if* the state is the creation of the people living in it, then state-sponsored medical research and health care are the way the citizen, as the creator of the state, acts to preserve himself. What 'fight and flight' are to the individual citizen, clinical intervention at the onset of illness or publicly mandated health measures against possible diseases are to the citizen as a part of the body politic. It is striking that the 1946 preamble to the Constitution of the World Health Organization, which states, "Health is a state of complete physical, mental, and social well-being, and not merely the absence of disease," could have been written by Virchow, Neumann, or Leubscher over a century ago.

It is also something very like this, we argue, that Descartes had in mind when he said, "I think, therefore I am." That is, *medical* thinking is the thinking that preserves: it is the only thinking that, *as* thinking, implies the continuous "I am."

Descartes stated precisely how important the study and science of medicine were to him. At the end of the sixth part of his 1637 *Discourse on Method* (his first published work), he wrote:

> I have resolved not to use the time left to me to live in any way other than to try to acquire some knowledge of nature of such a kind that one can draw from it rules for medicine [*règules pour la médecine*] more firm than those which have been attained up to the present; and I shall say that my inclination so strongly removes me from any other kinds of designs [*de toute sorte d'autres desseins*] . . . that if any occasions constrained me to busy myself with other designs, I do not believe that I should be capable of succeeding in them.[11]

Again, in a letter of 1645 to William Cavendish, the Marquis of Newcastle, Descartes stated, "The preservation of health has always been the principal end of my studies [*La conservation de la santé a été de tout temps le principal but de mes études*]."[12] Since Descartes wrote this eight years after he published his *Meditations* and four years after he had published his magnum opus, *The Principles of Philosophy*, those two works either supported his studies of "the conservation of health" or they were directly concerned with those studies.

That these two passages should have largely escaped generations of Descartes' interpreters is truly astonishing, but there is certainly no reason why we, in our turn, should be so accommodating as to carry on this tradition of misdirected reading of the texts. Reasons for this misdirection are touched upon in the following section. However, at this point we are particularly interested in the first of these two statements of Descartes' design (*dessein*), in which he distinguished between his medicine and his "studies of nature"—what we today know as mathematical physics. In making that distinction, Descartes clearly showed that he considered his mathematical physics to be only a step in his progress toward a more important goal—one associated with medicine. This means that his essential elaboration of analytic geometry prior to 1623, as well as his mighty works in optics, meteorology, cosmology, dynamics, and, of course, in medicine, all were intended by him to be unequivocally subordinate to his interest in "la conservation de la santé." We might expect, because Descartes was a great theoretical and original thinker, that theoretical pursuits would have been, of all studies, most highly valued by him, and that his social or philanthropic interests were a mere matter of necessity—designed, perhaps, to fight off the restrictions of a very repressive censorship exercised by both church and state. This, however, is simply not the case. Whatever charms the exercise of his own theoretical genius may have held for him, Descartes very seldom, if ever, failed to subordinate his theoretical speculations to his practical, philanthropic designs. For most men, the practical comes so much more easily than the originality of natural genius, that it is very difficult, but nonetheless absolutely necessary, for us to believe that Descartes valued the fruits of his practical, philanthropic activity far above his theoretical, speculative studies.

Descartes, no less than Virchow, envisioned a social revolution based on his philosophy of medicine. That his thinking helped forge the revolution known as the Enlightenment was shown in d'Alembert's 1751 preface to his *Encyclopédie*,[13] which identified Descartes both as a towering figure in the development of theoretical mathematics and as "the leader of a band of revolutionaries." Descartes' role as an architect of Liberalism via his medicine has been obscured, largely it seems, by his strange and puzzling disposition as a thinker: as few others have been able to do, he entirely subordinated his theoretical concerns to his concerns with public improvement. Descartes' philanthropy was supported, ultimately, by theoretical investigations into mathematical physics, and finally by the restriction of mathematical physics to living human bodies.

Descartes' medical theory is, of course, no more Liberal political philosophy than Virchow's epidemiology is Liberal political science, but medicine can provide very clear guidelines for social and political action. A simple illustration of such a support role can be seen in the relation of the modern hospital to its environment, into which it gives up the newly restored whom it has treated. If a hospital works *in vacuo,* to the extent that it turns out of its doors biologically and structurally sound humans into a desert lacking food or water, that hospital, although certainly concerned with "medicine," is only very partially concerned with "the conservation of health." Disease-free humans starve or die of thirst as well as the sickly (if not quite so rapidly). Thus, in its fullest signification, we can see sober grounds for taking Descartes' expression, "the conservation of health," as pointing to a design that locates healthy, sound, functioning humans in an environment that is productive enough to support them. Descartes' medical philosophy both challenged the prevailing philosophy and provided a model for a new kind of philosophy.

The philosophy that Descartes' medical theory helped to overturn was a Christianized version of the philosophy of the pagan philosopher Aristotle. Today we know that philosophy as Scholaticism, and its influence was as all-pervasive then as modern science is today. It provided the theoretical framework for every human enterprise, from sexual behavior to medicine, political thought, and theology. Moreover, it was widely used to support arguments in favor of monarchy as the most Christian form of government.[14]

Descartes used his medical theory negatively in his attempt to overthrow Scholasticism and all that it supported; he used it positively to provide a scientific model for a program that aimed to make humans happy. In order to clarify this, we here review the formation of Scholasticism, which largely prevailed throughout Europe in Descartes' lifetime, and, in particular, we consider the place of Aristotle in Scholasticism and the place of medicine in the overthrow of the Christianized Aristotelianism that comprised Scholasticism.

Translations of Aristotle's physical and biological texts became available to the Christian West in the period spanning approximately 1150 to 1250. Their effect was profound. The historian Émile Bréhier tells us, "These translations opened a virgin field to scholars and for the first time provided them with direct knowledge of pagan thought uncontaminated by Christian thought."[15] The first reaction to these translations was to realign the studies of the day into a mold following those presented by the new texts. Bréhier writes of an Archdeacon of Segovia, Dominicus Gundissalinus (d. 1151), who imitated the Arabic tradition of the great scientific philosopher Alfarabi, and taught Aristotle's texts in the following order: physics, celestial mechanics, zoology, and *only then* psychology.[16] As early as A.D. 1150, it was once again grasped that a scientific study of the psyche of the living animal, including humans, presupposed a thorough technical training in physics, astronomy, and zoology. However, this soon changed as the texts were Christianized. By the 1250s, the teacher of Thomas Aquinus, Albert the Great, was showing signs of the stress he was under to Christianize Aristotle. For, Bréhier tells us of Albert, that "in his *Summa of Theology*, he warns that there are two concepts of the soul, . . . the Aristotelian concept of the soul as the form of the organic body and the theological concept based on the writings of St. Augustine. . . ."[17]

Three hundred years later, near the time of Copernicus, Galileo, Gilbert, and Descartes, interpretation of Aristotle had become so Christianized that he was no longer viewed as a pagan philosopher whose thought could be used to combat official Christian doctrine. Rather, it was the unquestioned conviction of these men that to overthrow the (pagan!) philosopher Aristotle was to subvert one of the great foundations of Christian Scholasticism. Several of them underscored their quarrel with Christianity by appealing to non-Greco-Roman, but pagan, deities: Copernicus hymned the sun in Mithraic odes;[18] Gilbert appealed to the teachings of Zoroaster, Hermes Trismegistus, and Orpheus;[19] and Descartes speaks darkly of a wise age long preceding that of pagan Aristotle and Plato.[20] Thus, our age, the Enlightenment was founded on a rejection of a Christianized Aristotle, and its founding was deeply concerned with that rejection and with the subsequent overthrow of Scholastic thought based on a Christianized version of Aristotle.

Descartes is much easier to identify as one of the founders of the Enlightenment than to specify as the father of any discipline that is uniquely characteristic of it. However, a founder he was, and, as such, he had to address himself in detail to those aspects of the Scholastic-Aristotelian tradition that were particularly persuasive in its time. One of these was the clinical medicine based on the texts of Galen and his schools, and another was the actual teaching of Aristotle on which Galen and his school of medical practitioners based their clinical theory. That fundamental teaching was concerned with what can be termed "the nature of Nature."

Galileo's discussion of uniformly accelerated motion promised a replacement of the then-received Scholastic analysis of motion, but it did not thereby address the question of the development and growth of living bodies in the context of a universal physics. Until the school of Galen was overthrown in its entirety, including its presuppositions about the nature of Nature that it received from Aristotle, any great new medical discovery could only be considered a piecemeal correction by a great student of Aristotle, who remained "the Master." Thus, it required what can be called a *clinically oriented biophysics* to complete the overthrow of the ancient philosophy of Aristotle and the Scholastic-Aristotelianism of Roman Catholic Europe.

In 1628, William Harvey established the twofold circulation of the blood, and thereby that the blood did not enter the left auricle through invisible *foramina* (pores) in the septum between the atrial chambers of the heart. No less importantly, his book *On The Motion of the Heart and Blood in Animals [De Motu Cordis et Sanguinis in Animalibus]* showed that the blood in the body was not generated and consumed at the enormous rate that Galen's theory demanded. The body's organ systems and its vessels were thereby opened to extensively new interpretations: For, if the organs do not make and consume the blood, what do they do? And why are they *connected* to one another as they are?

Harvey's work on the circulation, as damaging as it was to Galen's theory of systemic circulation, left untouched the biology and physics behind Galen. Aristotle's teaching concerning Nature as a principle of rest and motion—in medical terms, a principle of biological growth and maturity—was largely untouched by Harvey's attack on Galen.

The Scholastic filter through which, even today, we receive Aristotle's teachings tends to obscure the fact that his theory of natural motion and rest contained in his book *Physics* applied equally to animate and inanimate bodies. This was just as true for Aristotle as it is for today's biophysicist. Harvey, although a marvelously adroit and subtle anatomist and what might even be called a "theoretical clinician," was an intellectual son of Galen; he was no Aristotle in the breadth, depth, or direction of his interests. Inanimate nature was a closed book to this wonderful anatomist of living and newly dead bodies of humans and beasts. At best, he could only mount brilliant ad hoc attacks on the Scholastic-Aristotelian tradition. Only a medical theoretician—not necessarily even a clinical physician—who was also a profound physicist could mount the necessary two-pronged attack on Aristotle's doctrine of Nature as being the principle of both animate and inanimate change. Descartes was both a medical theoretician and a physicist, and he indicated the way to our present-day radically non-Aristotelian biology based on his own radically non-Aristotelian physics.

PROBLEMS OF CARTESIAN SCHOLARSHIP

Descartes was born into the minor nobility of post-Reformation Roman Catholic France in 1596. At that time, France was surrounded by either conservative Roman Catholic countries or by countries containing at least enclaves of scarcely "liberal" Lutherans, Calvinists, Zwinglians, Waldensians, Moravians, Anabaptists, Socinians, and Antitrinitans, not to mention the Greek Orthodox and the Muslims. Descartes was born 53 years after Copernicus published *On the Revolutions of Heavenly Bodies [De Revolutionibus Orbium Coelestium]*, and he had partly finished a "Copernican" work, *Le Monde,* when in 1633 he heard about the trial of Galileo. Descartes suppressed publication of *Le Monde,* although he never abjured it. In short, the greatest part of Descartes' active intellectual life was lived during a period of considerable suppression of many styles of unorthodoxy. His own works were condemned—judged as damnable— by the church of Rome on November 20, 1663, "donec corregitur [until corrected]." Since Descartes died in 1650, the question of correction was perforce left to whomever wished to act as his apologist, and these have not been few: e.g., Gilson, Laporte, Gouhier, and, to a lesser extent, Kemp Smith and Balz, all of whom seem to agree that Descartes was in some important measure a misunderstood Scholastic, and hence Christian, thinker.[21] Since these and like-minded scholars have deeply influenced our present interpretation of Descartes, it follows that our present interpretation is partly of a "corrected" Descartes, and not of a thinker whose works really might have deserved the condemnation of the Holy Office, given the Holy Office's canons of judgment. As a consequence of this scholarship, Descartes tends to be viewed more as an *enfant terrible* than as "the leader of a band of revolutionaries"; this scholarship has prepared the readers of Descartes both to be puzzled by the prudence of this *enfant terrible* and, simultaneously, to be astonished by his boldness. At the least, we shall try to understand Descartes as a philosopher.

Another reason it is difficult to grasp Descartes clearly is also historical, and concerns the history of philosophy after him. Bertrand Russell has said that "modern philosophy has very largely accepted the formulation of its problems from Descartes, while not accepting his solutions."[22] There are two obvious reasons for this. On the one hand, Descartes' solutions are often incredibly wrong-headed, e.g., he simply refused to entertain the possibility that Harvey was right in saying that the heart was a muscle that *pumps* blood, but insisted that it was a container in which blood was heated so that it could expand, forcing it through the blood vessels. On the other hand, his views of the problems of physics, of philosophy, and of mathematics are often of unparalleled subtlety and, as such, difficult to grasp. "Wrong" solutions to difficult and subtle problems most often dim the glory of the discoverer of those problems and make us tend to forget their true meanings and weight in our efforts to find "correct" solutions to them. However, solutions aside, even the subtlety and complexity of his views tend to hide his reasons for holding them. To illustrate these last two points, we turn to his proof of the existence of God.

By means of his proof of the existence of God, Descartes set out to demonstrate to a very conservative Christianity that the analytic method of reasoning that found such success in the *Geometry* (the book in which he presents to the world his form of what we today know as analytic geometry), could also be used in what he saw as the theological dispute *par excellence*, that is, the rational and philosophically acceptable proof of the existence of a good and providential deity. To accomplish this, he proceeded exactly as he did so brilliantly and successfully as an algebraist—by starting from a known and proceeding to an unknown that he has expressed *exclusively in terms of that known*.[23] To do this, he took his own existence as known—and, indeed, what could be better known *to him!*—and then proceeded to define God by means of what he finds in his own consciousness, namely, certain of his own ideas. He knows clearly *that* he is, but not at all *what* he is. The idea of God he finds in himself is precisely the unique idea that is known only in knowing all that he can know about himself; it is *the* idea whose object is proven to exist purely by defining that idea in terms of the limitations of the mind holding that idea. With Descartes, the question of belief in God becomes infinitely personal, and the grounds, beyond all others, from which the need for toleration can be argued.

This oblique way of proceeding is indeed appropriate for an age in which religious and scientific heterodoxy could be punished by savagely cruel torments and executions reminiscent of the usage of Persian despots. However, his proof is also "of all seasons": to an age or polity of a more "tolerant" temper, Descartes' proof is merely a vicious circle. The orthodox in a less tolerant age or polity might well consider it a salutary attempt by philosophy to light the way for the (often regrettably squint-eyed) Faithful, whose darkened vision sometimes, sadly, has need of such ministration. The mathematically adept of the "free thinkers," anywhere, in any age or polity, might well view it as a splendidly refined piece of irony—true, to be sure, but true in the face of a web of apparently excessive ingenuity. To this small group of mathematically adept free thinkers, Descartes shows that there exists a whole rational theology that can be articulated both exclusively and exhaustively through that very same method he used to set up the equations of his analytic geometry and which was used even prior to him by algebraists in setting up equations for the solutions of difficult word-problems given them. In our present age, very many of the learned are tolerant agnostics who both extend and expect in return a very large degree of toleration. This fair-mindedness, this give-and-take toleration, implies, of course, that writers need fear no intolerance and therefore can and should express any intellectually or factually supported thought as openly and directly as possible. This postulate, profoundly characteristic of our age, suggests yet another reason why it is so difficult for us, today, to read Descartes: we tend to think that what is clearly understood by an author is to be just as clearly set down by him for us, his readers, in his writings. In principle, Descartes was entirely agreeable; but, in fact, the dangers that repressive orthodoxy presented to Descartes made such openness very dangerous indeed. This was further complicated by Descartes' rejection of many of the commonly accepted meanings of words in current use; he used them in ways that puzzled his own contemporaries, friend and foe alike. Our own taste for openness has led us to dismiss Descartes' explicit warning that his use of traditional terms, even of those found in the tradition's very deeply entrenched philosophic vocabulary, will be his own. In his *Rules* (Vol. X, p. 369, l. 8–10), he told his readers that his vocabulary is often that of the Schools, but not his meaning: ". . . what individual words signify in Latin, . . . I interpret in my sense, the sense which seems most apt to me." Descartes is here discussing his own use of the very important word *intuitus* (intuition), and he says that his use of the term is by no means that of the commonality of thinkers of the time. Prudence would suggest that in order to understand the key words of

Descartes' vocabulary, we should, in every instance, carefully study how *Descartes* uses them. Thus, when he uses such terms as *mens, corpus, animus, idea, cogitatio* (mind, body, soul, idea, thought), each must be taken as problematical until we find and establish its particular use in Descartes' texts. We cannot presuppose a traditional meaning for these words; thus, we cannot take it for granted that, for example, Descartes' use of the term *idea* is accurately translated either by the English word idea or by the Greek term ἰδέα. It is unquestionable that most of the tradition did not mean by the term 'idea' what Descartes meant by it, namely, what we are immediately conscious of because of a corporeal impression in the fleshy part of the brain (*Meditations*, Vol. VII, p. 160, l. 7, to p. 161, l. 3). As another example concerning the key word *intuitus* Descartes said (*Rules*, Vol. X, p. 369):

> Further, since someone perhaps may be troubled by my new use of the word *intuitus* (as well as other words) which I shall subsequently try to remove from their common signification in the same way, I here give general notice that I do not in the least understand in what way any words have been adopted in the schools, since it would be most difficult to use one set of words and to think entirely differently; in my case, I only attend to what individual words signify in Latin so that, whenever their proper significations are lacking in the school usage, I shall then interpret them in my sense, the sense which seems most apt to me.

As I show subsequently, Descartes' willingness to use terms appearing in both "ordinary" and traditional philosophical language in a most extraordinary manner led him to use such key terms as *dimensio, numero,* and *passio* in a way that has at least partially disguised the meaning of his teachings concerning these terms. Scholars of Descartes who do not take his warning seriously are very likely to be confused by the fact that he simply did not mean, in crucial places, what everyone else means by certain terms. (The context, however, can always be read so as to reveal the meaning when the usage is peculiar to Descartes.)

Descartes, we may safely suppose, knew Latin and French as well as his readers, who were often simply puzzled by his usages. Furthermore, since he was by no means a hermit, we may suppose that, if his diction was often decisively eccentric to that of many of his readers, it was primarily because his view of the subject that he was discussing was often distinct from theirs, not that he did not know theirs. Indeed, as we have just seen, Descartes says that his terminology is peculiar to him because his thoughts are entirely different from those of the Schools and he therefore cannot use their terms with their meanings. This warning was issued in 1628, before he felt endangered by (Galileo's) Church censors; after 1633, when he learned of Galileo's house arrest by the Holy Office, he had a further need to express certain kinds of thoughts very carefully.[24]

Whatever Descartes' final thoughts were about the teachings of the Church, at the very least he must have realized, after 1633, when he learned of the trial of Galileo, that clearly secular discussion of matters also pronounced upon by Church doctrine could be dangerous. Thus the Holy Office ("Inquisition") would tend to suspect anyone who evinced too much interest in the scientific truth of falsity of the Copernican system, not to mention anyone, such as Descartes, who reopened issues like those that defined the Pelagian heresy—the teaching of the perfectability of the individual human through self-discipline.[25] Descartes disguised his interest in these matters to a large degree by touching upon them in "scientific" contexts that would not easily be followed by the censors. Unfortunately, all too few Cartesian scholars have taken the trouble to read as widely in his "scientific" works as in his "metaphysical" work—unique in the corpus—the *Meditations*.[26] It seems likely that our present-day view of Descartes is largely taken from the text of the *Meditations*, and we are thus restricted to a view of Descartes as being almost solely preoccupied with doubts and fancies that, at the end of those very *Meditations*, he himself characterized as "laughable and excessive," while all along there was another Descartes for whom doubts held few charms.

This is not to claim that Descartes was not profoundly interested in many of the problems that were also dealt with thematically and at great length by the orthodox thinkers, i.e., by "the Schools." However, his own mathematical approach, even to problems also of interest to his contemporaries, was influenced by a relatively unknown tradition. Although this tradition was known to several important and well-known orthodox thinkers, it was not a major influence in orthodox thinking. So, yet another reason for a too narrow reading of Descartes is his debt to what he understood as the mathematics of a group he identifies as "the ancients." That is to say when he said, in the *Discourse on Method* (Vol. VI, p. 19), that his reading of those ancients led him "to imagine that all those things, able to come within the knowledge of men follow each other in the same manner . . . ," he identified a relatively unknown body of *mathematical* writings as his model for the true science that would reveal "all those things." While that body of writings certainly cannot be called "esoteric," it was not considered necessary for an educated man to be well versed in it. However, Descartes said very little about the mathematical writings of men such as Diophantos and Pappus, except to say that they almost hid more than they revealed. He also said, and possibly with some truth, that most men are not able to grasp both arguments used to solve problems addressed by mathematical analysis and by the metaphysical arguments of his day (*Principles of Philosophy*, Vol. VIII, p.

4, l. 3–6; Vol. IV, p. 46, l. 6–12; Vol. III, p. 691). In the foreword to his *Geometry* (Vol. VI, p. 368), he goes so far as to say that what he will include in that work cannot be followed by everyone.

Thus, not only does Descartes hide his debt to his Greek antecedents (out of contempt or vanity), but also, what is of still greater moment for us, he purposely excludes, almost always, explicitly "metaphysical" arguments from "geometrical-mechanical" works and "geometrical-mechanical" arguments from "metaphysical" works. Since he is the author of both sorts of work, he obviously does not include himself in that large majority of men who have difficulty following both kinds of arguments. Thus, a sufficient understanding of the Cartesian texts requires that the scholar read widely in both kinds—something that few have done, thereby giving us a one-sided view of Cartesian thought.

In addition, another major problem is that there is very strong evidence that Descartes *definitely* misunderstood the tradition of mathematics, even though he was deeply influenced by it; that is, he was deeply influenced by his own misreading of the mathematical texts that came down to him, especially those of Pappus (fl. A.D. 320).[27]

Generally, Descartes' sources are a complex problem. He said too little about the genesis of his insights. Except for the passage concerning the ancients in *Rule* IV (Vol. X, p. 376, l. 12ff.), he said almost nothing about the fact that he thinks that a crude adumbration of his own method existed (ibid., p. 376, l. 23) *prima aetate* ("in the first ages") but that men such as Pappus and Diophantus *perniciosa quadam astutia* ("with a certain low cunning") suppressed it in order to gain the more glory for themselves.[28] Because of this judgment of the Greek tradition as merely a dishonest transmitter of "ancient wisdom," Descartes' crucial dependency on this tradition is largely hidden, and a rich source of one whole side of his thought is largely unknown or obscure. This also makes the interpretation of Descartes' texts peculiarly difficult, and it tends to make Cartesian scholars take an unbalanced view of the importance for Descartes of the traditions of authoritarian Scholasticism and of Renaissance liberalism.

Among Descartes' antecedents there also occur the works of Bernadino Telesio (1509–1588), who, like Descartes after him, speculated about the first principles of Nature, using that term, again like Descartes, to embrace the elements of simple natural bodies as well as the rationale of all living organisms. Telesio postulated a universe of passive dead matter activated by heat and cold, heat emanating from "heaven" and cold from "earth." He considered sensation to be ultimately grounded in matter and attributed the superiority of animals over inanimate bodies to their superior organization. Self-preservation was held to be the goal of natural bodies.[29] Descartes' general cosmology also started out only with matter in motion, where what is sensed as heat is merely the effect of motion in matter. Descartes' derivation of living organisms proceeded in this same way. In his *Generatio Animalium [The Generation of Animals]*, Descartes considered the heart to be a retort in which otherwise "dead" matter is transformed into "spirits" that serve to give lifelike motion to an otherwise idle machine. He identified that matter, before it went through the retort of the heart, as being like the matter out of which earth is composed, and matter, after being transformed in the heart, as being more like the matter out of which the heavens are composed. Indeed, this is another side of Descartes that is both centrally important for him and, unfortunately, almost totally ignored by Descartes scholars. As a consequence, a well-hidden, almost totally ignored source of a noteworthy influence on his thought lies in the works of these iatro-physicists and iatro-chemists. However, this source in itself is perhaps merely of antiquarian interest if we are at the same time clear about the crucial role that his own "iatro-physical" and "iatro-chemical" thinking plays in Descartes' works and thoughts.

For instance, not unlike the work of Telesio and Descartes is that of the already mentioned iatro-physicists and iatro-chemists, such as Paracelsus. Hall points out that Paracelsus and the alchemists prescribed non-organic substances as specifics against syphilis. He writes that "inorganic chemical remedies were gradually introduced into medical practice, against strong opposition from the Galenists."[30] Renaissance hylozoism (i.e., the doctrine that life can be explained in terms of the attributes of matter) thus gained a sort of experimental verification in the success of the iatro-chemists' and the iatro-physicists' use of "dead" matter to cure living organisms. Descartes, as we have seen, held that life itself is altogether intelligible without any recourse to the idea of soul, which only thinks. It is worth asking to what degree the Cartesian program of reducing all organic processes to mechanical processes was influenced by the work of the doctor-alchemists as well as by the hylozoism of men whose thought was similar to Telesio's. Indeed, one of the central meanings of the term "philosopher" during Descartes' time, and even during several centuries before his time, was *alchemist*. For the alchemists—iatro-chemists—one primary goal was finding the elixir of life, the *aqua vita* that would be the panacea of all ills. Their program of discovery was essentially tied up with the notion that the adept could find the elixir only if he himself were initially healthy in spirit, so that he could be perfected, made "golden," by his research program, which he understood to comprise a sort of rule of living—not dissimilar to the idea of the monastic orders.

There is too little direct evidence to allow the claim that Descartes knew of and was significantly influenced by Telesio's or Paracelsus's books, but it is by no means too much to claim that Descartes must have known of this sort of speculation, which so interested him. Such speculation had strong affinities with his own thinking, and, since we today are liable to view the period prior to Galileo's house arrest in 1633 as a monolith of quasi-Aristotelian obfuscation, a notice directing the reader's attention to the splendidly rich variety of intellectual endeavors (including several that bear striking family resemblance to crucially important doctrines of Descartes) is appropriate.

In short, there is an aspect of Descartes' thought that seems to have been in remarkable harmony with the work and doctrines of the alchemists, e.g., Paracelsus, and the non-experimental counterparts of these alchemists, such as the "hermetic philosophers," e.g., Jacob Boehme. This side of his thought seems to have been almost entirely ignored by students of his thinking.

Hence, one goal of this study is to call attention to the immense importance of physiology for a balanced understanding of the Cartesian texts, and thus to call attention to the crucial importance of those Cartesian texts that report and analyze his physiological investigations. These contain the main justification of much that otherwise appears strained and irrational in his writings. An example is the ambiguity, remarked upon by Descartes himself (Vol. IV, p. 166), of his use of the word 'body.' Descartes was so fully aware of the ambiguity of his use of the term, that whenever he used it that ambiguity was evident. The primary reason he was so carefully ambiguous is that, on the philosophic side, using only *sa raison*[31] ("his own reason"), he saw it was possible to achieve freedom from blinding impulses that lead men to assign an "objective" existence to the soul's innate reaction to a very complicated machine's reaction—that is, the human body's reaction—to corporeal perturbations originating outside it. On the other side, by using this same freedom, men also can overcome those blinding prejudices that lead to indiscriminate adherence to authority, to any authority. What is more, it is by means of the same discipline that one comes to knowledge of anything, as well as to a total mastery of one's own passions, which are, for Descartes, the soul's reaction to perturbations in the body to which it is united.

It should be repeated that the most serious reason that the Cartesian texts tend to mislead scholars almost certainly relates to the role of medical physiology in the corpus. However, we do find some modern historians who are aware of this. Dr. M. Foster tells us:[32]

> If we judge Descartes from the severe standpoint of exact anatomical knowledge, we are bound to confess that he, to a large extent, introduced a fantastic and unreal anatomy in order to give clearness and point to his exposition . . . On the other hand, however, we must

admit that he did succeed in shewing [*sic*] that it was possible to apply to the interpretation not only of the physical but also of the psychical phenomena of the animal body, the same method which was making such astounding progress when applied to the phenomena of the material world. And indeed a very little change in the details of Descartes' exposition and some of that hardly more than a change in terminology would convert that exposition into a statement of modern views. If we read between the lines which he wrote, if we substitute in place of the subtle fluid of the animal spirits, the molecular changes which we call a nervous impulse, if we replace his system of tubes with their valvular arrangements by the present system of concatenated neurons, whose linked arrangement determines the passage and the effects of the nervous impulses, Descartes' exposition will not appear so wholly different from the one which we give today.

Foster was a practicing physician rather than a theoretician; however, in light of his intelligence and general accuracy, it is odd that, having said so much, he could still consider Harvey to be of greater importance than Descartes, the discoverer of the modern theory of psycho-physical medicine. Indeed, just as Harvey (who was sufficiently "modern" to give money to Hobbes when he needed it!) applied Copernicus's thought to his own theory of the body (in spite of his ignorance of the real existence of the capillaries, a point not to be lightly overlooked or undervalued), so did Descartes not only apply Copernicus's thought to gain his own elucidation of the blood-system, but also, extending him yet further, forge what is known today as the notion of arcs, of feedback mechanisms, loops, and the like. Modern thinking is, to be sure, profoundly fascinated by the concept of circulation—for instance, with the concept of monetary circulation, à la Montesquieu—but still more with neurophysiology and its conclusions. Concern with spiritual health has become a concern with mental health, and the older, uneasy liaison between the civil and ecclesiastical orders is echoed, astonishingly faithfully, in the liaison now obtaining between psychiatry and the law.

Many texts of Descartes are themselves *largely* concerned with this medical physiology. Indeed, as far back as the 1628 *Rules*, a considerable portion of the central rule, Rule XII—over 130 lines in the Adam and Tannery edition—discusses the physiology of perception. *Le Monde* greatly depends on the introductory physiological arguments for its subsequent "philosophical" development. Part Four of his *Discourse on Method* is largely taken up with a detailed account of the physiology of circulation, and *Dioptrics,* which he called an *essai* ("trial") of the method given in the *Discourse,* devotes very nearly one-half of its pages to a discussion of the physiology of sight. Even in the "metaphysical" *Meditations* there is a cursory discussion of "health" and "sickness" in the theodicy of Meditation VI; and Descartes ended Part IV of the 1644 *Principles of Philosophy* with an expression of hope that the cultivation of the principles that provide it with its basic subject matter will especially advance medical science. The entire first third of Descartes' 1645–46 *Passions of the Soul* discusses physiology as the foundation for a correct understanding of the passions of the soul, which for Descartes are the ways in which we are aware of our instincts for self-preservation. Finally, Descartes' last work, unfinished at the time of his death in 1650, *The Description of the Human Body/Concerning the Formation of the Animal,* is wholly occupied with questions pertaining to medical physiology and anatomy. In only one "trial" of the *Discourse*—that is, in his *Geometry*—and in the *Meditations,* we do find major works of Descartes that are not both intensively and extensively concerned with medical physiology. However, very few scholars of Descartes even briefly refer to his physiological investigations when they discuss such characteristically Cartesian problems as the "mind-body" problem. Is not that problem the mind-*body* problem?

A. R. Hall, a historian of science, is clear in his assignment of Descartes to a central place in the history of modern medicine. Hall says that "the application of mechanistic philosophy to biological problems was not attempted before Descartes."[33] Again, he says, "The old physiology postulated a variety of non-material souls or spirits, each charged with the management of a set of bodily functions; for Descartes, those functions were the result of mechanistic processes. . . ."[34] A historian of medicine, Charles Singer, says that Descartes was in the tradition of the iatro-physicists, or those who attempt "to explain the workings of the animal body on purely mechanical grounds."[35]

Speaking generally, the historians of medicine are quite clear about Descartes' central role in the founding of modern medical theory, even if they do not sufficiently appreciate the fact that it was Descartes who first tied the circulatory, hormonal, and nervous systems together; nor do they see how important he is as a founder of modern psychobiology and neurophysiology—and hence, ultimately, of analytical psychology and its derivatives. On the other hand, the historians of philosophy and science generally do realize his importance as a founder of modern mathematical analysis, and they agree that the tradition of rationalism received much of its characteristic flavor from his thinking. They do not, however, ask how these two are related, beyond a few words concerning scientific method, nor do they often ask why the same man who was a fundamental theorist in medicine and in mathematical physics also claimed explicitly that the goal of all his work was to establish an ethics (*la morale*) based on these two disciplines. It seems fair to say that this omission arises from the fact that they do not realize what Descartes meant by the term "ethics," any more than they understand what he meant by the term "medicine," nor their relation to one another. *La morale,* or ethics, was not for Descartes a private matter—unless, of course, tyrannous thought control required that it be so. In what follows, arguments are given for the view that Descartes' ethics largely addresses itself to what we today would consider the province of political science and sociology. For Descartes, the public realm comprised a sphere that was a moral realm, a realm of values.[36] Unless the reader of Descartes is clear about this, he cannot comprehend very much of cartesian thought nor, for that matter, very much of the moral passion of the Enlightenment, for all its fascination with what it called *"objective* reality."

Descartes' rational, nonreligious ethics is largely ignored by historians or, at the very least, is most usually considered to be identical with a sort of rationalized religious teaching.[37] Hence, when historians read d'Alembert's assessment of Descartes' place in the history of philosophy, they tend to be merely puzzled.[38] What d'Alembert has to say concerning Descartes' contribution to mathematics is perhaps somewhat shallow; his statements concerning Descartes' contribution to political theory show he understood it rather more deeply. Above all else, d'Alembert omits from his short account the role of medical theory in Descartes' thought and the enormous importance of it for the tradition, an omission that this present work attempts to repair.

D'Alembert says, in his *Discours Préliminaire de L'Encyclopédie:*

> Descartes can be considered as a mathematician or as a philosopher. Mathematics, which seemed to him of relatively little importance, is nevertheless today the most solid and least contested grounds for his glory. Algebra, in a certain sense created by the Italians and prodigiously augmented by our own illustrious Viéte, received new additions at the hand of Descartes. One of the most considerable of these is his method of indeterminates—a very ingenious and subtle artifice—which can be applied further to a great number of investigations. But, above all, what has immortalized the name of this great man is the geometrical use to which he put his algebra, an idea as vast and happy as any which the human mind has ever conceived, and which will always be the key to profound researches, not only in sublime geometry, but in all the physico-mathematical sciences.[39]

D'Alembert then continues a few lines later to assess Descartes as a political thinker:

> Descartes has at least dared to show men of real spirit how to cast off the yoke of Scholasticism, of opinion, of authority—in a word, of prejudice and barbarism; and by that revolt whose fruits we are nowadays gathering, he has tendered to Philosophy a service more difficult, perhaps, to render than all those performed by his illustrious successors. He can be regarded as the leader of a band of

conspirators who have had the courage to be the first to raise themselves up against a despotic and arbitrary power, and who, in preparing a glorious revolution, had laid down the foundations of a government more just and happy than any that has been seen to have been established.[40]

With the addition of medicine as the link between what d'Alembert has called Descartes' "physico-mathematical sciences" and his ethics, the goal of this present work may be characterized as an attempt to justify d'Alembert's assessment of Descartes as a revolutionary founder of a new ethical order.

GENERAL DESCRIPTION
OF THIS WORK

Descartes' medically based, and thus rational, ethics (*la morale*) presupposes the restriction of his own general physical science (*la mechanique*), to the consideration of individual humans as they use human institutions for self-preservation. This restriction requires that he show why and how humans can be reduced to objects that are no less accessible to his science than are any other objects; only then can he claim validly that his general science of nature, his mechanics, also can explain what is certainly one of the most characteristically human of phenomena, human institutions. This work proceeds by following the course of that restriction from the most general, i.e., metaphysical and theoretical-mathematical speculations behind Descartes' mathematical physics, through his cosmogenetic and embryogenetic reflections, on to his final goal, a human polity whose statutes are most ethical because they most faithfully reflect the laws of nature followed in the cosmogenesis and embryogenesis.

This study of Descartes' medically based ethics, that is, *rational* ethics, is presented in two parallel parts, where the first lays the groundwork for the second. In particular, the first part concerns the relation between thinking bodies and thought-about bodies, that is, between a highly organized individual living and thinking body that is able to understand objects mathematically because of the nature of the mind to which it is united, and body in general, "physical matter," which is an object that that unity of mind and particular body can understand. An individual, organized body is a highly qualified, modified, particular instance of general body; therefore, knowledge of that qualified body requires more than merely the knowledge of general, unqualified body. Knowledge of particular body presupposes a thorough mathematical knowledge of body in general or, as Descartes calls it, of *res extensa* ("extended substance"). Since, for Descartes, general body is logically prior to any particular body, and certainly to that highly organized particular body to which the human mind is united, the first part of this work begins with an examination of that general body. Descartes identifies it with "extended substance" or "general magnitude," that is, with "physical" body as completely knowable by means of a certain kind of mathematics. General, physical body is thus first established as essentially knowable by the (mathematically adept) human mind; then, in its turn, the human knower, a substantial unity of mind and organized body, is identified as being uniquely able to know the world around it precisely in order to preserve its biological life and, in particular, in order to preserve its union of mind and highly organized body. It is then shown that Descartes' restriction of general science to human objects constitutes what he often calls medicine; once medicine is established as a subsection and true part of general science, it prepares him to treat human institutions scientifically. The process and result of this medical treatment is the subject of the second part of this work.

The medicine articulated in Part I comprises Descartes' application of his mathematical physics of general body to the individual human body. Cartesian medicine is thus as original with Descartes as his mathematical physics, and even where Descartes is indebted to his predecessors for medical facts—e.g., to Harvey for the fact of the circulation of the blood—those facts are re-interpreted and explained by Descartes in light of his original physical theory. Part II of this work shows how Descartes' general physical theory of the formation of the heavens comprises general paradigms both for his theory of the embryogenesis of the human body and for his theory of the genesis of the sound, healthy "body politic" in which mature humans can live well. In Descartes' treatment, the development of the embryo, embryogenesis, is modeled after the earlier stages of the development of the ordered universe; cosmogenesis, and political genesis is modeled after later stages of that same cosmogenesis. Part II, and with it this book, ends with a sketch that was only hinted at by Descartes, of what he appears to have envisioned as a scientific, that is, rational, sound and healthy body politic. His death at age fifty-four prevented the elaboration of that sketch.

In short, Part I concerns the organization of the human body as being just sufficient to permit it to carry on the mathematical operations of the new mathematical physics that Descartes feels he has discovered, and Part II concerns in greater detail the anatomy of the human being's organized body in so far as it is fit to be alive and to carry on the intellectual operations of the mind with which it is united. It shows the human body as a problem-solving machine, which, with its paired muscles, interconnecting organs, and the like, has precisely the kind of organization best fitted to carry out the computations and solutions of its mind. Medicine, then, in Part II, begins to emerge as the science that keeps the body in just that degree of organization that is required for it to obey and carry out the computations and solutions of its mind. Only then can ethics emerge as the science that keeps numbers of organized individuals interrelated so that they can, acting as a compound, organized political body, best carry out the computations and solutions of the mind of that body.

NOTES

1. *Oeuvres de Descartes,* 12 vols. plus supplement, ed. Charles Adam and Paul Tannery (Paris: Leopold Cerf, 1897–1913), volume XI, p. 225, l. 26–31. (In some of the volumes there is only a posthumous French translation of a work, without the marginal numbering of the lines. Where this happens, only the volume and page number are given. [When *only* volume and page number are given, we are dealing with volumes I–V, which contain letters to and from Descartes.])
   The full title of the presently cited piece was apparently supplied by Descartes' literary executor, Clerselier, who was an intimate of Descartes, and who knew his works and temper very well. The title was, in full: "The Description of the Human Body and all its Functions, Both those which in no way depend on the soul, and those which do depend on it. Also, the principle cause of the formation of its constituent members." This is an entirely accurate description of the contents of the essay.

2. I. P. Pavlov, *Conditioned Reflexes* (New York: Dover Books, 1960 reprint of the 1927 Oxford University Press translation by G. V. Anrep).

3. Ibid., pp. 7–8.

4. Ibid., p. 12.

5. Ibid., p. 4.

6. J. M. Reiner, *The Organism as an Adaptive Control System* (New York: Prentice-Hall, 1968). The dedication to this work reads: "To Candida, my love, / because of whom / the rest of the universe / is worthwhile."

7. Pavlov, *Conditioned Reflexes,* pp. 7–8.

8. It is well worth questioning whether a "natural" body can be a truly constitutive unit in another "natural" body. Contemporary biology, significantly enough, seems to be energetic in its affirmation of that possibility. For example, see Lewis Thomas, M.D., in *The Lives of a Cell* (New York: Bantam Books, 1975), especially "Thoughts for a Countdown." Thomas, who is presently the president of the Sloan-Kettering Memorial Institute for Cancer Research, views cells "synthetically" as "historical" entities (so that Golgi bodies and the like are viewed by him as the remnants of cellular structures that once lived independently of other cells.) This view is almost certainly influenced by his view of society. Thus, only the elements are natural; the "society" formed by them is "late" and/or "artificial"; Dr. Thomas is a follower of Rousseau.

9. Here Descartes was in agreement with a very ancient tradition, of which he was almost surely ignorant: Aristoxenus reported of the Pythagorians that they held "Medical skill . . . the highest wisdom attainable by humans," and "that they do not honor least the sciences of music, medicine, and foretelling the future." Diels-Kranz, *Die Fragmente der Vorsokratiker,* 3 vols. (Berlin-Neukoellen, 1956), Volume I, p. 467, l. 3, p. 466, l. 9). See also L. Edelstein, *Ancient Medicine* (Baltimore: Johns Hopkins Press, 1963), pp. 58, 59.

10. George Rosen, *From Medical Police to Social Medicine* (New York: Science History Publishers, 1974). Although Rosen is unabashedly Marxist, his very interesting book, the historical value of which more than outweighs its bias, is well worth reading.

11. *Oeuvres*, Vol. VI, Discourse on Method, p. 78, l. 8–13.

12. Ibid., Vol. IV, p. 329, l. 16–19.

13. Jean le Rond d'Alembert, *Discours Préliminaire de l'Encyclopédie* (Amsterdam: Chatelain et fils, 1751), reprinted in Editions Gonthier, Paris, 1965, pp. 93–94, trans. R. N. Schwab and W. E. Rex, *Preliminary Discourse to the Encyclopedia of Diderot* (Indianapolis: The Bobbs-Merrill Company, Inc., 1963), pp. 78–80.

14. For example, Sir Robert Filmer, Bart., *Patriarcha or The Natural Power of Kings*. This work appeared posthumously in 1680, and was cited by John Locke as being representative of the ideas he was concerned with attacking. It is available as an appendix to John Locke, *Two Treatises of Government* (New York: Hafner Publishing Company, 1947), pp. 249–308.

15. Émile Bréhier, *The Middle Ages and the Renaissance*, trans. W. Baskin (Chicago: University of Chicago Press, 1967), p. 116.

16. Ibid., p. 119.

17. Ibid., p. 132.

18. John Hermann Randall, Jr., *The Making of the Modern Mind* (New York: Columbia University Press, 1976). *Sub.* "Mithra," p. 23.

19. William Gilbert, *De Magnete*, trans. P. F. Mottelay (New York: Dover, 1968), p. 309.

A lengthy search of the literature has resulted in only one author who saw the importance of Gilbert for Descartes, Maria Luise Hoppes, *Die Abhaendigkeit der Wirbeltheorie des Descartes von William Gilbert's Lehre vom Magnetismus* (Halle a.S. Kaemmerer, 1913). Other works on Gilbert of varying quality are: William Hale-White, *Bacon, Gilbert and Harvey* (London: Bale, Sons and Danielson, 1927), and William Dampier, *A History of Science*, Fourth Edition (Cambridge University Press, 1968). Interestingly, Dampier remarks (pp. 124–125) that Gilbert's discussion "seems to be the first realization of mass without reference to weight, and may have given the idea of mass to Kepler and Galileo." Without that distinction, a great deal of Descartes' physics is *impossible*.

20. This passage occurs in the *Rules*, Vol. I, p. 6, *Philosophic Works of Descartes*, 2 vols., trans. E. S. Haldane and G. R. T. Ross (New York: Dover, 1955, or Oxford University Press, 1967). (This is an adequate translation, but the notes are *very* suspect.)

21. *Vid.* Etienne Gilson, particularly, "Descartes et la pensée religieuse de son temps," *Annuaire d'Ecole practicque des Hautes-Etudes*, section des sciences relig. (1923–24, 1956–57). Also, his "La pensée religieuse de Descartes," *Revue de metaphysique et de morale*, 1925, 32: 519–537. Also, see Jean Laporte, particularly *Le Rationalisme de Descartes* (Paris: Presses Univ. Fran., 1945 and 1950), especially Chapter I; Henri Gouhier, *La pensée religieuse de Descartes* (Paris: J. Vrin, 1924). Also, see Norman Kemp Smith, *Studies in the Cartesian Philosophy*, (New York: Russell and Russell, 1962); and A. G. A. Balz, particularly his "Concerning the Thomistic and Cartesian Dualisms," *Journal of Philosophy*, 1957, 44:383–390.

Several good surveys of Descartes that touch upon the subject matter of this book, but that approach it from a different direction or upon different foundations, are: A. Boyce Gibson, *The Philosophy of Descartes* (London: Methuen, 1932); S. V. Keeling, *Descartes* (London: Ernest Benn, 1934); Anthony Kenny, *Descartes: A Study of his Philosophy* (New York: Random House, 1968); and, finally, there is Willis Doney's edition of critical essays, *Descartes: A Collection of Critical Essays* (Garden City, N.J.: Doubleday, 1967).

A syntoptical treatment of the Descartes literature is given in Gregor Sebba, *Bibliographia Cartesian, 1800–1960* (The Hague: Nijhoff, 1964).

22. Bertrand Russell, *A History of Western Philosophy*, 2 vols. (New York: Simon and Schuster, 1945), Vol. I, p. 564.

23. In the "Response to the Second Set of Objections," Descartes stated that his proof of God's existence in the *Meditations* is "analytic." (*Oeuvres*, Vol. VII, p. 156, l. 21, to p. 157, l. 17–26.)

24. However, his explanations are sometimes so bold that even today we find it difficult to believe that he meant them; for example, he wrote to a Jesuit priest that his own theory of *digestion* can account rationally for the Roman Catholic doctrines of transsubstantiation—that the host becomes the real body and blood of Jesus Christ at the time of consecration—and consubstantiation—that both bread and wine transsubstantiate. It may be argued that this proves Descartes to have been a good Roman Catholic; however, to me it argues that Descartes thought that Catholicism was only a mixed-up form of scientific thinking.

25. Descartes' 1648 *Passions of the Soul (Passions de L'Ame)* teaches something very similar to this doctrine.

26. Below, I argue that, in part, the *Meditations* was conceived and written as an adjunct to his *Dioptrics*.

27. It is not in the province of this work to show how Descartes misconstrued Pappus's definition of Greek mathematical analysis in order to solve one of the great unsolved problems of antiquity—the so-called *n*-line locus problem. However, in order to solve that problem by the use of Vieta's algebra (which Descartes calls ". . . that beautiful Analysis," [*Rules*, Vol. X, p. 82]), he had to posit something he called *magnitudo in genere* (or general magnitude—our "algebraic quantity"). In order to justify the intelligibility of general magnitude, Descartes had to make psychological assumptions of the greatest power. As is argued in Part I, Chapter 2, "The Human Body," it is largely out of this inquiry that Descartes derived his psychology, which provided the foundations for his consequent treatment of physics as a totally deductive science, borrowing its intelligibility from the fact that the intellect knows clearly and distinctly those few mental operations needed to think physics, psychology, and even *la morale*, ethics. As is further argued in Chapter 2 of Part I, the very passions of the soul—assuredly part of the subject matter of *la morale*—have, under their Cartesian treatment, the same cognitive status as most of our perceptions and are ultimately just as intelligible. (Indeed, it was likely on such grounds as these that the Roman Catholic Church condemned his works in 1662 as being "Pelagian.")

Descartes discussed Pappus in *La Géometrie* (Vol. VI, p. 377ff.). Also, for a clear presentation of the problem, see "Apollonius of Perga, On Conic Sections," trans. R. Catesby Taliaferro, in *Great Books of the Western World* (Chicago, London, Toronto: Encyclopedia Brittanica, 1952), p. 799ff.

The term *magnitudo in genere*, which we translate as "algebraic quantity," "general magnitude," or even "the genus of magnitude," first occurs in the tradition in Rule XIII (Vol. X, p. 431, l. 22) of his 1628 *Regulae ad Directimen Ingenii—Rules for the Direction of the Mind*.

28. In this thought, Descartes disassociated himself from one of the central prejudices that marks a "Renaissance" man, i.e., a certain high evaluation of classical antiquity, for which Descartes had nothing but contempt. *Prima aetate*, as Descartes explained in that passage, was long before the Greeks. Rousseau's etiology of civil man is here adumbrated. Generally, the impulse to historicize great events in order to discover why they appear on the scene only "now" and not "earlier" is distinct from the Christian epochal thinking, which locates the incarnation as a long-foreshadowed and unique moment in time. For, no Christian theologian would say that the incarnation of God in Christ as the fulfillment of prophecy would have taken place earlier "except for . . . ." At the heart of post-Cartesian historicism is a form of "resentment": the ever-present question is, "Why did this event

happen just when it did, and not sooner or later or in a different context?" The Enlightenment's eschatology, its view of the necessary movement of history in a definite, progressive, direction toward a goal of perfection, is entirely distinct from the Judeo-Christian form; the Enlightenment almost always "blames" historical events for *lack* of progress, whereas the Judeo-Christian view of history views it as entirely timely, i.e., as transpiring "within Heaven's own good time."

29. *Vid.* Frank Thilly, *A History of Philosophy* (New York: Henry Holt and Co., 1914), pp. 236–237; also, John Herman Randall, Jr., *The Career of Philosophy* (New York: Columbia Univ. Press, 1962), pp. 201–206; William McDougall, *Body and Mind* (London: Meuthen & Co., 1928), p. 43. It appears from Hall's evidence (see Note 32) that the ancient Stato of Lampsicus (circa 270 B.C.) had a hylozoism.

30. A. R. Hall, *The Scientific Revolution, 1500–1800* (Boston: Beacon Press, 1960), p. 150.

31. *Sa raison* is usually translated as "*the* reason" in the English version of the full title of the *Discours.* This is entirely wrong and very misleading. "Sa" is the personal possessive pronoun in French, as Descartes certainly knew. "Sa raison" thus must be translated into English as "one's own reason" or "his own reason."

32. M. Foster, *Lectures on the History of Physiology* (New York: Dover Publications), p. 268.

In connection with the traditional misevaluation of Descartes' importance in medicine, the reader is directed to: L. Euler, *Letters to a German Princess,* "Letter LXXXI, *Of the Union between the Soul and the Body.*" [Published originally as *Lettres à une princesse d'Allemagne sur divers sujets de physique et de philosophie,* Leipzig, Steldel et compagnie, 1770, where that letter is number 96. In the 1795 edition, trans. Henry Hunter (London: H. Murray), it is LXXXI.] In that letter, Euler gives a very fine and complete survey of the principal points in Descartes' neurophysiology, but then, presumably for "nationalistic" reasons, he gives us "Letter LXXXII," in which he makes some little sport of Descartes; then, in the following letter, he praises Leibniz. Still, Letter LXXXI contains a very fine encapsulation of Descartes' principles of psychology.

33. Hall, *The Scientific Revolution,* p. 129.

34. Ibid., p. 150.

35. Charles Singer, *A Short History of Medicine* (New York: Oxford Univ. Press, 1962), p. 127. Singer, as opposed to Hall, thinks that the iatro-physicists had a mechanics behind their physiology.

Singer certainly is correct in saying that Descartes was in the tradition of the iatro-physicists, but he takes neither Descartes nor the iatro-physicists seriously enough.

36. This is not to claim that, in principle, political science is the same as social science; that claim involves the assertion that polity is society and society is polity, an assertion that must be very much qualified before it is valid. We can say here, however, that the parallel between Descartes' accounts of the ontogenesis of the human body and his cosmogenesis leads directly to a political science whose immediate foundations are "psycho-biological" or even "neurophysiological," and whose ultimate principles are embedded in a natural law theory articulated in Descartes' three laws of body, together with his doctrine of divine providence.

37. An exception to this rule is to be found in Richard Kennington's "Descartes' 'Olympica'" (*Social Research,* Summer, 1961), pp. 171–204. Given the assessment of d'Alembert, and given Kennington's work, if nothing else, it is simply astonishing that so little attention has been paid to Descartes' political teaching or to its central place as a continuous source of nourishment for political theory. The answer, in part at least, seems to be the modern age's extreme distaste for any theological dimension to "truly scholarly" work; another, again very partial, answer may well be this age's extreme distaste for anything

infringing on our freedom—and recognition of founding fathers and the like makes demands on that freedom that are often deeply onerous to us. Descartes, on his part, considered generosity and its proper complement, gratitude, as central conditions for any great improvement in the human condition. Leninists and Maoists seem to agree.

38. Except for M. Leroy's remarkable writings, e.g., "Descartes precurseur du social moderne" (*Revue de synthèse*, 1948, 63:9–67), there is very little appreciation expressed for Descartes as a founder of liberal democratic theory (again, excepting Kennington).

39. D'Alembert, *Discours Préliminaire de L'Encyclopédie*, pp. 93–94.

40. Ibid., p. 94.

PART I

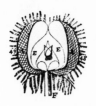

THINKING BODIES
AND THE BODIES OF
MATHEMATICAL PHYSICS
Preparation for
Medicine and Mechanics

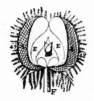

Introduction

DESCARTES' NOTION OF body derives much of its power from an ambiguity that has managed to charm both physics and medical physiology. An instance of this ambiguity is found in the title of Meditation II, which announces that it is concerned "with the nature of the human soul, and that it is easier to know than the Body." There, "the Body" refers primarily to merely physical body and not to the human body. Although Meditation II discusses the difficulty of clearly conceiving a piece of wax (*une morceau de cire*), there is not one word in it concerning a *human* body. Furthermore, Descartes never did discuss a living body in any detail in any of the six Meditations, although the general title of the *Meditations* announces that it is concerned with demostrating the real distinction "Between the Soul and the Body." Only in the "Abridgement" to the French translation do we find (Vol. IXA, p. 10) that "the premises on which one can conclude the immortality of the soul, depend on the explication of the whole of Physics." To make sense of that title, it seems to imply that: Physics deals with the general body out of which particular bodies are formed; medicine deals with particular, mortal bodies that are alive and that have souls united to them; and, finally, ethics deals, at least in large part, with doing unto others as you would have them do unto you—especially in matters of life and death.

Descartes often wrote, however, as if his interest in medical matters, and hence particularly in organized body, arose early—long before his interest in physics. Indeed, he even told the Marquis of Newcastle (Vol. IV, p. 329, l. 16–17) that, "the conservation of health always has been the principal goal of my studies. . . ." In another place, (Vol. IV, p. 221, l. 5–11), speaking to a close confidant, Princess Elizabeth, he said that he was quite sickly as a child and that the doctors despaired of his life. However, he learned to overcome his illness by his temperament:

I believe that the inclination that I have always had of considering things which come up from a point of view which could enable me to render them most agreeable, and to make sure that my principal contentment depended on me alone, is the reason that this indisposition which came to me as if it were natural to me, has little by little entirely passed away.

Thus, there is evidence that the problem of health, and hence of the organic body, was of concern to Descartes long before he began his mathematical studies of the nature of merely physical body, whose only essential attribute is that it occupies space, i.e., that it is extended. What, then, led Descartes to invent a mechanistic biology, that is, a biology founded on strict physical principles without any appeal to life forces, souls, and the like, in order to understand the phenomenon of living, organized body?

Descartes gave us indications of his answer. In Article 71 of the first part of his *Principles of Philosophy* (Vol. VIII, p. 35), he wrote that the first and principal cause of error in a human being arises from his judgment, first formed in childhood, that things exist outside him in the same form that he perceives them. He then said that *anatomy* shows that this could not possibly be the case, since the nerves leading to the brain from the eyes are not able to transmit the whole shapes of things that we perceive. All that nerves can transmit, he said, are differences in intensity or magnitude, motion, and the like. However, these are precisely what he felt to be the subjects of mathematics, and they are properties that body has merely as body, that is, merely as physical body. It seems, in short, that neuroanatomy implies that one must study something like mathematical physics to understand what it is that the nerves carry to the brain from the external senses. Consequently, Part I of this study begins with an examination of the sorts of things that the nerves carry from the external senses to the brain.

However, study of Descartes' mathematical physics as it relates to neuroanatomy presents us directly with another problem: Descartes' physics is a *mathematical* physics, and, according to Descartes, his view of mathematics does not in the least imply the existence of any body whatsoever, organized or even merely extended. Concerning his view of mathematics, he first stated that:

> I wanted to find . . . other truths, and having proposed to myself the object of the geometers, which I conceive as a continuous body, or an indefinite space extended in length, width, height (or depth), divisible into various parts which can have various shapes and sizes, and which can be stationary or transposed in all ways, because the geometers suppose all that in their object . . . [Vol. VI, p. 36, l. 4–11]

Then, five lines later, he stated that "I also took note that there was nothing at all in the writing of mathematicians that assured me of the existence of their object." Consequently, Part I of this work continues by examining *how Descartes came to think that his mathematics does have some-*

thing to do with real, existant body, and thus with medicine. Only this examination can reveal how Descartes justifies his use of mathematics to analyze and to understand the physics of the nerves leading to the brain, and what it is that those nerves carry from the external senses to the brain. That task occupies the rest of Part I, Chapter 1.

The nature of the mathematics performed by the computational, problem-solving machine that is comprised by the human body dictates that the mathematician using it have the ability to distinguish between what he knows and what he does not know, and, moreover, that he be able to *anticipate* solutions to his problems on the basis of what he does know. Chapter 2 of Part I, addresses this topic and prepares the way for the general cosmology and developmental anatomy given in Part II, "Compound Bodies in General."

CHAPTER 1

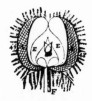

Physical Body

THIS CHAPTER IS divided into five main sections. the first section, "Solids and Super-solids," describes Descartes' truly astonishing and absolutely original introduction, into the tradition of geometrical studies, of the concept of geometrical constructs of more than three dimensions—"super-solids [*sur-solides*]." This concept leads to the question of the degree to which our perceptions of external reality are faithful images of that external reality, mediated as they are through the agency of the brain and nerves. Descartes, the primary inventor of analytic geometry, rejects the view that our perceptual field contains faithful images of an external world. This, in turn, raises questions, very important for both philosophy and science since his time, about the biological nature of perception. Furthermore, it raises the critical problem of justifying the replacement of the geometry known prior to Descartes with "symbolic" mathematics, that is, with algebra and its derivatives.

The second section of this chapter, "Dimension," concerns the general concept of dimension in Descartes' thinking, a concept already either completely or very nearly fully realized in the early (1628) *Regulae*. This section includes some of the immediate consequences of the concept of "solids" that have more than three dimensions; we also indicate how the Cartesian concept of dimension leads to a notion of rational explanation, and hence science, that defines its subject matter as being comprised of just so many "dimensions"—or "factors," as we say today— as there are distinct and clear concepts or ideas involved in our theories about that subject matter.

The third section presents an introductory sketch of Descartes' notion of mathematical analysis, against the background of the tradition from which his notion of analysis was a momentous departure. The section indicates how his comprehension of analysis justifies his concepts of dimension and geometrical super-solids.

The fourth and fifth sections address the problem of the relation between simple experience and the constructs of Cartesian mathematics, which include "geometrical solids" of more than three dimensions: For example, what is the relation between mathematical body, body as grasped by Cartesian geometrical algebra, and "naive" body, body as grasped by the senses in everyday experience? This problem is a central consequence of Descartes' analytic mathematics, since it seems that "geometrical analysis" (or "algebra") can only give a mathematics of the phenomena—it does not seem to be able to address itself to our daily experienced and impassioned involvement with them, nor to explain such phenomena as "innate" or "instinctive" desires, repulsions, or reactions, without which the most gifted and learned of Cartesian mathematicians would not live to practice his art for half a day.

SOLID BODIES AND SUPER-SOLIDS: BODIES OF MATHEMATICAL PHYSICS

Descartes invented a version of what we today call "analytic geometry" when he was a young man. Analytic geometry is, by definition, concerned both with analysis and with geometry. Since Descartes, and others of his time, identified analysis with algebra, analytic geometry is a sort of geometrical algebra, and, to the extent that algebra has many similarities to and affinities with arithmetic, it is a sort of arithmetical geometry. However, this gives rise to a problem. On the face of it, geometry and arithmetic are very different. Indeed, Descartes himself seems to address this problem at the beginning of *La Geometrie* (1637), the book in which he gives the world his own newly invented analytic geometry. The book begins with his announcement that any problem of geometry can be solved by treating it as if it were a problem in arithmetic, and hence by using only arithmetical operations. He wrote:

> and as all arithmetic is composed of only four or five operations which are: addition, subtraction, multiplication, division, and extraction of roots . . . ; so, has one anything else to do in geometry, touching the lines one seeks, in order to prepare them to become known, than to add certain of them to others or subtract them from others? And I shall not be afraid to introduce terms of arithmetic to geometry, since I wish to make myself more intelligible. [Vol. VI, p. 369, l. 8–p. 370, l. 14]

Concerning the novelty and superiority of his own treatment of these matters he said (Vol. I, p. 479, l. 2–8) that it is "to ordinary geometry what the rhetoric of Cicero is to the a,b,c's of children." However, we all know what the objects of geometry look like, and even that the figures that geometry deals with look like things we see every day. What about the objects of arithmetic? What do they look like? What experience do we have daily that presents us with things that look like what we do when, for instance, we multiply a number by itself 6 times? Furthermore, in arithmetic, any arithmetical object can be multiplied times itself *any number of times* (e.g., "2 times itself 6 times" equals 64), but what does *a line* look like if we multiply it? A line in geometry multiplied by itself 3 times gives the volume of a cube (a box 2 feet on a side is "2 cubed" or "8 cubic feet" in volume), but what does a line give when multiplied by itself 6 times? Is there some sort of solid of more than three dimensions, some sort of "super-solid"?

Geometry and arithmetical algebra seem to be very different kinds of mathematics, because the things with which they deal, their objects, seem to be very different. The objects of geometry are inherently visible, and they often look like things we see with our eyes in everyday experience; the objects of arithmetic are inherently invisible. What is more, this difference is paralleled in the operations we can perform on the objects of each science: the objects of geometry are visible, but they cannot be given in more than three dimensions; the objects of arithmetic are not visible, but we can multiply them by one another any number of times and still have an arithmetical object. However, Descartes still held that, "I shall not be afraid to introduce terms of arithmetic into geometry." He even went so far as to say that (Vol. VI, p. 378, l. 23–28):

> the scruple that kept the ancients from using certain arithmetical terms in geometry (which would not have happened except that they did not see their relation sufficiently clearly), caused much obscurity and embarrassment in their manner of expressing themselves.[1]

That is, Descartes saw none of the problems that we have pointed out, even though he knew that mathematicians belonging to the very ancient tradition preceding him had scruples sufficiently powerful to keep them from confusing the objects of arithmetic with those of gemoetry.

Why did Descartes put aside those scruples, and what was the result of his "unscrupulousness" in these matters? The first and most obvious result was that Descartes did not distinguish between the numerical quantity of arithmetic and the linear quantity of geometry: Descartes' analytic geometry deals with a species of objects that are no more imaginable than, but just as imaginable as, the objects of arithmetic—which we "imagine" to ourselves by means of symbolic numerals. However, this means that the lines we use to draw the objects of geometry are no more "natural" than those conventional numerals with which we represent to ourselves the objects of arithmetic. Descartes' geometry is, therefore, the science that deals both with what he characterized as "a body . . . extended in length, breadth, and height . . ." *and* with the numbers of arithmetic. It has affinities with that universal mathematics that includes all other branches of mathematics; indeed, insofar as its objects are not

particularized as either numbers or linear magnitudes, Cartesian geometry *is* a "pure" mathematics.

The Cartesian scholar Jean Laporte discusses the ambiguity of the
object of Cartesian geometry:

> [The conception of analytical geometry such as Descartes elaborated]
> could not be a matter of a simple application of algebra to gemoetry,
> but, of a veritable reduction of geometry to algebra . . . To under-
> stand the properties of the circle, for example, there is no need to
> look at the shape; it is sufficient to study and discuss the equation "x^2
> $+ y^2 = r^2$." But, on the other hand, an algebraic equation is, *per se,* a
> stranger to space. It is a matter of pure quantity.[2]

As Laporte says, Descartes' geometry is not concerned with the
shapes of bodies any more than arithmetic is. The question then arises:
What is Descartes' mathematics a mathematics of? For, if it does not have
a definite object outside the mind of the mathematician, what good is it?

Descartes' mathematics is the mathematics that claims that it can
solve each and every question that any human being can put clearly to it.
Its general object, which Descartes sometimes refers to as "lines [*lignes*],"
is whatever it is that we use to solve particular problems. Although it
does not have a definite object outside the mind (for what definite object
could be at the same time the object both of arithmetic and of geometry?) it does have a sort of object. *Descartes' mathematics has as its object
classes of problems.* Indeed, later writers were to refer to it as "specious
arithmetic," that is, as the general mathematics that was concerned with
species, or classes, of problems," as treating of species, classes, or genera
of objects, it is a general mathematics.

Descartes' geometry provides mathematical proofs concerning one-,
two-, and three-dimensional geometrical constructs, but, insofar as it is
at the same time arithmetical, it can also provide proofs concerning
geometrical constructs of any number of dimensions. Cartesian geometry, however, uses lines to make visible, geometrical forms. A question
then arises about the relationship between the figures of everyday things
we see with our eyes, and the figures that Descartes' geometry constructs: if Descartes' geometry is just as much a sort of arithmetic as it is a
sort of geometry, then what sort of thing is it that we see, when we look
at the constructs of his geometry? Are we looking at a numberlike thing?
At a bodylike thing? The geometrico-arithmetical character of that geometry implies that all its objects are, *at one and the same time,* both
numberlike and bodylike; consequently, how do we distinguish between
what we see when we look at a metal cube and what we have constructed
by means of Cartesian geometry? The metal cube is not a numberlike
object of arithmetic, but anything that can be addressed by Cartesian

geometry would seem to be both arithmetical and geometrical at the same time. In other words, the constructions of Cartesian geometry are purely imaginative or imaginary, but the perceptions we receive through our eyes in everyday experience often look just like them. Is there some aspect of real, three-dimensional body "out there" that we by nature, i.e., instinctively, and pre-mathematically, grasp through perception? How do we distinguish between it and our imaginative constructions of geometry?[3] (This is not a verbal exercise: whenever we "mathematically" determine the volume of a cubical container existing outside us, we treat it as if it were a mathematical construct, and we make no distinction between the perceived cubical container in front of us and the cube we imaginatively construct in order to determine a volume.)

Descartes stated that in order to determine the objective status of anything of which we are conscious, and thus to determine whether it is real or merely imaginary (Vol. X, p. 448, l. 21–22), "it belongs more . . . to the physicists to examine whether or not their foundations should be real."[4] Thus, for example, it is the physicists who can tell us whether we feel hot because of the way our bodies react to external body, or whether we feel hot because of the heat *in* some distinct body. (The medical consequences of this are clearly a importance—for example, in the formation of a theory of fever and chills.) However, abstract geometry, what we today call theoretical, mathematical physics, investigates methods for determining whether sensible qualities of bodies, such as heat and cold, heaviness or lightness, color, etc., are perceptions of things in external bodies that are faithfully mirrored in the way we perceive them. Thus, abstract geometry must first determine what it is we are conscious of as heat and cold before we can discover whether they really exist, "out there"; in Descartes' terminology, abstract geometry investigates the "what it is" (the *quid sit*) of all qualities that we perceive, and physics investigates the "whether it is" (the *an sit*) of particulars. Abstract geometry, he said, investigates questions concerning the way we use our minds to solve problems. There is also "another kind of geometry whose goal is to explain the phenomena of nature. For . . . my Physics is nothing else but geometry" (Vol. II, p. 268, l. 9–14). He then continued, "I have resolved to leave abstract geometry . . . in order to have more leisure to cultivate [that] other kind of geometry." The 42-year-old Descartes thus left theoretical, mathematical physics for applied physics—what we can call "mechanics."

In that abstract geometry concerns the scientific use of the mind, it is not interested in any particular physical quantity; it is only concerned with those mental operations that the physicist will use in his applied physics or mechanics to solve any and all particular problems. Abstract geometry, "that is to say, the investigations of questions which are only mental exercises" (ibid.), has for its object the object of that pure, general mathematics that is alike arithmetical and geometrical: its object is pure, nonspatial quantity or "magnitude in general." The other sort of geometry, mechanics or *applied* geometry, has for its object what Descartes called "extended body [*cors estendu*]."

This leads us to the following perplexity: if there exists an abstract mathematics (algebra or pure geometry), and an applied mathematics (applied geometry, physics, or mechanics), what is algebraic quantity in relation to physical quantity? In other words, if physicists think about physical bodies of three dimensions and their properties, what do abstract mathematicians think about? Reason's inherent taste for symmetry demands an answer that is something like: physics, which is *applied* mathematics, deals with physical bodies, and abstract mathematics deals with abstract bodies. But then we must ask what an abstract body is, and what is the relation between the rational abstract body of pure mathematics and the "out there" physical body of the physicists. That is, do abstract bodies have "abstract dimensions"?

Descartes wrote (especially Vol. III, p. 691, l. 3 to p. 692, l. 20) that mind thinks, and *only* thinks. Therefore, it could not concern itself with any particular physical quantity, but only with those intellectual *operations* that are used in physics to solve, i.e., to think through, any and all particular problems that arise with particular bodies having particular shapes, positions, and quantitites of matter, etc. Consequently, the dimensions of abstract bodies must be just those abstract dimensions that define abstract bodies as being *definite* abstract bodies. This leads us to ask how Descartes understood and used the term "dimensions." (It is certainly not the way in which it is generally used.)

As we discuss in detail in the next section, the *operations* used in any instance of problem-solving are considered by Descartes to be the "dimensions" of that problem. In the case of pure geometry, those operations are those of his "arithmetic," i.e., of our algebra, and it is Descartes himself who, sometime before 1628, invented an abstract geometry that is widely held to consist in a partially arithmetical re-interpretation of geometry.[5] In common speech, the term 'dimension' means exactly what it means when we say "the dimensions of this box are $3 \times 4 \times 7$ inches." The new Cartesian use of the term 'dimension,' however, is not in the least dependent upon the concepts of space or of body, but only upon the concept of "arithmetical" operations. These operations can be performed without any restriction being placed on their possible objects; therefore, the Cartesian overthrow of the traditional dimensional restrictions upon performing "arithmetical" operations on "geometrical" magnitudes is equivalent to providing the tradition with a new calculus whose objects are n-dimensional "geometrical" constructs, "super-solids": arithmetic knows no limit to the number of operations we can perform on *its* objects.

Descartes first publicly referred to this n-dimensional quantity in the *Geometry.* He wrote "it should be remarked that by a^2 or b^3 and the like, I usually have in mind only completely simple lines—although, in order to conform to the usage of algebra, I call them squares, cubes, etc." (Vol. VI, p. 371, l. 16–20). Thereafter he continued, "the square or the cube or the square of the square, or the super-solid . . . should be equal to what is produced by the addition or subtraction of two or more other quantities" (ibid., p. 373, l. 9–12). By the expression "the like" in this passage, Descartes meant expressions like a^4, a^5, or, for any number, a^n, or where he explicitly broke with Vieta and Fermat, $a^2 \times b^3$. The English translators, Smith and Latham, remark, in a footnote to that passage, that "At the time this was written, a^2 was commonly considered to mean the surface of a square whose side was a, and b^3 to mean the volume of a cube whose side was b; while b^4, b^5 . . . were unintelligible as geometric forms."[6] Aside from the problem of understanding what *geometrical* meaning the expression a^5 could have, what could Descartes have had in mind when he said that a^2 can be both a square as well as a completely simple line? What sort of a line is that? And what sort of "geometrical" construct is comprised of the sum of, for example, a square and a cube— $a^2 + b^3$? How can one add a square and a cube? Obviously, a^2 and b^3 do not refer to squares and cubes as we think of them geometrically.

Descartes said that he calls a^2 "a squared," and b^3, "b cubed," in order to conform to common usage; but his definition of these terms does not conform to *any* prior usage. This usage began with Descartes. In the expression a^b, for instance, or, to be general, a^n, n does not refer to the number of spatial dimensions of a geometrical construct; it serves only as the index of the number of times the base a was "multiplied" by itself in a certain way.[7] The index n thus refers to the number of times an intellectual operation was performed, and *not to what is constructed by performing that operation.* Thus, for example, if we construct three lines (where the unit length is an inch) of 3, 9, and 27 inches respectively, the last, in the Cartesian usage, is "three-dimensional" with respect to the first, i.e., $27'' = (3'') \times (3'') \times (3'')$. Considered operationally, the quantity a^n is not essentially different for any value of n; that is, a^3 is no more clearly grasped than a^{15}, insofar as both are defined as the construction comprised by multiplying the "quantity" a times itself either three times or fifteen times.

The fact remains, however, that whereas a^3 can be considered either as a length that stands in the triplicate ratio to the unit length a or as a cube with side a, no such relationship is true of a^n for any values of n greater than 3. a^{15} can only be grasped as a "geometrical" entity by considering it as a length standing in the ratio of 15:1 to the unit length *a*. In this case, however, although the operation of multiplication is applicable both to numbers and to lines, a^{15} has no representation beyond a "symbolic" one, e.g., the symbol a^{15}. Once we deal with constructs of more than three dimensions, it is clear that we are considering something that can never be directly—"naively"—presented to our perceptive capacity through the senses in the way in which we "see" cubical solids. Super-solids, such as a^{15}, insofar as they are presented to our imaginations at all, must be presented in the form of *arbitrary* "symbols" by means of which we represent to our senses nothing but the operations of the intellect—as when we construct symbolic systems to represent mathematical operations. However, we can certainly also use this mathematics to solve problems of three dimensions; then, in considering these three-dimensional figures, we are exercising our intellects to understand clearly and distinctly what is given to us, originally, by our senses in "naive" experience, without any intellectual effort. *This* use of the intellect is what Descartes called "physics," in distinction from "abstract geometry," and he identified this physics with "applied geometry." Once again, when these constructs are viewed as aids in exhibiting the mind's purely intellectual operations, we are dealing with what he calls "abstract geometry."[8]

Crucial problems still to be faced are: what is the relation between this nonspatial, pure quantity and physical matter, or, as Descartes referred to it, "a body . . . extended in length, breadth, and depth. . . . "; furthermore, why is the question of this relation so central to Descartes' thought—even requiring him to prove the existence of God in order to relate his pure mathematics to any physical object?

In his physical works, such as *The World* and *Principles,* Descartes assumed without a word of justification that all of space is filled with that "extended body," and in his medical works he even attempted to show how *live* bodies are generated from that "extended" body. However, in the second part of the *Discourse* he said that geometers prior to him did not prove the existence of body, although their method of demonstration seemed to him to yield many trustworthy results. In the *Meditations* he went so far as to doubt the very existence of body. Why are some of Descartes' writings so preoccupied with discussions of the existence of solid body of three dimensions when others assume it without question? Furthermore, what was he meditating on, thinking about, when he began to see the existence of solid, three-dimensional body as a problem? He ended the *Meditations* by calling that doubt "excessive and laughable." Or, to ask the question in "scientific" terms, what is the relation of mathematics to physics? That is, how is mathematical physics even possible? And, if Descartes' algebraic geometry is "alien to space," and in no way presupposes the existence of physical objects, how can we use it in the solution of problems concerned with physical objects?

Part of Descartes' greatness as a thinker and philosopher is that not only did he contribute largely to the invention of physics and its mathematics,—an achievement on which many thinkers would have easily rested their claim to fame—but he also pointed our a myriad of problems associated with those discoveries, and then undertook to give deep foundations for his answers to his own questions about his own discoveries. That search for deep and sure foundations to his science he calls, not altogether historically inaccurately, "metaphysics."[9]

What Descartes calls his "metaphysical" doubts about the existence of three-dimensional body were not begun *in the course of* "metaphysical" speculation at all; these speculations were carried on largely after the fact. Upon what, then, was he meditating when his "excessive and laughable" doubts about the existence of solid body occurred to him? He wrote in the Second Part of the *Discourse:* "I wanted to seek . . . other truths, and having proposed to myself the object of the geometers . . . I also took note that there was nothing at all in them that assured me of the existence of their object." It appears that his doubts about the external existence of bodies arose as a consequence of his meditations on "the object of the geometers," as *he* understood that object. As he understood it, that object was by no means merely three-dimensional body.

Then why would he present these doubts, arrived at while meditating on geometry, as if they were the fruit of metaphysical speculations? Did Descartes think that problems dealt with in metaphysics prior to him were in truth "meta-mathmatical" rather than "meta-physical" problems?

Descartes wrote that there are two sorts of people, who appreciate two sorts of arguments—one metaphysical, the other mathematical. In the Foreword to the *Geometry* (Vol. VI, p. 368), for instance, he wrote: "Up til now, I have tried to make myself understandable to everyone; but, where this treatise is concerned, I fear that it cannot be read except by those who know already what is in the books of Geometry." That warning might, to be sure, simply mean that many people happen not to have read the books of the geometers and so are not prepared to follow his proofs, but this is apparently not his point. For, in the dedicatory letter to Princess Elizabeth in the *Principia* (Vol. VIII, p. 4, l. 3–6), he wrote, "It happens in almost every case that those who are versatile in Metaphysics abhor geometry; if, however, some are good in geometry, they do not grasp what is written concerning First Philosophy. . . ." In a private letter to Princess Elizabeth (Vol. IV, p. 46, l. 6–12), he continued in the same vein:

Experience made me realize that most of those intellects which have the ability to understand the reasoning of Metaphysics, cannot grasp that of Algebra, and reciprocally, that those which understand easily the latter, are usually incapable of the former. . . .

In still another letter to her (Vol. III, p. 692), Descartes qualified his former distinction by saying: "Metaphysical thoughts . . . serve to render familiar to us the notion of the soul; and the study of Mathematics, which exercises principally the imagination in the consideration of figures and movements, accustoms us to form quite distinct notions of body. . . "[10] Descartes' doubts concerning the existence of body thus seem to be a metaphysical version of his mathematical speculation, a version that presents mathematical meditations in a metaphysical guise, i.e., *directed at the non-mathematicians.*

Descartes' introduction, into mathematics, of a pure geometry that concerns *all* the operations of the mind, including those that can provide the imagination with representations of bodies of only three dimensions, brings up the metaphysical problem of the relation between body conceived geometrically—"imaginary" body—and body conceived in relation to questions of life and death, nutrition, pleasure, and pain—"physical" body. Physical body is entirely pre-mathematical; how could it be deduced from an algebraic notion of body? Indeed, so distinct are these two kinds of awareness of body that the mathematics dealt with in the *Geometry* (which was published by Descartes himself as the third and final "essay" on, or trial of, his *Discourse on Method*) does not at all prepare us for its application in another "essay" of that same *Discourse,* i.e., in the *Dioptrics.* In the *Dioptrics* Descartes dealt with the solutions of problems concerning our perception of color, distance, figure, and the like, together with the design for machines to grind lenses for eyeglasses to correct faulty vision. Descartes himself, however, tells us that his mathematical physics involves a mathematics that does not seem to have anything to do with physical objects: it makes no essential distinction between solids and super-solids. How, then, can it be used to solve physical problems?

Furthermore, what could a textbook of the neuroanatomy of vision, the *Dioptrics,* have to do with the metaphysical *Meditations,* which addresses "the existence of God and of our souls"? Also, Descartes published the *Dioptrics* as an introductory, companion piece to the *Geometry,* with its super-solids; whatever super-solids are, they hardly seem to be concerned with the neuroanatomy of vision—no more, indeed, than arithmetic is concerned with it.

The remainder of this section addresses the question of the need for a metaphysical foundation for the neuroanatomy of *Dioptrics.* (Later sections of this chapter consider the details of the relation between the mathematics of super-solids and the neuroanatomy of sight, between, that is, the *Dioptrics* and the *Geometry* that it introduces.)

Descartes the mathematician-neuroanatomist was very clear about the need for a bridge to connect the extremely abstract mathematics of works like the *Geometry* with other very practical works, such as the *Dioptrics.* The *Meditations,* even in spite of its metaphysical arguments and proofs, provides such a bridge in Descartes' published works. In 1630 he told his good friend and confidant, Father Mersenne, that he would publish a work concerning "dioptrics," but that he was afraid that he would not be understood, and that he would probably have to write another work, a treatise on metaphysics, which would discuss the existence of God and the immortality of the soul. He wrote:

> I will test in the *Dioptrics* whether I am capable of explaining my concepts, and of persuading others of a truth—after I have persuaded myself of it! I do not think I will be able to do it, but, if I can, then who knows but that one day I might finish a small treatise on Metaphysics which I started . . . and in which the principle points are to prove *the existence of God and that of our souls,* when they are separated from the body, from which their immortality follows. [Vol. I, p. 182, l. 13–22]

That is, the metaphysics of the *Meditations* is designed to examine the thinking soul when it is not directly dealing with physical bodies: "when our souls are separated from the body." A few years after he wrote to Father Mersenne, he published the *Dioptrics,* and a few years after that he published the *Meditations.*

In the *Dioptrics,* he presented, among other things, a neuroanatomy of vision, and (in the accompanying *Meteors*) the physics of a wave-particle theory of light. On the basis of his results, he calimed to prove biologically that the Aristotelian theory of vision (which he incorrectly said involves the late medieval theory of "intentional species"[11]) cannot be correct since the structure of the optic nerves is such that they can react only to particles of matter in motion; Descartes' neuroanatomy sets out to prove that the optic nerves *cannot* transmit whole figures. He traced the optic nerves to the brain and undertook to show how they transmit different impulses of varying intensity to a certain area deep inside the brain where the pineal gland (*corpus pinealis*) is located. That gland, Descartes said (incorrectly!) is very delicately attached to the floor of ventricle III of the brain, so that the least motion in the nerve endings causes it to swing into a new position. In Discourse V of the *Dioptrics,* Descartes first refers to the pineal gland in the context of tracing the path of nerve impulse up to the interior of the brain. He says (Vol. VI, p.

129, l. 19–22), "and from there I could further transport it up to a certain little gland, which is found within the middle of these concavities, and is properly the seat of common sense."[12]

Up to this point, Descartes had discussed the pure mechanics of vision. A few pages later, in "On Vision," however, he ceased what we might consider an empirical neurophysiologic investigation of sensation, and made a "metaphysical" assumption of great power, without any remarks to that effect. Describing the relation between nerve impulses as they affect the pineal gland and the contents of consciousness, he said of these impulses:

> These are the movements by which they are composed, movements which, acting immediately against our soul, is so far as it is united with our body, are instituted by Nature to make the soul have such sensations. [Those sensations are] light, color, position, distance, size and shape. . . . [Vol. VI, p. 130, l. 11–15]

In a letter to Chanute, the French ambassador to the Protestant Queen of Sweden, Christina, dated February 26, 1649, Descartes addressed himself directly to the relation between his anatomical studies and his mathematical studies. Discussing the relation of magnitude, figure, and motion to what we sense as light, figure, motion and the other elementary data of consciousness, Descartes said:

> Although I consider nothing in body except magnitudes, figures, and the movements of their parts, I claim nevertheless to explain in my treatise [i.e., the *Principles of Philosophy* of 1644] the nature of light, of heat and of all the other sensible qualities; furthermore, I presuppose that these sensible qualities are only in our senses in the way that tickling and pain are in them; and I presuppose that they are not all in the objects which we sense, in which there are only figures and movements which cause the sensations which we call light, heat, ect. [Vol. V, p. 291, l. 28 to p. 292, l. 10][13]

The soul is so constituted by nature that these objects of abstract mathematics--magnitudes, figures, and movements—provide the occasions for the soul to come to be aware of just that class of perceptions that can be viewed objectively.[14]

Descartes continued this mathematical biology; he said of our simple responses to magnitude, figures, and movements that those responses alone properly belong to the sense of sight, and that: "it is necessary to think that our soul is of such a nature, that the force of movements, which are found in the places of the brain from whence come the small filaments of optic nerves, makes the soul experience the sensation of light" (Vol. VI, p. 130, l. 20). He said of our visual perception of magnitude that it is derived from perception of distance and situation (Vol. VI,

p. 140, l. 2). The visual perception of distance is derived from the shape and setting of the eyes, in which a motion is begun that ends in the pineal gland, "in a manner instituted by Nature to allow our soul to perceive this distance" (Vol. VI, p. 137, l. 14–15). Of our visual perception of situation or place, he said that change of place of the sighted object causes a change in the pattern in which particular optic nerves at the back of the eyes are affected by incoming light rays, and that this "is instituted by Nature not only to make the soul know in what place each part of the body is which it animates with respect to the others; but also to make it transfer its attention to all the places contained in straight lines . . . and determine their locations" (Vol. VI, p. 134, l. 31 to p. 135, l. 17).

In the *Dioptrics*, then, the soul's perceptions are primarily viewed as its natural reaction to mechanical perturbations affecting the equilibrium of the pineal gland that are transmitted to it through the agency of the optic nerves.[15] [Descartes touched upon other sources of "internal," "endocrinological" perturbations only as needed, leaving to the later *Passions of the Soul* (1645–46) and the *Description of the Human Body* (1648) the task of exhaustively accounting for all such sources.] The six parts of the *Dioptrics* are almost entirely concerned with how all occasions for the sensations of light, figure, motion, and the like can be reduced to simple corporeal motion; in the first two parts he considered motion initiated outside the body, and in the last four parts he considered motions modified by the structure of the body itself. The soul, Descartes said, has perceptions as a consequence of motions simply because it is its nature to react in a particular way when the pineal gland is moved in a particular way. The *Dioptrics* includes no justification for or discussion of that happy involvement of the soul with the motions of bodies, and the relation between the two appears profoundly arbitrary and merely the counsel of despair. The *Meditations*, on their part, are largely concerned with things of which we are conscious that do not seem to be occasioned by corporeal motion, for instance our idea of God. Indeed, the *Meditations* proceed as if even those perceptions identified in the *Dioptrics* as being caused or occasioned by motion in the pineal gland were merely constructs of the mind, and hence divorced from body entirely. It thus seems that Descartes' doubts concerning the existence of material things that are found in the *Meditations* are manufactured by him to introduce his metaphysical defense of his doctrine of "natural institutions" set forth four years earlier in the *Dioptrics*. Without that doctrine, which is specifically designed to give an objective reality to those perceptions (dealt with in *Dioptrics*) that are occasioned by perturbations of the pineal gland, perceptions and thoughts about body, and any other thoughts, are left with a merely formal existence in the mind and with no subject basis outside it.[16]

To sum up, the doctrine of the natural institutions plays the same logical role in the *Dioptrics* as the proof of the existence of material things plays in the *Meditations*. The two works are thus essentially complementary to each other. The one begins with the reality of body and shows its connection with our consciousness of the visible world containing bodies, while the other begins with the reality of what thinks and validates its thoughts about body. In Descartes' mathematical terminology: the *Dioptrics* is "synthetic," and the *Meditations* are, *as he himself said*, "analytic." The former proceeds from body to conscious perception, and the latter from consciousness to body.

In short, Descartes was fully aware of the power of what he calls the "metaphysical" assumption to which he was led *as a mathematical physicist*. He saw that his treatment of his physical and mechanical physiology of sensation led to an immense gap separating mind from body, and which required a very special hypothesis to be bridged, namely, an hypothesis that had to be consonant at one and the same time with his view of physics and with his views on the nature of mental activity.

DIMENSIONS

Descartes thoroughly investigated the concept of dimension prior to the 1628 *Rules*. In the *Rules*, Descartes wrote that a "subject" has as many dimensions as there are aspects of it that can be measured. Since for him all that can be clearly understood concerning body can be quantified, his characterization of dimension implies that there are at least as many dimensions in any body as there are distinct and characteristic qualities in it.[17] Also in the *Rules*, Descartes defined "dimension" as:

> nothing other than the mode or way according to which some subject is considered to be measurable: so that, not only length, breadth and depth are dimensions of body, but gravity is also a dimension, that according to which a subject is weighed, and speed is the dimension of motion, and an infinity of others like these . . . It is clear from this that there can be an infinity of differing dimensions in the same subject and that they add nothing more to what is measured in things; rather, they are to be understood in the same way whether they have a real foundation in their particular subjects or whether they have been thought up in accordance with the discretion (or: free power) of our minds. . . [Vol. X, p. 447–448]

In classical Latin, the term *dimensio* referred either to the dimension of a solid or to the extent of something.[18] The term was apparently not used except in reference to area, volume, and the like. However, the only time *dimensio* had this restricted meaning for Descartes was when the subject, such as a point, a line, a surface, or a solid body, was being considered as an extended surface and nothing else. Descartes' own use of the term is, to say the least, a generalization of the classical sense. In his usage, distance and time, for example, are dimensions of a moving body considered only in terms of its speed, entirely parallel to the more ordinary usage, which spoke of length, breadth, and depth as dimensions of a solid body considered in terms of its volume. Length, depth, and breadth are thus sometimes to be considered as dimensions of body, but only in terms of its volume; therefore, when Descartes said that his geometry is physics and it has for its object extended body (*cors estendu*), he did not mean merely that the subject of his physics is the extended body in its aspect of being extended: such a physics could only tell us that extended body has three dimensions. Rather, Descartes saw physics as being essentially concerned with all the significantly characteristic, *and measureable,* properties, "dimensions," of that "three-dimensional" body that he refers to as "extended body."

As shown in the previous section, it was Descartes who first said that a^3 could be interpreted to refer either to a "three-dimensional" solid of side a, or to some numberlike quantity "multiplied by itself three times." We also saw that, according to mathematicians prior to Descartes, a^4 (or a to any higher power than 3) cannot be understood as referring to a "geometrical" construct. For Descartes, a, a^2, a^3, as well as, say, a^{20} or whatever, refer to lines (*lignes*), and not to what prior mathematicians understood as a subject of gemoetry.

What are these *lignes* of Descartes, and what do they have to do with the familiar geometrical lines of high-school geometry—which serve to define the dimensions and shapes of geometrical objects? What do these "lines" have to do with lines we perceive by means of our optic nerves?

To understand the answer to these questions, we must first understand that Descartes did much more than free algebra from its dimensional, quasi-geometrical restrictions. For Descartes, that so-called "freeing from dimensional restrictions" that Scott refers to did not even primarily apply to constructs of more than three dimensions; indeed, Descartes saw absolutely no inherent, *theoretical,* distinction to be made between "three-dimensional" constructs and, say, "21-dimensional" constructs, except for precisely the number of "dimensions." These expressions, 'three-dimensional construct' and '21-dimensional construct,' did not, for Descartes, refer to distinct objects that only two different and distinct sciences can grasp—i.e., geometry dealing with up to three dimensions, and arithmetic thereafter. Descartes' pure geometry is universal mathematics (*mathesis universalis*), and, consistent with that name, the objects of universal mathematics are species or kinds of mathematical objects. Newton referred to it as "universal arithmetic," and others called it "algebra or specious arithmetic."[19] This new mathematics is generally considered today to deal with objects that are distinguished from one another and arranged in distinct "species" or "kinds" only by their dimensions. The question of the dimensions of the problems *about* bodies determines the *species* of body: the *kind* of the body is replaced with the *way* we solve problems about it. From this moment on, "species" belongs to *mind*, and not to vision, and a principle foundation of modern philosophy has been laid down.

The dimensions of an object of this new universal mathematics determine the "specific" kind of mathematical object it is, and the kind of mathematical object, that is, its "species," is precisely determined by *how* that kind of object is mathematically grasped. Since the "arithmetical" operations of addition, subtraction, multiplication, division, and extraction of roots were for Descartes generally applicalbe to any and all mathematical objects, these operations merely determine that their objects are mathematical, that is, are related to one another as quantities are related to one another. The dimensions of a mathematical object do not necessarily determine which arithmetical operations are applicable to it. Rather, the term 'dimension' refers to the way we must consider a given object to determine the best way to solve *any* problem concerning it— using, to be sure, the operations of addition, subtraction, etc. Thus, for example, the *volume* of a cubical container is a three-dimensional mathematical object, i.e., it is determined by multiplying together length, breadth, and width. However, the *weight* of that container when it is filled with certain materials, such as feathers or sand, is a four-dimensional object for Descartes, i.e., it is a mathematical object that depends on three-dimensional volume "times" the density factor of whatever is in the container, since a cubic foot of feathers weighs less than a cubic foot of sand. But even that density factor varies somewhat between sea level and 40,000 feet above sea level; thus, if height above sea level is a consideration—a "factor," as is said algebraically today—then the weight of the filled container is a five-dimensional mathematical object. Its five dimensions are length, breadth, depth, density factor at sea level, and height factor to compensate for distance above sea level. All these must be considered together to give a complete mathematical concept of the weight of the filled container located 40,000 feet above sea level. The new physics, mathematical physics, is not a physics that deals with bodies that "by nature" fall into distinct categories or species; mathematical physics groups its objects according to the *mathematical* procedures by means of which problems concerning bodies are solved. Instead of having natural classes of objects, the world is rearranged into classes of objects that are subject to the same group of operations.

In this light, the concept of dimension appears very similar to "consideration": a given object has as many dimensions as there are distinct

things that we must take under consideration if we are to grasp it mathematically. But then it follows that the dimensions of a mathematical
object are the same in number as the considerations or notions that
comprise our ideas about that object when we are solving particular
problems concerning that object. The dimensions of an object are thus
each and every aspect of the object that can enter into the solution of any
problem that the object poses. For Descartes, "lines" represented distinctly, and thereby articulated, *the various elements of solutions to problems:*
they are the way we refer to and keep before our immediate attention all
those aspects of problems that must be taken into consideration in order
to solve them (see especially Vol. X, p. 438–443).[20]

The soul as the thing that thinks is beginning to emerge as what
seeks "solid" solutions to its problems. At any rate, in place of an intellectual faculty that directly sees the truth once the obstacles to clear vision
have been cast aside (as in Plato, *Republic*, Book VI, especially
510b–511c, and in Aristotle, *Posterior Analytics*, 99b, l. 27–100b, l. 4),
Descartes presented a new faculty for seeking and grasping the truth.
That new faculty uses "factors" or "dimensions" to construct mathematical objects, and then performs operations on the dimensions of those
mathematical objects in order to arrive at a solution that is "the answer
to" or "the truth about" the question. That solution has *exactly* as many
dimensions as the problem.

According to Descartes, these constructs are the best means we have
for keeping all the parts of a problem together, but distinct, before we
have entirely solved it (and the only means we have of preventing ourselves from confusing the terms of distinct problems with one another).
"Lines" are thus also the means that thinking humans have for anticipating the solution to unsolved problems: according to Descartes, they enable us to show ourselves precisely what we do not know in order to
permit us to come to know it—a way of representing the dimensions of
problems we are trying to solve.

It follows from this that the power we human beings have of creating perceptible images for ourselves, of imagining, is, for Descartes,
closely bound up with our ability to think about solutions to problems
about subjects. Insofar as this power of imagination is bodily, which it
certainly is in part, the definition of the human body involves an aspect
that is profoundly in the service of intellectual problem-solving. (Anticipating ourselves: we can define medicine as a species of scientific
thought that is essentially concerned with the human body insofar as it is
in need of intellectual and scientific solutions to its bodily problems, or
sickness; as a consequence, medicine emerges as the science of the living
human body precisely insofar as that body is united to a mind that thinks
mathematically, using imagination to discover the dimensions of prob-

lems that beset it.) Body itself becomes a means to the solution of problems. As such, it loses its "out there" aspect and becomes matter for the working out of solutions to problems. Two hundred years after Descartes, Charles Darwin realized the full implications of Descartes' insight concerning real body as being exhaustively intelligible as a solution to a complex problem. For the orthodox Darwinian, and for the contemporary life-scientist, the living organism with, say, 2,000 biologically significant attributes, represents the real solution, effected "mechanically" through evolution, to a "2,000-dimensional" problem. For them that is what a living body *is*.

Thus, just as the expression a^4 can have a perfectly precise referent in physical reality, so can it be for Descartes that $2^4 = 16$ is a four-dimensional construct, because in that expression 16 is considered not merely as numbering a definite number of definite things, but as something constructed by a human thinker who does something to something four times in order to be able to solve some problem. The expression '2^4' thus represents the "specific" (species-wide) answer to all questions whose answers can be derived by multiplying 2 times itself 4 times; '16' represents the "solution," the "super-*solid*", and the expression '$2 \times 2 \times 2 \times 2$' represents the dimensions of the problem.

As Laporte reminded us, Descartes' geometry is "a true reduction of geometry to algebra" ("une véritable réduction de la géométrie à l'algèbre"). This means that the solution to geometrical problems is accomplished by the use of "arithmetical" operations performed on "lines," our "algebraic quantity." As Laporte also said, the equations of algebra are inherently non-spatial, and thus alien to the property of being necessarily no more than three-dimensional. All restrictions inherent in the dimensional character of geometrical objects are obliterated in treating them as objects that are accessible to the operations of arithmetic—where one can multiply any number of numbers together and still remain strictly within the domain of arithmetical objects. In his unrestricted use of all the arithmetical operations in the solution of geometrical as well as what his antecedents considered strictly arithmetical problems, Descartes obscured the distinction between bodies as the object of mathematics and numbers as the object of mathematics. This results in a hybrid use of arithmetical operations in geometry—as in our analytic (i.e., *algebraic*—and hence quaisi-arithmetical) geometry. The mathematical object of algebraic geometry is neither number nor body; it is a pure, abstract magnitude that is common to the domains of sensible, bodily quantity *and* purely intellectual, numerical quantity. This object, considered by "all the particular sciences which are commonly designated by the name mathematics," Descartes described by saying:

seeing that although their objects might differ, and that they still agree in the respect that they are concerned with nothing but the different relations or proportions found in them, I thought it better for me to examine only these general proportions and not to suppose them except in the subjects which served to render their knowledge easier for me. . . .[Vol. VI, p. 20, l. 1–7][21]

Earlier, in the *Rules*, Descartes said that general proportions, like particular ratios, presuppose some unit of measure common to each and every term in the proportion or ratio. He called this common unit the "equality" underlying the difference of magnitude of the terms, and he said of this equality that:

It should be remarked . . . that nothing can be reduced to this equality except what can be considered under the aspect of greater and less, and further, that all such is comprehended by magnitude: so that, after . . . the difficulties in terms have been abstracted from any subject . . . we then only consider ourselves to be dealing with magnitudes in general (or: with the genus of magnitude). [Vol. X, p. 440, l. 21–27][22]

In his partial fusion of the realm of geometry with that of arithmetic, Descartes at first sight seemed to transform the bodily or physical into the abstract and purely "ideal"; however, to be entirely accurate, this is not quite what he did. The "lines" of "pure geometry" ("algebraic quantity," as we refer to them today) are real, i.e., *visible*, lines, and they are essentially imaginable: they are perceived through the functions of a bodily organ, such as the brain, which is able to present a determinate quantity to our perceptual faculty. For Descartes, those "lines" are not best considered as abstractions from true body; they are genuinely perceived quantities that are entirely serviceable as means for solutions of problems (*Rules*, Vol. X, p. 438, l. 8–10). They are physical matter in the service of problem-solving mind—and, as such, they are *a strange sort of essential union of mind and body*, in that "[the parts of a question] are to be transferred to the real extension of body, and presented to the imagination only using bare figures: for they are in this way perceived far more distinctly by the intellect."

Consequently, we can refer to Descartes' "mind-body" problem as his imaginary-body/physical-body problem. The point is *not* that he abstracted from body to get "lines"; rather, he transformed physical quantity into an instrument useful for the process of thinking.

Descartes' mathematical object, his algebraic quantity, thus can be called a materialization of algebraic concepts: we can call the object of Descartes' geometry "mathematical body," body purely as an instrument of problem-solving. This is shown clearly at the beginning of the *Geome-*

try, where the operations of arithmetic are used to solve the problems of geometry, "touching the lines which are sought for in order to prepare them to be known [*touchant les lignes qu'on cherche, pour les preparer à estre connues*]." J. Babina has described Cartesian geometry as constituting a general method for solving problems (as constituting a general "heuristic") by showing how the formulae of algebra are to be interpreted geometrically.²³

Since this general method of solving problems was entirely unrestricted with respect to mathematical problems, and since for Descartes mathematics dealt with magnitudes, the general terms or symbols of the discipline had to deal with general magnitude. However, confusingly enough, at first sight there seem to be two kinds of general symbols in general mathematics. In the second part of the *Discourse*, Descartes referred to them as "lines" as well as "certain ciphers [*quelques chiffres*]." In his algebraic geometry (analytic geometry), Descartes used symbols for numbers when he wished to consider a single proportion, and lines, or even whole figures, when he wished to consider several together. For Descartes, however, a point, a line, or a figure is *just as much a symbol* in this general mathematics as is an empty cipher. This point cannot be stressed too much, as when, in the *Rules*, he said:

> it can be easily concluded that it will be more than a little profitable
> if we transfer what we understand to be said concerning magnitude
> in general to that species of magnitude which, of all, is most easily
> and distinctly pictured in our imagination: however, it follows from
> what has been said that this species of magnitude is the real
> extension of body, grasped by disregarding all else except the fact of
> its being figures . . . because in no other subject are all differences of
> proportion more distinctly exhibited. [Vol. X, p. 441, l. 4–15]

The essential difference, then, between abstract geometry (which for Descartes is only a method for general problem-solving) and physics is that the questions of physics deal only with those questions concerning attributes—of however many dimensions—that have as subject what he calls "true body."²⁴ That is to say, physics is "practical." In its completely practical aspect, Descartes calls it mechanics.

When Descartes chose the term 'dimensions' to refer to any important factor that must be included in a problem's statement if we are to solve it, he was materializing concepts, ("concretizing" them), and not abstracting concepts from matter: Descartes certainly knew how the rest of mankind used the term 'dimension,' and his use was a *fundamental* extension its common usage.

That the thinking soul or mind represents to itself the presence of its own body's chemical secretions as emotions and feelings *about* what caused the nerves to send messages to organs to secrete those chemicals, is a natural abstraction of a "feeling about" something from our 'perception" of something. We reverse the natural act of "biological" abstraction when we consider an emotion as merely an added dimension to what we are perceiving—namely, as the "subjective" dimension. Finally, the concept of dimension is essentially tied to our perception of bodies, and our perceptions of bodies are the pre-eminent objects of scientific mathematics. Consequently, treating all discernibly distinct aspects of feeling and perception as dimensions of the thing perceived prepares us to deal with experience as rationally as humans can. Dimensional analysis is thus the first preparation of the imagination for Descartes' subsequent rational, medical treatment of day-to-day life.

ANALYSIS AND PROBLEM-SOLVING

One reason that Descartes' contribution to the tradition is assessed at such widely differing worth by different scholars is lack of agreement concerning the place of the scientific, and particularly the medical, studies within his work as a whole. Descartes, however, is not the only great thinker and philosopher who has received this treatment: ironically, the thinker identified by Descartes as his archenemy, Aristotle, has suffered much the same fate. The scientific anthropology behind the teachings of Aristotle's *Ethics* and *Politics* have been largely ignored for a millenium, and generations of Aristotle specialists, even specialists in his ethics and political thought, have, on the whole, given little weight to his biological works, which are a very large portion of his published works. (As has already been discussed, the historian Bréhier tells us that Dominicus Gundissalinus, Archdeacon of Segovia, who died in 1151, imitated the Arabic tradition of Alfarabi in insisting on the following order for teaching Aristotle's works: physics, celestial mechanics, zoology, and, only then, psychology. We have also seen that Albert the Great, a century thereafter, rejected this protocol in favor of a more "anthropocentric" view based on Augustine's Christology.) What school of Aristotle studies insists on a thorough grasp of Aristotle's physics, celestial mechanics, and then of his zoology as a foundation for the study of his *Ethics* and his *Politics*? Is there a living teacher who insists on anything like the same order for reading Descartes?

As is argued later at length, the proper order for reading Descartes' works is unexpectedly parallel to that in which, according to Alfarabi and Dominicus Gundissalinus, we should read Aristotle: namely, physics (along with its mathematics), celestial mechanics (the subject matter of Part II of Descartes' *Principles of Philosophy*), zoology (which Descartes tells us at the end of the *Principles* is the next work he will address), and, finally, psychology (the subject of the 1648 *The Passions of the Soul*).

Descartes' psychology presented his theory of man, or anthropology. It was new to the extent that the disciplines on which it is based were new—and it was new! Mostly because of Descartes' teachings, our age believes that any human being who does not spend his life actively solving problems is not a fully productive member of society. *Homo sapiens,* "man the knower," has become *Homo faber,* "man the maker," i.e., the one who knows *how*. Paleoanthropologists, such as the late Louis B. Leaky, Mary Leaky, and Richard Leaky, arguing from evidence found in the Olduvai Gorge, tell us that the child of a Pithecanthropoid union was a true human *because* it made a tool. This section is concerned with Descartes' transformation of *Homo sapiens* into man the problem-solver. If we wish to follow the broad outlines of that transformation, however, we must involve ourselves somewhat in Descartes' mathematical theory. That is, we take Descartes strictly at his word when he wrote at the end of the *Discourse*—his first published work—that his mathematics, physics, optics, and whatever else would be entirely subordinated to improvements in medical practice. However, at crucial places there are developments in his medical philosophy that are so deeply influenced by his mathematical work that we must touch upon the mathematics if we are to understand some of the most important underpinnings of his medical theory.

The theoretical mathematics of Descartes' mathematical physics is analytic mathematics. The history of the mathematical aspect of analysis was contained in a book which we know Descartes read, because he quoted from it in the *Geometry* (Vol. VI, p. 337, l. 9ff.). It is the so-called *Mathematical Collection* of Pappus of Alexandria, who lived in the third century A.D.[25] In Chapter IV of his book, Pappus proposed some problems that he said no one could answer; Descartes elaborated a mathematics that is very much like what we today know as analytic geometry precisely in order to solve those problems, the so-called "*n*-line locus problems" (see Appendix 1).

Also contained in Pappus's history of mathematics (Chapter VII) is a definition of mathematical analysis (and synthesis) that he found to be current in antiquity.[26] That definition is contained, with several modifications, in Descartes' discussion of ways in which he can prove, of all things, the existence of God (Vol. IX, pp. 121–122); indeed, he even stated that his famous proof of God's existence in the *Meditations* is modeled on mathematical analysis. His mathematical mechanics is, he wrote, a foundation of his ethics.

Pappus's discussion of analysis can be summarized as follows: a distinction is to be made between two kinds of questions; one kind is theoretical and the other is concerned with problem-solving.[27] Theoretical questions are concerned with truth and falsity of a statement which is usually an answer to a question. For example, "What is justice?" "Justice is being fair and giving everyone an equal share" is the answer to a theoretical question. According to this view, no matter how serious the consequences of an incorrect answer to the question "What is justice?," the question is theoretical—it is concerned with *what* something is, not whether it is or how to get it. On the other hand, the question "Given a rectangle $4'' \times 7''$, how can we find a line a'' long such that the square with that side a'' long equals the area of the rectangle $4'' \times 7''$?" is a *problem*. One wants the right answer; truth and falsity are not the question. Finding whether such a line exists, and then finding out how to get it, are the primary interests, and they are the kind of mathematical problem dealt with by a problematic analysis. More generally, however, problematic analysis was, as early as Aristotle, considered to be concerned with action that follows methodical deliberation—in situations like medicine or carpentry, where what one does does not always turn out the same way every time. Thus, as Aristotle wrote (*Ethics*, 1112,a21–1112,b28), a carpenter does not deliberate about *whether* to build a porch or lay floors, but *how to*, in a given instance. In particular, Aristotle pointed out (1112,b20–b28, Rackham translation):

> For, when deliberating one seems in the procedure described to be pursuing an investigation or analysis that resembles the analysis of a figure in geometry—indeed it appears that though not all investigation is deliberation, for example, mathematical investigation is not, yet all deliberation is investigation—and the last step in the analysis seems to be the first step in the design. Then, if they have come up against an impossibility, they abandon the project—for instance, if it requires money and money cannot be procured; but if on the other hand it proves to be something possible, they begin to act.

Thus, according to a tradition that began at least as early as Aristotle, problematic analysis is a methodical deliberation performed by highly trained and skilled practitioners of arts, crafts, and sciences, e.g., medicine, carpentry, and geometry, whose goal is, first, to discover whether a particular project is feasible, and then, if it is, to discover through deliberation the best way to apply the rules of one's art, craft, or science to succeed in a plan.

It is especially noteworthy for our development of Descartes' psychology and anthropology that, in the distinction that Pappus makes between the two sorts of analysis, theoretical analysis "searches for the truth," whereas problematical analysis shows us how to get something ("supplies a construction"); for Pappus, only problematical analysis is concerned with how to find "lines" or figures. Descartes ignored this distinction between the two sorts of analysis, and treated them as one.[28]

Furthermore, in theoretical analysis, the search for the truth begins by assuming that whatever it is that is under consideration is "given and true"; it does not begin by assuming that something is possible or attainable. Theoretical analysis ends when it arrives at the conclusion either that whatever was under consideration is true or that it is false: it always concludes with a statement of truth or falsity and never with the statement that it is theoretically impossible to determine whether something is true or false—that is, an impossible something is never true *or* false.

Problematic analysis is far different. It begins with the proposal to obtain something that is lacking and wanted, something that is known to be lacking and wanted; it proceeds by supposing that whatever it is which is lacking either has been obtained or that it is obtainable, although at the beginning we know we have not yet constructed something, and that we do not know if we *can* construct what we want. Problematic analysis ends when we can conclude that what we have supposed is either possible and obtainable, or impossible, and hence not obtainable. In tabular form, this reduces to:

	Theoretical Analysis	*Problematical Analysis*
Beginning:	An opinion or some conclusion assumed as true.	A proposal for constructing something in a way or manner that leads to it.
End:	Conclusion of truth or falsity.	Something possible and either known with respect to how it can be obtained or known as impossible to be obtained.

When we fill in the details, we have:

Theoretical Analysis	*Problematical Analysis*
1. We suppose that what we are examining both exists and is true.	1. We suppose the thing set out in the proposition* to be known**.
2. We proceed through consequences that follow from that supposition (where these consequences are admitted as true *only* because they are in agreement with that initial supposition).	2. We proceed through consequences that result from that supposition (where these consequences are admitted as valid only because they are in agreement with that initial supposition).
3. We end when we have something we know in some other way, namely, by common assumption or some previous proof, or even	3. We end at something agreed upon. a. If it is possible, or is given because it has already been

which we simply know or agree to be false.

    a. If we simply know it is true or agree to it, then what we are considering is true, and the proof of it is merely the reverse of the steps of the analysis.

    b. If what we come to is false, then what we are considering is false.

proven previously, the thing set out is also attainable and the demonstration is the reverse of the analysis.

    b. If it is agreed to be impossible, the problem is impossible.

---

*That is, we suppose that we know that we can construct something and how to do it.

**"Known" here means "found" or "constructed *and also* proven to be the thing which we sought to construct."

Therefore, *if* we confuse the two sorts of analysis—theoretical with problematic—*then* the true becomes equivalent to the possible, and the false becomes equivalent to the impossible. Whatever can be either is or will be, and analytic thought concerns only the way to the solution of a problem, the way to get something.

Descartes ignored Pappus's distinctions, and he therefore identified the task of determining the truth or falsity of a statement with the task of determining either how a thing can be obtained or that it cannot be obtained; that is, he confused the question of truth and falsity with what Pappus and the tradition saw as the distinct undertaking of determining whether a thing can be constructed "in lines" by determining how it can be constructed, and hence, whether it can exist.[29] In theoretical analysis, something is assumed to exist and to be true, and the consequences of the assumptions are examined for a contradiction; in problematic analysis, something lacking and wanted is assumed to exist in order to find out if and how it could be constructed in order for it to exist.[30] Once that construction is found, the existence of the thing is thereby also demonstrated. However, it cannot be repeated too often, theoretical analysis does not assume something to be true or to exist in order to find out whether it can be obtained or made; that assumption is the task of problematic analysis.

In the identification of theoretical analysis with problematic analysis, Descartes implied something that he more or less fully realized in the course of his work. That identification implies that to know is *to know how*, and, what is most momentous for this present study of Descartes, to see or to perceive is *to see or to perceive a way*. This means, when taken to its limit, that our psychic responses to nervous impulses are reducible to means for, and ways to, the solutions of problems confronting precisely that union of body and psyche that has nerves and a psyche to respond to nervous impluses. In particular, the identification of seeing with seeing a way challenged Descartes to discriminate between precisely what aspect of our perception images its external physical causes, and what aspect of it is merely a consequence of our anatomic structure. In the realm of external physical causes, we find number, figure, motion, and the like—the so-called common sensibles; our anatomy is primarily involved in all the other elements of our perceptions, such as heat, pain, tickling, and our feelings about whatever we perceive. Thus, if we are terrified of a house cat, we have one sort of problem; if we don't see it in front of us, we have quite a different sort of problem.

Our perceptions of heat, pain, fear, etc., involve us in the "subjective" realm, a realm that, under the scientific scrutiny of medicine, will produce answers to questions about the structure and biochemical state of our bodies as highly organized entities. Thus, in contemporary terms that closely parallel developments found in texts of Descartes (see, especially, Art. 102 of *Passions of the Soul:* "Concerning the Motion of the Blood and Spirits in the emotion of Love"), sexual desire, *as a perception*— and what is desire if it is not perceived?—indicates the physical presence in the blood of "hormonal" secretions. What is more, sexual desire can be exhaustively understood, scientifically, by appeal to the species-perservative consequences of having such prominent secretions at certain times and not others. Our very *perception of*, that is, *awareness of*, those hormonal secretions which we perceive as desire, and not as hormones in our blood, is an element in a solution of a biological, species-perservative, problem. (Poets and composers, for instance, are not employing their inner states as part of a direct solution to a biological problem; we say, in our attempt to be consistent, that they are "sublimating" those desires, that is, they are not using their perceptions of such desires to address directly the solution to species-preservative problems. Rather, they are presenting us, and themselves, with biologically useful outlets for relieving the stresses on our biology induced by convention.)

In the "objective" realm of our unemotional perception of figure, of multiplicity, motion, and the other common sensibles, or "mathematicals," a strikingly parallel situation obtains. Descartes said, for instance (Vol. X, p. 450, l. 10–12):

> As for figures, . . . we can form the ideas of all things only using them; it only remains to be pointed out here that, of the innumerable species of figure, we are only going to use those by means of which differences of relationships or, if you like, proportions [*habitudium sive proportionem*], are most easily expressed.[31]

Thus, a few lines later (p. 450, l. 21–24), Descartes illustrated the relationship of a father to two children by means of an equilateral triangle.

Again, referring to figures by means of which "we can form ideas of all things," Descartes said (p. 452, l. 17–21):

> For these uses, we need nothing except either surfaces shaped into rectangles by straight lines, or even straight lines alone, which we also call figures because we can just as well imagine a truly extended subject using a straight line as by a rectangular surface

From this it is clear that for Descartes the ideas of everything we can possibly conceive, under any circumstances, can be replaced by one of a set of figures chosen purely because they clearly express certain relationships (Appendix 2). This objective realm of ideas extends to the emotions, because they can, according to Descartes, be exhaustively reduced to our natural awareness of certain secretions produced by our organs to make us disposed to a proper response to dangerous situations, in order that we might react much faster than we would without the secretions. Thus, what we are emotionally aware of as a sort of fearful anger is, according to the Cartesian analysis of *The Passions of the Soul,* our awareness of certain substances secreted into the blood such that we are better prepared to withstand shocks to our system than we would be otherwise. By means of these medical analyses, our emotions lose their subjective, impulsive character and are reduced to objective changes of state in the composition of our blood. In contemporary terms, the chemical *formula* for, say, adrenaline, becomes the form or figure we choose to replace our naive emotion of fearful anger in order to make it accessible to rational treatment. Therefore, the chemical formula for adrenalin— complete with its chains of organic compounds by means of which we express its formula—is the scientific replacement for the naive, prescientific form of emotional perception. This replacement is responsible for the birth of social sciences like crisis intervention, which examine how situations affect the biochemistry of the participants, rather than the "subjective" merits of the case.

According to the analytic view (which, we are arguing, derives from a re-interpretation of Pappus's description of theoretical and problematic analysis), there is nothing in human life that is not a beginning to a solution to a problem. Thus, for example, when we laugh, we are releasing tension that, if not released, would make us ill, through disturbance of psycho-physiological homeostasis. Do we feel affection for someone? Then we are conscious of the need for a regular and dependable relationship (*habitudo*), and, probably, a replacement for one of our parents. The list of such interpretations of everyday experience is exhaustive, and it is formed with an eye to the identification of every aspect of our conscious life as a means toward finding answers to personal problems.

Descartes stated that, "of the innumerable species of figure, we are only going to use those by means of which differences of relationship or, if you like, proportion, are most easily expressed" (Vol. X, p. 450, l. 10–12). Therefore, the ultimate intelligible natural species are, for Descartes, not at all what appears to us naively and pre-scientifically; rather, they are mathematical, and are related to one another by, and chosen according to, mathematical considerations. For Descartes, what can be referred to as the ultimate natural species are figures having such properties that "we can form the ideas of all things only using them." Thus, Descartes' neuroanatomy of vision denies that our nerves *transmit* visible forms. All our nerves need to do is transmit "dot-dash" impulses to the brain, which then translates them into "symbols"—that is, into the visible world as potentially intelligible according to the rules of the new algebra, the rules of which Descartes' teacher, Vieta, called *symbolae*. For the new age of the two sciences consisting of Cartesian mathematical physics and the neuroanatomy of vision based on that mathematical physics, the visible world itself is the soul's symbolic representation to itself of forms that are either immediate, innate responses to external events or that are generated by performing mathematical operations on lines.[32]

It is one thing for Descartes to insist that we are free to take figures out of the storehouse of geometrical shapes and use them to represent to ourselves the ideas of relationships and mathematical ratios between magnitudes; it is quite another thing to justify the figures that we choose as being more than merely convenient ways of talking about relationships—as more than visible metaphors (as in the expression "love triangle"). Descartes undertook that justification by showing that, given the *symbolae,* the rules of algebra as interpreted by his own analytic geometry, he could take relationships and ratios between magnitudes and construct unique figures, in order to present to the sense of sight otherwise invisible things. Furthermore, the magnitudes whose interrelations are addressed symbolically by these figures were also dealt with by Descartes as if they had no more independent existence than abacus beads on a string. He said, "However, whatever at any given moment does not require our mental attention, but which we will later need to solve a given problem, is much better designated by the briefest possible notation than by whole figures" (Vol. X, p. 454, l. 10–12). By whole figures he meant squares, lines, triangles, etc. "It is useful here to notice how every rectangle can be formed into a line, or conversely, how a line, or even a given rectangle, can be transformed into another rectangle. . ." (p. 468, l. 7–11). That is, when it is more convenient for the solution of a problem, figures can simply be represented by *notae,* our algebraic symbols.

It is clear by now why Descartes saw it necessary to ignore Pappus's distinction between theory and problem-solving. For, if all the contents of our consciousness (and this centrally includes our consciousness of our purely rational, mathematical thought processes) are only symbolic representations of sequences of nerve impulses coming to the interior of the brain, then the "objective reality" of these symbolic representations must relate to real, present, external agents that cause those sequences of nerve impulses. It is neurophysiology, hand in glove with analytic geometry, that teaches that any perception of change in consciousness states has a physical cause, ultimately outside us, and it is the particular province of medicine to determine in what way a given change is inaugurated by something going on "outside," and to what extent it is inaugurated by something going on "inside." The particular province of ethics, in its turn, can only be defined once medicine has accomplished its task, since ethics presupposes that we can disassociate feeling (which comes from something happening "inside") from pure perception of what begins "outside." Consequently, we can do what is rational, i.e., objectively realistic, in spite of how we may happen to feel about it at the moment because of something going on inside us—for example, a previous experience may have disposed us to feel fearful even upon occasions when it is not in our best interests to be fearful.

In this scheme, all perceptions and all experiences are caused more or less directly by physical bodies that affect our nerve-endings in such a way that, corresponding to each and every distinct percept, there is a distinct physical event. Thus, our inner life can also be ordered parallel to the order of our external world. Also, the more technological the outer world is, the more the parallel will be historically, intentionally, and experientially reached. In only 100 years after Descartes' death, the axiom of human progress and the attendant necessity of technological progress came to be very widely accepted.[33] Technological progress follows the progress of what Descartes calls "mechanics," our "technology." Problem-solving in mechanics replaces anything like theoretical, contemplative pursuits. Neuroanatomical science shows, according to Descartes, that all our visual pictures are "symbolic" representations of more or less linear impulses in the nerves leading to the interior of the brain. Because his analytic geometry includes clear and unequivocal (i.e., algebraic) rules—Vieta's *symbolae*—by which we can construct mathematically any and every conceivable shape we could ever experience, those symbolic representations are in strict accord with mathematical rules or "symbols"; and, because of the harmony between neuroanatomy and analytic geometry, perception itself can be viewed symbolically— that is, as a strictly and purely *rational* process. Consequently, for Descartes, to perceive is to think, to feel is to think, and to will is to think (Vol. IXA, p. 22). Descartes can say this only because he can give a *scientific,* mechanistic neurophysiology of perception; a *scientific* endocrinology of feeling-states, where those feeling-states are viewed scientifically as the way we naively represent to ourselves certain "dimensions" contained in the biological agents that disturb the brain. Finally, volition or willing is the subject matter of scientific ethics, which addresses itself to the way we represent to ourselves the dependency of all the powers of our soul on the health of our own body and the help of other humans.

Descartes consciously ignored the tratitional distinction between bare lines, their magnitudes, and the relative comparison or measure of those magnitudes, i.e., magnitude considered as length. Since, according to this view, bare lines are our immediate psychic reaction to nerve impulses, they have no particular significance beyond the fact that they provide the material for extension; a bare line is the vehicle for "extendedness." Magnitude viewed within this scheme becomes extension, whose only significance is that it is to be measured and thus transformed into length. Descartes' "magnitude" is an indeterminate length, and when he used the term 'line' (*ligne*), he was referring to a perceptible something whose only meaning can be supplied to it by measuring it; measure provides determinate, numberlike form to magnitude. Once a group of magnitudes have been measured, they can be ordered in a numerical sequence[34] according to their real lengths, and their interrelations can all be expressed in arithmetical terms, e.g., one line is four times another.[35] Indeterminate length is unmeasured, but essentially measurable, magnitude.

In the geometry to which Pappus refers, the magnitude of a given, perceptible line was of particular interest in that, when compared to any other line, the magnitude of the first line exceeded, equaled, or fell short of the other lines. The precise extent by which the one differed in magnitude from the other was not an essential part of the concept of the magnitude of a line. The magnitude of a given line was only one of many characteristics of any line: for example, a line could be curved in many distinct ways—as a circle, as an ellipse, or as a cusp; it could be "bent"; it could be straight and parallel to another line, or it might not be parallel. In all such cases, the relative magnitude of the line is immaterial—for Pappus and his tradition, that is. Furthermore, for the earlier tradition the length of a line only concerned the relation of its magnitude to the magnitudes of other lines that could be stated precisely: in mathematical terms, the statement (in words or in written letters that can be pronounced because of conventional rules of pronunciation) gives the "ratio" of a number to a number. Thus, to say that a line is "3 inches long" is to say that its magnitude, when compared to another, unit magnitude, is three times the first. Length is thus a peculiar composite of two different things: namely, it is a composite of multitude ("3 times the unit") and magnitude. Magnitude belongs to the thing; multitude and its measure belong to the sphere of human activity. The phrase "3 inches long" expresses in speech (where "speech," "word," and "utterance" all equal *ratio*, in Latin) a ratio between a unit magnitude and a measured magnitude. Measuring, and thus the determination of length, is not in any simple way a natural act for the tradition referred to by Pappus; the use of the term *ratio*—which always meant "word, utterance, speech," whatever other meanings were loaded into it—shows this. Speech and speaking are intentional, contingent activities that, except for humans, would not even begin to exist in nature. The length of a line requires that we *talk* about something, namely, about one of many characteristics of a perceptible something in front of us: about its magnitude.

In Rule XIV (Vol. X, p. 438, 441), Descartes said that everything true of general magnitude, that is, of line as the vehicle for extendedness, can be said of particular lines:

> it will be more than a little useful if we transfer all those things
> which we understand to be said of general magnitude to that species
> of magnitude which, of all, is more easily and distinctly pictured in
> our imagination; this, however, [is] the real extension of body
> abstracted from all else except that it is figured . . . [for] we conceive
> of the imagination itself, with extended ideas in it, as being nothing
> else than real body, truly extended and possessing figure.

Consequently, the line that we perceive because of the structure of our neuroanatomy and the impulses it receives from outside is, before it is measured, a visible, but indeterminate length (Appendix 2). Determinate length presupposes a ruler, which is chosen for convenience—a person who is 6 feet tall in the U.S. is 1.8 meters tall in Switzerland. Furthermore, since our bare perception of a line is a psychic reaction that is symbolic (as is shown by the fact that we can thoroughly manipulate it according to the rules, *symbolae*, of arithmetical algebra), what we really perceive in response to nerve impulses in the brain, according to Descartes, are objects that can be used to solve problems. For Descartes, we are incapable of any perception that cannot be used as an instrument for solving some problem: in contemporary terms, all our faculties are adaptational survival mechanisms. What has already been solved has no existence except as information for the solution of new problems. Not a single perception that we have as a response to nerve impulses is, according to Descartes' re-interpretation of Pappus's description of analysis, material for contemplation or insight. Perceptions are material for problem-solving, and for nothing else. They have no inherent meaning beyond the meaning we supply to them in our self-realization as a more or less precarious union of body and soul. From this concept philosophic history and a theory of progress are born.

DISCIPLINE OF THE IMAGINATION

Starting from the doctrine of super-solids, and proceeding through his teachings concerning dimensions and the "lines" and figures of mathematical analysis, Descartes at this point seems to be far removed from his announced goal of founding a new and better medicine to improve the lot of humanity, and even fruther from the ultimate goal of establishing an ethics, which is the final degree of wisdom (*le plus haut degrée de la sagesse*). Indeed, he seems to be proceeding in a direction that is very nearly opposite to that in which such a goal might be expected to lie.

This is merely an appearance. Descartes' doctrines of super-solids, dimensions, and the like are the background for his more important doctrines of body viewed "emotionally" or "subjectively." That is, his mathematical treatment of body prepares the stage for his doctrines concerning bodies that are naively perceived by us to be helpful or harmful, or, as Descartes says, good or bad for us. Up to this point the notion of body with which we have been dealing is primarily concerned with how body is known mathematically; however, we each begin life by viewing bodies very unmathematically, as good or bad in relation to us. Therefore, we must investigate the way in which we change our perspective so that we come to view bodies "objectively," i.e., not as being harmful or helpful to us, but as aids to mathematical knowledge. We must ask, How do we sophisticate ourselves?

When we are considering body scientifically, that is, objectively, mathematically, and unemotionally, we are, according to Descartes, using it to represent to our minds certain relations between "lines" that we perceive because we imagine them. When we imagine lines, we unemotionally experience body—after all, lines are "only imaginary." In several places, Descartes was clear about the relation between mathematical thinking, imagination, and these lines. For instance (*Rules:* Vol. X, p. 440, l. 26, to p. 441, l. 13):

> after the terms giving us difficulty have been abstracted from any given subject, we understand ourselves . . . to be concerned with generic, abstract magnitudes [*circa magnitudines in genere*].
> However, in order that we should present ourselves with pictures [*imaginemur*], we do not use pure intellect but add specific details (*species*) depicted in the imagination [*in phantasia*]: it should be understood quite carefully that nothing can be said of generic,

abstract magnitudes [*de magnitudinibus in genere*] which cannot be referred as well to any specific magnitude whatsoever.

It follows from this immediately that it will be more than a little useful for us also to apply those things which we understand to concern generic, abstract magnitudes to that species of magnitude which is, of all others, most easily and distinctly pictured in our imagination [*in imaginatione nostra*]: but, from what has been said . . . it follows that this is the real extension of body abstracted from all else except that it is figured. And here we conceive that imagination itself [*phantasiam ipsam*] with ideas extended in it, is nothing else but true body really extended and figured.

In other places, Descartes even spoke of these figures formed out of lines as being "ideas," and thus affecting us unemotionally—indeed, we can sometimes even use a perception of a shape as the idea of the thing perceived (*Rules:* Vol. X, p. 416, l. 17, to p. 417, l. 3):

For, since the intellect can be moved by imagination or, contrarywise, imagination by the intellect, imagination can therefore be active with respect to the senses by applying them to objects (using its motive power), or, working in the contrary direction, objects can be applied to the imagination through the senses' motive power, so that, for instance, they depict the images of bodies; . . . of course . . . when intellect acts in situations where there is nothing bodily or even like body, imagination cannot help its faculties to function; in such situations, however, in order that intellect not be bogged down in these things, it should be insulated against sensation and imagination in so far as possible, and all distinct impressions should be banished. But, on the other hand, if the intellect proposes to itself something for examination which can be referred to body, its idea ought to be formed in the imagination as distinctly as possible. This is done best when the thing itself which that idea is to represent is exhibited to the external senses.

Finally, there is the famous passage in the *Discourse on Method* where Descartes discussed "the object of the geometers" and its relation to rational proof (*Discourse,* Part IV: Vol. VI, p. 36, l. 5–11):

proposing to myself the object of the geometers (which I conceived as a continuous body, or a space extended indefinitely in length, breadth, and depth or height; as divisible into distinct parts; which could have different figures or magnitudes; and which could be moved or carried in different ways—for the geometers suppose all this in their object) . . .

In short, if we are thinking about anything that can in any way be referred to body (and this includes human life, sickness, health, weight, light, motion, figure, etc.), we ought to use our bodily power to imagine real body and then use what we imagine as an idea. However, this means that instead of reacting blindly and "emotionally" to what we perceive around us merely because it strikes us as either good or bad for us, we can use our perception of body in a mathematical manner that is both rational and completely under our powers of choice rather than under the powers of automatic instinct.

According to this view, the world of physical bodies can be considered either instrumentally or causally: we consider it instrumentally when we treat our perceptions as the subject of a mathematics that *uses* material images to represent constant relationships; we consider it causally when we think of these perceptions as being caused by bodies that can help or hurt us. In a completely controlled environment, produced by mechanics—the ultimate fruit of the technological enlightenment—all aspects of all bodies would be manipulated to express relationships. This idea is exemplified in Cubist art, the unbroken repetition of the elements of a Mies van der Rohe building, Calder mobiles and stabiles, Bauhaus furniture and utensils, stream-of-consciousness literature, Piagetian education (with the "new math" of relationships), Fritz Perl open relationships (always changing, always expressing new relationships and new facets of old relationships), balance-of-power governmental structures, which are defined only in relation to other structures, and homeostatic medicine. However, before that dream of total control over all surrounding bodies can be realized, those bodies that, willy-nilly, strike us as good or bad, pleasant or painful, must be emotionally neutralized for the viewer. Emotional neutralization means a control over the emotions, which is the first intimation of a deep relationship between ethics, which certainly involves self-rule and self-control, and analytic mathematics, which involves the totally rational manipulation of our perception of bodies for the sake of problem-solving.

The process of emotional neutralization is, perhaps, Descartes' greatest contribution to the modern era. The foundations of emotional neutralization are found at the beginning of his new mathematics, in which we take a perceptible line or figure and turn it into something that is totally "symbolic," i.e., chosen as an aid in problem-solving.

Emotional neutralization must be performed methodically. Before a given linear magnitude is placed within a given coordinate system, it has no determined length: it is merely something that strikes us because we have eyes and are conscious. At this pre-analytic, pre-scientific stage, the object of sight is merely a "thing." It is merely "noticed." It enters the world of rational investigation only when it is, by means of an intentional act on the part of the thinking human being, actively, willfully considered as unknown. Then it is further transformed into something known in an indeterminate way—"Let the unknown be x"—by our considering it as knowable in terms of something already known. As Meno asked in the Platonic dialogue that bears his name, (80 D–E):

> And in what place will you seek, Socrates, for something about which you know nothing at all? What sort of thing which, although you do not know it, you are inquiring about, will you present us with? Or, even supposing the best; if you happen to trip over it, how will you know that it is this which you do not know?

Descartes certainly intended to improve upon Plato when he said:

> we consider the matter entirely in this way: first, something must be unknown in every question, for otherwise our search would be fruitless; secondly, that very same unknown ought to be designated in some way, for otherwise, we would not be clearly set on the track after this rather than any other unknown; thirdly, that unknown cannot clearly be distinguished other than by being designated in terms of something already known. [*Rules:* Vol. X, p. 430, l. 16–22]

He continued this thought several pages later:

> Now, whenever we are going to call on the help to be given by the imagination, we must take note that every time some particular unknown thing is deduced from something else already known, we do not thereby discover some new kind of entity; rather, all we do is extend our first knowledge to what we have just deduced from it. We thereby perceive that the thing sought for [*rem quaesitam*] in some particular way participates in the nature of those things which were given in the proposition stating the question. [p. 438, l. 12–18]

In Descartes, the body that is at first merely noticed is then intentionally, willfully considered as unknown; it is next transformed into something knowable in terms of something already known. At this juncture it is considered as being known indeterminately. Descartes represents this stage *geometrically* by placing the unknown in a coordinate system, in terms of which each and every linear magnitude can be determined as being of a definite length; *algebraically*, the unknown is included in an equation containing knowns. We take a linear magnitude, which we arbitrarily, willfully assume to have measurably definite end-points, and we locate it within a coordinate system.[36] However, before we can do this, we must cease to view the given lines merely as something we see because there is a pencil trace on paper, a source of light, and working eyes; each perceivable line must be "analytically" transformed into a magnitude of an unknown length. To take a given linear magnitude and assign to it definite end-points is to transform that merely perceived line into a linear magnitude possessing an indefinite length. When we do this, we leave the world of naive experience and enter into the world of rational choices; the gateway into that world is the intentional transformation of a given, visible line into a magnitude of unknown length. The primary power of the intellect is thereby manifested in the act whereby it rejects something as happened-to-be-perceived in order to consider it as something-to-be-known. This analytic procedure is both the mathematical model of and justification for embarking on a program that begins with universal doubt.

We see the relation between the method of analysis and doubt in Descartes' first published work, the 1637 *Discourse on Method*, where he wrote that the first step into the method is programmatic, intentional, doubt:

> when I am only considering the investigation of truth . . . I should reject as absolutely false all that in which I am able to imagine the least doubt, in order to see if there might be something remaining in my belief which might be altogether doubtless. [Vol. VI, p. 31, l. 24–30]

Also, in the *Principles* (1644), Descartes stated "In order to seek the truth [*pour examine la verite; veritati inquirendi*], it is necessary, in so far as possible, to place all things in doubt once in your life" (Vol. XI, B, 25: Part I, Art. I). Only when we have prepared ourselves in this way can we pursue the sought-after; the world that is doubtful is a world that can be considered as being indeterminate with respect to the truth, and, as we have seen, Descartes fused the notions of truth and the possible or obtainable. Therefore, the world as doubtful is the given world reduced to a possible world in order to better view it according to our wishes and needs. Mathematically, the world is viewed as being prepared to be known by being assigned a set of coordinate systems. "Ethically," the characteristically human world is reduced to a vast store of belief-systems or intellectual coordinate systems into which all human events can be fitted. In either case, we entirely reject the world as given and replace it as sought-after. However, this stance implies a powerful moral neutrality and unlimited toleration. Its only palliative is our innate fear of death, which alone warms that cool objectivity. It is not by chance that the foundations of so many of the scientific governments during our "age of reason"—meaning primarily the age of reasonable government—have been founded on a reign of terror, and that, as our medical expenditures reveal, fear of death is the very heart of our modern rational life. This is one of the great contradictions central to our age.[37]

Contrary to doubt is our prejudice that things are as we perceive them; the impulse to affirm the simple existence of objective correlates of ideas is innate, and can be traced, according to Descartes, to the fact that any act of affirmation or rejection is anticipated by a person's perception of what is helpful or harmful to him.[38] Descartes' neurophysiology teaches that our naive perceptions of the world around us have a form instituted by our own natures, and not by the natures of the things that seem to occasion them; accompanying these, we find "blind and rash" impulses, for example, to approach or avoid, flee or face, etc. Those impulses are also instituted by nature, and thus Descartes transformed the central Roman Catholic doctrine concerning the will, which chooses wrongly as a punishment for original sin, into a naturally instituted correlate to our perceptions, a correlate naturally instituted precisely to help us distinguish between body as viewed "objectively" and body as viewed under the aspect of help or harm—viewed "subjectively" as we say today. Thus, to be a mathematician, and hence to view the body "objectively," requires that the individual be able to view body outside "good and evil." It is precisely Descartes' "geometry" that provides the proof that we can do this systematically, and that shows us how to proceed. Descartes' geometry thus occupies in his general strategy the place of an essential, but only preliminary, discipline; it constitutes the first preparatory step in the direction of a doctrine of ethics.

It has been said by R. C. Taliaferro, a deep scholar of Descartes, that "the power of symbolizing is . . . placed by Descartes at the very center of knowing.[39] To the degree that this is true, the discipline of the imagination that allows the thinker to view much of the contents of consciousness as symbolizing some aspect or other of processes and relations that are found in external reality is the central preparatory discipline of Cartesian philosophy. (When the content of consciousness is not strictly symbolizing some aspect of external reality, it is symbolizing an aspect of the soul, which has no naturally instituted mode of representation. For example, the peacock serves as the symbol for the passion of pride, which, although we feel it naturally, does not have a naturally instituted form that we clearly distinguish.) The discipline of the imagination is, for Descartes, analogous to what the mortification of the flesh was for other seekers who sought other sorts of truth.

Descartes himself seldom if ever used the term 'symbolic.' He often referred to algebraic symbols as ciphers (*chiffres*) and to the soul's reaction to corporeal perturbations in the brain as thought (*cogitatio*). When Taliaferro speaks of the importance of symbolic thinking for Descartes, he seems to refer to Descartes' opinion that the mind's operations, although very much concerned with body, can still be considered strictly under the aspect of the primitive and innate notion of mind itself. For Descartes, the mind, using mathematical physics, can consider the body strictly as an intellectual phenomenon. As an illustration, according to *Meditation III* (in the French *only;* Vol. IX, p. 32), all our ideas of things are works of the operations of the mind—"*mais on doit a sçauoir que toute idee estant un ouurage de l'esprit. . . ."* On the whole, men's ideas of physical bodies are considered under the aspect of the union of body and soul, and hence as caused in the soul by the real presence of bodies; however, if they are viewed only insofar as they are products of the operation of the mind, they are emptied of intentional content and become mere "signs" of intellectual activity in its rational concern with body. Our thoughts or notions concerning corporeal things are in that case "symbolic," by which we mean that they are to be considered only as the manifestations of mental operations. They are, however, symbolic of the activities of the mind, and not directly of the characteristics of anything alien to the mind that might be somehow connected to them. Descartes identified this view of notions (as mere signs of intellectual activity) as metaphysical, and said that this means we consider only the soul and its attributes.[40]

As an example of Descartes' presentation of the notion of symbolic thinking—thinking about the *operations* whereby the mind thinks "things," and not about the subject of thought—Taliaferro quotes from Descartes' *The World* (Vol. XI, p. 4 of Taliaferro's translation), "But if words, which only signify by the institution of men, can make us conceive things they have no resemblance to, why cannot Nature have established a certain sign to give us the feeling of light although this sign is nothing in itself which resembles this feeling?"[41]

Taliaferro concludes from the passage:

> Thus the sensations of light can be explained in terms of extension, figure, and motion; the ones are the symbols of the others . . . This act of symbolization is further discussed in a famous passage of the *Diotrique* where the relation of the sensation of color to the corresponding motions in the realm of clear and distinct ideas is compared to the knowledge a blind man has of the things around him in terms of the reactions of the end of a stick which he holds in his hand. And the strange arbitrariness of the power of symbolization is finally placed by Descartes at the very center of knowing in the letter to Mersenne of July 22, 1641, where he says: "And finally I hold that all these ideas which include no affirmation or negation, are *innate* in us; for the sense organs bring us nothing which is like the idea which awakes in us on their occasion, and this idea must therefore have been in us before."[42]

Thus, the *first* preparation required of men before they can set about arriving at "objective" truth, that is, truth in the sciences, is concerned with how they are to consider that class of their perceptions that they naturally, i.e., "impulsively," take as accurate images of external things. Through this preparation, we can learn to deny the contents of the imagination any inherently meaningful character; we thereby place ourselves in a position to confront our perceptions as if they comprised a text filled with suspicious ciphers whose *designations* are entirely unclear and doubtful. "Instinct" then supplies "natural" meaning to "natural symbols," and this philosophical, analytic discipline of the imagination severs emotion from perception, guaranteeing that each and every meaning that forms and shapes are to have is a meaning *intended* by the perceiver insofar as he is rational and actively intending or volitional. The figures formed by the lines of analytic mathematics have no meaning other than the rational meaning assigned them by the thinker. This is precisely how the world dealt with by Descartes' geometry is symbolic.

Our tendency to regard the contents of consciousness as intentional arises from what Descartes called a "blind and rash impulse [*aueugle et temeraire impulsion*]." It is the power of that impulse that gives rise to the need for a countering discipline. Descartes wrote:

> by a blind and rash impulse, . . . I believed that there were things outside of me, and different from my being; also, I believed that through my sense organs, or through some other way in which this could occur, they send in to me their ideas or images, and imprint their resemblances there.

The principal part of the preparatory discipline to Descartes' philosophy, then, is concerned with overcoming that blind and rash impulse to believe that most of our perceptions faithfully image their external causes. The new, Cartesian man must become able to consider his perceptions as representations of his own mental operations and not as consequences of physical causes. Once this is accomplished, a means is found whereby all perceptions, even those obviously having physical causes, can be explained in terms of intellectual operations—the means of "mathematical" physics. (This means that the laws of nature apply both to bodies and to minds.)

To judge from the letter to Mersenne (which Taliaferro characterizes as crucial), the *Meditations* sets out to persuade those men ignorant of medicine and anatomy that their notion of the union of mind and body is by no means sufficiently wide to justify their thoughts about many things that they assume to fall under such a notion. They think, for example, that they can clearly and distinctly conceive of a simple piece of wax or a ten-sided solid by means of their naive notion of the union of mind and body. But what about that piece of wax as it is continuously changing, under the influence of heat, from a clearly shaped solid through an infinite series of transformations into a pool of liquified wax? And what about a solid as more and more sides are added to it? Starting with the fundamental assumption that there is an active aspect of thought that is totally independent of anything not thought, Descartes *analytically,* i.e., by arguing backwards, isolated the primitive notion of mind; he then *analytically* isolated the primitive *notion* of a body, without thereby proving the physical existence outside the mind of anything corresponding to that notion of body; and, finally, he analytically isolates the primitive notion of the union of mind and body. That primitive notion of mind is the first that must be isolated.[43]

To sum up: Descartes viewed his analytic method, which assigned causes to all particular events, as being the right way to empty our daily experience of innate intentional content. For, armed with this method, we may view all individual phenomena initially as to-be-deduced phenomena, that is, as "indeterminate." It seems likely that this is the ultimate reason for the importance of doubt in his program. That is, Cartesian doubt is not unlike judicial indictment: the accused person is in some way "indeterminate" until proven guilty or innocent. And surely the indicted citizen, even if he is free, on bail, to walk the streets and to sleep at home and not behind bars, is not altogether a citizen. So it is with the phenomena that the deductive physicist faces before they have been proven to be the effects of certain given, general causes—the laws of nature.

Thus Descartes' mathematics of super-solids and his physics of n-dimensional bodies give the first indications of how his ethics, the supplier of clear sight to the powerful but blind impulse for self-preservation, is necessary. That is, the logic of his philanthropic program (which considers mathematical physics a foundation for a biophysics that advances human health) implies that we must cast into doubt our consciousness of the impulse for self-preservation; but that impulse is no less blind, than powerful, and so its way must be illuminated by Descartes' ethics.

CREATIVE USE OF THE
DISCIPLINED IMAGINATION

In the *Meditations,* Descartes presented the beginning of philosophy as universal doubt. Similarly, Part I, Art. I of his *Principles of Philosophy* begins with the thought that, "in order to examine the truth, it is necessary once in each person's life, to place all things in doubt in so far as it is possible." This doubt is both the beginning of philosophy and the intellectual preparation for mathematical analysis. It has two objectives, each of which is pursued in philosophy no less than in analysis: one is the systematic weeding out from the mind of all opinions placed there by minds other than the thinker's own mind; and the other, allied objective, which involves ethical considerations, is the rejection of the "emotional," subjective judgment that the images we perceive resemble external reality. We here examine how these two objectives are related, and how we are to use the imagination to accomplish them both.

Descartes was freed from the power of the opinions and precepts of others (to which, he tells us, he at one time subscribed) early in his youth. The opinions presumably included the teachings of his preceptors at home and at school, of his parents, and of his king. Then, when he rejected those teachings entirely, he could reestablish them on grounds lying within his own mind (Discourse II: Vol. III, pp. 11–14).[44] Descartes carried this rejection of other men's opinions so far as to place in doubt even the theorems of the geometers until he himself could prove them *in a certain way*. He called that "certain way" the "way of analysis":[45]

> The method of demonstrating is two-fold: one is done by analysis or resolution, and the other by synthesis or composition. Analysis shows the true path by which a thing has been methodically discovered and it makes clear how effects depend on causes; so that, if the reader cares to follow it, and carefully to peruse all that it contains, he will understand no less perfectly the thing so demonstrated, and he will make it no less his own, than if he had himself discovered it. [Vol. IXA, p. 121]

Synthesis, or composition, examines causes by means of their effects. The synthetic method "does not give, as does the other, an entire satisfaction to the minds of those who desire to learn, because it does not teach the method by which the thing had been discovered." Synthesis is not the philosophic way of proceeding to demonstrate truths because it never reveals how the thing was found in the first place. As a consequence, proofs learned by a student following a synthetic argument are really only forms of prejudice! The student has to accept without any questions the axioms and postulates of a science if it is presented synthetically. For Descartes, Greek geometry was largely an instrument of intellectual suppression.

Truly philosophic thinking, for Descartes, is thinking that starts from the true beginning, and the true beginning is the nature of the mind that grasps both the problems and their solutions. For example, in *The World* (suppressed by him in 1632 because of the danger of its Copernican presuppositions), Descartes wrote (Vol. XI, p. 32, l. 7–8) that we are to suppose that "God creates anew all around us. . ." a sufficient quantity of matter to allow him, Descartes, to present this visible world to us. Descartes held in particular that, if we follow his methods, we can take this matter with its "laws" and "suppose that God creates nothing more than that which I have said, and even that He puts together a Chaos . . . ; these Laws and this matter are sufficient . . . to produce . . . the form of a perfect world, and one in which can be seen . . . all the . . . things that appear in this real world" (Vol. XI, p. 35). Here, the solution to the problem "How did it all begin?," no less than the question "What is it?," involves *creating* the problematical thing itself—surely a principal part of Descartes' legacy to his heirs. In Part III, Art. 45 of the *Principles,* written eleven years after *The World,* in 1644, Descartes repeated this sentiment:

> For there is no doubt whether in the beginning the world might have been created with all its perfection: so that the Sun and the Earth and the Moon and the Stars existed in it . . . But it is still the case that, in order to understand the natures of plants or men, it is far better to consider in what way they have been created by God at the first origin of the world . . . In this way . . . we can expose their nature far better than if we were only to describe them in the way they might have been then. . . .

In a letter addressed to Mersenne in 1632, he referred to the order in which the stars are arranged in the sky and claimed that he could deduce that order from his own principle (*a priori*), which he held was the best way. He wrote:

> I dare now to seek the cause of the position of each fixed star . . . and the knowledge of this order is the key and the foundation of the highest science that men can have touching material things; in so far as by this method one could know *a priori* all the various forms and essences of terrestrial bodies, whereas, without it, we must be content to divine them *a posteriori* and by their effects. [Vol. I, p. 250, l. 20 to p. 251, l. 2]

Descartes' *a priori* science is a deductive science, "the highest . . . that men can have," and it is analytical and shows "the true path by which a thing is methodically discovered and made to see how the effects depend on their causes."[46]

By means of his analysis, Descartes could scientifically construct an *imaginary* world that is "quite perfect, and in which can be seen . . . all the . . . things . . . which might appear in this true world." Such a world is not, according to Descartes, the "true" world; it is a simulacrum of, the "exact image of," the true world, but a simulacrum that is entirely intelligible and "quite perfect"—i.e., in every way complete. Furthermore, this *a priori* science yields knowledge of "forms and essences of the terrestrial bodies [*formes et essences des cors terrestres*], and *not* knowledge of forms and essences of things in the true world, because (Vol. III, p. 418, l. 5–8) "the sense organs tell us nothing which is like the idea which is awakened in us on their occasion, and thus, that idea must have been in us before."[47] Therefore, Descartes' "highest science" deals with a simulacrum, an exact image, of the world, and not with an external world that "causes" these ideas in us. Descartes defined the *Principles,* and from these we can "deduce," that is, *construct in imagination,* the very world that, naively and pre-philosophically, we take for granted as being the *cause* of our perceptions. Descartes' principles of philosophy are thus designed to replace actual, active, physical bodies as the causes of our conscious experience; rational principles concerning the action and interrelation of bodies replace the bodies themselves as the cause of our ideas. Only by doubting all the evidence of our senses can we empty the world of experience, thereby permitting ourselves to reconstruct it on rational, scientific grounds. The reconstructed world is the thinker's world.

Descartes' rejection of the intentional, i.e., inherently significant, aspect of the content of consciousness is, however, by no means purely destructive. Using the findings of his medicine, we can reduce the emotional aspect of the way we experience the world to our consciousness of the way our body's internal systems prepare themselves to help the body respond to what its soul perceives. Using the findings of mathematics, Descartes took certain aspects of his sensations and converted them into aids to understanding. He considered lines, squares and the like to be just as symbolic as the symbols (ciphers) of algebra, and they were used as symbols and nothing more. Rule XV spells this out in its title: "It also helps in many ways to draw these figures and exhibit them to the external senses so that our attentive thinking is thereby retained more readily." The title to the next Rule continues this thought: "However, whatever things do not require the present attention of the mind, even if they are necessary for the conclusion, are much better designated by the briefest possible notations than by whole figures. . . "

Considered mathematically, there is no distinction whatsoever between those "shortest possible notations" (the letter-symbols of algebra) and the "whole figures" of our natural perception. Even the forms and shapes of everyday experience can serve as mathematical symbols, but only because they have been stripped of all "subjective," emotional content.[48]

None of these figures or "notations" is either sacramental—like the sacred words of the sacraments—or naturally intentional; the only meaning they have is the meaning the thinker assigns to them. We must learn to exercise our "ingenuity" (e.g., *Rules,* Vol. X, p. 363, l. 24; p. 365, l. 24; p. 367, l. 18; p. 370, l. 17) to teach ourselves to think even about body without precipitously affirming that it truly exists outside us in the way it appears to us. Body conceived of in such a way is the "symbolic" object about which the geometers knew so much without inquiring whether or not it existed outside them. The symbolic object that they presented to their minds did not lead them to affirm or, indeed, even to pose questions concerning its external existence. That "symbolic" object, according to Descartes, is arrived at by analysis, which allows men to think about body as it might exist but without the need for affirming that it does exist. Further grounds for this conclusion are given by medicine's study of the physiology of sight; that inquiry, according to Descartes, proves conclusively that the relation between perception and what we perceive is in large part determined by processes occurring in our optic nerves and brain. However, we are so constructed that we automatically—"precipitously"—react to almost all of these perceptions precisely as if we were perceiving things directly and as if they existed outside our nervous system. Analysis, together with medicine, gives us rational grounds for denying emotional content to these perceptions. This analytic-medical way of considering body does not make Descartes susceptible to the blind and rash impulse to affirm its existence "outside of me" ("hors de moi"). After he has identified the shapes he is conscious of as being merely complex ciphers, they no longer have emotional content for him, and therefore he does not consider them to represent anything "outside of me."

The analysis of the geometers, Descartes stated in the second part of the *Discourse*, taught him that the "true way" of demonstration is analytic. This means two things: It means that all scientific demonstration deduces effects from causes, and, consequently, it also means that the scientist must proceed by treating the objects of his science as if they were constructs of precisely those intellectual operations that the scientist employs to think.[49] Thus, the true analytic scientist thinks about his perceptions of things as if they were only symbolic forms of things; that is, the true analytic scientist is concerned with perceptions that he conceives of as being entirely rational in origin.

To think using ciphers does not mean simply to contemplate wholly conventional marks on paper. The drawing of symbols on paper does not constitute anything even remotely approximating thought for Descartes, or for any serious thinker. For Descartes, however, a variant on or development of Vieta' s algebra constituted a sort of arithmetic, a calculus, of such symbols. This calculus supplied him with just that way of defining intellectual activity that is best suited to treat the data of consciousness intelligently—i.e., as if the data of experience were given by the mind to the imagination (see *Rules*, Vol. X, p. 416, l. 17, to p. 417, l. 3).

In short, to avoid the danger of precipitously (i.e. "passionately," "subjectively," "emotionally") affirming the existence of things presented by the imagination, but still giving a science of the real world, Descartes reestablished his perceptions of what was originally given to him by the senses upon the operations of his own mind. To accomplish this, he treated all the data of the senses as if they were derived from the operations of pure thought aided by imagination; he treated that data as symbolic.

Symbolic Thinking, Medicine, and Ethics

If the intellect can represent all incoming ideas of external things as if they were its own constructs, how can we ever be sure that these are ideas *of* anything and not mental fictions? The answer is that the "ingenuity" required to effect such representations is never exercised without our being aware that we are exercising it. Indeed, in the *Second Responses* to the *Meditations* (Vol. VII, p. 107, l. 4), Descartes stated that nothing happens in the soul of which we have no awareness. This is a fundamental postulate for Descartes. Moreover, his own "analytic" geometry factually demonstrates how a great part of the original data of visual sensation can be re-created by forms analytically derived from algebraic operations symbolizing general operations of the intellect. Descartes held that in order to give an intelligible account of the data of sensation, that is, of the day-to-day phenomena of life, we must treat them as if they were constructs of the mind thinking about them. An intelligible account of the phenomena is, for Descartes, a matter of representing them through their re-creation, using only the operations of the mind and not at all the material of the dramatic poets—the emotionally charged data of the senses, which take their meaning and power from our instinctive response to them. If, as Descartes said, it is analysis that allows us to treat what is given to us as if we ourselves discovered it, then the forms of Cartesian analytic geometry constitute, as far as they go, an entirely rational re-creation of, and thus replacement for, the initially given data of sensation and consciousness.

This point is central. For, if Descartes could not show a method for deriving the contents of our perceptions, insofar as these are the lines and figures of geometry, then Cartesian science could never be assured of being more than a formal game played with algebraic symbols alone. However, if he could methodically image all possible forms of sensation only using the operations of his mind, then he could be sure that his science was not "subjectively" tied to an innate impulse to consider those forms more than its own internal structure.

Descartes stated in the *Discourse* that his physics is the basis for his medicine, and we have just seen that his pure geometry is the intellectual advance guard of his physics. He also addressed himself to the relationship between physics and medicine in a work first published in 1664, fourteen years after his death: *The Description of the Human Body and All its*

Functions, Both those which do not depend on the soul as well as those which do. And also the principal cause of the formation of its members. [*La Description du Corps Humain, et de toutes ses Fonctions, Tant de celles qui ne dependent de l'Ame, Que de celles qui en dependent. Et aussi la principal cause de la formation de ses membres.*] In this work, he stated that "There is nothing with which one can occupy oneself more fruitfully than to try to know oneself. And the utility which one has a right to hope for from that knowledge concerns [*regarde*] not only Ethics [*La Morale*] . . . but especially also Medicine. . ." (Vol. XI, p. 223, l. 10, to p. 224, l. 11). Consequently, "one does not attribute to the soul the functions which depend only on the body," a mistake that he ascribed to "ignorance of anatomy and mechanics." Thus, just as pure geometry is the problem-solver, "engineer," for applied geometry or physics, so mechanics is the problem-solver for medicine; the two together are the problem-solvers for *la morale*—ethics.

Descartes' mathematical notion of body can, perhaps, be characterized most generally as a *rational* notion of body. In his view, the great task facing the philosophic man is not so much understanding what is intelligible about natural bodies as it is beginning at physical laws and then showing the rational source of our *perception* of natural bodies. For, by means of his new analytic geometry, Descartes gave Christian Europe a way to inviolably connecting certain operations of the intellect to perception of body, and thereby a reasoned account of the shapes and figures of unreasoning bodies. Indeed, is not the most "Cartesian" aspect of Descartes' thought his constant preoccupation with justifying the "inner life" of men? Does not the very term "rationalism" carry with it a powerful optimism concerning this inner life, especially when contrasted with the often "other-worldly" skepticism of Christian thought in these matters? Thus the *Meditations* provides a brilliant rhetorical device for countering that skepticism: in that work he lets the validity of the inner life of man be subjected to the most monstrous and nightmarish doubts; but within man is found the seed of his redemption—his reason. In its light, such doubts—largely based on Christian doctrine—appear "excessive and laughable" (*Meditations*, Vol. VII, p. 89, l. 11–20).

When man's reason is properly applied, it can validate many aspects of our perception of physical body, however "chaotic" the beginnings of that body may be imagined to be, however "remote" from man's soul its perfections as found in the world around us. In short, the doubts that he characterized so contemptuously as "laughable and excessive" are almost surely not *Descartes'* own doubts so much as the statement of the ultimate excesses of skepticism on the part of the largely Christian public. Descartes' answers to those doubts were more than persuasive to many of his contemporaries: they were fascinating. Such intelligence, coupled as it was with a lofty philanthropy, and free as it was from "dogma," could not help but be fascinating to many, and the independence of its speculations to many more. (The Holy Office found them "damnable.")

In the next chapter we discuss the relation of the functions of the body to the idea-producing mechanism of its soul. At this point, however, an anticipation of that discussion is required in order to complete this reflection on the role of imagination and its symbols in Descartes' thought.

Descartes told Princess Elizabeth that "body, that is to say, extension, figures and motion, can also be known by pure intellect, but much better by the understanding aided by the imagination." The aid given to the understanding by the imagination is deeply involved in Descartes' view of what Taliaferro calls "the power of symbolizing," which is "placed by Descartes at the very center of knowing." As Descartes told Elizabeth, however, it is not altogether necessary for the understanding to have the aid of the imagination in order to know body! Furthermore, in its knowing of itself, pure reason does not use imagination at all (*Rules*, Vol. X, p. 416, l. 17, to p. 417, l. 3), and thus would not seem to require *any* symbolic activity for that so very important knowledge. We explain this difficulty as follows.

Pure understanding (*l'entendement pur, mens pura*) understands the soul, which Descartes identified with mind, insofar as it understands its own operations. Those operations, when directed toward body, are best symbolized by the algebraic operations of addition, subtraction, multiplication, division, and the extraction of roots—operations expressed by Descartes with the respective symbols $+$, $-$, x, a/b, and $\sqrt[n]{\ }$. These operations also occur disguised, as, e.g., the passions of love and hate—replacing the operations of adding distinct things into a unity, or of taking a whole and replacing it with distinct and separate parts. (Multiplication and division were understood by Descartes as being repeated addition and subtraction.) The extraction of roots is replaced by the passion or emotion of wonder. These assertions are dealt with further in the next chapter in the context of Descartes' 1645–46 *Passions of the Soul*, but taking these assertions here as provisionally true for Descartes, we can see more clearly the role of symbolizing in his thought.

There are two sorts of symbols for Descartes. One kind is "naturally instituted" and the other is ingeniously composed by men using "intellectual convention [*arbitrium mentis*]." For Descartes, the use of these intellectual conventions presuppose the God-given freedom to judge the most *suitable* convention to represent what is in itself either not "naturally" given to consciousness in any spontaneous way (e.g., the operations of the mind), or, what is given to consciousness spontaneously, but only in a confused and "meaningful" way (e.g., light, heat, color and pain). The powers of the mind are an example of the sort of thing that is represented to the mind clearly *only* through certain human artifacts, that is, by means of representation, such as the signs of the algebraic operations. Descartes' analytic geometry was thus understood by him to be proof that operations that were very nearly the same as those used in the algebraic analysis of his predecessor, Vieta, were precisely those that the intellect used both when it concerned itself with the figures, motions, and ratios of the problems found in Pappus's collection of problems solved by the geometrical analysis of the Greeks, as well as when it was applied in his mechanics (our mathematical physics). Our initial, irrational perceptions of light, heat, color, pain, and the like need mechanics and medicine for a completely rational, biophysical account of these perceptions as symbols of body in motion.

Symbolic thinking, for Descartes, is not a matter of "thinking in symbols." It is an intellectual process involving non-intentional marks ("chiffres," "notae") to represent directly to the thinker those distinct operations of the mind by means of which he is thinking of anything at all; it is also a *methodical* thinking, which proceeds according to clearly stated rules—Vieta's "symbolae." Symbolic thinking, always and at every moment, refers to the mind whose operations are being performed in any given case. Imagination is so important for Descartes in this matter because under the free, ingenious, use of his geometry, it allows the thinker to represent to himself, to imagine, the powers of *sa raison*—of his own mind. It thereby also makes clear to the thinker that even thought processes are profoundly rooted in the operations of the mind, using the imagination, which is itself profoundly rooted in the processes of the thinker's body. Only by means of what we might call the "discipline or art of the imagination" can the thinker realize that all thoughts are in some radical way the fruits of the power of *one's own mind*. As a consequence, the scientist must be entirely free to choose, in each and every case, the best way possible to "imagine" the operations of his own mind as he grapples with first one and then another problem. This procedure implies, as its absolutely unquestionable foundation, *freedom of thought*. This concept provided one of the deepest springs for Enlightenment and post-Enlightenment political theories of freedom and, in particular, it provides the reason why men as sophisticated as Diderot and d'Alembert looked to Descartes, "the inventor of the method of indeterminates," as also, and even primarily, a principal founder of modern revolutionary thought. That is, Descartes' method presupposes a broadly free environment as a necessary precondition for symbolic procedures. The Cartesian doctrine of the individual's imagination as being the corporeal basis for performing symbolic procedures chosen in each case purely on the grounds of their particular usefulness, assigns to every rational human being the obligation to realize, insofar as possible, that he alone is responsible for all judgments, affirmations, denials, doubts, and, to speak generally, for any and all intellectual endeavors concerned with the human solution to human problems. Therefore, whereas the laws of Christian Europe were based on the Old Testament accounts of creation and Sinai, and the New Testament account of Jesus Christ as the messiah, Descartes' doctrine required each man to reconstruct the visible world of Genesis for himself, insofar as it is intelligible to him through the use of his own intellect. That is, Descartes' doctrine implies the replacement of Eden, Sinai, Bethlehem, and Golgotha by the constructs of his own mathematical physics. Finally, ethics, *la morale*, Descartes' own science of man, is the final fruit of his physics. The discipline of the imagination is thus ultimately Descartes' preparation for freeing humans from the teachings of both Old and New Testaments and from the civil law based on them.

NOTES

1. That is, Descartes was suggesting that the ancients thought that they should use terms from arithmetic in geometry, but that for "unmathematical" reasons they did so as little as possible.

2. Jean Laport, *Études D'Histoire de la Philosophie Française au XVII Siècle* (Paris: J. Vrin, 1951), p. 14.

J. F. Scott, a historian of mathematics, calls Descartes' use of arithmetical operations in geometry "momentous," because:

> Not only are geometrical problems to be reduced to questions anent the length of lines, and so ultimately to algebraic problems, but . . . by reducing all algebraic calculations to a few irreducible primitive ones, and all geometrical constructions to a few irreducible ones again [Descartes was able to] detect fundamental parallelisms of structure between the two sciences.

[J. F. Scott, *The Scientific Work of René Descartes* (London: Taylor and Francis Ltd., 1952), p. 88.]

Speaking in a similar vein, the mathematician Kleene says:

> The analytic geometry of Descartes (1619), i.e. the use of co-ordinates to represent geometrical objects, constitutes a general method for establishing the consistency of geometrical theories on the basis of . . . the theory of the real numbers.

[S. C. Kleene, *Introduction to Metamathematics* (Princeton: Van Nostrand and Co., 1952), p. 54.]

3. Descartes himself said:

> For I do not prove the [outside] existence of material things from this, that their ideas are in us, but from this, that they come to us in such a way that we are conscious that they did not arise from us but entered in from elsewhere.

[Vol. III, p. 428, l. 30 to p. 429, l. 2]

That proof of the existence of material things is *identical* to Descartes' proof of the existence of God. And well it might be! In order for Descartes to develop a mathematical physics ("applied geometry," or "mechanics"), his mathematics must be applicable to physical bodies.Descartes must thus show how his pure, "abstract," *algebraic* quantity relates to *physical* quantity.

4. As is discussed later on, the notion of "objective reality" belongs to ideas—and never to the things of which they are ideas.

5. J. F. Scott discusses this arithmetical (or operational) character of Cartesian geometry in the context of his discussion of the relation between Descartes' mathematical investigations and those of his great contemporary, Fermat. In the context of arguing his claim that Fermat did not know Descartes' work, Scott says:

> Much more weighty evidence lies in the fact that had he been familiar with Descartes' works . . . he would not have stopped short at equations of the second degree. Above all he could have discarded the trammels of Vieta with regard to the nominal homogeneity of all the terms of an equation, and thus by liberating algebra from the fetters of reference to physical quantity prepare the way for its arithmetization. [*The Scientific Works*, p. 88]

Scott rightly judges that a major contribution of Descartes' mathematics lies in his "liberating algebra from the fetters of reference to physical quantity," i.e., from questions of what we today usually call "spatial dimensions." For, in Vieta and Fermat, a^2 means only the square of side a, and $a \times b \times c$ could only mean the solid with sides a, b, and c. As a consequence, a^4 could have no meaning except in arithmetic, i.e., a in a^4 could not, *in geometry*, stand for the side of a figure a units in length. Scott, discussing the novelty of Descartes' treatment of algebra and geometry, says:

> It is a momentous liberation when Descartes throws aside the dimensional restrictions of Vieta and lets the second power a^2 measure a length as well as an actual square, and the arithmetical first power a measure a square as well as an actual length . . . Just as an arithmetical problem may involve the operations addition, subtraction, multiplication, division and the extraction of a root, . . . so also in geometry . . . to determine the lengths of certain right lines, it is only necessary to add or subtract other right lines . . . and so on. This is a momentous point. [Ibid., p. 95]

6. René Descartes, *The Geometry of René Descartes*, trans. Smith and Latham (New York: Dover Books, 1954), p. 5, fn. 6.

7. In the beginning of the *Geometry*, for example, Descartes defined the "quantity" a^3 as follows. Given the "line" a, a^3 is not found by constructing a cube on a side of a length a. Rather, using Euclid II, 14, Descartes finds a second "quantity" m, such that $1/a = a/m$ (i.e., "cross multiplying" $m = a^2$). Then, a^3 is the quantity such that $1/a^2 = a/m$. Repeating this process, we can construct a^4 as the quantity such that $1/a^3 = a/m$, and so on indefinitely. These "squares," "cubes," etc., are merely *general* magnitude for Descartes, and they apply equally to lines, surfaces, volumes, etc., and are only defined by the *operations* required to arrive at them. Descartes' "quantity," m in this example, thus belongs to the domain of geometry as well as to that of the real numbers, and thus to neither; m is a symbol of "algebraic quantity," that is, its only definition is within the context of the equation in which it occurs. In a like way, the quantity a^n is defined entirely by the operation of repeated multiplication by which it was reached.

8. This abstract geometry, although it directly leads to questions that can be answered only by metaphysics (as Descartes understood—or misunderstood—that term), is not metaphysics as his contemporaries understood it. Descartes said that metaphysics considers only the soul in itself, whereas abstract geometry considers only that power of the soul whereby it knows. For Descartes, metaphysics considers all of the operations that belong to the soul, i.e., perception, understanding, and volitions, and questions about why they are operative in this world. As is argued at length in the second part of this work, his metaphysics is also used by him—and, knowingly or unknowingly, by his successors—to establish a general foundation for his social science.

9. Since Descartes' day, Western thought has been largely divided into problem-solving efforts and reflection on the subsequent fruits of those problem-solving efforts: the former portion comprises science and its ancillaries; the latter comprises academic philosophy. Thus, when Karl Marx persuaded many of Europe's thinkers that the job of philosophy was henceforth to begin *doing* things, he thereby transformed political philosophy into political science. What was left of academic philosophy was academic history of philosophy and academic metaphysics. Academic metaphysics has two branches: one is Ethics (which is usually vaguely religious), and the other is self-consciously and sometimes militantly unethical, and is best represented by linguistic analysis.

Because today's metaphysics is addressed to discovering foundations for and implications of the solutions to problems that are the fruits of scientific thinking, both in Descartes, and even more after him, it has been mainly, although not altogether, seen as a sort of formal exercise that is apart from the real work of life. (Something in Descartes was not quite happy with this view, but his disgust with the [truly horrendous] state of academic philosophy of his time, together with his desire for the glory of laying down the practical foundations of a new, secular, and populist age, muted his sense of the true worth of metaphysics.)

The prejudice about metaphysics held in our age is clearly illustrated by the fact that the only places I have ever been that truly appreciated the power and subtlety of Descartes were seminars whose participants were mature neuroanatomists, psychiatrists, and psychophysiological clinicians. Academic philosophy has largely been persuaded that philosophy is either history, ethics-religion, or some form of philosophy of science.

10. As I show later, even the mind "acting alone" in abstract geometry or pure mathematics is indirectly concerned with body. Descartes held that only when the object of thought is explicitly the powers of the mind itself are its thoughts not concerned with body. Such thoughts he called "metaphysical." However, elsewhere (*vid.* Vol. III, p. 694, l. 15 to p. 695, l. 3) he suggested that even metaphysical thinking is somehow concerned with body. Indeed, given his doctrine of mathematical body, it must be.

11. This concept of intentional species, which was taken by Descartes to have started with Aristotle and to mean that the body is so constructed that it senses directly the form of things that are brought to the senses through the medium of air, sound, etc., seems to begin with St. Bonaventura (fl. 1248), whose teaching about intentional species (see *In Lib. 1 Sent, d. 31, p. 2, a.i., q. 3 concl.*) is very nearly what Descartes later referred to as the "objective reality of an idea." As is so characteristic of Descartes, he threw out the received opinion and substituted his own, which is only a well-disguised version of the reject.

The concept of intentional species concerns the likeness of an idea to that of which it is the idea; it is the one likeness shared by the thinking mind and the thing that mind is thinking about.

In Part II of this work, we clarify both the extent of Descartes' neuroanatomical mistakes as well as their likely cause. For now, all we need remark is that the pineal gland does for Descartes very much what the optic tectum of the occipital lobes of the neocortex (along with the reticular formation) does for our neurophysiology of sight.

12. In his *Almagest*, the astronomer Ptolemy (A.D. c. 100–c. 178) said that, according to certain distinctions to be found in Aristotle: "the kind of science which shows up quality with respect to forms and local motions, seeking figure, number, and magnitude, and also place, time, and similar things, would be defined as mathematical." [*The Almagest*, Book I, Preface, trans. R. Catesby Taliaferro, in *Great Books of the Western World* (Chicago: Encyclopedia Brittanica, 1952, Vol. 16, p. 5.) Although to my knowledge Descartes only referred to these qualities of physical bodies as being what affects the common sense or pineal gland, the well-known source, Ptolemy, says that what are identified as common sensibles in Aristotle are precisely the objects of the science of mathematics. This passage of Ptolemy should be compared with Descartes, Meditation VI (Vol. IX, p. 69, in French,

which he preferred to the Latin text; Vol. VII, p. 86, l. 16–19, in Latin), and Aristotle, *On the Soul* (418a, 16–19; 425a, 14) and *On Sensation* (437a,8).

Descartes assigned to the pineal gland more or less what is now, in modern neurological parlance, assigned to the reticular formation, along with the optic tectum of the occipital lobes of the neocortex.

13. These "mathematical ideas" have the peculiarity that only in their case is what Descartes called the "objective reality" of those ideas directly traceable to the "formal reality" of their "object." That is, in this one case, the form of the idea faithfully images the shape of the thing whose idea it is. Hence, the truly existent shapes, magnitudes, and motion of matter are not the objective reality of our ideas of them. As Descartes said:

> that manner of being objectively [*de estre obiectivement*] belongs to ideas, because of their proper nature, just as, on the other hand, the manner or fashion of being formally belongs to the causes of these ideas . . . by their proper nature. [Vol. IX, p. 32]

The relation between the forms of ideas and the forms of objects of ideas is discussed in the fourth section of Chapter 2.

14. Anticipating ourselves, the human body's mechanical response—"reflex" response, as we say today—to these motions in matter outside us gives rise to how we feel about what we perceive, precisely because the mathematicals cause the soul, the "thing which thinks," to ideate those percepts *directly;* but our body's "personal," "endocrinological" response to these percepts gives rise to such "passions" as fear, love, etc. The whole of Part II of this work concerns this side of Descartes.

15. As is discussed in detail later, all ideas, even "clear and distinct" ideas, are, strictly speaking, *corporeal* impressions affecting the pineal gland and thence the soul. This point should never be lost sight of. It should also be mentioned here that what Locke and the subsequent tradition called "ideas," Descartes called "perceptions" and "thoughts," i.e., *pensées.* Descartes perhaps did not always conform to his own definitions of these terms (*vid.* Vol. VII, p. 160ff., for the definitions.)

16. As is argued later, when we exclusively attend to the *form* of the corporeal impression that gives rise to some thought, then, and only then, does that thought "grasp" an idea. Otherwise, something in the thought is merely "subjective," i.e., caused by the relation of mind and body. In some degree, however, we "think" ideas insofar as our thoughts are *about* ideas.

17. We address this question of quantification of qualities in more detail later. For the background to this critical concept, refer to: Paul, Eph. IV: 7, and references to it in Peter Lombard, "Opera Omnia," Tom. II, p. 566 (Migne, *Patrologiae cursus completus*), which in turn were, it appears, picked up by Nicole Oresme, "*Tractatus de latitudinibus formarum*" (Biblioth. Mathem. 1912/13, 13(1): 115–145. In that same series, see also Heinrich Wieleitner, "Ueber den Funktions begriff und die graphische Darstellung bei Oresme," ibid., 1914, 14(3): 193–282). There is an English translation of the *Tractatus de latitudinibus formarum*, as: *An Abstract of Nicholas Oresme's Treatise on The Breadth of Forms*, trans. Charles Glen Wallis (Annapolis: St. John's College Press, 1941); a translation of the Latin text accompanying the Weileitner commentary can be found in: "Nicole Oresme and Medieval Geometry of Qualities and Motions/A treatise on the Uniformity and Difformity of Intensities known as *Tractatus de configurationibus qualitatum et motuum*," ed. with English translation and commentary by Marshall Clagett (Madison, Milwaukee and London: University of Wisconsin Press, 1968). On p. 1033ff., Clagett discusses the importance of Oresme for Galileo, and on p. 106, Descartes' name is mentioned, with a reference to A. Koyré, *Études Galiléennes*, Vol. 2, pp. 25–54, and his *The Science of Mechanics*, pp. 417–418.

18. Lewis and Short, *A Latin Dictionary* (Oxford: Oxford University Press, 1958), s. v. "*dimensio.*"

19. Readers who recall their introductory algebra will remember that word-problems are taught by species: for example, mixture problems, age problems, rate problems, etc. This is precisely what the seventeenth- and eighteenth-century thinkers meant when they referred to algebra as "specious arithmetic." Vieta's *Isagoge in Artem Analyticem* (1596) was accurately and intelligently translated by J. Winfree Smith in 1955 at St. John's College, Annapolis, Maryland, and his translation appears as the appendix to Jacob Klein's *Greek Mathematical Thought and the Origin of Algebra*, trans. Eva Brann (Cambridge, Mass.: MIT Press, 1968). Chapter VI of Smith's translation of Vieta is given as, "On the precepts of the reckoning by species," and according to Vieta that reckoning "operates with species or forms of things, as, for example, with the letters of the alphabet" (p. 328).

20. "Lines" are the dimensions of, the way we keep track of, all those essential considerations that, when taken together, comprise a definite, solvable problem that we can ask about a definite body under definite circumstances. In a way, "lines" do indeed form "super-solids," namely, to the extent that when we take all the conditions of a problem together and perform a set of mathematical (often quasi-arithmetical) operations on them, we end up with a "product," the solution itself, which is analogous to, *but only analogous to*, what we term the "volume" of a solid, which we obtain once we have "multiplied" together all the dimensions of the solid. The solution of a real, definite problem is, in this way, analogous to the volume, which is the result of multiplying only three dimensions together. The "answer to" or "truth about" any given questionable thing is thus a unity, and a single, identifiable object of the mind, because of this volumelike aspect of the answer—which makes truth quasi-"solid"!

Two examples help show what it could mean to speak of a "quasi-solidity" belonging to the multidimensional constructs composed of Cartesian "lines." The most obvious example is continuity: a number of points (often a very small number of points) are connected to one another by a (usually) smooth curve, a curve that is "nowhere interrupted"— following Descartes' dictum of the necessity for a "continuous and nowhere interrupted motion of thought [*continuo et nullibi interrupto cogitationis motu*] (Vol. X, p. 407, l. 3–4). The curve, of course, has an infinity of points on it, but we postulate that all the points that represent the intersection of the dimensions of a problem—e.g., plotting time against distance to get velocity—belong to, "lie on," and indeed, *actually compose* the continuous curve. (We discuss this notion of curves soon.) The statistical approach of probabilistic mechanics is an algorithm for dealing with just this problem.

Again, the Leibniz-Newton treatment of an *integral*, and, in particular, its interpretation as the "area under" (or "volume under," whichever applies) a curve, points even more strongly to this characteristic of quasi-solidity. Analytic mathematics, starting from Descartes, has a powerful tendency toward the materialization of concepts; it is possible that the central Christian doctrine of the Incarnation, that is, of the *logos* (John 1:1), where *logos* means "word," "form," even "formula," is a model for this way of thinking. For Descartes, whatever we can clearly and distinctly—non-contradictorily—imagine can be brought into existence; this is the power of what Descartes calls *ingenium*, a term that has a derivative in 'engineer.'

21. The genesis of this view is not within the province of this work, but it is probably to be found in his reading of Pappus's account of locus-problems, of Oresme's attempts to quantify quality, and of Vieta's work with symbolic algebra. *The* work on this point is Jacob Klein's *Greek Mathematical Thought and the Origin of Algebra* (see Note 19,), especially Part I, Chapter 7, and Part II, Chapters 11 and 12. Kelin's work on the subjects we deal with in Chapter 1 of this text is incomparable.

The reason that these general proportions are so important for Descartes is touched upon below, when we examine the relation between *datum* and *quaesitum* (between the given in a problem and the sought-for). For now, it must suffice to say that proportions appeared to Descartes to provide a formal bridge for thought between the given and the known, e.g., if *a:b* as *c:d* . . . as *m:n*, then *a* and *m* are related to one another formally; and, if *a* represents the given, *a* to *b*, the given ratio, then, if *m* is the sought-for, that continued proportion provides the bridge or rung (*gradus*) between *a* and *m*. It is, apparently, this insight that led Descartes and his succesors to value continuity so much. Furthermore, basing their argument on the notion that the continuous and the truly extended are one and the same (*vid.* especially Rules V–IX, and compare with the *Geometry*, Books II–VI, pp. 391–395), men would later call geometry itself a "rational mechanics," where Descartes himself calls his physics "applied geometry"—implying that, *mutatis mutandis*, geometry itself is in some way a matter to be comprehended by physics.

The Euclidian (more accurately, perhaps, "Eudoxian-Theatetian") theory of proportions exemplified in Book V of Euclid's *Elements* is couched in terms of magnitudes that are "equal to, less than, or greater than" one another. The fundamental definition of sameness of ratio (Def. 5, Book V, *The Elements*) is stated in just such terms. Then (using modern notation), a proportion between magnitudes *a*, *b*, *c*, and *d* is expressed as $(a/b)=(c/d)$. [These look like fractions, *but they are not*. Rather, the expression is to be read: "By however much the magnitude *a* exceeds, equals, or falls short of magnitude *b*, so the magnitude *c* exceeds, equals, or falls short of magnitude *d*." This has nothing whatsoever to do with fractions (*vid.* Klein, *Greek Mathematical Thought, sub.* "fractions."] This expression enables us to "cross-multiply," and thereby to transform a proportion into "an equation": if $(a/b) = (c/d)$, then $(ad) = (bc)$.

The point here concerns Descartes' claim about "all the particular sciences which are commonly designated by the name mathematics"; namely, his statement that, "seeing that they are concerned with nothing but the different relations or proportions found in them, I thought it better for me to examine only these general proportions and not to suppose them except in the subjects which seemed to render their knowledge easier for me . . ." (Vol. VI, p. 20, l. 1–7). But, since the source of these equations is the definition of proportion in Book V of *The Elements,* which deals with magnitudes that equal, exceed, or fall short of one another, Descartes meant by "the subjects which seemed to render their knowledge easier for me" magnitudes insofar as they could be ordered in respect to size or extension. Then, Descartes next identified that aspect of extension as being that because of which we can know anything about magnitude, and he thereby invented two things at once: on the one hand, he offered the notion of extended substance (*cors estendu,* or *res extensa*) from an abstraction on the magnitudes under consideration in Book V of Euclid, and, on the other hand, since each and every linear magnitude can be ordered with respect to size or extension, he offered the concept of magnitude in general (*magnitudo in genere*), our "algebraic quantity." Algebraic quantity is real body, which has the one property that can be used to come to mathematical solutions of problems. Thus, the human brain and the human nervous system are the organized correlates to algebraic quantity. One of the primary goals of this book is to lay out the most important details of Descartes' teachings concerning this correlation.

22. It is in this obscure context that Descartes in effect tells the world that anything which really exists in physical reality can be grasped in its entirety by the methods and procedures of his mathematical physics; for that physics is guided by a mathematics whose object is "magnitude in general": anything which has magnitude, or which can be reduced to magnitude (in, for instance, the way social psychologists "quantify" choice by setting up "forced choice" questionnaires and statistically analyzing the results) can be treated by the methods of Descartes' mathematical physics.

23. Babina says:

If the equation contains only one unknown, its solution will yield the line segment which determines the geometrical problem; if the geometrical problem is "indeterminate," the equation will contain two unknowns (and if one of these is represented by a variable segment, one of whose extremes determines, on a fixed straight line, the segment represented by the other unknown, and the other extremity describes a line which resolves the geometrical problem, thus outlining the fundamental concept which will later be that of the Cartesian coordinates). With this process, all the resources of algebra—the theory of equations, algebraic transformations—are applied to geometry, and the 'empty letters' of that science are satisfied by the geometrical content. Possessed by its cosmological desire, it will pursue the process, and, generalizing the concept of dimension . . . all the science of nature will satisfy the formal marks of algebra. . . . [J. Babina, "La Matematica en Descartes y El Mundo Exterior" *Escritos en Honor de Descartes* (La Plata, Argentina, 1938), p. 15].

24. Although Descartes developed a theory of n-degree curves for his studies of refraction in the *Dioptrics,* he had to show that those cruves were generated in the media (i.e., in air, glass, the fluid of the eyeball, etc.), because of certain "physical" properties of the media, e.g., distortion of figure, dampening or quickening of motion, rest, etc. Indeed, a good part of the investigations of the second and third books of the theoretical, "abstract" *Geometry* are taken up with discussion of how to generate curves of degree greater than three (i.e., of super-solids) by means of machines, where he had to justify his constructions using only the physical properties of the machines. That is, he had to show that the curve drawn by a machine with such and such a structure was in fact the curve having such and such a formula. [For a view of modern, i.e., post-Darwinian biology that characterizes it as the study of organisms as "biological loci" of curves whose force-moments are geophysical/mutational events, see Richard B. Carter, "What states are made of: New questions," *International Studies in Philosophy,* vol. XIV, no. 1 (Spring, 1982), pp. 1–16.]

25. *Pappi Alexandrini Collectionis quae supersunt e libris manu scriptis edidit, latina interpretatione et commentariis Instruxit Fridericus Hultsch* (Berolini, 1876, 1878), 3 Vols. in 8º. A French translation, with copious notes, is available: *Pappus D'Alexandrie, La Collection Mathematique,* 2 Vols., trad. Paul Ver Eecke (Paris & Bruges: Brouwer et Cie., 1933). My own translations refer to Hultsch's Greek text, which is, happily, faced with his own Latin translation. Although all the Pappus citations herein refer to Ver Eecke's text, they are based on the Greek, Latin, and French texts. The present citation is Ver Eecke, Vol. II, pp. 477–478.

For a masterly treatment of this matter from the perspective of the history and philosophy of mathematics, see Jacob Klein, *Greek Mathematics,* fn. 232 on p. 166, and pp. 166–172 of the text.

26. In the *Geometry,* we find a long Latin quotation from a sixteenth-century translation of Pappus of Alexandria's Συναγωγή or (mathematical) *Collection,* which dates from about A.D. 320. Descartes took his quote from the beginning of Book VII, the "Treasury of Analysis" (as translated by Commendinus in 1560). In that book, Pappus describes the history of mathematical analysis and gives the *sometimes conflicting* opinions about it which were current in antiquity. He first describes analysis as the discipline to be learned by those "who, after having acquired the common elements, wish to pursue in lines the ability to discover problems which are laid down for them, and for this alone it is useful." However, Pappus then distinguishes between two species of analysis—in what could be taken as a direct contradiction to his first, general definition of analysis as being concerned only with the relation between "lines" (by which he means geometrical constructions, some of which were very sophisticated curves), and "the ability to discover problems." He says that one sort of analysis is called "theoretical" and the other "problematic" or "poristic" (θεωρητικòν

and ποϱισικὸν). Only problematic analysis ("poristic," as it was to be called in the sixteenth century and thereafter) concerns "lines." Theoretical analysis concerned only truth and falsity; it did not *in the least* concern the discovery of a geometrical construction for the solution of a problem.

Pappus wrote:

That which is called the analytical reasoning . . . is, in summary terms, the particular matter prepared for those who, after having acquired the common elements, wish to pursue in lines the ability to discover (solutions to) problems which are laid down for them, and for this alone it is useful. This matter has been treated by three men: by Euclid, the author of *The Elements;* by Apollonius of Perga; and by Aristeas the elder, and it is approached through analysis and synthesis. Analysis, then, proceeds as follows: we first suppose that we in fact have what is being sought after, and then, proceeding through the orderly consequences of that supposition, we finally arrive at something admitted through the synthesis. For, in the analysis, we assume the sought-after as having been accomplished or done, inquiring out of what this results, and again, of the latter, we inquire for its predecessors, and so thus retracing, we arrive at something already known or something which is on the order of principles; and such an approach is called analysis—as being a backward solution. [This is the literal translation of ἀναλύσις.] In the synthesis, on the contrary, supposing the thing already perceived by the analysis as being already obtained, then disposing its consequences and its causes in their natural order, and then connecting them with one another, one at last arrives at the construction of the thing sought; and this is what we call synthesis. There are two sorts of analysis, the one which searches for the truth and is called theoretical, and the other which supplies that set out (to be found) and which is called problematical. Now in the theoretical kind, we assume the sought-after as existing and true, and then, by means of orderly conclusions considered as true and existing because they are in agreement with the hypothesis, we arrive at something admitted [or: about which we are sure]: hence, if what has been admitted be true, the sought-after shall also be true and the proof will be the contrary order of the order of the analysis; if we arrive at something admitted to be false, that sought-after will also be false. In the problematical kind, we assume as known what is sought-for and then, by means of orderly conclusions supposed as true, because they follow from that supposition, we arrive at something admitted; if the admitted be possible and obtainable (this is what is called *the given* by the mathematicians) the proposed as known shall be possible and obtainable, and then the proof will be the contrary order of the analysis; however, if we arrive at something admitted to be impossible, then the problem shall also be impossible.

27. The mathematical foundations of this present study are in part parallel to the matter in Jacob Klein's book, *Greek Mathematical Thought and the Origin of Algebra,* and are very often guided by it, although they are not often taken from it. Klein's work is extraordinarily difficult and dense, and thus mostly inaccessible to many thoughtful readers who would greatly welcome the opportunity to grasp its subject matter. Parts of it, however, are worth anyone's effort, especially pp. 197–211, "The concept of 'number' in Descartes."

In spite of my great debt to Klein's work in this section, a caveat is necessary here: at certain crucial places it is more proper to address some issues in the context of neuroanatomy and what can be called generally "medical physiology" in Descartes, rather than in the grand philosophic tradition, as Klein has done. Descartes was both a philosopher and a philanthropist. As such, perhaps, he lacks what Klein called "the immoderate moderation" of ancient philosophy, which, although was often deeply philanthropic, was never primarily so.

28. I owe this particular, crucially important point to detailed private conversations with Jacob Klein during 1961–1962. The development contingent upon this point is, however, my own.

29. Klein points out (*Greek Mathematical Thought*) that it is in the actual synthesis that follows problematic analysis—*and only in problematic synthesis*—that the line or figure must be entirely determined. We must add, however, that such a determination is not, for Pappus and the tradition, a determination of length, i.e., determination does not in the least presuppose a universal unit of measure or a universal ruler based on such a universal unit of measure—or, more particularly, the determination of line or figure does not presuppose a "Cartesian coordinate system" to specify its ratio to a unit length in order to be a determinate magnitude.

Here is an example of the use of problematic analysis from Pappus, Book VII, Prop. 105 (Ver Eecke, Vol. II, pp. 640–642). This problem illustrates precisely the province of problematic analysis and *its* synthesis.

PROBLEM: To find a broken line, DBE, touching a given circle at B from the two given points D and E, such that, if DB and BE are produced to meet the circle again at A and C, AC is parallel to DE.

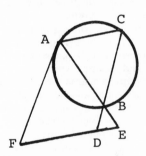

Analysis	*Synthesis*
1. Suppose the problem solved and draw the tangent from A.	1. Let there be a circle ABC and two points, D and E given in position.
2. Since AC is parallel to DE, ∡ ACD = ∡ CDE.	2. Construct the rectangle FE × DE equal to the square on the tangent from E (this gives the line EF).
3. But, ∡ FAE = ∡ ACD.	
4. Thus, ∡ FAE = ∡ CDE (& ∡ FAE + ∡ FDC = two right angles).	3. Draw the tangent from F to A on the circle.
5. Thus, points F, A, B, and D are on one circle.	4. Draw AE.
6. Thus, rectangle AE × EB = rect. FE × DE.	5. Draw DC through B and connect A and C.
7. Now, rect. AE × EB is given, since it equals the square on the tangent from E.	*I say that AC is parallel to DE*
	DEMONSTRATION
	6. FE × ED is constructed equal to the square on the tangent from E.

8. Thus, rect. FE × ED is also given.
9. Thus, FE is given in position and in length.
10. Thus, its end-point F is given in position.
11. And, since FA is tangent to the circle given in position, FA is given both in position and length.
12. And F is given, so that A is given.
13. But E is also given in position.
14. Therefore AE is given in position.
15. Since the circle is given in position, the point B is given.
16. Since D and E are given, DB and BE are given in position, and *the line BDE is given in position.*

7. But rect. AE × EB is also equal to the square on the tangent from E.
8. Thus, rect. FE × ED = rect. AE × EB.
9. Thus, the points A, B, D, and F are on one circle.
10. And ∡ FAE = ∡ CDE.
11. But, ∡ FAE = ∡ ACD.
12. Thus, ∡ CDE = ∡ ACD.
13. And these are alternate angles;
14. Thus, AC is parallel to DE.

Correspondence between steps in Demonstration and in Analysis:

Demonstration	Analysis
Step 6	8
7	7
8	6
9	5
10	4
11	3
12	2

30. A revealing example, which is similar to what Pappus calls theoretical analysis, is to be found in Plato's accounts of Socrates arguing with men such as Thrasymachus, Theatetus, Gorgias, Polus, and Callicles. Plato used a form of analysis so often in his Socratic writings that there existed in antiquity a tradition that Plato himself invented analysis. (*Vid.* Proclus, *In Euclid.*, ed. Friedlein, p. 211, l. 19–22, and Diogenes Laertius, III, 24. Also, *vid.* Klein, *Greek Mathematical Thought*, fn. 216 on p. 154. Klein, in this matter, as in so many others treated here, is incomparably helpful.)

31. For Descartes, the pineal gland seems to be the brain structure that can act as an "origin." There is a certain neutral position for it, and depending on how and to what degree this position is diverged from, one is conscious of this or that shape and emotion. Modern neuroanatomy has rejected Descartes' pineal gland as the origin, but it still seeks a replacement for what it rejected—namely, *Descartes'* invention!

32. Klein (*Greek Mathematical Thought*, p. 208 and fn. 324) cites Eustachius à Sancto Paulo (who published a *Summa philosophica* in 1609), and E. Gilson's *Index scholastico-cartesien* (Paris: Alcan, 1931), p. 107. Concerning the scholastic doctrine of Intentions, Klein points out (p. 210–211) that, "Extension has . . . a twofold character for Descartes. It is 'symbolic'—as the object of 'general algebra,' and it is 'real'—as the substance of the corporeal world." Klein then speaks of the symbolic objectivity of extension, and places that objectivity "within the framework of the *mathesis universalis.*"

My own sense is that this account could well be supplemented by reference to Descartes' medical investigations. Whatever the original source of Descartes' understanding of these matters, the question that Klein so well calls "the symbolic objectivity of extension" cannot be correctly appreciated outside a context that includes as its central concern Descartes' psychobiology. What is more, the whole question of the bridge between the true extension of body and the extension imagined by the soul in response to nerve impulses was complicated for Descartes, requiring quasi-theological reflections that address the Christian doctrine of the Incarnation, e.g., if Jesus the son of Joseph is God incarnate, then whatever has been said of the infinite, omnipresent God now applies to a living human being who had a home, mother, etc. This exemplifies "the second intentionality of Descartes' use of extension" (Klein, ibid., p. 208), better than Eustachius à Sancto Paulo, William of Ockham, or a host of other Scholastics. Also, Descartes took the relation between nerves and our consciousness center as a relation "instituted by nature" (Vol. VI, p. 134, l. 31, to p. 135, l. 1; p. 137, l. 24–25); this natural institution was instituted to preserve the union of body and soul. That providential institution is the starting point for the oddly passionate religiosity of some of Descartes' greatest students.

33. Rousseau's 1750 discourse, "Has the restoration of the sciences and the arts tended to purify morals?," no less than his *Letter to D'Alembert* on the arts, show, by the vigor and power of his attack on the notion of technological progress, how widespread and firm its defenses were.

34. The nineteenth-century mathematician Richard Dedekind defined irrational "numbers" as "cuts" that determine sequences of greater and lesser magnitudes. He then draws a purely Cartesian conclusion: that the magnitude whose "irrational" end-point is the "irrational cut," is called a length. In spite of this, his initial insight seems to be that the irrational "interval" is primarily a magnitude whose only property is that it is greater than some magnitudes and less than others. Again, he subsequently ignores the distinction he first made between magnitudes and lengths. [Richard Dedekind, *Essays on the Theory of Numbers*, trans. W. W. Beman (La Salle, Illinois: Open Court Publishing Co., 1948), pp. 8–24.]

The existence of irrational—more exactly, "incommensurable"—lines seems to show beyond a shadow of a doubt that not all lines can be classified according to their lengths. Plato's contemporaries Theatetus and Eudoxus in antiquity, and Dedekind in modernity, show, however, a way of ordering all lines with respect to their magnitudes, *as strictly opposed to their lengths*. In fact, this procedure neither reduces lines to magnitudes nor magnitudes to lengths; for example, considering the "analytic" property of a tangent to a curve, in their algebraic expression, the line and the curve share one and only one pair of values, which does not at all comprise a true reduction of lines to lengths.

35. That is, given numbered coordinates, we can exactly locate the end-points of magnitudes, and thus specify how many of the units on the coordinates the magnitude matches; we can exactly measure the magnitude, and thereby turn it into a length. "Lines" are a form under which we perceive; as such, they are initially perceptible, not mathematical. "Lines" that are set out to be measured, but that have not been actually measured, are indeterminate in length for Descartes; when they are measured, i.e., when we locate them within a coordinate system, they become automatically determinate in length. Magnitudes are, for Descartes, indeterminate lengths, and lengths are determined magnitudes. This is in contrast to the development in Plato's *Meno* concerning the diagonal of the square. For Descartes, the diagonal of that square is not just the side of the double square; it is "the square root of 2 units long," when compared to the side of the first square as the unit length.

36. In algebra there are two ways to measure a line segment. One way is to place a marked ruler or measuring rod parallel to the segment and to measure, the other way involves a line segment that is not parallel to the ruler, but that is drawn at an angle. This is the usual situation in any case where two or more lines meet one another at different angles, as in angles or triangles. In that case, we cannot simultaneously have one ruler parallel to more than one line, so we must measure the line at some determinate angle and multiply the length we get times another number—the so-called sine or cosine of the angle at which we measure the line segment. When we set up two such rulers to measure any number of lines, we get what is known as a set of Cartesian coordinates; when we set up three such rulers at right angles to each other, we get solid coordinates; and when we set

up more than three such rulers, we get what is needed to measure so-called n-dimensional manifolds. In short, any number of linear magnitudes located within the domain of a system of measuring rulers can be directly determined in length. Linear magnitudes, considered exclusively as entities that can be determined by coordinate systems are thus transformed into magnitudes whose lengths are indeterminate—into Descartes' "lines," which were originally given to us through neurophysiology. A "line" thus becomes a magnitude *known to be knowable in length,* and thus known in an indeterminate manner. We label such magnitudes by symbols that "stand for" unknown quantities.

37. Cf. Franz Kafka, *The Hunger Artist,* with Hobbes, *Leviathan,* Part I, Chapter XIV.

38. An "objective correlate" to an idea is what corresponds in "external reality" to the "objective reality" of an idea.

39. R. Catesby Taliaferro, "The Concept of Matter in Descartes and Leibniz," *Notre Dame Mathematical Lectures,* no. 9 (Notre Dame, 1964), p. 5.

40. Cf. Kant's use of the term *Vorstellung* in his second edition of the *Critique der Reinen Vernunft* of 1787, especially (B 202) *Axiome der Anschauung, das Prinzip derselben ist: alle Anschauungen sind extensive groessen.*

41. Taliaferro, "The Concept of Matter," p. 5.

42. Ibid.

43. Pappus defines analysis as a backwards solution (where synthesis is the straightforward solution): if we make use of a method of investigation in which what we end up with is the elements of what we started with, we are treating something analytically, in that we are proceeding from the particular question or problem to those elements in light of which we are able to draw certain conclusions concerning it. In that we do not return to the original problem, but analyze it (in order to get rid of it or in order to determine which of a number of its causes or elements is responsible for something we wish to eradicate), *we never do any synthesis,* in Pappus's sense of the word. Thus, because ignorance is temporally prior to knowledge or accomplishment, the method that reveals the way, analysis, is prior to the way that gives us knowledge or accomplishment. We must learn "how to" before we can act. Modern uses of analysis—chemical analysis, psychoanalysis, philosophic analysis— are curious in that they all treat problems at hand not as things to be understood and then accepted or rejected, but rather, as things to be solved—in some way, to be dis-solved!

44. The *Discourse* is concerned with "La Methode Pour Bien Conduire Sa Raison." Again, I have checked many translations, in several languages, and all of them translate *sa raison* as if it were *la raison,* but *sa* can only be a personal possessive in French. In English, this title should be given as "Discourse on the Method of Rightly Conducting One's Own Reason."

45. It is not altogether amiss to wonder how much place pride had in his taste for analysis. Descartes does reject all other mathematics! Also, Descartes' statement of what analysis and synthesis comprise is much more simple than Pappus's statement—which he certainly read.

46. This, I think, is the root of Descartes' *a priorism* [cf. Rule XIII (Vol. X, p. 435).]. Ultimately, Descartes justified his *a priorism* as a solution to "Meno's paradox" (*vid.* Rule XIII (Vol. X, p. 430, l. 17–22). (There is the possibility that Descartes' *a priorism* comprises an adumbration of Hegelian historicism. Descartes seems to divine something akin to an evolution in *L'Esprit.*)

47. It seems very likely that what the tradition came to know as "innate ideas" are first found in Descartes as generic physiological characteristics (that is, physiological characteristics of the human body as opposed to canine body, etc.) that give rise to certain thoughts. It is interesting that John Locke, a physician, was silent about the relation between physiology and psychology.

48. It may then be asked why Descartes was not content to use only "whole figures" of perception as symbols. What good are the letter-symbols of algebra if we can use the figure-symbols of geometry as well? When do we use each, and why?

One answer is simply that we can attend to only one thing at a time. Thus, figures, which have many parts, at times can confuse the issue by causing the mind to stray from particulars in its attempt to grasp the whole. At such times it is better to manipulate letters. There is, however, a far more urgent reason for use of letter-symbols in the Cartesian scheme. That is, letter-symbols, which are obviously arbitrary and conventional, do not look like anything "natural," and therefore natural impulse does not cause anyone viewing them to attribute any natural meaning to them. Since letter-symbols look like nothing except arbitrary, conventional marks on paper, they obviously do not naturally belong to that chain of causation that affects the well-being of the thinker. Because the light of nature so instructs us, we tend to believe that images in the imagination truly represent things outside. In order to overcome this "impulsive" teaching of nature, we must, whenever we can, present to the brain only such forms as would never be taken to be natural— such forms, that is, that are clearly only conventional, arbitrary symbols formed by the conventional, arbitrary motions of a writing instrument used in making marks on paper. When we have done this, and *only* then, can we use our percepts entirely according to our own needs of the moment. (This is another form of Descartes' neutralizing of perception. Curiously, it is novelist Albert Camus who, in *The Stranger*, presents the most clear picture of the results of this neutrality *vis à vis* the day-to-day life of humans.)

49. An excellent example of present-day fidelity to Descartes' procedure is found in the classic college calculus texts by Richard Courant, *Differential and Integral Calculus* [2 vols., trans. E. J. McShane (New York: Interscience Publishers, 1952) Vol. I, p. 91]. Courant states that we should consider the phenomena as constructs of our thought, the better to deal with them. He says:

> Now the fact that the problem of differentiating a given function has a definite meaning apart from the geometrical intuition of the tangent is of great significance. The reader will recall that in the case of the integral we freed ourselves from the geometrical intuition of area, and on the contrary based the notion of area on the definition of the integral.

However, the notion of an area is a notion derived from *naive* experience; Courant replaces this with the mathematical "definition of the integral." He says that:

> We . . . avoid the difficulties which arise out of the indefiniteness of the geometrical view, since we base the geometrical definition on the analytical and not vice versa. Nevertheless, the visualization of the derivative as the tangent to the curve is an important aid to understanding, even in purely analytical discussions. [p. 92]

Echoing Descartes, Courant uses "visualization of the derivative as a tangent" as "an important aid to understanding." He continues:

> The velocity is therefore the difference quotient of the function c + b . . . From this new meaning of the derivative which in itself has nothing to do with the tangent problem, we see that it really is appropriate to define the limiting process of differentiation as a purely analytic operation independent of geometric intuitions. [pp. 93–94]

"Velocity" is no more an experienced phenomenon for Courant than for Descartes; for both it is an idea concerned with an operation, e.g., differentiation. It is plausible that the author arrived at that idea somewhat as follows: First, he had to withdraw himself from all the immediately significant evidence of his senses, that is, he had to accustom himself to deny the primacy of his *intuition* of a tangent of a curve. Then, when he had arrived at clear and distinct thoughts that were intelligible to him, he reviewed, in light of his withdrawal, all that he thought that he had known and all that was given to him prior to that withdrawal, readmitting only that part of it that could be directly justified in terms of something not affected by the withdrawal, but only readmitting it insofar as it could serve as an aid to understanding. After such withdrawal, velocity is no longer what was once discerned by simple intuition. It is now "the difference quotient of the function c + b," or, in Cartesian terms, an intelligible image of what was "given" as a "phenomenon."

CHAPTER 2

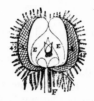

The Human Body

INTRODUCTION

IN TWO REMARKABLE letters to his Jesuit disciple Père Mesland[1] (Vol. IV, pp. 161–170, 345–348), Descartes discussed the ambiguous character of the common use of the word 'body.' In the first letter, he distinguished two senses of the word, one referring to "general body [*d'un corps en general*]," and the other to "the body of a man [*du corps d'un homme*]." In both letters he wrote that what distinguishes and identifies the human body is its "disposition" to receive the human soul.

These two letters to Mesland, written in 1645 and 1646, are primarily concerned with Descartes' *physiological* explanation of the mysteries of transubstantiation and concomitance, mysteries pronounced upon in the crucial counter-reformation Council of Trent of 1562. The former mystery concerns the real presence of Jesus Christ in the host at the time of consecration, and the latter concerns the real presence of Jesus Christ in *both* species of the host at the same time. Descartes considered these mysteries in terms of his own theory of the digestion and absorption of food. The point of his explanation lies in his theory of how the living body assimilates nonliving matter and how the assimilated nonliving food becomes a real part of the living body that it nourishes, even though in some respect it remains identical with the foodstuff it comprised before it was assimilated into the living body. Descartes pointed out that the digested parts remain, for a time, within the body, and so they are all "informed" by the soul of that body (Vol. IV, p. 168, l. 14).[2] The digested parts form, on the one hand, a true part of that body because they are all assimilated into the body having that particular soul, and, on the other hand, assimilated food can also still be considered to be the same bread or wine it was before it was assimilated for as long as all its parts remain collected together within one body until evacuated.

Descartes was precise about the difference between body in general (*magnitudo in genere*) and body that comprises a part of a living human body and is thus "informed" by a soul. In the first letter to Mesland, he distinguished between two uses of the term 'body':

Firstly, I consider what the human body is, and I find that this word body is very equivocal; because, when we speak of a body in general, we understand a determined part of matter, and, at the same time, the quantity of matter of which the universe is composed, such that one could not leave out any portion of this quantity, however small, which would not make us judge immediately that the body is less and that it is no longer whole; nor could one change one particle of this matter such that he would not think thereafter that the body is not entirely the same, or *idem numero* . . . . [Vol. IV, p. 166, l. 1–12]

He then continued that this description does not apply to the body of a man, because:

[by] a human body, we do not understand a determinate portion of matter, nor a part which has a determined size, but only . . . all the matter that is united together with the soul of that man . . . and we believe that this body is whole while it has all the dispositions required for conserving this union.

Thus, it is because of certain dispositions that the union of body and soul is conserved; it is, therefore, *not* the case that the absence of a soul causes the body to die, or that its presence causes the body to move as a living body. Indeed, in his 1648 treatise, *The Description of the Human Body*, Descartes stated:

And although all movement ceases in the body when it dies and when the soul leaves it, one should not infer from this that it is the soul which produces movements; but only that it is one and the same cause that makes the body no longer able to produce movement, and that makes the soul depart from it. [Vol. XI, p. 225, l. 26–31]

In short, the human body is precisely "all the matter which is united together with the soul of that man"; and it is the body itself that produces motion in all the matter informed by or united with the soul. The first part of this chapter discusses the dispositions (*les dispositions*) that give life to a body and make it fit to unite with, or be informed by, a human soul.[3]

Death of the body is caused by a change in the dispositions of the body required for a soul to be united with it. Thus, it is not primarily the loss of matter that causes death; it is the loss of *structure* that causes the body to lose its disposition to be informed by the soul. No loss of magnitude changes the living body, Descartes said, unless that loss involves "the organs of the human body necessary for life" (Vol. VI, p. 168, l. 20–21). Therefore, however distinct the thinking substance that comprises the human soul may be from merely physical, extended matter, there must be some aspect of the thinking substance that is dependent upon a certain disposition found in matter precisely when it forms a human body. The second section of this chapter concerns the disposition of merely physical, extended matter (*res extensa*), whose only essential changes are quantitative, within an organism fit to be united with and informed by the thing that thinks (*res cogitans*), whose only activity is thinking. Finally, the last section of this chapter asks in what way physical, extended matter (*res extensa*) makes it possible for the thinking soul (*res cogitans*) to be conscious of its thoughts, and thus in what way and to what degree the thinking soul really depends on purely physical matter in order to carry out its operation of thinking—even though Descartes said that the two substances are truly distinct and independent of one another.

How are we to translate *res* in the key expressions *res extensa* and *res cogitans*? The usual English translation is "substance," although sometimes we find the more literally accurate translation "thing." Both translations are potentially misleading. The Latin *res* often has the same force as *thing* in English or *chose* in French (and Descartes indeed translated *res cogitans* as *la chose qui pense* or as *une chose qui pense*). In English, "thing" has the peculiarity that, although grammatically it is always used as a predicate and never as an attributive—i.e., we speak of blue things, and not of thinged blue—it still never has the force of a true predicate, of that *of which* we say some particular. Quality may be attributed to a 'thing,' but when we speak of "things," the point always concerns what is *said about* the thing, *and not the thing itself*. Indeed, we use the term 'thing' precisely in order to refer to a quality of 'something or other,' where the quality is the point of the utterance. 'Thing' thus seems to have the force of an indefinite substance, which is no substance at all, and is only correctly used in order to talk about an attribute that, so to speak, "must be thinged" in order to be located.

Thus, *res extensa, extended thing* (and, with the appropriate substitution of terms, *res cogitans*), refers to an extensive*ness* and not to the fact that some body *is* extended. In Rule XIII (Vol. X, p. 443, l. 11ff.), Descartes used the expression "extension occupies space [*extensio occupat locum*]" and said that, "for it is certain that I conceive the same thing if I say: *extension occupies space*, as if I were to say: *the extended occupies space*." *Res extensa*, and by the same token *res cognitans*, are thus clearly "-nesses," that is, "examples of extendedness," "examples of thinkingness"—and nothing else. Descartes' "thing" is not far different from "the definite intersection of a number of quality-classes—intersections of Venn diagrams." The world, for Descartes, is what we said a curve was for him—the togetherness of all its intelligible properties. (It is on similar grounds that Spinoza, in his *Ethics*, can say that only God is a substance.)

Therefore, in this chapter we lay the groundwork for the analogy that: as local concentrations of primary elements comprise the organic foundations for bodies that contain a number of organs, so living human beings comprise the organized foundation for political bodies or associations, and, as medicine is the science whose object is the live, organized human body, so ethics is the science whose object is the compound body politic.

THE ORGANIZATION OF
BODY AND LIFE

This section discusses the causes and genesis of those dispositions found in general body (*corps en general, magnitudo in genere*) that so qualify it as sometimes to make it fit to be informed by or united with a human soul, that is, as sometimes to make it a living human body.

To begin, Descartes' usage in his first letter to Mesland makes it clear that the reason a body has the dispositions that are required for a soul to be united with it is that it has organs. In this letter he spoke both of (Vol. IV, p. 166, l. 21–22) "the dispositions needed in order to conserve that union [*les dispositions requises pour conseruer cette union*]" and of (Vol. IV, p. 168, l. 20–21) "the organs of the human body necessary for life [*les organes du corps humain necessaries a la vie*]." What is more, he specified that these organs are composed of "particules" of matter. Consequently, we can infer that the dispositions of a human body can ultimately be traced to dispositions of particles of matter, composed of particles of general physical body. The particles are of three distinct orders of magnitude: the largest is "earthlike"; the medium sized are "liquid"; and the finest or smallest are "gaseous." Instead of the five Aristotelian elements (air, water, earth, fire, and ether), "quintessence" forming heaven itself, Descartes proposed three states of matter that are distinguished from one another both by the size of their constituent parts and by the degree of motion found in them—by their "kinetic energy levels," as we say today.

The disposition of the particles of matter (more or less what we today consider either molecules or crystals and the like) are for Descartes the "organs" of even those bodies that do not have a soul united to them. Descartes' strained use of the term 'disposition' is strikingly reminiscent of Cicero's usage in his *Oration concerning Brutus* (Chapter 19):

they arrange [*disponunt*] their words as painters arrange their colors, referring each to every other [*verba ita disponunt ut pictores varietatem colorum, paria paribus referrunt*].

In this section we shall see that it is precisely because all the organs in a body "refer each to every other" that the living body has its peculiar disposition to receive a soul, and that the term 'disposition' is second in importance to no other single term in Descartes' often excruciatingly idiomatic vocabulary.

We find that the term 'disposition' has three meanings for Descartes:

1. An interrelation of parts, and thus something very close to the primary meaning of λόγος in Greek and *ratio* in Latin;

2. The readiness or inclination to act that is a consequence of that interrelation of parts, and thus something very close to the primary meaning of ἕξις in Greek and *habitus* in Latin;

3. An individual's mood or stance with respect to the world around him.[4]

The first of these meanings is manifested most clearly in mathematics: for example, figures express relationships of magnitudes and a formula expresses the relation existing between knowns and unknowns. The second meaning is manifested most clearly in mechanics and anatomy (and anatomy is only biological mechanics), where the precise interrelations of parts determine precisely what the body and/or machine can do. The third meaning is manifested most clearly in ethics, in which a personal discipline prepares us to relate certain perceptions with feelings other than those we experienced first as children, so that, for example, instead of fleeing danger, we can consider the possibility that we might do better to stand and fight. Thus, a thorough analysis of the term 'disposition' can show the relation between medicine, mechanics, and ethics.

The disposition of the particles of matter gives rise, for Descartes, to the "organs" of even those bodies that do not have a soul united to them. Hence, a dead human body is, on the whole, an organism composed of smaller "organisms" and, ultimately, the disposition of the organs of that corpse is caused by or traceable to the dispositions of the organisms in that particular piece or "neighborhood" of general body that comprises the gross bulk of the corpse. It follows from this that medicine is ultimately based on mechanics, which studies what laws the particles of matter obey to form distinct bodies with distinct properties.

Although the human body has the dispositions required for it to be informed by and united with the soul, Descartes did not consider that the human body is at all primarily intelligible in terms of the soul.[5] Rather, the principles guiding the formation and maintenance of the human body are physical principles, and these principles are identified explicitly by Descartes as being the ones he employs in the *Principles* to explain the generation of the visible world out of the three elements described both in Part Three of that same work (Art. LIIff.) and in *The*

World (Vol. XI, Ch. V). Thus many inanimate bodies are also to some degree "organized" bodies, whose activities, whatever they are, depend on their primary "organs," i.e., the elementary particles with their definite interrelations. In the *Principles,* even those three elements are considered to be generated out of "body in general," and each kind of element differs from the other two kinds primarily in the degree of "force of agitation" (Vol. VIII, p. 105, l. 13–14) present in it. The elements are therefore the truly primary constituents of all individual bodies. The elements are also the first level of organization found in general matter, and, by being elements of something else (bodies), are analogous to the "lines" of geometry, since those "lines" are also both indeterminate magnitudes (lengths) and purely of use for solutions to problems.

When we are considering the qualities of elements only as bodies, then we are engaged in the mathematical study of mechanics, that is, in the study of the way hard bodies of different shapes and degrees of motion interact; however, to have a medical science based on mechanics, we must consider the way bodies composed of large numbers of elementary particles affect our mechanism of perceptions, so that, for example, one green, light body smells sweet but tastes sour, etc. Such qualities of large, perceptible bodies are the result of the imperceptible qualities of their elementary constituents. (This is the theoretical justification for a "reductionist" biology of perception: in perceiving, we are reacting to the sum total of the compound activities and qualities of elementary particles, which we do not directly perceive at all.) It is on these grounds that Descartes can justify his reference to the structures of inanimate bodies as their "organs." That is, on the whole, the perceptible qualities of bodies are a result of the way their imperceptible elements interact with one another.

In the cases of magnitude, figure, and motion, the perceptible attributes of compound bodies are also the attributes of their imperceptible constituent elements. All other attributes of external bodies are, in fact, only the way we are aware of what Descartes called the internal "dispositions" of external bodies; Descartes designated them as the causes of such sensations as light, taste, and smell. Concerning these sensations, Descartes said:

> In all events, it should be concluded that those things noticed by us—which, in external objects we call by the names of light, color, odor, taste, sound, heat and other tactile qualities—are absolutely nothing else than various dispositions of those objects which cause our nerves to move in different ways. And excepting magnitude, figure and motion—which I have described to be found in every single body—everything else placed outside us is sensed as light, color, odor,

sound and tactile qualities; and it has thus been demonstrated that these are nothing else, or, at least are not comprehended by us to be anything other in objects, than certain dispositions consisting in magnitude, figure, and motion. [Vol. VIII, p. 322, l. 26, to p. 323, l. 13]

What the tradition came to know as "secondary qualities" are for Descartes the soul's response to dispositions of "primary qualities" that are only found in the elements.[6] All attributes perceived through our senses, such as flavors and odors, are complex psycho-physiological responses to compound motions initiated by compound bodies. These compound motions, the immediate causes of motions in the nerves, Descartes called "dispositions of external bodies." They are complex motions compounded of the individual motions of individual elementary particles having determinate sizes and shapes. It is our own organs, particularly of sense, that permit us to sense light, color, and the like. Consequently, the compound dispositions of bodies outside us whose motions are compounded out of the motions of elements give complementarity here: the disposition of our organs permits us to "sense" the dispositions of the primary elements of bodies.

How are these elementary particles, with their elementary attributes, connected to their compound bodies with their "compound" attributes, which we sense as heat and color, for example?

A physical body derives its qualities and powers (e.g., heat or magnetism), as a consequence of the motions, sizes, and shapes of its smaller constituent parts and, ultimately, of its elements. These smaller constituent parts are thus the "organs" through whose activities compounded bodies present their compound qualities and powers.[7]

In this scheme of things, individual perceptible bodies are usually formed by the three elements mixed together in differing proportions and local concentrations. To take an example from Part Four of the *Principles,* iron has magnetic properties because the grossest, third, element, of which it is primarily composed, so directs and forms particles of the finer second element (which permeate it through channels left by the absence of the third element) that the particles of the second element are threaded—forming what Descartes calls *particulae striatae* or *parties canelees.* The direction of these threads is such that the threading channels in a piece of iron will thread the particles that pass through it so that they can enter another piece of iron in only one way—hence the polarity of magnetized iron! These channels may be said to be the true organs of magnetic iron, that is, the means by which iron has magnetic powers. The reason that the parts of the third element do not evaporate from the surface of the mass of iron is that they are surrounded either by other bodies composed of heavy elements (when in the ground) or by an infinity of smaller particles of the first and second elements, which constantly bombard the grosser particles of the third element and keep them in their relative positions. In general, a distinct compound body is an aggregate of the three elements localized in a ratio differing from the constituent ratio of the elements in its contiguous neighbors.

In this account, bodies are aggregates of the three elements, which differ primarily in their respective shapes, magnitudes, and degree of agitation. The interaction of these elementary particles ultimately gives rise to compound motions on the surface of the compound bodies, and these compound motions are the immediate external source for the motions transmitted to our senses and perceived as light, heat, color, etc. Since their compound motions are dependent upon all the parts of the body, and since each of those parts has a determinate magnitude that is constantly modified by the attributes of its contiguous neighbors, it follows that for Descartes all dispositions of a body (such as light and heat) ultimately consist in magnitude, figure, and motion. It is thus that Descartes considers the threading channels inside a piece of iron to be responsible for the magnetic properties of iron; those channels are the true organs of magnetic iron, and hence the notion of organ becomes relative for Descartes in precisely the way that the notion of dimension has become relative for him: an organ is always defined with respect to a given power that arises from it.

The Generation of the Human Body

The remainder of this section is concerned with Descartes' use of this general scheme to demonstrate how the compound human body is generated so that its inner organs and outer sensory apparatus together constitute its peculiar disposition to be united with or informed by the human soul. We will then be one step closer to seeing how the organized human body itself acts as the organ of the larger complex "civil body."

Article 188 of Part Four ends Descartes' *Principles of Philosophy*. In that final article he stated that he would leave the work unfinished and that its true completion would require two more parts, "the fifth, in particular, concerning living things, or animals and plants, and the sixth concerning men." In a letter dated January 25, 1648, two years before his death in February of 1650, he told Princess Elizabeth (Vol. V, p. 112, l. 12–15) "I have now another piece on the way . . . it is the description of the functions of men and beasts." He said that he had finished it some years before, but that its reception was bad and so he had to express it more clearly. A few months later, in what the editor of Descartes' works,

C. Adam, calls (Vol. V, p. 145) the account of "a conversation between Descartes and Burman, in Egmond, April 16, 1648," Burman relates of Descartes that:

> when he wished to explain animal functions alone, he saw that he could scarcely do this without explaining what was necessary concerning the conformation of the animal as a result of its conception in the egg; he remarked that this followed from his principles in such a way that he could state the reason why the eye, nose, brain, etc., existed, and he plainly grasped that the nature of those things was so constituted from his principles that they could not be otherwise. [Vol. V, pp. 170–171]

The only major works that are dated after the 1644 *Principles* are the *Passions of the Soul* (1645–1646) and the unfinished *Description of the Human Body*, believed by Adam to have been begun prior to 1648, and found among Descartes' papers after his death in 1650. This last work is developmental, and deduces the effects from principles. It begins the account of the human body *ab ovo* (from the egg), and refers to the doctrine of the three elements, specifically referring the reader to the relevant passages of the *Principles*. I therefore conclude that the missing Parts V and VI of the *Principles* were meant to be supplied by the unfinished work *The Description of the Human Body/Concerning the Formation of the Animal.*

The *Description* has five parts in its present form. Part One is the Preface; Part Two is entitled "Concerning the Motion of the Heart and Blood"; Part Three, "On Nutrition"; Part Four, "Concerning Parts formed in the Seed"; and Part Five, "Concerning the Formation of the Solid Parts." In what follows, I refer mainly to the texts of Parts Four and Five (pp. 252–286 of Vol. XI). First, however, we need to consider Cartesian methodology.

Chapter 1 of this work shows that Descartes' faithful adherence to the deductive procedure is deeply involved both with his mathematical insights into the symbolic character of our perceptions as well as with his final goal of establishing a general ethics, on the basis of which men could affirm, deny, or merely view any and all perceptions. It was there pointed out that if the phenomena were approached as to-be-deduced from general principles, they were thereby reduced to a sort of "indeterminate" realm with respect to assent or denial of their real, "objective" existence as well as with respect to their character as helpful or harmful to us.

Furthermore, as we saw (in Chapter 1, in the section concerning analysis), understanding even truth or falsity was for Descartes a matter of finding a construction. Thus, in his view, deduction and construction are essentially interrelated. In particular, the deduction of a particular phenomenon from a general law of nature entails the discovery of exactly how the particular phenomenon in question was caused, how it came to be. Thus, we are not to be surprised to find both that his physics is deductive and that his explanations are etiological—concerned with discovering sufficient causes. The general causes or laws that regulate particular effects are, for Descartes, the basis of the intelligibility of the particulars subsumed under those general laws. Deduction, for Descartes, is primarily a reduction of particulars to "compounds" of general causes. He even went so far as to say, in Rule XII (Vol. X, p. 427, l. 3–6), that all we ever know is these principles and their mixtures or their compounds.[8] Thus, Descartes did not consider that particulars are interrelated by some sort of logical chain of cause and effect. Rather, as Leibniz saw so clearly in Descartes, particular effects exemplify, or "mirror," the general causes. Since, further, Descartes denied the notion of potentiality, causation does not, as with Aristotle, involve a coming-to-be whose beginning can be traced to a distinct cause. Rather, an effect of a given cause is a true and real reproduction, or "mirroring," of that cause, as, for example, the motion in one particle of matter is transferred to or reproduced in another particle when the first "causes" motion in the second. Causal principles are always and at every moment entirely active for Descartes. A description of any change thus involves, almost exclusively, the way in which causes are related in a particular case at any particular moment.

In *The World,* Descartes insisted that God primarily preserves His creation as it was from the beginning (*ab initio*). He archly remarked that any other "activity" on God's part would contradict His immutability. *Cartesian physics is absolutely conservative:* no matter how much things seem to change, they really and truly stay the same.

A general statement of Descartes' commitment to the deductive mode of procedure in the sciences is found in the *Principles,* Part Three, Article 45:

> There is no doubt that the world was at the beginning created with
> all its perfection, so that in it there existed the Sun, Earth, Moon and
> Stars and, further, that in the Earth were not only seeds of plants,
> but the plants themselves, nor that Adam and Eve were not born
> infants, but were created adult humans. This the Christian faith
> teaches us, and in this natural reason also plainly persuades us . . . .
> But nonetheless, in order to understand the nature of plants or men,
> it is far better to consider in what way they could have arisen from
> seed than in what way they might have been created at the first
> origin of the world. . . . [Vol. VIII, p. 99, l. 27, to p. 100, l. 11]

Concerning that account of Genesis, Burman relates from a conversation he had with Descartes that Descartes was of this rather dubious mind (Vol. V, pp. 168–169): "he describes the creation of the world, in so far as found in Genesis, sufficiently out of his philosophy . . . perhaps that narration of creation which is contained there is metaphorical and as a consequence should be relinquished to theology . . ."

Finally, in the fourth part of the *Description* Descartes stated his procedure in that text. He said, "to the end that the knowledge one has of animals already formed does not hinder one's conception of the shape they have when they begin to form, it is necessary to consider the seed as a mass, from which the heart is first formed . . . " (Vol. XI, p. 264, l. 11–16).

In his account of embryogenesis, Descartes did not relate the organs of sensible, inanimate bodies to those of animate bodies by what he considered only a convenient metaphor. According to his description of the formation of the fetus, every stage of growth *results from* the activity of the primary bodies regulated by the principles of geometry and mechanics, following which motion and magnitude can be diversified by each other. The human body is a machine in the way that any natural body is a machine. In Descartes' own words (Part Four, Art. 103 of the French version; Vol. IXB, pp. 256–257), "it is certain that all the rules of mechanics pertain to physics . . . in such a way that all the things which are artificial are also natural." He could have added that all those things that are natural are also artificial.

The notion of an artificial natural body seems contradictory, but Thomas Hobbes, the English political theorist (who is also the author of *The Third Set of Objections* to Descartes' *Meditations*), began his major work, the *Leviathan,* with the words: "Nature (the Art whereby God hath made and governes the World) is by the *Art* of man, as in many other things, so in this also imitated, that it can make an Artificial Animal."

Descartes' account of the generation of the fetus is an account of the construction of a machine, the parts of which are the three elements that are instrumental in the generation of the larger parts of the body, the organs that are large enough to perceive. These organs of the human body are on the order of magnitude required for the naked eye to perceive them as fully formed organs, and their function is almost solely to make aliment available to the body. Aliment comes to the body in the form of a chewed up, and thus relatively unorganized, compound of the three elements. The local concentrations of elementary particles—having determinate shapes and magnitudes—are for Descartes the organic building material for true machines, the organs of the body, which are of sufficient complexity to permit them to construct larger machines or organs, which together form an "organism."

It is not at all stretching a point to say that, for Descartes, the egg and sperm, at the moment they join with one another, form an organism (we call it a zygote) whose activity is to "mold" the nutrition supplied in the womb into a fully formed fetus.[9] Descartes strictly distinguished between embryonic development, which entails that "molding" and nothing more, and fetal development, which entails only growth in volume of the fully articulated and formed embryo. The fetal stage begins when the embryo is fully formed, and the newly fertilized seed is a microorganism or very small machine that constructs the embryo until it is finally a fetus.

What food is to the fully formed adult body, complete with its fully formed organs, so is what Descartes considers the "volatile portion" of a fertilized seed to the mass encased within the womb-wall or eggshell.[10] The mass encloses a seminal mixture that Descartes likened to the volatile mixture of fermenting green wine (*vid. The Description*, Part IV; Vol. XI, p. 253ff.). The formation of the fetus consists in the settling of the three elements, which occur in the seminal mixture in exact proportions. The solid parts of the fetus are formed by the settling of the third, earthlike element; the spongy organs, such as the lungs, are formed by the settling of the second (*aérienne*) element; the nervous system, including the brain, whose cavities are filled with a thin, serous fluid like that found in the spinal column, is formed by the passages forced by the first, most subtle, element present in the seminal fluid. That element is too tenuous to settle in any one part of the body, and is found in all parts, but mostly in the region of the brain.

The machine that is the human body is thus a construct of a true machine of a lower degree of organization, the fertilized seed. The spiritous part of the seminal mixture, largely composed of the first, least dense element, forces its way throughout the body of the mixture contained within the seed-case—which is contained within the womb, and which acts just like DNA—and prepares a path for the other denser parts of the fluid. They, in turn, settle off their denser parts as they travel down the paths and tubes forced by the first element, all the while regulated by the laws of matter, which govern "the way these three things can be diversified by each other." Descartes described, for example, the production of the nervous system from the seminal mixture:

> it is necessary to consider the seed as a mass from which, first of all, the heart is formed . . . After this, the spirits having mounted a little higher than the blood in the direction of the head where, being collected in some quantity, they take their course . . . as close to the surface of the seed as their force can carry them . . . And when they have followed this course, their small particles are so disposed as to allow them to pass by all the other paths which are easiest for them to proceed by . . . Now I say that the spirits which prepare the path for the nerves in the seed take their course in it towards the outside

because they are pressed by the surface of the womb—not having any passages free enough to receive them; but they find such passages towards the front of the head. This is why . . . certain spirits are separated from the others without their thus being different and tracing in the forepart of the head the path of the nerves . . ." [Vol. XI, p. 264, l. 14, to p. 265, l. 22]

So mechanical and automatic is the formation of the body from the seed that Descartes claimed that knowledge of the structure of the seed would allow one to deduce the final shape of the human, and vice versa:

if one knew well all the parts of the seed of some species of animal in particular, man, for example, one could deduce from that alone, from reasons entirely mathematical and certain, the whole shape and make-up of each member; and, reciprocally, in knowing a few peculiarities of this make-up, one could deduce the composition of the seed. [Vol. XI, p. 277, l. 1–9]

Descartes would have rejoiced over the discovery of, and claims made for, DNA.

For Descartes, the fully formed body is comprised of three systems: the nervous system, the circulatory system, and the alimentary system. (Descartes seemed to consider the reproductive system part of the nervous system.) In the fully formed body, the nervous system is the record, i.e., what we might call the "biological locus," of the action of the spiritous part of the seminal mixture; the circulatory system is the biological locus of the part of the seminal mixture that is composed mainly of the second element; and the solid parts of the body are the biological locus and record of that part of the mixture composed mainly of the grossest, third element. Once the parts of the fetus are fully formed, they constitute a mechanical system, a machine, whose main activity in the womb is to break down aliment into concentrations of the elements that can then be assimilated by those parts of the body initially formed by concentrations of the elements present in the seminal mixture. Thus, in aliment, the least dense part, similar to the constituent matter of the nervous system, nourishes the nervous system, in that it is assimilated to its material and replaces any that might be lost. Similarly, in the other two systems, each part of the fully formed body assimilates such parts of aliment as are identical to those present in the seminal fluid that were responsible for its initial formation. Thus, any differences between formation, growth, and bare sustenance are matters solely of the accessibility of sources of supply of the material out of which the parts of the body are made. *In complete agreement with his physics, Descartes' physiology is absolutely conservative.*

The human body, when it is fully formed, can thus be said to consist of the interaction of the three parts of general body, which are diversified only in terms of magnitude, figure, and motion. Just as the interaction of the elements constituted out of general body gives to the sensory apparatus of a man those motions perceived by the soul as light, heat, etc., so it is that the interconnection of the organs gives to certain of the fluids of the body those physical states that we are conscious of as hunger, sadness, sexual desire, and the like. Precisely because of these interior sensations, a man knows that a certain body, among all others, belongs to him, i.e., is united with his soul. In Descartes' own words:

> We must also conclude that a certain body is more closely united to our soul than all the others in the world, because we perceive clearly that sadness and several other emotions come to us without our having foreseen them, and that our soul, by a knowledge which is natural to it, judges that these emotions do not come from it only . . . because the soul thinks, but because it is united to an extended thing that it moved by the disposition of its organs, which is properly called the human body. [*Principles*, French version, Vol. IXB, p. 64]

Just as the interconnection of the organs of a given living body are the reason why the body is fit to receive a soul, so the interrelation of men, as defined by their political institutions, emerges as the reason why that union of body and soul is conserved: the living human is a compound organism that continues to live because the mind to which it is connected as a whole is concerned with health. "I think, therefore I am."

As is examined in Part II of this work, Descartes' theory of alimentation falls within the wider framework of his cosmology, and, in particular, of his theory of *tourbillons*, or whirlpools, of matter. This cosmological theory is, for Descartes, imaged faithfully in his particular accounts of ingestion, assimilation, and evacuation, i.e., the process tends to be a circular. For now, however, it is enough that we see that his theory of assimilation gave Descartes a model of how inert matter and, generally, *external* things, are pulled into the soul's "sphere of influence," and are informed by it for the sake of conserving the union of body and soul.

In Part Four of the *Principles* (Art. 189; Vol. VIII, p. 315, l. 23–24), Descartes stated that the human soul "informs the whole body [*totum corpus informet*]," which phrase he gave in the subsequent French translation as *unie a tout le cors* ("unites with the whole body"). This translation is his interpretation of his own Latin usage, and it indicates that the soul and the body are united because the soul "informs the whole body." Bread and wine, the staples of French life both secular and spiritual, are thus united to a living body when they are ingested and they become "informed" by the soul that "informs" the body of which they become a part. By extension, it is easy to see that any body potentially ingested into the human body is thereby potentially informed by or united with a human soul. By yet a further extension, anything whatsoever that is used as an instrument or organ of the conservation of this union can itself to that degree be said to be informed by the soul of the body conserved by or through its instrumentality.[11] Thus, the stick that a blind man uses as a substitute for his missing organs of sight is informed by his soul in the same way that his food, had he healthy eyes, would be assimilated into the matter of his healthy eyes.[12] Indeed, the very matter of the stick is assimilated "by information," so to speak, into the total complex of organs useful for conserving the union of soul and body of the blind man.

By yet a further extension along the lines of the last one, if we consider human political association to be primarily an instrument of the conservation of its constituent members, then the institutions of that association can be justly viewed as the organs of the body politic, which conserves the soul-body unions of its constituent members.[13]

THE SOUL'S USE OF THE HUMAN BODY IN PERCEPTION

This section considers the mind-body problem in scientific terms as a psycho-physiologic problem. In this section, we describe the dividing line between the psychological concerns that Descartes treated in his "metaphysical" *Meditations* (concerns arising primarily in the context of reflections on the soul as distinct from all body) and the physiological concerns treated in works like the *Passions of the Soul* (concerns arising from reflections on the union of the soul with a particular body). The problem confronted in this section is one of Descartes' central problems: the character of the common borderline that divides soul from body. Because it is a shared borderline, it provides, so to speak, the "shapes" of each of the two.

In the next section we will particularize the mutually defining borderline by investigating the soul's use of the body to represent to itself its powers, an investigation that leads into Descartes' doctrine of the will, which is an essential part of Descartes' doctrine concerning the soul's use of body. This brings into high relief his treatment of the "free will versus determinism" dichotomy, which so preoccupied post-Cartesian, Enlightenment, Europe until the times after Hegel and Freud, and which were abroad in his own times under such guises as the Scholastic problem of free will in the light of God's foreknowledge of His creation, and Calvin's doctrine of election. To say the least, this problem was a delicate one for Descartes, one which preoccupied his philosophic successors.

While our contemporary schools of thought simply ignore this question, Descartes *did not* ignore it, even though his own mechanistic physics posed the problem to him in a particularly difficult form. We look at the place of the will in Descartes' teaching and, in particular, its relation to imagination, in the fourth section of this chapter.

It must be admitted, however, that such an inquiry seems well outside the ken of ethics or medicine. How is it that this manifestly "metaphysical" problem is of concern to here?

Spinoza's *Ethics* indicates something of the kind of work required to show the ethical and social relevance of the precise distinction between body and soul.[14] However, to see clearly the very practical importance of the question of free will (involving as it does the individual's accountability), we need only consider the situation of the legal acceptability of the plea "innocent by reason of insanity," which is often entered in cases of particularly repulsive crimes of violence.[15] Descartes lived in an age scarred with the horror of men, women, and children being brutally killed because they were legally considered to possess superhuman powers; we live in an age in which men and women are held *not* accountable for their deeds precisely because of the brutal nature of their crimes, which we say no one in possession of his powers would commit. We have returned to a non-Cartesian psychology of possession, and, as a trade-off for our increased lenience, we have, *in theory*, deprived citizens of their powers of responsible choice. Descartes would not approve.

Descartes was certainly an archenemy of unchecked ecclesiastical power, but he faced this astonishingly tangled puzzle of freedom in a mechanistic world with admirable clarity and wit. We would do well to seek our own answers to this question by re-examining his attempts, which were made in spite of the difficulties he faced from his own mechanistic physics.

Finally (and perhaps much more momentously for the future of the Enlightenment than all his other contributions), in this inquiry into the defining border shared by soul and body, Descartes revealed his grounds for unbounded confidence in the ability of every human being to correct himself through "spiritual mechanics," that is, by employing certain characteristics of the brain and nerves to overcome impulses that tend to enslave us, and that, if *not* overcome, tend to justify the necessity for our being ruled by moderating rulers. Without this quasi-medical inquiry, later theorists like Rousseau would not have had what they considered objective, nontheological scientific foundations for their doctrines of the innate perfectibility of men, and hence for their doctrines concerning the possibility for self-rule. It is, to a large extent, Cartesian medicine that fed their optimism. So that, for example, in *Passions of the Soul*, where Descartes is concerned with ethics, the work is a *medical* text that is concerned with ethics and it presupposes the mechanics of the *Principles.*

Descartes' ethics is specifically designed to replace the political science of Aristotle's *Politics* (along with its foundations in Aristotle's biologically based anthropology, as is found in *On the Soul*). This replacement proposed by Descartes presupposes the following particular substitutions: his own *Passions of the Soul* for Aristotle's *On the Soul,* his *Principles of Philosophy* for Aristotle's *Physics,* his *Discourse on Method* (together with its essays) for Aristotle's *Organon* (or *General Logic*), and, finally, his *Meditations* for Aristotle's *Metaphysics.* Indeed, writing to the French ambassador to Sweden, Chanute (Vol. IV, pp, 440–442), Descartes apologized for sending his *Principles* to a worldly man of affairs, who must be primarily interested in the manners and ways of mankind (in *les moeurs* or *la morale*), but as he pointed out to Chanute:

> the general notion of heaven and Earth which I have tried to give in
> my *Principles* is very far removed from a detailed account of the
> Nature of Man—concerning which I have not as yet treated at all.
> Still, because I do not want you to think that I wish to sidetrack you
> from your studies [*de vostre dessein*], I will say, confidentially, that
> whatever notion of physics I have been able to acquire through my
> own efforts has been very useful to me in establishing certain
> foundations for Ethics . . . [Vol. IV, p. 441, l. 19–27]

Accordingly, we should be at least open to the possibility that Descartes' ethics is intended to be a replacement for political science.

This is not to suggest that works like the *Meditations* are not important or that the *Discourse* is not an extremely difficult work that indeed can and should bear much explanation. Rather, the point here is that the key to certain of the problems any serious reader is likely to raise concerning Descartes' thought is likely to be found in his works treating on physics, medicine, and ethics, and not merely "metaphysics." For example, the only straightforward accounts of *how* the body and the soul are united with one another are found in the earliest and the latest of his works, in the mathematical *Rules* of 1628 and in the ethical *Passions* of 1646.

The *Rules,* a work in abstract algebra, seems to have been suppressed by Descartes because crucial parts of its argument depended upon a Galenic view of the motion of the blood, which taught that it ebbs and flows like the tides. Harvey, in the 1628 *De Motu Cordis,* showed that the blood circulates, in that it is pumped from the right ventricle of the heart to the lungs, thence to the left atrium, then to the left ventrical, and then, via the aorta, throughout the whole body and back to the right atrium. Descartes came to accept all of Harvey's description except for the detail concerning the motive power that causes the circulation. He insisted that the heart is like an alchemist's flask—a "retort"—and that the blood in it is heated to such a degree that its expansion forces it out into the body. In the body, because of its great heat, the blood readily gives off its more spiritous parts as it meets with the very narrow passages, which allow only very refined parts to pass through, leaving the coarser parts to continue on through the larger arteries. A Cartesian heart is a sort of steam engine!

The role played by the least dense, most highly refined parts of the circulating blood in Descartes' works is very great indeed; so great, it seems, that Harvey's 1628 publication made Descartes leave off writing the mathematical *Rules* in order to begin anatomizing the heads of various animals to find out "what composes common sense, memory, etc." It was not until the *Passions,* written some eighteen years later, that Descartes completed the investigation he had begun under the Galenic point of view, but abandoned when Harvey's discoveries were first published. The question of the blood's circulation involves crucial issues, including: alimentation; the production of spirits—which include the production both of our "chemical" and of endocrine secretions at different organic sites throughout the body (and hence of slightly differing sorts of volatile chemicals or "spirits," which alone give the soul a clue about the true foundation [*fundamentum*] and source of certain of its perceptions); the generation of the human body as an organism fit to be united with a soul; and, finally, the role of the spirits in producing motions within the brain so that the soul can sense and perceive at all. Descartes explains *all* these questions using the circulation of the blood.

We have already touched upon the questions of alimentation and the production of the spirits and return to them in detail in Part II of this work. Also, Part II discusses in detail the question of the formation of the body from the circulating blood. At this time we are prepared to examine in detail only the question of the role of what Descartes saw as the least dense, spiritous part of the blood (what we call the cerebrospinal fluid), in producing motions within the brain so that the soul can sense and perceive.

In the *Passions of the Soul,* Descartes wrote with some precision how it is that the complex of soul and body interact; that is, he described how the body acts upon the soul joined to it and how the soul affects its body. He said that certain secretions of the organs, together with volatile distillates of the blood, which he collectively called "spirits," differ from one another because of the different dispositions that result from the different sizes and degrees of agitation found in the elementary particles comprising those secretions and spirits. Depending on their source in the body (that is, whether they have their origin in the blood, liver, heart, or spleen), the elementary particles comprising these secretions have different sizes, shapes, and degrees of motion.[16] Descartes' mechanistic psychobiology involves a genuine, even if relatively unsophisticated, biochemistry, and it is appropriately first presented comprehensively in *Passions of the Soul,* his work that describes the entire relation between the characteristics of these spirits and secretions and the reaction of the soul to them. The soul's moods, emotions, and passions are its responses to the presence of what we know as "biochemicals."

In the first article of *Passions of the Soul* (Vol. XI, p. 328), Descartes wrote that the terms 'action' and 'passion' are to be understood to refer to the same thing according to two different aspects: when we primarily consider one subject as the cause of some activity in another subject, what the first subject does to bring about an effect in the second is an *action* in it and a *passion* in the other. For Descartes, "action" and "passion" are identical to "cause" and "effect" when they refer to conscious human beings.

In the second article, he described the immediate consequence, which is that, since nothing is united more closely to or acts more immediately against the soul than the body to which it is joined, what is an action in the body is a passion in the soul. As a consequence, whatever we can discern in a living human body that need not be attributed to the action of the soul but that can be explained by the action of inanimate body (Vol. XI, p. 329) must be the action of the body alone, and, to the contrary, whatever there is in the soul that "we do not understand how in any manner can be concerned with a body" belongs to the actions of the soul.

Having said this much, Descartes then proceeded, in a manner quite unlike that used in the *Meditations,* to set forth an anatomical disquisition on the extent that the live human body can be considered to be a machine—that is, how far it can be understood strictly in accordance with the teachings of his mechanics.[17] When he had exhausted the possible effects of the body as machine, he then addressed himself to the soul insofar as it is merely conscious of what happens in the body. Only at this point did he feel that he could state the unique contribution of the soul to the complex of mind and body. All the particular operations or actions of the soul are, for Descartes, in each instance, indissolubly bound up with the soul's perceptions of some action in the body. Descartes did not discuss the nature of the soul when it is really apart from the human body, even though he often discussed powers of the soul where it is united to a body, but that cannot be reduced to the action of that body. In other words, although Descartes' *Meditations,* for instance, discusses the nature of the soul as a substance that we can clearly distinguish from extended substance or body, he did not subsequently discuss the operations of the human soul when it has left the body. A sober understanding of Descartes requires us to realize clearly that the soul that distinguishes between itself and body is united to a body at the very moment that it is making the distinction. It seems likely that the reason many students of Descartes have so neglected his medical works is that they have not recognized just this point. Indeed, someone may perhaps infer from the Cartesian texts that the soul *thinks* after it is separated from the body; but works such as the *Passions* strongly imply that a body is required if the soul is to have any perception of the fact that it thinks. Perception (or awareness) requires a body, *even perception of what Descartes said is substantially distinct from body*.[18] For Descartes, even the soul's perception of itself requires a body to which it is united at the moment it perceives itself. And it is medical science that shows not only how the soul has perceptions directly concerned with body, but how the soul has perceptions of itself, and thus of something that is substantially distinct from body. Perhaps the soul, for Descartes, can *think* without body; however, it is not *aware of its thoughts* without body.

Under the right circumstances, the soul can perceive anything that takes place in the body; however, the soul's very perception of any modification in the body in turn causes a further ("feedback") modification in the body, which the soul perceives as its own activity. For example, when the soul, in whatever way, causes the hand of "its" body to write down algebraic equations, this represents to the soul not only its own thinking operations concerning body, but also the result of the soul's action on the body, i.e., the writing hand writing the symbols chosen by the soul *as* symbols.

Concerning the soul's perception of the body's activities, two cases must be distinguished. On the one hand, because of the natural relation between motions in the body and the soul's perception of those motions (e.g., light, heat, hunger, anger, etc.), the soul of even the most untutored savage occupied in making arrowheads ordinarily perceives all that can be perceived by the soul of the most educated man. On the other hand, by means of medical science, men are empowered to find certain motions and activities in the body that are never perceived as those motions, but only as the results of more complex motions. For example, what men ordinarily perceive as a passion has its roots, according to Descartes' medicine, in the organic manufacture of certain secretions within the body; these secretions then allow for extraordinary activity in the nervous system. Thus, in an oblique way, medical science, according to Descartes, can bring to the attention of men certain otherwise unperceived motions as the precise bodily cause of perceptions.

Concerning the way the activity of the soul disposes the body so that it, the soul, can become aware of its own activities, there are two cases analogous to those just mentioned. Ordinarily, men know what is going on in the soul because the soul's activities somehow cause the body to give the soul some perception of its, *the soul's,* own activity. However, those representations of its own activity that the soul receives from the body are often confused with activities having their origin strictly within the body itself. It is only by means of a species of mathematics that deals strictly with those operations that the soul needs in order to come to know something, namely, the algebraic operations, that the true activities of the soul as something that thinks can be isolated and identified.

It is in this respect that Descartes' analytical geometry is the exact mathematical analogue of his medical science. For, having first identified the algebra of his time as precisely the discipline that was essentially involved with the symbolic representation of the operations of the mind, Descartes then identified all the operations of geometry (which is concerned with figures, and hence with something the soul initially perceives only because it is naturally united with the body) with the operation of algebra. When the powers of the mind are considered algebraically, we absolutely minimize any bodily contribution to our consciousness, but even that consideration of mind is not complete without a complementary consideration of the mind as united with body. Descartes' "medical" teaching, and thus his ethics, must be considered against the theoretical perspective of his mathematical analysis as presented in the *Rules* and the *Geometry.*

There is a problem here: What could it mean to say that the soul uses the body in order to represent to itself its own distinct operations and activities? In the course of answering this question, we shall see the way the soul uses the body in order to represent to itself the very mental operations through which the soul can know anything at all about its "own" body or any other body, living or nonliving. The answer to this question is drawn from the first two parts of Descartes' *Passions of the Soul* (Vol. XI, pp. 327–442), and leads us to the topic of the next section, "The soul's use of the body's dispositions: the will."

THE SOUL'S USE OF THE BODY'S DISPOSITIONS: THE WILL

Descartes' last work, the *Treatise on the Passions of the Soul,* can be read as a completion of what was begun in his earliest work, the (1628) *Rules for the Direction of Ingenuity (Regulae ad Directionem Ingenii).* Since for Descartes the mind is the complete soul, both works refer to one thing— the mind that comprises the totality of the human soul. Both works address ways in which the soul uses, and relates to, the body and the dispositions of its organs.

On its part, the goal of the *Rules* was explicitly to show the human body's adaptations that enable it to represent to its soul or mind that mind's own (mathematical) operations, and how we should use our ingenuity, or inborn force of the mind, to make use of those bodily adaptations. In the *Passions*, on their part, Descartes was not so much interested in the way the soul or mind employs its inborn force in order to know, as he was in the character of the *obstacles* it must overcome in order to be fit or disposed to know. Consequently, the *Passions* has very little to say about the products of that force—mathematics, physics, ethics, etc.—once the soul or mind has overcome obstacles to its knowing; rather, the *Passions* is addressed to the character of the obstacles that threaten the mind's inborn force, and it sets out to provide the mind with a scientific, methodical way to overcome those obstacles, since it is primarily our passions that confuse the mind or soul and lead it astray, according to Descartes. In order to lay bare the nature and cause of those passions, as well as to teach us how to put them to good use, Descartes instructed us how the soul acts upon the body and how it can turn the very relation between body and soul, which is the reason the passions are so dangerously powerful, into the best possible way for the soul to exercise its rule over the body.

The same relation we find between the *Rules* and the *Passions* is also found between other works of Descartes. For instance, the *Geometry*, which is the last part and "trial" of the *Discourse,* is addressed to the strictly mathematical productions of the soul, which, although unhampered by the body, to be sure, are still essentially aided by the body. The *Meditations,* to an important extent written as an explanation of some difficult points in the *Discourse,* considers the soul as "withdrawn from" the senses, but certainly not as absent from the body.[19] That is, the *Meditations* discusses certain aspects of the nature of the operations of the soul after it has successfully overcome its natural impulse to consider all of its perceptions as faithful representations of external bodies. "Withdrawal from the senses" therefore means "conquest over their dangerous aspects." If the *Meditations* explains the metaphysical foundations of the *Discourse,* then the *Discourse* itself presupposes conquest of the natural impulse to affirm our trust in our senses. However, it is in the *Passions* that we first find the anatomical details of that conquest, the details of how it can be accomplished. Therefore, we must consider that work in some detail.

The *Passions* is Descartes' last work; his first work, the *Rules*, asks questions about the source of the soul's power to freely create both "symbolic" means to knowledge and means to overcome what in his later works is described as the "blind and rash" natural impulse (our "biological urge") that inclines the individual to affirm the objective and external existence of what we perceive. The *Passions* goes much further than the *Rules:* it addresses the question why it is or is not good for us to comply with this or that natural impluse, i.e., passion. Therefore, its questions and answers are foundations for all of Descartes' earlier works. The *Passions,* of all Descartes' works, discusses issues that we, today, would consider to be ethical.

For Descartes, ethics concerns the human soul only as it is united with the human body, and thus ethics is not at all a kind of "metaphysical" speculation on the "abstract" nature of good and evil. The *Passions* is a work in which medicine, mechanics, and ethics are finally united in the search for corporeal principles governing a human body's actions with respect to the soul's discernment of good and evil, and which includes Descartes' conclusions about how the soul can employ its power, i.e., its will, to make ethical use of the power that the body has over the soul. The *Passions,* then, primarily deals with two concerns: how it is that we can sometimes separate perception from emotions, and how, in other cases, the mechanics of the brain are instituted by nature to make the soul perceive those activities in one and only one way. Furthermore, it deals with the power the soul has to dispose the organs of the body so that the actions of the complex of body and soul shall not be altogether controlled by the laws of its mechanics (in the way that the blind actions of a machine are functions of its design). In the *Passions* we find that we are psychologically capable of preparing, that is, of predisposing, the body so that it will react to events taking place around it in the manner most conducive to the preservation of the union of soul and body. The power of the will, for Descartes, is the power to dispose the body in one way rather than another—that is, to dispose one's own body, to prepare it to act, in the way that is most beneficial to oneself. However, since that disposition is relative to its environment, the will's disposition of the body implies the will's further disposition of the body's effective environment. This is the heart of Cartesian ethics: the study of the soul's proper environments, starting from the inner environment of the body and reaching ever further outward. Ethics gives sight to the soul joined as a true unity to a living machine.

The passions of the soul, according to Descartes, are the soul's perception of the "biochemical" agents that are secreted as an immediate, natural effect of the perception of external objects that are by nature able to harm or help us in our struggle to preserve the union of body and soul; the difference we experience between particular passions and emotions—the distinct "flavor" that characterizes the way we experience distinctly two passions, such as fear and love—is a result of the soul's distinct perception of different biochemicals that are secreted by distinct organs and that, therefore, can affect the pineal gland, which Descartes considers the brain's consciousness center, in distinct ways. Our consciousness of different passions is, for Descartes, entirely reducible to the presence of different endocrine agents that act against the pineal gland so as to affect it in different ways: whatever the number of distinct secretions that reach the gland, that is the number of distinct passions or emotions that are perceived. According to Descartes, these organic secretions are produced by the secreting organs as they become disposed in a manner required to preserve the body: the heart beats faster at the sight of danger, and we are thereby better prepared to run without getting tired.

As a more complex example, we can consider the secretions of the spleen. For Descartes, the sensation of a certain hurtful object outside, or even the memory of it, leads the nerves to agitate the spirits in the brain so as to open up the pathway between the spleen and the brain; this causes the soul to perceive the emotion of anger, because the spirits coming directly from the spleen are not like those coming from other parts of the body, and we are naturally constituted to "read" the chemical substances secreted by the spleen as anger.

Generally, our passions or emotions—our "subjective states"—are the way we represent to ourselves the inner disposition or state of preparedness of our body with respect to something going on outside it (and often either remembered or imagined as going on outside us). Thus, to take a contemporary example again, our perception of certain events going on around us excites the renal medulla to produce adrenalin, which, when in our blood, makes us less liable to go into shock if we are wounded. Thus, the emotion of fearful anger that we experience when we "get a shot of adrenalin" prepares us to undertake punitive measures against what we perceive. Our emotions or passions are thus our consciousness of our bodily disposition to act with respect to the object that arouses that emotion in us.

Our passions are the kind of perception we have when, for example, we are cut by a knife: "objectively" we perceive that the action of the blade on our body causes our flesh to part; "subjectively" we feel pain and fear, and a disposition to pull away. Our perception of the blade cutting "some" flesh is distinct from our particular perception of the pain and fear that only results from the circumstance that "some" flesh is in this case "our" flesh—that is, "some" flesh is the flesh to which the soul must be united if it is to perceive *anything*. Volition essentially concerns a perception involving the union of what perceives, i.e., the soul, and that by which it perceives, i.e., the body; therefore, for Descartes, the understanding of the will implies a thorough knowledge of human anatomy. Only that knowledge can give us the details of the complex systems that, according to this view, define the human body as a set of problem-solving mechanisms. Our emotions or passions are our way of being conscious of the particular systems that are on alert and are disposed to act immediately. In any given instance, what we ultimately will or do not will is that some systems of organs be disposed to make us act in such a way that the organs necessary for the soul that is united to this body are not so damaged that the body is no longer fit to be united with the soul that perceives what is happening.[20]

The soul and the body are essentially distinct for Descartes; however, volition, the power of willing, which is concerned with noncontradictory, clear perceptions, is still primarily concerned with the union of body and soul—two mutually distinct substances. Because they are distinct, the concept of their union must either be a contradiction (and then the will would be essentially self-contradictory—indeed, no better than what the most pessimistic Christian country priest would say it was), or it must be concerned with a true substantial unity of mutually distinct substances. Western philosophy took a portentious course when Descartes said that the soul and body, although distinct substances, nevertheless form a third distinct unity in the living human thinker. In that case, opposites are identified by means of their substantial union, the living human being.

Volition is immediately concerned with the preservation of the real union of the mind with the body; but body is a complex entity composed of a number of organ systems, and those organ systems are so interconnected that severe damage to any one of them is likely to result in the destruction of the system as a whole, and thus the dissolution of the union. Therefore, just as there exists a "natural institution" that determines that motions of a certain kind involving certain sensory nerves will result in our perception of figure, motion, rest, and the like, so there also exists a yet more discriminating mechanism that permits the soul to distinguish the different secretions originating at distinct organ sites. There is thus a profound complementarity between our ability to discriminate between sensory activity by means of our ideas of figure, motion, number, and the other mathematical objects, and our ability to discriminate between organic secretions as distinct emotional states.

Those "unemotional" perceptions can, via medical science, include all perceptions; even such passions as love and fear can be viewed objectively (as the way we are conscious of changes of inner body states), just as objectively as we view our perceptions of triangular figures on paper. It is Descartes' conviction that all emotional states can be reduced to distinct physical events, and that the soul, using its power to will, can control its emotions and how we feel about things we perceive. That is, we find in Descartes the surprising thesis that it is precisely because the soul has control over body that it can control its own emotions. Certainly the soul can no more simply control how it feels about something than it can control what it perceives when it looks at something; but, because it can willfully associate different emotions—each of which has a distinct set of physical causes within the endocrine system of the body—with different perceptions, it can control what it feels about what it perceives. It can do this only because ideas in the brain are in some significant way corporeal.

Descartes sometimes said outright that ideas in the brain are corporeal and obey the laws of physics; the perceptions of the soul, the perceptions of distinct things, are *not* corporeal for Descartes; but, an idea, "that form, by the immediate perception of which I am conscious of that very thought" (Vol. VII, p. 160, l. 15–16), *is* corporeal. There is a good reason why Descartes is so misunderstood on this point. Although in many places he specifically referred to patterns physically impressed on the pineal gland as ideas, he sometimes modified this by saying that such patterns are not ideas except insofar as they inform the mind. The term 'idea' refers not only to the perception the mind has because it is informed by such a pattern, but also to the immediate corporeal cause of that perception. In his 1633 *Treatise on Man,* for instance, Descartes said, "I suppose that the body is nothing other than a statue or machine of earth . . . " (Vol. XI, p. 120, l. 4–5). In the course of the discussion, he considered the way the pineal gland of this statue is moved when its "sense organs" are moved by some external object, D, which has its ends and middle—A, B, C—that cause the spirits to strike the pineal gland at corresponding points a, b, c. Descartes said:

> while this gland is held inclined toward some side, it is hindered from so easily receiving the ideas of objects that act against the organs of other senses. Conformable to this . . . , almost all the spirits . . . leave from points a, b, c . . . From which you can see how ideas hinder each other, and why one cannot concentrate on several things at the same time. [Vol. XI, p. 185, l. 22ff.]

At the end of that treatise, he again referred to "ideas" in this inanimate, clay statue:

> I want you to consider, after this, that all the functions I have attributed to this machine, such as the digestion of food . . . ; the reception of light . . . in the external organs of sense; the impression of their ideas on the organ of common sense and imagination; the retention or imprint of these ideas on the memory . . . : I want you, I say, to consider that these functions follow naturally in this machine from only the dispositions of these organs, no more nor less than the movements of a clock or any other machine . . . [Vol. XI, p. 201, l. 29, to p. 202, l. 19]

If robots have ideas, ideas are no less material than the robots are.[21]

How do these forms depicted on some part of the brain inform the mind? And what did Descartes mean when he specified that these bodily forms are ideas *only insofar as* they inform the mind?

Descartes said, in effect, that the reason a man cannot think about two things at the same time is that two bodies cannot occupy the same space at the same time. This means, once again, that the individual acts of the mind tend to follow the operations of mechanics. This is not to say that the mind is matter. It is only to say that, since the mind is capable of perceiving only what comes to it as a result of the action of matter, i.e., in the pineal gland, its perceptions are profoundly qualified by the laws of matter. Descartes had stated that the essence of his method lay in his discovery that all the things that can be studied by science are linked together in a fashion closely imitating the long chains of altogether simple and easy proofs employed by geometricians; he had also told us that his geometry is really mechanics.

This is not to say that Descartes, along with Alexander Pope, considers that "What is, is good." For Descartes, "What is, is natural," and what is natural can both hurt man as well as tell him that certain things are good for life, for the union of body and soul. For Descartes, the passions that attend upon the perceptions of the soul, (and, indeed, all the passions are initially incited by the soul's "objective" perceptions) lead the mind to consider the question of good and bad with respect to those perceptions. Our "sense" of good is, for Descartes, the emotion that accompanies our imagination of ourselves as possessing something helpful; our "sense" of bad is the emotion that accompanies our imagination of ourselves as possessing something hurtful. In contemporary terms, our senses of good and bad are the emotions we have that accompany the fight-flight, or arousal, reflex. Of the six primitive passions, five concern good and bad, in that (Article 52) "they make the soul disposed to want things which nature tells us are useful to us, and to persist in this wish. . . ." The six primitive passions are: admiration (or wonder), love, hate, desire, joy, and sadness. Except for admiration, they can all be derived from love, by inversion and/or repetition, i.e., hate is the inverse of love. In Article 96, Descartes said that the latter five all have a common cause: the movements of both the biochemicals in the blood and the cerebrospinal spirits; only in the case of admiration do the spirits within the brain alone suffice to give rise to a primitive passion.

The passion of admiration arises when some motion is new and unexpected. Then the soul perceives not only the things that cause the motion, but also the fact that the parts of the brain that carry the spirits that move the gland so that the soul perceives the thing have not hitherto been employed in this way.[22] In Article 72, Descartes said that when the parts of the brain that have not previously been used as channels are used for the first time, the soul perceives the resultant novel heightened sensation as the passion of admiration (or wonder). In Article 71, he wrote that only for admiration and its derivatives is it true that a passion has no concern for good and bad. Love, in a quite different way, is the soul's perception of spirits excited by something external, together with those spirits that come from the heart. In particular, according to Article 80, the passion of love is excited in the soul when the spirits cause the soul to imagine oneself as united with something perceived as good, and the passion of hate when those spirits lead one to imagine oneself as separated from an object perceived as harmful: admiration is the "objective," and thus, "scientific," passion; love and its derivatives belong to the "subjective" sphere of ethics.[23]

Both love and hate concern separation or union in a future not far removed from the time that these perceptions take place. According to Article 86, it is the passion of desire (which is, for Descartes, *distinct* from willing or wishing) that leads one to imagine oneself united with an imaginary (absent) good. This passion has no contrary since inquiry (*la recherche*) into the future attempts to find the good in it and not the bad. In the case of desire, the two perceptions involved are the perception of oneself—certainly present—and the "perception," which Descartes calls the imagining, of something good that is not present. Article 91 says that the passion of joy consists of the soul's pleasure in a good, which "the impressions of the brain represent it as its own. . . ." In Article 94, Descartes says that joy follows upon pleasant sensations when the objects of sense excite such motion in the nerves that, were the body not strong and in good health, it could not overcome possible (i.e., clearly imagined) hurt from these objects. Thus, the soul can perceive not only possible danger from the objects of sense but also the fact that the body to which it is joined can overcome that danger; this excites joy in the soul by means of a perception "instituted by nature." (This, Descartes said, is the reason men take joy in horrible spectacles presented on a stage.) Sadness is the naturally instituted perception of our weakness, in that we cannot overcome some danger, that is, that our body is not, and cannot presently be, disposed to meet that danger.

We see, then, that the primitive passions all involve the perception of something present along with the perception of something not present. (In case of admiration, we perceive that a given perception has not previously been perceived.)

How the Body Acts Against the Soul So That the Union of Body and Soul Both Perceives and Wills

Although volition is always concerned with our perceptions—that is, with our naturally instituted reaction to a mechanical event taking place in the brain—there are two naturally instituted reactions connected with any neural event. One reaction is permanent and unalterable, and it is this class of reaction that determines that, under certain conditions, we must always perceive light, heat, color, etc.; we cannot change this unless we destroy nerves or organs of perception. The other class of naturally instituted perceptions, however, is, although naturally instituted, also, because of the will, variable.[24] Thus, the fear excited by a rushing lion is an example of the sort of emotion-charged perception that accompanies the bare "objective" perception of a threat to our well-being; indeed, we can train ourselves to the extent that we become fearless in such cases. It is the soul's power to change our naturally instituted passions or emotions, which are attached to the perceptions of the class of alterable, but still *naturally instituted* perceptions, that is the primary discriminent of will. The constant exercise of the will is, for Descartes, learning.

Descartes' first step in his investigation of how the body acts against the soul was to locate the organ site of psychic activity. Descartes remarked, in Article 31 of the *Passions,* that in his time it was commonly believed that the soul, although united with the whole body, exercised its functions in two particular parts, the heart and the brain. He said that he thought this to be incorrect, and that the soul does not in the least (*nullement*) exercise its function in the heart nor even in the brain as a whole, but only in the "most interior of its parts"—the pineal gland, which is suspended in the passage through which, according to Descartes, the cerebrospinal fluids (spirits) of the third and fourth cavities (ventricles) of the brain communicate, so that the least movement in the gland changes the course of the spirits traveling through the passage, and the least movement in the spirits traveling through the passage is communicated to the gland.[25] He specified the importance of the role of the gland in Article 34, where he said that, "the little gland which is the principal seat of the soul is so suspended among the cavities which contain the spirits as to be moved by them in as many different ways as there is a diversity of sensibles in objects. . . ." He said that this gland is not only moved by the spirits which surround it, "but . . . this gland can also be moved in various ways by the soul, which is of such a nature that it receives as many diverse impressions in it, that is to say, it has as many diverse perceptions, as the gland receives diverse movements." According to Descartes, for each change in position of the pineal gland there is a corresponding perception in the soul, and the soul, in the other direction, can further move the gland by the mere fact that it has perceptions.

Here Descartes first said that the soul can move the body, but then he characterized the soul by its ability to receive impressions from the motion of the gland. He did not, as one would expect, say of the gland that it is of such a nature that differences among the perceptions arising in the soul cause differences in the motions in the gland. Rather, he merely characterized the soul as being of such a nature that differences of motions in the gland give rise to differences in the perceptions of the soul. This is perplexing and disappointing, since it is in this passage that the reader would hope to find the answer to the great question to which the concept of the soul acting upon body gives rise: can the soul be the absolutely original cause of any motion in matter if that matter is ruled by laws of conservation of the total quantity of motion in the universe? Those perceptions in the soul are themselves the soul's "natural," automatic reactions to motions in the gland. Are there any motions in the gland that are originated by the "natural" power of the soul, that is, because of the soul's volition? Why didn't Descartes discuss here the relation between the soul's powers and its will, rather than merely remarking that the soul responds to motion in matter by having certain impressions or perceptions? As we shall see, Descartes cannot answer the question of how the soul moves the body without addressing himself further to the character of those impressions that arise in the soul because of motion in the gland. For, in Descartes' view, the will operates only through those perceptions that are passions in the soul, that is, that are *originally* caused by *motion in the gland*. Descartes thereby definitively rules out any direct supernatural "fixing" of the will, be it celestial or demonic, and therefore, any attempt to discount Descartes' thinking on the grounds that he was "orthodox" is to be dismissed. Descartes' neurophysiology excludes the direct operation of both divine grace and demonic possession.

Descartes ended Article 34 by saying that, whenever the pineal gland is set in motion, and however slight the motion, it pushes the spirits surrounding the gland within the brain's central cavity (ventricle III) toward the walls of the cavity, where there are pores (nerve endings); these pores lead the spirits, via the nerves, into the muscles, which are disposed to be easily moved when the spirits inflate their nerves, so that they contract or expand and the body moves.

The motion of the spirits in the brain thus "hydraulically" operates the machine that is the body. As is seen in the 1633 (posthumously published) *Treatise On Man*,[26] this function can be entirely understood by the laws of mechanics and does not require that a soul be united to the body. Before the entering (afferent) spirits that come into the central cavity at its anterior end can transverse its length to reach the more posterior end, where the tubes leading to the rest of the body are located, they must strike against the pineal gland suspended in that cavity. This alters their direction and determines precisely what sort of efferent (leading-out) motion there will be. Thus, when two afferent impulses strike the gland at one time, they can so affect the gland's position that they leave the cavity by tubes that neither of them would have found had they each struck against and reflected off it singly.[27] However, all this is purely mechanical, and Descartes discussed this situation in detail in the *Dioptrics* and the *Treatise on Man.*

In the *Passions,* however, the perceptions arising in the soul because of the motion in the pineal gland that is caused by the brain fluid (spirits) are only of interest when they are related to the course they follow *after* they have been reflected off the gland. Descartes says that the soul can relate its perceptions of external objects to its perceptions of the ultimate goal of particular infusions of spirits; the goal of the spirits or hormones, etc., aroused by a given perception causes the soul to have certain "feelings" about that perception. The sight of a cabbage in front of us, for instance, not only makes us perceive the presence of food, but also leads us to perceive whether or not our stomachs are empty. On the other hand, the emptiness of our stomachs makes us imagine food, even when it is not present in front of us. It also makes us feel good about food that we imagine to be present and in front of us, and, if we are hungry to the point of discomfort, it makes us feel bad about food that we imagine to be not present and not accessible. The soul views what comes to it either as a bare perception or as good or bad for its union with the body. Up to a point, it views the mechanical results much as an infinitely unsympathetic physician might view a patient "objectively"; but, added to this, there is, according to Descartes, a natural disposition in the soul to view its perceptions in light of the general good of the complex of mind and body—"subjectively." In Article 52 or the *Passions,* Descartes wrote that "nature tells us [*la nature dicte nous*]" that some of the things we perceive are useful and some are hurtful; in the former case, there arises in the soul the passion of love, and in the latter case, the passion of hate. Article 79, which discusses love and hate together as simple contraries, says that the passion excites the soul to wish to be joined to the objects represented by that perception and that appear agreeable to it. It is then that Descartes concludes that "hatred is an emotion caused by the spirits which incite the soul to want to be separated from the objects which present themselves to it as harmful." (The parallel between this description of the two emotions and the usual description of mathematical addition and subtraction is obvious.)

Descartes stated clearly and simply that the passions that incite the soul to will something are *perceptions.* Article 27 gives a general definition of the passions as "perceptions, or sentiments, or emotions of the soul." In Article 28, he said that he calls them sentiments because "they are received by the soul in the same manner as the objects of the exterior senses . . ."; and that he calls them emotions because, of all the thoughts (*pensees*) that the soul can have, no others agitate and inflame it so much.

They are kinds of perceptions (*des perceptions*) merely because we are aware of them.

In Article 19, Descartes said that our perceptions are of two sorts: those caused by the body and those caused by the soul. Those that depend on the soul "are the perceptions of our will, and all the imaginations and other thoughts which depend on our will." He then continued that, although the soul's will, i.e., volition, is an action, the soul's perception of its own volition (we perceive our will "by the same means that we will") is a passion. He says that a volition is called an action only because it is customary to refer to a thing by the more noble term, although "this perception and this volition are, in effect, the same thing. . . ." He continued, in Article 20, that it is by means of an application of the soul that we can imagine either a nonexistent thing or something that is entirely intelligible, "for example, . . . the soul's own nature. . . ." He says that this application of the soul to the imagination of things depends principally on the will, which brings it about that the soul notices them, or, in Descartes words, "which brings them to its attention." Article 21 states that the body causes both perceptions of bodies, largely depending on the nerves, and imaginations. Some of these "bodily" imaginations are caused by the random course of the spirits in the brain, which is the cause of the dreams of sleep or derangements of illness or drunkenness, and is largely the result of an irregular stop in the motions caused by external bodies in the nerves.

Summary

For Descartes, the passions of the soul are passions in it only because they are initiated outside the soul. Volition is essentially tied to the soul's sensitivity to the activity outside it that excites a given perception within it; any given volition is directed to a perception. Volition therefore concerns the soul's perception of its union with a body, which can affect it with respect to perception. Volition is the perception of a thing under the aspect of its being helpful or harmful to what perceives because it has a body and a soul that are united to one another in a very special way.

All the perceptions in the soul arise as an immediate result of motion in the pineal gland; that is, whatever powers the soul might possess, it cannot cause itself to perceive unless there is also, at the same time, the motion in the gland that would also naturally give that perception to the soul in the presence of an external object. However, the soul is not constrained by a given motion to perceive only what is naturally or customarily associated with that given motion in the gland—unless it is very violent. Nor is the soul totally preoccupied with the motions that originate outside the body. The soul, according to Descartes, also perceives what we today call the biochemical character of the secretions, the "spirits" that act immediately against the gland. The soul therefore perceives both "objects" and the source in its own body of the spirits that come to the brain, as well as their destination after they leave the brain.

With this account, we can now look at how the soul imagines what it has never seen and remembers what it once saw.

WILL AND IMAGINATION

Throughout the *Passions,* Descartes addressed himself primarily to the origin and purpose of the passions, and only incidentally to their force and "flavor." With the help of Cartesian medicine, the passions can be viewed with entire "objectivity" as being the results of certain organic secretions and motions in the spirits; they thus cease to have any prescriptive, impulsive value with respect to external objects, and instead turn the mind toward the corporeal causes of emotions within the body of the impassioned man. For Descartes, the polite, civilized, and ethical man is a man who understands the sources of his passions and hence how to govern them; his manual of instruction is neither the Bible, *The Book of the Courtier,* nor a handbook of fencing, but a medical treatise.[28] The age of progressive optimism begins with the age of Descartes' medicine. So does modern ethics, which is based on that medicine, which teaches us that since every action in the soul is also a passion, there can be no question of a war between the soul and the passions, or of a man's being "of two minds." Such irresolution, according to Article 47 of the *Passions,* arises only when the spirits move the gland in rapidly alternating ways; the two resultant perceptions, one seemingly good and one seemingly hurtful, follow so closely upon each other that the contrary passions that they excite are confused. In Article 45, Descartes said that our passions cannot be directly excited or dismissed by the action of our will, "but they can be indirectly, by the representation of the things which are by custom joined with the passions we want to have, and which are contrary to those we want to reject." That is, the soul has the power to use the imagination to represent to itself images of things that are absent and that are contrary to the present perception caused by the present action of the spirits upon the pineal gland. The soul's power with respect to its passions is the power to remember the past and to imagine the future, and thus to be attentive to something other than what is presently caused in it. In this way it can indirectly cause a change in the usual effect of a given motion in the spirits. When a representation is the repeat of a past motion in the spirits, the soul is said to remember; when a representation is the result of motion in the spirits that is caused by no past experience or present object, then the soul is said to imagine. To imagine something possible is, in a way, to perceive the future.

In Article 42, "How one finds in his memory the things one wants to remember . . . ," Descartes addressed the problem of how the act of willing to remember something is related to motion in the gland. The simple willing to remember does not cause the gland to move directly toward a certain place in the brain where traces of a former experience are found. To do that would be to remember a memory without remembering the content of the memory. Rather, the gland is in constant motion because of the constant influx of impulses in the spirits, and sooner or later the gland must, willy-nilly, move toward the place sought by the soul's will to remember; when this finally happens, a representation of the sought-after former experience occurs in the soul. The soul's will to remember does not consist of a particular wish to move the gland in one way instead of another; rather, the will to remember is a disposition of the soul toward attending to or keeping in view one particular representation among all those that come to it while it actively seeks to remember.

In Article 43, Descartes discussed how the soul is able to be attentive to one perception rather than to another. It is only in this article that he says that a particular wish has the force to do something to the gland. He stated that, "when one wants to arrest his attention to consider that object for a period of time, this will retains the gland, during this time, sloping towards the same side. . . ." It is also in this unique article that Descartes says that, when one wills to walk or move one's body in some way, the simple act of willing brings it about that the gland pushes the spirits toward the muscles that serve to that effect.

Descartes here stated clearly that the soul, upon the occasion of a certain perception in it, has the power to actually preserve the position of the gland by its will; however, this implies that, in consequence of the soul's will, the motion of the gland seems to abandon the laws of mechanics. If this is true, then there seem to be instances in which motion in matter cannot be explained by mechanics: if one's will can arbitrarily change the direction of motion of the spirits in the brain when one wishes something to be accomplished other than what would have been accomplished without that exercise of will, then, at the moment when the spirits come into close proximity to the gland controlled by the will, their future path ceases to be deducible from their past mechanical behavior. The state of the will at that time becomes a true dimension of the problem, and that state is hardly a matter of mechanics.

It is not clear, however, that Descartes held that the path of the spirits becomes unpredictable in the neighborhood of the gland when it is moving in accordance with particular volitions. For, first of all, it is a fundamental postulate of Descartes' that our acts of will, that is to say, our volitions, are always constrained by nature in such a way that we always will what is perceived as being good for us. We simply cannot will otherwise. (There cannot be any demonic possession for Descartes, nor any essential wound of Nature.) When we are observed to will something that is bad for us, it is because we mistakenly perceive it as good for us. There are no bad or defective souls for Descartes; error in choice is a result either of diseased or malfunctioning bodies, or of ignorance. This means that rehabilitation—re-education—must replace punitive responses to crime, which can be a result only of either neurophysiological malfunctioning or mistreatment. In Article 44 of the *Passions*, Descartes said that "nature or habit" can join "in different ways each motion of the gland to each thought"—where by "thought" Descartes merely means "sensation" or "percept." We have already seen that all our acts of will are dependent on passions excited by predictable motions in body, and, from the second part of his *Discourse,* we are aware of the importance for Descartes of those of our early experiences that are regulated by our elders' experience—so that our habits and prejudices are largely matters of our own experience and a great deal of what we today would call acculturation. Thus, it follows that only new experiences will lead us to new acts of will—most of our decisions and volitions being habitual. However, if we are knowledgeable about medicine and mechanics, we will be able to identify what is good for the continued healthy union of soul and body, and this always constrains us to will in an unambiguous or doubtless way. This estate of always willing what is good for us would be the ultimate moral or ethical condition, and it is "according to nature." Also, it cannot be stressed too much, that that nature is at one and the same time both moral (or ethical) nature and the very same nature that "gives" regulations to matter; it is the source of the laws of nature of Part II of the *Principles of Philosophy* ("The Principles of Material Things"), and of that medico-ethical work, the *Passions of the Soul,* which was meant by Descartes to supplement and complete the *Principles.*

    This account is not a reading of contemporary deterministic behaviorism back into Descartes. On the contrary, it is taken from the texts of the *Passions,* and it points to the inescapable conclusion that, if we were to know all there is to know about a given man's experience, then, *because* he is entirely constrained by nature to choose what he naturally knows to be the better for himself, we can exactly predict his volition in any given situation. There is an apparent contradiction in the idea of will operating in a world ruled by mechanical laws, but since Descartes thought that what concerns man's welfare is taught him by nature, and hence is natural, the contradiction can be resolved by determining whether or not there is a science of what is good for man, i.e., a prescriptive social or ethical science, in accord with the natural teaching of the *Principles of Philosophy*. Indeed, if the laws of nature of his *Principles of Philosophy* did not apply equally to men and the human order, man would have to be under another, nonnatural law; however, if humans were under a nonnatural dispensation, what could guarantee that the authority of that nonnatural dispensation would never extend its sphere of influence into the area treated of in the *Principles,* and hence arbitrarily overrule nature itself? If man's highest good can be achieved by means of a science of nature, then nature fixes his will and makes him will in strict accord with the productions of that natural science. If he does this, then his will can never act in an unscientific, unnatural, unpredictable way.

The predictability of the will of man, based upon the natural constraint to will what he sees naturally as good for him, thus resolves the apparent contradiction between Descartes' psychology and his physics—between free will and determinism. To the extent that an ethical science is possible that can show man how to surround himself with only the things that are choiceworthy, it follows that man's will is absolutely predictable. If, further, the ethical science were based on medical physiology, which includes mechanics in its foundation, the will would be predictable with geometrical accuracy. Barring the fruits of such a science, all Descartes could, and likely would, say is that, given the detailed and complete socio-medical history of any individual human, an observer could predict precisely how he would react in any given situation, i.e., what volition would arise when excited by a given perception of the situation.[29]

This argument seems somewhat sophistical, since did not Descartes say that, whether the body is growing, healthy, or decomposing, its parts each obey the laws of nature? Therefore, why should health be "naturally" better than sickness? Does not his doctrine of this "natural" teaching concerning what is good or bad for men seem merely an artificial importation, sincere or not? Descartes' rejoinder would, I think, be as follows.

Since thinking determines my being, and since thinking always involves perception, and, finally, since perception requires that the corporeal organs of sensation be in good working order, a sound body is an absolutely necessary condition for a soundly operating mind. As a consequence, our perception of anything contains an aspect that indicates the importance of health for its smooth and accurate functioning—for instance, the passion of joy.

However, this presupposes a natural disposition for making the right choice every time that a decision is demanded. Ultimately, indeed, Descartes' program seems to comprise a universal institution for aiding human decision-making. The ultimate goal of his program (*dessein*, as he called it in the sixth part of the *Discourse*), is to establish a medical-mechanical basis for making the right choices—always. Out of this *dessein*, I believe, comes the profoundly "liberal" dimension of his work, since the act of making the right choice is, by definition, a biological act belonging equally to all men, *as* men. On this showing, the soul's acts of will are essentially involved with its clear perception of its dependence upon the body for the operation of its powers, together with the natural disposition for the *medically* right. Since perceptions of what is present (and the thinker's body is always present in the form of the gland) are usually more lively (*plus vite*) than perceptions of what is not present (*Passions*, Art. 28), the soul's perception of the body's contribution to perception arrests its attention when perception is new.

How the Soul Wills to Imagine

According to Descartes, the brain itself is affected by "new ideas" differently from the way it is affected by memories, which are traces of "old ideas." The question remains, then, about how the soul "wills to imagine." That is, what is it that the soul is passionate to or perceptive of when its action causes the gland to move in such a way that the next perception in the soul is new, i.e., is really different from any it has ever had before? This seems to be a crucial case, since only in Article 43, where Descartes discussed how we imagine and are attentive, did he actually say that the gland is pushed by the soul in order that we have "imaginative" perception or an "attentive" perception. Upon a close reading of this article, however, we see that the power of the soul to move the gland may not be the real issue: Descartes said that a volition has the power to move the gland in a certain way (Vol. XI, p. 361, l. 4–5), "when one wants to imagine something one has never seen. . . ." But just when is that? If each and every passion in the soul is paired with a perception, the will to imagine cannot be altogether unconditioned, because, as a passion, an act of will is excited only by a perception. Further, that will must be to imagine either something similar to something we have already seen or, at the very least, something that, when imagined, can be recognized as what satisfies the will to image just thus and not otherwise. However, if we have never seen the thing before, how can we recognize it as what we willed to imagine when it is finally represented to us? Indeed, if we have never seen the thing before, how is it that we have the will to imagine it at all?

The answer to this question lies in Descartes' view of the mind's "analytical" power to represent to itself, as if it were known, precisely what it is seeking. Indeed, much of the theoretical mathematical development of the *Rules* is taken up with showing when this is necessary and how it is possible; and what else is an algebraic equation except a way of representing the unknown as if it were known, in that the given terms of the equation provide the "conditions" or information necessary to exactly determine or solve for that unknown? Descartes' statement of the possibility of and necessity for just this procedure is found in *Rule* XIII:

> First, in each question it is necessary that something be unknown, or otherwise it is sought in vain; secondly, that unknown thing ought to be designated in some manner, for otherwise we would not be determined to the investigation of one thing to the exclusion of all else; thirdly, it cannot be designated in this way unless by something which is known. [Vol. X, p. 430, l. 17–22]

In short, the mind can will to imagine new things if it is able to imagine some "mark" or symbol as representing something unknown and sought for; it is able to consider that mark as signifying one particular unknown rather than any other only because what symbolizes the unknown stands for something that *can* be known because of something definite that is already known—the way of Descartes' analytic mathematics.

In this light, even the will to imagine something new and hitherto unperceived moves the gland because of something that has previously been perceived and that is determinate and known relative to what is to be imagined. In this way, even the crucial case of the will moving the gland reduces, exactly as in analysis, to expressing a new thing in terms of other things already perceived, i.e., to expressing the unknown in terms of the known. Descartes' doctrine of the will is exactly based on his reflections on algebra.

At this point we are finally in a position to see how the soul employs the imaginative mechanisms of the body to which it is joined in order to represent to itself its own mental operations.[30]

In Article 34 of the *Passions*, "how the soul and body act against each other . . . ," Descartes said that the pineal gland, which supplies the exact location at which the body and soul interact, is so suspended within the cavities of the brain that contain its spirits that those spirits can move it in as many different ways as there are sensible differences between objects.[31] Furthermore, the motion of that gland can be modified in different ways by the soul, which receives as many diverse impressions or perceptions as there are differences in movement in that gland. Since there are only six primary passions, and since the soul wills nothing except when excited to it by a passion, the way in which the soul moves the gland is closely related to the way in which the gland moves the soul. (Again, for Descartes, the will is also a perception and hence also a passion.) Admiration (or wonder) alone, Descartes stated in Article 70, has knowledge for its object, and not good and bad. Admiration is the scientific passion.

What motion in the body, involving the will attending upon the passion of admiration (which is itself excited in the soul by the perception of something novel) helps the soul to come to know?

Article 70 defines the passion of admiration by saying that, "admiration is a sudden surprise of the soul which makes it consider closely those objects seemingly rare and extraordinary." Thus, admiration causes the soul to consider certain objects attentively. Article 43 tells us in detail "how the soul is able to imagine, be attentive, and move the body." In particular, the soul can be attentive when it wills to arrest itself to the attentive consideration of an object: for the will then "causes" the gland to be held in the position required for the soul to have the same perception presented to it for some time.

Descartes said that this passion, which leads us to be attentive to what we have not seen before, "disposes us to the acquisition of knowledge." But then can we not immediately infer from this that the most admirable and fruitful of all sciences is that in which the soul most fully utilizes its power to be attentive to what it has not seen before—that is, to imagine? For it is by using the body's power to imagine that the soul can represent to itself things it has never seen before. It seems that it is a form of this inference that led Descartes to explain both the power to be attentive and the power to imagine in the same article, separate from the article discussing the soul's power to remember what it has seen. For, although Descartes had very little good to say about "arts," which proceed as if to be admirable were solely to be new and different (Article 74 calls this love of novelty for its own sake, a defect of the passions), still, if science is to lead us to see things that heretofore have not occurred to us, the disposition to admiration must be closely allied to the disposition to imagine readily.

Article 20 considers the power of imagination:

> "when our soul applies itself to imagining something that does not exist . . . and also, when it applies itself to considering something that is only intelligible, not imaginable, for example, to consider its own nature, the perceptions that it has of these things depend principally on the will that allows it to perceive them.

But, concerning those things that are not at all imaginable, such as the soul itself, Descartes in another work said:

> As imagination uses poetic figures of speech in order to conceive bodies, so the intellect uses certain sensible bodies such as wind and light in order to picture to itself spiritual things; so that, by philosophizing profoundly, we are able to carry the mind to sublime cognition. [Vol. X, p. 217, l. 12–16]

That is, although there are many things that the soul cannot "naturally" perceive, in that there are many things that never directly act on the gland to make it move in ways required to excite certain perceptions in the soul, the soul can nevertheless apply its will to imagine in such a way that it can cause perceptions to arise as a result; it can then consider them purely as "figures for," and not at all as "images of," things. For the soul perceives that, in a way, these "highly imaginative" figures originated within it; that is, the soul can attend to the origin and purpose of that sort of perception and entirely disregard the image or idea except as it conveys its origin and purpose. Such a figure presents to the soul what might be usefully referred to as an intentional symbol. The power to construct these symbols gives Descartes a proof that humans can absolutely distinguish, in actual fact, between the intentional aspect of perceptions and the "objective" aspect of perceptions, between what body causes and what will causes us to perceive by the soul's use of body to perceive. In Article 44 of the *Passions*, Descartes discussed a similar relation obtaining between our idea (or perception) of words and their meaning. He said, "and when in talking, we think only of the sense of what we wish to say, we would move the tongue and the lips better and much more promptly than if we thought to move them in all the ways required to make the same words." Indeed, the soul's ability to distinguish between the matter and the form of perception allows men to overcome the rashness and impulsiveness of the passions themselves.

INTELLECT AND BODY

This section considers in what way and to what degree it is true to say that, for Descartes, thought depends upon the corporeal substance of the brain.[32] In particular, we shall see that for Descartes there is no *conscious* thinking without the body, because without the body the soul would lack the means to represent anything to itself. We show that all psychic activities of which we have any awareness are, for Descartes, somehow associated with uniquely corresponding corporeal activities, and that it is these corporeal activities that diversify the power of the "thing that thinks [*chose qui pense*]" into conceiving, doubting, affirming, denying, willing, not willing, imagining, and sensing.

How Body Is Concerned with the Soul's Representations of Its Activities

It is in the second *Meditation* that Descartes ruminated:

But what am I? A thing which thinks. What is a thing which thinks? It is to say a thing which doubts, which conceives, which affirms, which denies, which wants, which does not want, which also imagines and feels. [Vol. IXA, p. 22]

From what source does one thing (*une chose*) acquire the power to accomplish all these different activities?[33] How could Descartes identify the mind (which thinks) with the soul (which "doubts, conceives, denies," etc.)?

When Descartes asks "What am I?," he seems to be asking what Rene Descartes, the thinking man, is. Could that answer reasonably be, "a substance which thinks [*une substance qui pense*]"? More likely, the answer is "a person," as he writes to Elizabeth: "it is one single person [*une seule personne*] who has a body and a thought together which are of such a nature that the thought can move the body and feel the accidents that happen to it" (Vol. III, p. 694, l. 2–6). The members of the enumeration that comprises his answer to "What is a thing which thinks?" are, except for doubt and its opposite (which can be termed "conception"), treated in the *Passions*, under the heading of things excited in the soul by corporeal motion in the brain.[34] All the others in this list are dealt with in detail as passions arising in the soul because of its conjunction with the body. Although the point is not developed in the *Passions*, the list presents the way in which even doubt and conception in the soul can be seen as radically dependent upon the body for their definition.

Descartes seldom, if ever, discussed the soul as acting entirely apart from the body. When prudence forced him to mention such things as the soul's joy after death, with an eye to the Christian doctrine of the beatitude of the blessed elect, he left the question with a vague reference to "les Divines" or to "la Revelation." The thing that thinks and perceives that it thinks is viewed by Descartes primarily as a compound organism that thinks only in conjunction with something unlike it, namely, a mind or soul. (Again, for Descartes, the mind is the whole soul.)

As early as the *Rules*, Descartes unequivocally stated that all the soul's powers are reducible to one single power. We may therefore infer that this simple power of the soul or mind must be differentiated in its operations by differences in something that is not soul, in particular, by certain distinct organs of the body. The body is compound; the soul is simple. Descartes wrote:

We should understand that the power by which we properly know things is purely spiritual and no less distinct from the whole body than blood is from bone or the hand from the eye; and that it is every single one of the following, namely, what receives figures at the same time from common sense and the fancy, as well as what forms new figures—with which the imagination is so occupied, that often it is not capable of receiving ideas from the common sense and at the same time of transferring those ideas to the motor force in accord with the dispositions of pure body. In all of which cases, this cognitive power is sometimes passive and sometimes active, and so in one way imitates the stylus and, in another, the wax tablet; here, however, this is to be taken only as an analogy, for nothing is found in corporeal things which is altogether similar to this power. [Vol. X, p. 415]

The points made in this passage differ in no important respect from the teachings of the *Passions,* written 18 years later. However, the *Rules* generally addresses the intellective acts of the soul, the *Passions* more the sensitive reactions of the soul, which, although they are sensitive, are the reactions of what only thinks. The *Passions* also supplies a fuller account of the mechanics of the way the soul receives figures from a certain part of the brain, and specifies both how the soul applies itself to remember and how it forms new figures in the imagination. Both the *Passions* and the *Rules,* the latter of which is often occupied with extremely "abstract" mathematics, specify the details of how the imagination, when preoccupied with the figures in it, is often rendered incapable of receiving more figures. Indeed, in the *Passions,* this mechanical detail leads to a doctrine of how to rule over the passions entirely, that is, by so preoccupying the (corporeal) imagination with either memories or constructs, that the soul cannot attend to the perceptions usually connected to these passions. And, in a very real way, the deft use of the imagination supplies, for Descartes, the way to a total conquest of hurtful passions.

Descartes said in Rule XII that the soul's intellective power is no less distinct from the whole body than blood is from bone or hand from eye. This is not a great distinction. Furthermore, as Descartes said both in Rule XII and in Article 47 of the *Passions,* the soul is absolutely simple, completely lacking anything like parts. It is "one and the same thing [*uniquamque*]" that perceives, remembers, or forms new figures. In Article 47 of the *Passions,* he wrote that, "there is in us only one soul . . . : it is the same soul which is sensitive and reasonable, and all its appetites are its volitions." If, then, this soul is one, and is no more distinct from the body as a whole than blood from bone (bone being for Descartes generated from and nourished by blood) or the hand from the eye (and the hand grasps what the eye sees) it follows that the several powers belonging to that simple soul are differentiated according to the different organs in the body, which the soul "uses" at different times and in different ways. This, it seems, is what Descartes meant when he said in the *Passions* that the actions of the soul are also its passions For, depending on whether one or another action in the body excites a corresponding reaction in the soul, the reaction in the soul may be considered as sense, reason, or will. With respect to the body, all three are passions in the soul, since those movements begin in the body. When referred to as perceptions in the soul, sense, reason, and will are considered as actions in the soul and passions in the body. A question thus arises about what action in what part of the body excites the soul so that it acts in a *reasonable* way.

In order to act reasonably, the soul must act through the agency of some part of the body; otherwise, sense, reason, and will would be identical, since the soul, whose powers they comprise, is one. In order to will, the soul acts on the pineal gland, so that it pushes the surrounding spirits (in modern terms, we initiate voluntary nerve impulses), which then mechanically control the body's movements in such a way that the soul can consequently perceive the object of its volition, because it is at last present. The soul can sense because ideas, if they are depicted on the gland, are instituted by nature to make the soul perceive. These ideas are corporeal impressions caused by configurations of individual impresses made by spirits issuing from similar configurations of nerve endings in ventricle III, the middle ventircle of the brain.

Under what corporeal circumstance is the simple, uncomplex soul excited in such a way that it comes to a knowledge of truth? And does that corporeal circumstance operate on a single occasion or over a long period of time?

Thought, even "pure" thought, must involve ideas (as Descartes called the "forms of perception") impressed on the gland by the spirits. Consequently, we should expect to find some aspect of ideas that acts as the corporeal agency associated with intellective operation of the soul. It is ideas, insofar as they give the soul occasion to perceive distinct and differing forms, with which the soul is occupied when it operates intelligently. The perception of the forms of its sensations gives rise to the intellective operation of the soul, for it is only its perception of differences in the forms of its ideas that leads the simple soul to an awareness of anything beyond itself (Vol. III, p. 428, l. 30, to p. 429, l. 2). The formal aspect of an idea, together with its aspects of being immediately caused by spirits and originally caused by agitation more remote from the gland, thus gives to each idea impressed on the gland a threefold aspect. It is in its ability to distinguish between these three aspects of a given idea that the soul can distinguish between an idea as 1) a representation of external causes, 2) a representation of internal causes, and 3) a distinct form. In the last case, the soul is largely concerned with its own operations, which leads it to realize that it could not give rise to form without the aid of the body. The soul's unconditioned power to attend to any one of the three aspects of an idea to the momentary exclusion of the other two enables it to resolve the naturally deceptive aspect of all ideas, namely, that they tend to appear as representative of their causes. This power to attend to one aspect of an idea, and thus to disregard the others, is the source of the soul's power to conceive, as opposed to its power merely to perceive.

Descartes explicitly distinguished between these aspects of an idea in his "geometrical" proof of the existence of God, which he gives at the end of the *Second Responses* to the *Meditations*. There (Vol. VII, p. 160) he said that he includes under the name of thought (*cogitatio*) all that is within us of which we are immediately aware; in particular, "all operations of will, intellect, imagination and sense." In the next definition, he said that an idea is "the form of each thought" by the immediate perception of which he himself is aware of or conscious of that thought. He also said that by the name "ideas" he is referring to those images depicted in the fantasy, i.e., in the region of the pineal gland, only insofar as they can inform the soul as it considers that part of the brain. In the next definition, Descartes defined the "objective reality of an idea" as the "entity of the thing" represented by the idea. This addresses that part of the ideas that is not contributed by the soul. He said, in the Latin edition:

> By *the objective reality of an idea* I understand the entity of the thing represented through the idea, in so far as it is in the idea; and in the same way one can speak of the objective perfection or, if you please, the objective artifice, etc. For whatever we perceive as if in the objects of ideas, those things are objectively in the ideas themselves. [Vol. VIII, p. 161, l. 4–9]

"The objective reality of an idea" concerns some aspect of the *soul's* perception of an idea depicted on the gland together with some aspect of that perperception that is not contributed by the action of the soul. He clarified this definition by saying that whatever it is we perceive to be "as it were" in the object of the idea is *objectively* in the idea. The objective reality of the idea is primarily that of which the soul is aware in an idea that connects that idea to what truly causes it "outside." The objective reality of the idea of a horse, for instance, is that aspect of an existing horse that causes an impression or pattern to be imprinted upon the pineal gland so that we consciously perceive a horse, as entirely distinct from any other impression. The objective reality of most ideas is the slender thread that connects the soul's "natural" reactions to the primary nonpsychic causes of agitation in the gland; the objective reality of an idea is that, *in the idea,* that gives a clue to the true source of the motion in the gland that excites the soul to perceive the idea (see Appendix 3). In the French translation of the Latin original (cited above), which serves as a partial gloss on the Latin, Descartes said:[35]

> by the objective reality of an idea, I understand the entity or the being of the thing represented by the idea, in so far as this entity is in the idea, and in the same fashion one can speak of an objective

perfection, or an artificial perfection, etc. Because all that we conceive as being in the objects of ideas, is objectively, or by representation, in the ideas themselves. [Vol. IXA, p. 124]

In short, then, ideas, as mere excitations in the gland such that we
are aware of them, are the causes of perceptions. However, since perceptions differ from one another, there must also be a cause for that difference. This cause cannot be the simple soul, for, as Descartes said in
Meditation III, the soul is the simple, but common, basis of all perceptions. Hence, any knowledge, even that of one's own existence, is in part
dependent upon the soul's simple power of being differentiated by
something that is not soul.

Once again, if the soul is truly one thing, then its multiplicity of
operations and thoughts cannot be understood without recourse to a
nonpsychic agency for the definition of those operations and thoughts.
We have seen that the objective reality of an idea is one cause of distinction between the forms of thought; we have seen that differences in the
various sources of cerebrospinal fluid effect different emotions in the
soul; and we have seen that biochemicals, secreted by various organs into
the blood, effect different emotions in the soul. Now let us look at the
operations of the soul with respect to these causes of different states of
consciousness: for, whatever the action of the gland, the reaction is the
soul's reaction, and, considered as really and uniquely characteristic of
the soul, those reactions are the actions of, activities of, the soul—*its*
operations. In examining them, we are looking at the match between the
corporeal actions of the gland and the correlative actions of the soul.

One can gather from Descartes' accounts found in the *Rules* of 1628,
in the *Geometry* of 1637, and the *Passions* of 1645 that there are only five
fundamental operations that are performed by the differentiated operations of the soul. These are: 1) the operation of taking a whole and
considering it as consisting in equal parts—mathematically formalized as
division; 2) the operation of considering several groups, each of equal
number, together—formalized as multiplication; 3) the operation of taking two things and considering them as one thing—formalized as addition; 4) and the operation of considering a group as separate from a
larger group of which it might properly be considered a part—formalized as subtraction; and finally 5), the discovery of causes—formalized as finding "roots." It is fair to say that there are "informal"
versions of these operations in the *Passions*, where, for example, hate
arises when the soul perceives itself as "subtracting" its body from something it judges harmful to it; it then wills separation, which causes the
body to "subtract" itself from its situation. Love is "additive," and admiration is the seeking of root causes, and so on. In Rule XVIII (Vol. X,

pp. 461–468), Descartes described these operations as they apply in his mathematical writings, but he insists that the soul is simple and one, and that it has no parts. Thus, these five fundamental operations must be reducible to varied applications of one single power of the soul.

Descartes said that, when the soul is presented with many perceptions at once, it can entertain one of them to the exclusion of all others. That one perception may be of a remembered or imaginary object. Thus the soul can attend to just one perception out of many because of its power to use the memory or the imagination in such a way that it is preoccupied to the exclusion of any other perception. In the *Passions*, Descartes identified this power as the true "arsenal" of the soul against the waywardness of the passions. This same power appears mathematically in Rule XVI (Vol. X, p. 451, l. 21 to p. 452, l. 6), and in the second part of the *Discourse* (Vol. VI, p. 20, l. 18–21), as the power to set aside one object presented for consideration in order to attend more closely to another. When a man wishes to represent several things together, Descartes said that he should use figures; when he wishes to take several things apart and consider them one by one, he should use *chiffres*—the symbols of algebra.[36]

Descartes said time and time again that the soul is best understood by pure understanding—*l'entendement pur, intellectus purus*—aided by imagination; therefore, perhaps we should not look principally to mathematical operations, which concern how we conceive of and understand body, in order to show in what way the soul uses the body to think and to come to understand. Is there not a real question about whether and how the soul operates through the agency of the body when it wishes to understand *itself*?

Not really. For, as early as in the *Rules* of 1628, Descartes distinguished between three kinds of notions—one of pure body, one of pure soul, and one of their union. In Rule XII, where he said that it is one power that understands, senses, imagines, and remembers, he also spoke of the soul "acting alone" and thereby understanding. He said:

> And it is one and the same power which, if it applies itself with the imagination to the common sense, is said to see, touch, etc.; if to the imagination alone, in so far as endowed with diverse figures, it is said to remember; if to the same thing in order to make new figures, it is said to imagine or conceive; if, finally, it acts alone, it is said to understand. [Vol. X, p. 415, l. 28, to p. 416, l. 4]

The sense of this passage is echoed fifteen years later in two 1643 letters to his protegée, Princess Elizabeth, concerning the character of the soul's union with the body. Descartes said that we can conceive of that union only because of a primitive, innate notion of it, and that "of the soul alone, we have only the notion or thought, which includes the perceptions of the understanding and inclinations of the will" (Vol. III, p. 665, l. 18–20).

However, we have seen that for Descartes the term 'thought' includes everything of which we are immediately conscious, and that he defined the term 'idea' as the form of each thought. Furthermore, Descartes said that there are certain corporeal impressions in the brain that, insofar as they also inform the soul, are called ideas. Then how can he say that the soul ever acts alone without any help from the body, as when it conceives its ideas of itself? In other words, Descartes seems to say both that the soul acts alone when it considers the primitive ideas within it, and that the soul is aware of its thoughts only because it is informed by ideas depicted on the brain.

In a second letter of 1643 to Elizabeth on this point, Descartes said that "the body, that is to say, the extension, the shapes and the movements" can be understood by the understanding alone, "but much better" by "the understanding aided by imagination" (Vol. III, p. 691, l. 24–26). The notion of the union of the body and the soul "is known only obscurely through understanding," but very clearly in the senses. The soul "does not conceive itself except through pure understanding" (ibid., l. 22). In all three cases, it seems, albeit in varying degrees of clarity, the soul acting alone and without the aid of corporeal agents can conceive its primitive notions!

In Rule XII (Vol. X, p. 419, l. 6–23), Descartes called the three primitive notions "simple natures [*naturae simplices*]," and said that "We can never understand anything more than these simple natures and a certain mixture or composition of those things" (Vol. X, p. 422, l. 6–7). Writing to Elizabeth in the same vein fifteen years later, he said: "I consider also that all human knowledge consists in distinguishing these notions, and in attributing to each of them those things which belong to each" (Vol. III, p. 665, l. 25–30).

The Withdrawal of the Soul from the Body

If the final goal of science is to grasp firmly these three notions and their compounds, as well as to identify their objects, then it appears that the thing that thinks [*chose qui pense*] arrives at knowledge *only after* the long exercise of all its operations: *only mature* scientists can grasp these notions firmly. Insofar as, and only insofar as, these operations individually require the body for their differentiation is it true to say that the soul uses the body in its acquisition of knowledge. Differences in "external reality" are not the root cause of this definition of psychic powers; such differences are merely "dispositional" and effect differences only in particular perceptions. *The foundations of Descartes' physiology require that the cause of the differentiation be in the structure of the human body—not primarily in external objects.* There seems to be an ascent from the soul's operations involving its union with the body to an activity involving only its *own* notions; for, even its own notions generally concern the objects formerly represented to the soul through its operations requiring the body. For Descartes, then, the ultimate science that he described to Elizabeth is achieved only *after* one masters the particular sciences: abstract geometry, which is concerned with the powers of the mind; physics or mechanics, which is concerned with the powers of body; and medicine, which is concerned with the dispositions required in a body before it is fit to be united with a mind or soul. Descartes did not use his abstract geometry to distinguish between irreducible "primitive" notions of mind and body; rather, the geometry concerns body merely as *knowable by* mind, without any question of its existence. (Cf. Vol. III, p. 694, l. 15 to p. 695, l. 3, where Descartes spoke to Elizabeth about the intelligible counterparts of body.) The perfection of these three sciences—abstract geometry, physics or mechanics, and medicine—enables a man to distinguish clearly between the three primitive notions of mind, body, and their union; Descartes even said (Vol. X, p. 215, l. 5–10) that men incapable of grasping all three can become more astute judges of the truth by becoming conversant with their teachings. As he said in the preface to the *Principles,* the fruits of the tree of philosophy can be gathered only after its parts have been cultivated. The soul's primitive notions are the ultimate object of its peculiar activity, *but these cannot be clearly distinguished from one another without the aid of geometry, physics, and medicine.* Without the help of these disciplines, one might be led to think, as Descartes said the ancients were, that, for example, purely intellectual passions exist; whereas, as he wrote Elizabeth, it is the union of body and soul which causes "its sensations and passions [*ses sentimens et ses passions*]" (Vol. III, p. 665, l. 10–12). As a consequence, our knowledge of the primitive notion of the soul requires that we not try to understand the soul's peculiar powers merely by looking at its presumed peculiar passions. There are none: our primitive notions of mind, of body, and of their union can be clearly distinguished only as a result of the soul's particular "reflection" upon its own specific operations, through which it perceives either body, the union of mind and body, or, as in the case of the mind's own notion of itself, "the perceptions of understanding and the inclinations of will."

The place of long intellectual experience in Descartes' teaching concerning soul, body, and their union can be seen in another way as well. For Descartes, the ultimate test of the worth of a given philosophy lies in its fruitfulness, that is, not so much in the range and richness of the truths it contains as in the power of its principles to enable us to constantly discover new truths. Indeed, it seems as if Descartes distinguishes between "philosophy" and "science" mainly on the grounds that philosophy is static and science progressive. We see that, in the preface to the French translation of the *Principles,* he dismissed Aristotle precisely on the grounds that his philosophy has made no progress since he expounded it. He said: "and one cannot better prove the falsity of the principles of Aristotle than by saying that no one has been able to progress in that way for the several centuries that have followed" (Vol. IXB, p. 18, l. 29, to p. 19, l. 1). Whereas he said that the primary value of his own principles is that "one can, in cultivating them, discover a number of truths which I have not explained" (Vol. IXB, p. 18, l. 18–19). We can conclude from this that any philosophy that is based on principles that do not lead to substantial progress in the course of time is based on false principles. However, if their essential lack of fruitfulness makes them false, then it is likely that it is fruitfulness that makes principles true.

As we have seen, Descartes said that the final goal of thinking is the ability to clearly distinguish between the three primitive notions of mind, body, and their union. The perception of these three notions is itself a perception of what is general to, shared by, all three genres of perception. These primitive notions are abstractions from the generality of our perceptual experience and the single perception of all three together is a perception on the highest level of abstraction. The progressively higher levels of abstraction through which the thinker must pass before reaching his goal are progressively further removed from the immediate perceptions that the soul has because it is united with the body. On the highest level of abstraction, the soul utilizes the body only in order to present to itself its own abstractions. Hence, progress in the sciences does involve something like a withdrawal of the soul from the body, but a withdrawal that always presupposes body. This withdrawal is effected by the constant interposition of the soul's abstractions from immediate experience between itself and immediate experience until all its perceptions are composed of abstractions. The contents of the mature thinker's consciousness are then like those of an ideal physicist surrounded by measuring devices in a windowless laboratory lighted only by artificial light. In such a case, the soul is in what Descartes considered its true element: its own artifacts.

This view of the soul (*l'ame, mens, l'esprit*) compares in a most revealing way with Aristotle's view of the mind (νοῦς) as we find it in Book XII of his *Metaphysics.* He says (1074b, l. 35) that the mind's understanding of itself is a "thinking which is a thinking about thinking."

The conclusion to this development is that only a very special sort of man ever arrives, through his experience, at the place where he can be said to *know* simply and without any direct use of a corporeal instrument beyond sensed speech or writing. A man who is deeply conversant with *Cartesian* geometry—both pure and applied—and who is in possession of sound and healthy senses, and he alone, can realize clearly the distinction between those ideas that result from the union of body and soul and those ideas of body (which here have been referred to as "the object of the geometers" and as "mathematical body") that lead him to conceive clearly certain ideas as purely intellectual reactions to body. Only after he is clear on these two points can he then, by an act of intellectual abstraction, really conceive of ideas as the artifacts of the simple, pure intellect. Such a concept of ideas is a conception of the purely intellectual complement to true body in motion. It must be stressed once again that this final concept cannot be antecedent to the speculations of pure geometry; for once these speculations have led the mathematician to see the "boundary lines," as it were, between the actions of true body in motion and the reactions of the simple intellect, then those boundary lines define the limits of pure intellect. To judge from the passages quoted from the *Rules* (Vol. X, p. 415, l. 28, to p. 416, l. 4; p. 419, l. 6–23; p. 442, l. 6–7) and the 1643 letters to Elizabeth (Vol. III, p. 665, l. 10–20; p. 691, l. 24–26), the single clear knowledge of the simple intellect is of those boundary lines, and of nothing more.

In Part II of this work, we examine this complementarity to discover how general physical body in the course of eons came to form first a "heaven" and a "solar system"; next, how it formed a living body fit to receive a mind that thinks about true body; and, once this was done, how numbers of living bodies with minds complement one another so that they form a compound body, a body politic (or *res publica* or social union) whose sole aim is the conservation of the union of the live body and mind of each single participant who is a compound of "thinkingness [*res cognitans*]" and "extendedness [*res extensa*]."[37] This last formation takes place in a manner that recapitulates that in which the planets of any sun's solar system are formed, and it functions in a manner that images the way the planets of a solar system make a union of individuals whose individuality is a necessary precondition for the solar system itself.

NOTES

1. Mesland was finally sent to Canada for defending Descartes' thought. He died there among the Indians.

2. In the *Principles*, Part Four, Art, 189 (Vol. VIII, p. 315, l. 23–24), Descartes stated that the human soul "informs the whole body," which he gives in the subsequent French translation (Vol. IXB, p. 310) as "soit unie" ("is united"). *Descartes' translation is his interpretation of his own usage.*

3. Disposition—order and interconnectedness—is a critically important concept for Descartes. In what follows, the concern with disposition will be seen to obtain from the most elemental level right on up to a point where we can extend it to man in his political interconnections.

4. The place of disposition in modern thought is worthy of a book of its own. For example, the *way* our muscles are opposed to one another, and their extreme sensitivity to very minute impulses, no less than the bilateral symmetry of our body, permit very great effects to follow relatively small causes—e.g., the motion of the whole body because of very small nerve impulses. (It seems that *disposition* replaces δυναμὶς and *potentia.*)

In his development concerning the genesis of light, Descartes referred to the spheres or balls of second element that primarily enter into light production as follows (*Principles,* Part III, Art. 56): "elles sont tellement situeés et desposeés à se mouvoir, qu'elles s'en éloigneroient en effet, si elles n'estoient [they are so placed and disposed to be moved that they would actually remove themselves if they were not being at the same time held back by some other cause]."

As another example, we see that the whole of *Mathesis Universalis* proceeds by "setting up" equations such that there is a clear and distinct disposition between each of the knowns and between the knowns as a whole on one side of the equation, and the unknown on the other side of the equation. Thus the equation manifests in symbols precisely the disposition that must exist between known and the unknown in order for us to arrive at the solution.

5. We might do well to refer to Plato and Aristotle on this subject: Plato, *Timaeus* 34C; Aristotle, *On the Soul,* 402a–403b, l. 19 (esp. 403a, l. 28); then Plato, *Laws,* 884–890 (esp. 886D). If Plato, in the *Laws,* is even partly correct, Descartes' treatment of organic body as mechanically self-generated, and thus in need of no psychic agency, is lethal to good polity. The *ultimum finis* of this book is to give grounds to conservatives and liberals alike for re-examining their Cartesianism—which is powerfully supported by technology (which charms the political right by its increased productivity, and the liberal left by its promise of cheap abundance for all without the threat of slavery for any) and by its medical programs, which speak so forcibly to our fear of death.

6. Cf. the title of Art. 203, Part Four of *Principles:* "How we know the figures and motion of insensible particles." Descartes was saying that the magnitude, figure, and motion "which are in every single body" are the magnitude, figure, and motion of the elements; these attributes are not directly sensed as belonging to the elements of bodies, but are sensed as belonging to the compound bodies themselves (the motion of the particles of a body is sensed by us, for instance, as the *body's* heat, not the motion of its particles). Only these three attributes are present both in the elements and in the bodies they constitute as elements, only they are present both in *every* element and in *every* compound body—every element, and every compound, no matter how complex, has figure, motion, etc. It should be stressed that Descartes did not mean that these three attributes of elements are unlike all others in being *immediately* sensed as they occur in external bodies; he denied that this is true of *any* attributes of external bodies. Rather, these three attributes are unlike all others in that their effect upon the nerves results in various motions, which, happily enough, the soul subsequently perceives in the same general form as that in which they in fact occur in external bodies. This is a fundamental presupposition for Descartes (and for contemporary neuroanatomy), one which he cannot prove.

The Cartesian account of the neurophysiological structure of the eye and optic nerves leading from the eye to the brain forces a momentous *ad hoc* postulate—namely, that not even the figure, motion, and rest of external things are directly perceived "inside"— although it appears that, for example, an oblique triangle on paper "outside" is faithfully "represented" by an oblique triangle shape "inside," where the same general proportions of length and angles are reproduced. It is an open question whether Descartes is more to be blamed or to be praised for his courageous consistency here.

In a passage found in Part Four of the *Principles* (Art. 103), Descartes gave a remarkably clear and succinct account of his thinking in these matters. He stated that one might well wonder how he knows so much about the constituent particles of matter since he has said that they are insensible because of their smallness. His answer is that he has considered all the clear and distinct notions (French *notions*, Latin *principia*) concerning material things and that he has found that there are no others besides magnitude, figure, and motion, together with "the rules, following which these three things can be diversified by one another—which rules are the principles of geometry and mechanics." As a consequence, he continued, "all the knowledge which men can have is drawn from these alone," and he claimed he could show that, of necessity, whatever men do perceive of large bodies is a consequence of the actions of insensible bodies. He then stated that the simile of artificial machines strikes him as apt, and that all natural bodies are related to their insensible parts in the way that artificial machines are related to their parts, which are necessarily large enough to have been seen by their makers. Then, in the Latin text, he stated that "natural effects almost always depend on certain organs so small that they escape all the senses." In the French text, that strange phrase is replaced by what can be translated as "the tubes or furnaces which cause the effects of natural bodies are ordinarily too small to be perceived by our senses." In short, Descartes held that the human mind is of such a nature that it grasps clearly only the ideas of motion, figure, and magnitude, and that, as a consequence, all intelligible accounts of the physical world must have these as their principles. However, since the intelligible elements of the bodies of the physical world are insensibly small, any intelligible account of that world must show how these larger bodies are dependent on their parts in the way that understanding a man-made machine requires an understanding of how the parts work together to make the machine do what it does. These intelligible elements of sensible bodies are the insensibly small "organs" of these bodies in the same way that the viscera of the human body are the organs that make it behave in the way that it does.

7. In Part Two of *Principles* (Vol. VIII, p. 52, l. 29 to p. 53, 2), Descartes stated concerning motion that "all variation of matter, (or if you like, all diversity of its form) depends on motion." Two paragraphs later, in Art. 25, he stated what he meant by the term 'motion' (*motus*): "by motion ought to be understood . . . the *translation of one part of matter, or of one body, from the vicinity of those bodies which immediately touch it and as it were are considered at rest in the vicinity of others*" [emphasis in the original]. He then specified that "by *one body*, or, if you like, *one part of matter*, I understand all that which is transferred together." By "one body [*unum corpus*]" and "one part of matter [*unam partem materiae*]" Descartes meant compound bodies, which are distinguishable from their neighbors only in that the moving of the aggregate does not necessarily affect the motions within that aggregate. Such motion merely puts the body or part of matter into a new neighborhood and does not change its characteristics. On the other hand, considered within itself, certain motions can and do affect the characteristics of a given piece of matter. For, by determining that certain particles that are contiguous to one another will be considered together, but others are neighbors, we are able to direct our attention to only the former. These motions then comprise the motions of the elementary particles of the body, since they are within the confines of their neighboring particles. Descartes justified this procedure in *Principles*, Part Two, in the titles to Articles 28 and 29, as follows: "Motion properly understood is only to be referred to bodies contiguous to the body moved," and "Nor should it be referred to those contiguous bodies if they are not considered as if at rest." Not only does this view imply that motion is altogether relative—a view useful for a seventeenth-century speculator who wished to avoid the church's anti-Copernican censure—but also it implies that the limits of a body are entirely ambiguous and relative. Since Descartes' universe is a *plenum* (i.e., without any empty space or void), any given body, whether compound or elementary, must be at all times contiguous to other bodies everywhere on its

surface. Indeed, in his accounts of the three elements, he spoke of the second and third (relatively gross) elements, corresponding roughly to liquid and solid states, as being surrounded by a "sea" of the finest, gaseous, "first" element.

8. He wrote, "all human science consists in this one thing, that we should distinctly see how these simple natures concur simultaneously in the composition of other things [*omnem humanam scientiam in hoc uno consistere, ut distincte videamus, quomodo naturae istae simplices ad compositionem aliarum rerum simul concurrant*]."

Thus, if *res* A causes some modification in *res* B, for Descartes it means that some causal quality of *res* A is truly transferred to *res* B. This usage accurately manifests what Descartes means by *res*, i.e., the vehicle for qualities; once having said that, it follows of logical necessity that causes are transferred. We can, perhaps, see what this means if we compare it with Aristotle's notion of *dunamis* in his *Physics: dunamis* (or, *intrinsic basis for a to-be-realized act*) is in the thing that is activated by a distinct cause, where that distinct cause is the activity of the agent that causes, and, as such, cannot be in any way taken from it or shared by any other thing. We see just what Descartes means in the modern locution "upon impact, billiard ball A loses to billiard ball B just the quantity of kinetic energy required to make B move in reaction to being struck by A." In that locution, a definite quality of something is taken from one *res*—billiard ball A—and given to another *res*—billiard ball B. When kinetic energy is the dimension in terms of which we measure the action of the two billiard balls, then the billiard balls themselves are "the dimensional correlates" of that quantity of kinetic energy. As in the present section, where we discuss the relativity of body and motion, *res* is the aspect of present body—of body in front of us here and now—that is entirely relative to what we want to know about it. (*Res* is body about-to-be-known through dimensional analysis.)

9. Because, for Descartes, the elements of sensible bodies are the insensibly small "organs" of those bodies, the developing body—as well as the mature body—is a product of the activity of those organs. Therefore, there are no organs in the original sense of that word, i.e., "instrument." On the contrary, the living body is the effect of these Cartesian "organs," and they are not exhaustively intelligible in terms of the living body of which they are, in the *pre*-Cartesian (that is, Aristotelian) sense, "instruments." This is the basis of some of the difference between "vitalism" and "mechanism," and perhaps even between Lamarkians and Darwinians, since the former consider "species" to be instruments of evolution and the latter consider them results of it.

10. In modern terms, rather than being considered a chemically active soup, the zygote (or newly fertilized egg cell) is a mass of "mother cells" (stem cells) that themselves give off "daughter cells," which are the cells that ultimately form the parts of the body. Functionally, Descartes envisaged a chemical, quasihydraulic method of accomplishing what we explain, in the example of brain development, by the division of stem cells (neuroepithelial cells), which results in new daughter cells (neuroblasts); the daughter cells "migrate," sometimes for considerable distances, and, when they have reached their destination, stop and mature into nerve cells (neurons).

Functionally the degree of agitation of the first element does for Descartes what the migrating daughter cells of the stationary stem cells do in developmental embryology: rather than having stationary stem cells that form distant parts of the body through migratory daughter cells, Descartes has the heart—formed at once after conception, as we are led to believe by looking at the development of a chick embryo—which sends out a sort of efficient-cause agent (the high-energy first element), to distant sites. For Descartes, a form of thermal physics, rather than histology, is the ultimate foundation of what we know as biology.

11. This use of "organ" as "instrument" follows Aristotle's usage. Descartes thus seems to have two theoretically disjunctive notions of "organ." The reader might glance at

Gilbert's 1600 *De Magnete (On the Magnet)*, where the notion of "sphere of influence [*orbis virtutis*]" plays a prominent role. It is this notion of Gilbert's that permits Descartes to use the Aristotelian notion of organ along with of his own "mechanistic" use. [*Vid.* William Gilbert, *De Magnete*, trans. P. Fleury Mottelay (New York: Dover, 1958), pp. 203, 258.]

12. This is a likely *locus classicus* for the strikingly "metaphysical" Chapter 17 of Part Five of Marx's *Das Capital*, which is concerned with the labor theory of value.

13. This metaphor of "body politic" has become obscured by the use of the cell concept in considering the body a *synthesis* of cellular component-citizens. "Body politic" as used in this work refers more to the concept of an organism as it was conceived after Harvey showed the heart to be a pump and Kepler showed the planets to be a chorus of dancers encircling the sun.

14. A thorough understanding of Spinoza's *Ethics* helps one understand what Descartes means by *la morale* [see Martial Gueroult, *Etudes sur Descartes, Spinoza, Malebranche et Leibniz* (New York, Hildesheim: Georg Olms Verlag, 1970), pp. 75–78, and especially fn. 26 on p. 76].

15. In the very recent past, we have even begun to specify the chemical agent of legal innocence: for example, alcoholism has become a valid plea for U.S. senators who accept bribes and for U.S. congressmen who vote against bills for the toleration of homosexuals, but who are subsequently caught soliciting male prostitutes. If we dismiss these astonishing events as part of some sort of widespread social breakdown, we miss a very important point: namely, there is a seed of such views implicit in the medical philosophy that is deep in the soil of the Enlightenment. Soviet Russia's treatment of dissidents, however gratuitously brutal and vengeful, is only the other side of the philanthropic coin stamped by men like Descartes, Locke, and Virchow. Law courts that, *now,* accept pleas of innocence on the grounds that criminal deeds rooted deep in character are really only the results of alcohol usage, can, in the future condemn sincere political dissidents to drug therapy without any contradiction.

16. Descartes had a clear notion of the need for the concept of molecules composed of more elementary particles of matter to explain numerous physiological processes. Instead of "atoms," however, Descartes had a concept of minute agglomerations of matter that act in a way that is distinct from the actions of the immediately surrounding matter— for example, the eddies in a swiftly flowing stream are discrete neighborhoods of water particles that act in concert, even though they are surrounded on all sides by more water. However, modern physics, in which atoms are defined probabilistically, is something like what Descartes had in mind.

For an interesting treatment of the "psychobiology" of this section, compare Gueroult, *Etudes sur Descartes*, Ch. IX, passim. James Collins, in his *Descartes' Philosophy of Nature* (Monograph No. 5, Oxford, 1971), pp. 22–24, treats this question as a problem of the history of ideas!

17. Descartes' proof of the immortality of the human soul consists ultimately of remarking that all so-called vital functions of the living body are organic functions. As a consequence, the soul is not ever, strictly speaking, alive; *ergo*, it can never die. (Cf. Plato, the *Republic*, Bk. X, 608c–610d, for a strictly "physiological" proof of the immortality of the soul.) See also Gueroult, *Etudes sur Descartes*, pp. 38–40, for a discussion of the soul and the mechanism it somehow inhabits.

18. From the interpretation of Descartes for which I now argue, the "substantial distinctness" of body from soul refers to its *powers*. I argue that the soul's power to perceive *anything* presupposes its powers in conjunction with those of the body, i.e., their union. (Cf. Gueroult, *Etudes sur Descartes*, and Collins, *Descartes' Philosophy of Nature*, pp. 29–34, 80–87.)

19. In his *Second Responses* (Vol. IXA, pp. 121–122), Descartes said that the *Medita-*

tions proceeded analytically, i.e., in the way that shows "how effects depend on their causes [*comment les effets dependent des causes*]." This procedure forced him to prove the real existence of what is given ("les effets"). Thus, his treatment in the *Meditations* of soul *sans* body means only that soul is proven to exist (through the "I think") before body is proven to exist. For the more or less standard treatment of the question, see Collins, *Descartes' Philosophy of Nature* pp. 42–45, 61–65, 68–69; and Sylvie Romanowski, *L'Illusion Chez Descartes* (Paris: Editions Klincksiech, 1974), pp. 61–63.

20. In close agreement with this analysis, Article 7 of the *Principles* (Vol. VIII, p. 7, l. 5–7) states that "it is repugnant" for us to suppose that what thinks does not exist at the time it thinks. *Repugnat*, in Latin, means both "is distasteful" and "is logically contradictory." "Distasteful" or "disagreeable" is obviously the primary meaning, and "logically contradictory" a derived meaning. Indeed, the French translation, which was thoroughly revised by Descartes himself, says (Vol. IXB, p. 27) "for it is so distasteful for us to conceive. . . ." In French, *repugnance* never means "logically contradictory"; it means "distasteful" or "disagreeable." Hence, in his strange and famous argument to "prove" his own existence, Descartes certainly means, whatever else, to characterize the thing that thinks as the sort of thing to which the perception of contradiction is fundamentally distasteful. In other words, the thinking thing naturally rejects what is inherently confused. It is for similar reasons that we can speak of man's will or impulse to clear perception, since the perception of a thing and its opposite together provide the very type of a confused perception. To deny the force of this argument, the reader must be willing to say that Descartes, the Frenchman, knew what *repugnat* meant in Latin, but that he did not know what *repugnance* meant in French.

21. On the other hand, he addressed himself somewhat differently to the notion of corporeal ideas in his *Second Responses* (Vol. VII, p. 160, l. 19, to p. 161, l. 3):

And so I do not call those bare images depicted upon the corporeal imagination [*phantasia*] ideas; indeed, I do not here in any way call those things ideas in so far as they are in the corporeal imagination which is depicted in some part of the brain, but only in so far as they inform the mind itself when turned to that part of the brain.

Thus, in his response to objections raised to his *Meditations*, not only did Descartes include under the name "idea" bare images depicted upon the corporeal organ of imagination, but also he even calls those images "ideas" only insofar as they inform the mind when it is paying attention to that part of the brain.

For a somewhat different light on this question, see Gueroult, *Etudes sur Descartes*, pp. 36–37; and Jonathan Rée, *Descartes* (New York: Pica Press, 1975), pp. 83–84.

22. This is Pavlov's "what is it?" reflex (Pavlov, *Conditioned Reflexes*, p. 12).

23. It is not inaccurate to contrast science after Descartes with philosophy before Descartes by saying that the "objective" science of the Enlightenment cannot be characterized as an erotic undertaking, whereas philosophy prior to Descartes was, as Plato described so eloquently, erotic from its very conception. This erotic element in philosophy was very strong as late in 1619 in Kepler's *Epitome of Copernican Astronomy*, Book IV [trans. Charles Glen Wallis in *Great Books of the Western World*, R. M. Hutchins and Mortimer J. Adler, eds. (Chicago, London, Toronto: Encyclopedia Brittanica, Inc., 1952), pp. 848–851]. Kepler was, so to speak, the last of the ancients and the first of the moderns among scientists.

For an astonishingly faithful repetition of Descartes' analysis of the emotions, see Constance Holden, "Behavioral Medicine: An Emergent Field," *Science* 209 (July 25, 1980): 479–481. However, although the author and her references thought that they were replacing Cartesian categories—they were all faithfully recapitulating his *Passions!*

24. Addressing the question of how the body acts against the soul, we point out that

the soul has the power, through the will, to use its body to represent to itself things that it has never seen before. Symbolic mathematics and all disciplines based on ingenuity in creating symbols are based on that power. However, the exercise of that power presupposes the politically guaranteed freedom for each man to use his own reason (*sa raison*); for Descartes, as for Copernicus' Rheticus, this freedom is seen as an ethical imperative that is pre-political: it is, so to speak, a natural imperative. Its effectiveness or lack of it in a polity then becomes the fundamental measure of its excellence for those superior new orders of which d'Alembert said Descartes was the founder.

As for Rheticus, see *Three Copernican Treatises* [trans., with an introduction and notes, by Edward Rosen (New York: Columbia University Press, 1939)], in which "The *Narratio Prima* of Rheticus" (pp. 107–196) is prefaced with "Free in mind must be he who desires to have understanding," and attributed by Rheticus to Alcinous. (There is reason to believe that Rheticus got this sentiment from the *Didaskalos*, written circa 150 A.D., perhaps by Albinus.) At any rate, that sentiment provided the war cry of liberalism in the sixteenth to eighteenth centuries. (The Greek for this is, interestingly enough: δεῖ δ ἐλευθεριον εἶναι τῆ γυώμη τὸν μέλλοντα φιλοσοφεῖν.)

25. Indeed, the pineal body is located medially and rostral to the inferior and supperior calliculae, seemingly commanding the sulcus lateralis cerebri, which connects ventricle III with ventricle IV. Because the dissection techniques of Descartes' time led him to locate the gland imprecisely, he did not realize that the pineal body is *exterior* to the brain mass.

26. Thomas Steele Hall has very well translated the work, as *Treatise of Man* [French text with translation and commentary (Cambridge: Harvard University Press, 1972)]. Hall's commentary is occasionally very fine; most often, however, he does not follow his own good intuitions. Concerning our present development, see Hall's commentary, pp. 22–32.

27. As a consequence of Descartes' doctrine that all preceptions are "jogged" into consciousness by occasional perturbations in the brain fluid (or whatever), looking at, listening to, smelling, tasting, and touching have no real meaning. This is perhaps one of the principal roots of a certain aspect of our contemporary ennui: we are locked up in a windowless room with no hope of even glimpsing the world around us. The taste for horror films that is characteristic of the technocratically minded progressives today might well have something to do with this doctrine. Modern, technocratic man is *bored*.

28. Descartes proudly wore his sword as the badge of his birth into the (minor) nobility of France, and he knew how to use it with considerable skill, indeed once overcoming a band of brigands on a small boat who set out to rob him. He was very proud of that fight—as well he might have been! There is a deep tension in his work between nobility and egality, a tension that all scientific attempts to popularize science have not overcome. If science is the preceptor of humanity, then those humans who are exceedingly adept at learning it are somehow natural preceptors.

29. Descartes' doctrine of the will, however, still seems to suggest that, when the will to attend or imagine some new thing affects the pineal gland in a given way, we in fact do have a case of a motion in matter that cannot be explained by Cartesian mechanics as based on his three laws of nature. However, perplexingly enough, we have two sets of such laws, both from Descartes' own hand. The first is contained in the 1633 (but posthumously published) *The World* and is identical to the second set, contained in the 1644 *Principles*, except for one provision in one of the laws: namely, in the *Principles*, Part II, Articles 40–52, Descartes imagined a case involving the meeting of two bodies where that meeting does not alter the amount of force in one of the two bodies. In particular, he said there that we can suppose two bodies to hit one another, where one is very much larger than the other; it can then happen that, although the larger body causes motion in the smaller, it

does not subtract any force from the larger. In the earlier, unpublished edition of the laws, this is not the case: any body that causes motion in another body thereby loses just as much of its own motion as it gives to the other.

Why did Descartes' view of this point change? It is likely that it may have been because of his questions concerning the size of the pineal gland relative to the size of the particles of animal spirits in the brain that strike it. For, if the soul "wills" or "attends," a very small deflection of the gland could result, which in turn could cause a very small deflection of a very small number of very small particles (without contravening this special sub-case, found only in the *Principles*), if, that is, the body were in a "hair-trigger" state of readiness to react to a very small action. (Again, we see the importance of the disposition of the body's parts: i.e., if it is not disposed in such and such a way, all the willing in the world will not cause any significant effect in it—the mere volition to play a difficult instrument is nothing without preparation.)

Nor should the reader too hastily reject this solution as unworthy of Descartes, that is, as being too artificial and limited in scope. What else do we do, when we take a limit, t, other than say that the absolute value of the difference $(t-x)$ becomes arbitrarily small— "less than any epsilon," as L'Hospital's rule has it?

30. This view, which holds that for every psychological event there is a unique neurological foundation, is one reason why we today consider that all theory directly concerns practice and, ultimately, that each and every thought in some way is revealed through an action in the body. Hence we find in a recent article in *Scientific American* [E. V. Evarts, "Brain Mechanism in Movement," Vol. 229 (July, 1973): 96–103] the conclusion that:

> In the past most attempts to describe the higher functions of the brain have been made in terms of how sensory imputs are processed from the receptor on up to the higher cortical centers. A strong case for an alternative approach has been made by Roger W. Sperry of the California Institute of Technology. I shall end with his comment: "Instead of regarding motor activity as being subsidary, that is, something to carry out, serve and satisfy the demands of the higher centers, we reverse this tendency and look upon the mental activity as only a means to an end, where the end is better regulation of overt response. Cerebration essentially serves to bring into motor behavior additional refinement, increased direction towards distant, future goals, and greater overall adaptiveness and survival value. The evolutionary increase in man's capacity for perception, feeling, ideation, imagination and the like may be regarded not so much as an end in itself as something that has enabled us to behave, to act, more wisely and efficiently."

Even with almost no change of technical vocabulary, Descartes could have written that paragraph.

31. Again, Descartes located the pineal body at the rostral portion of the sulcus lateralis cerebri, which connected ventricle III with ventricle IV.

32. These sections may seem dreary in their detail to many readers, but the importance of the study of the present foundations of our ethics makes it imperative that we investigate Descartes' scientific doctrine of the soul—Descartes' above all others, since it is his mechanistic biology, his neurophysiological psychobiology, that has overwhelmingly tempted enlightened scientists, such as Freud and Skinner, to mention only a few, to throw out the soul. (Freud's "psyche" is no soul.) A glance at Skinner's *Walden II* will indicate what that loss can entail.

S. V. Keeling substitutes "self" for soul, in *Descartes* (New York and Oxford: Oxford University Press, 1968), pp. 290–301.

33. As we argue in a later section, Descartes' notion of the unity of the soul is one of

the many ways he used to disassociate himself from the Christian doctrine of the soul, which is based on texts like Paul's *Letter to the Romans.* The reader should never forget that the soul *is* the mind for Descartes.

For an interesting treatment of this question from the tradition of "Ideengeschichte," see Detlef Mahnke, *Der Aufbau des philosophischen Wissens nach Rene Descartes* [Epimeleia Beitraege zur Philosophie, Band 8 (Munich, Salzburg: Verlag Aton Pustet, 1967), Ch. IV].

34. Affirmation and denial are acts of will. Consonant with what is remarked below concerning the "will to perceive," conception is contingent upon absolute clarity of perception. As is pointed out in the last section, clarity of perception involves the distinctness of the tools at our disposal with which we can solve problems—be those tools anatomical, the figures of geometry, or the symbols of algebraic equations.

35. Descartes here particularly stressed that the objective reality of an idea is that aspect of the being of the object of the idea that is represented by the idea. (If Descartes thought that some aspect of the object of the idea is not representable, he did not explicitly say so.) There is thus some aspect of the being of the objects of ideas that is, for Descartes, representable. Although Descartes did not say as much explicitly, it seems reasonable to infer that the representable being of an object must be what in fact causes some specific representation of itself, *and no other,* merely because it is what it is. Purely intelligible objects of thought must also admit of being so represented that the perception of the representation necessarily involves a perception of the being of the thing. In the case of a machine, the aspect of our idea of the machine that is representative of its being is precisely our perception of what it does. For, as Descartes said in the Summary to the French translation of the *Meditations,* a clever man can figure out the inventor's plan of a machine if he sees what the machine can do. As Descartes explained it, the idea of an externally existing machine *represents* the purely intellectual artifice that was required for the inventor to invent it. That intellectual artifice represents an aspect of the being of this machine here in front of me. The best representation of any clear and distinct idea is the representation that most clearly reveals the operations of the object of the idea. In only one instance, perhaps, does it happen that the representation of the object of an idea exactly corresponds to the idea itself; the instance of our ideas of motion, figure, and magnitude. Here ideas and their objects are presumed to be entirely similar in form. Descartes defined this case in defining the "formal reality of ideas," where he said that the being of the thing is "in itself" such as we perceive it through the representation of its idea (Vol. VII, p. 161).

The literature on this question is extensive, but for a good general view, see Wilhelm Halbfass, *Descartes' Frage nach der Existenz der Welt* (Meisenheim am Glan: Verlag Anton Hain, 1968), especially Ch. 4.

36. For example, if a man wishes to consider together the class of equal quantities that are related to each other as squares to rectangles, he need only represent to himself a right triangle inscribed in a semi-circle with a line x perpendicular to the hypotenuse (which forms the diameter of the semi-circle). This divides that diameter into segments a and b. x being the mean proportional between a and b, $x^2 = b$ times a. In this situation, he disregards everything about the figure except for that one property. If, however, he wishes to determine how to construct a rectangle on a given line such that the rectangle is equal in area to a given square, he uses the form $x^2 = a$ times b and solves for a or b. In the former case his imagination is not preoccupied by the multitude of cases that exemplify the rule; in the latter case, he directs his attention to one case out of the multitude and disregards all others.

In the former case, the figure itself, considered only as a right triangle whose hypotenuse is intersected by a line dropped from the right angle, represents the relation obtaining between all rectangles and the squares equal to them.

For another approach, see Romanowski, *L'Illusion Chez Descartes,* Ch. II, "Du symbole a l'algebre. . . ."

37. The necessity for a philosophy of history can be directly inferred from this section, and, with it, the "secularization" of theology. Karl Jaspers' work is of interest here; see his *Descartes und die Philosophie* (Berlin: Verlag Walter de Gruyter, 1956), pp. 95–98.

PART II

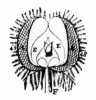

COMPOUND BODIES
Living and
Nonliving Systems

*The aim of biological science is to formulate the laws
governing cells, organisms and societies of organisms. At
the molecular level, this process has led to studies of the
crystallization of proteins . . . Workers at other levels
study the electrical properties of nerve, the nervous control
of endocrine secretion, the function of kidney tubules, the
emission of behavior units by pigeons in Skinner boxes, or
the transmission of news and gossip among the members of
human groups.*
—J. M. Reiner. *The Organism as an Adaptive Control
System*

*U.S. Urged to Rely on the Behavioral Sciences: Report
asks Government to Utilize Insights to Help in Formulation of Policies.*
—*New York Times* (September 3, 1968, headline)

Introduction

DESCARTES IS NOT famous today because of what he said about what we consider the subject of ethics, let alone because of what he said about what we consider the subject matter of political theory. Yet such highly sophisticated political thinkers as d'Alembert refer to him as a prime founder of a vast new "political order," and Descartes himself said that his physics is the foundation for an exalted ethics. What, then, is it about Descartes' work that would so impress these thinkers as being fundamentally revolutionary in the sphere of human interrelations? It is not likely that they were all simply misguided in their judgments; it is much more likely that they read Descartes' texts in a way that, for whatever reason, has fallen into disuse.

In Part II, we argue that they did indeed see something crucial that has been either ignored or undervalued by later commentators on Descartes; namely, the vast cosmological horizons of the foundations of the Enlightenment's new theory of the correct, scientifically defensible way in which humans should relate to one another.

The particular goal of Chapter 3, is to bring to light the theoretical link between Descartes' general natural law theory, with which he accounts for the generation of the heavens, and his ethics, that is, his theory of the individual human being in the society of other humans, which he clearly intended to serve as a permanent replacement for the political science that was based on Aristotle's *Politics* as modified by Christian teachings such as those found in Augustine's *City of God*. Descartes, no less than his contemporaries and his intellectual heirs up to the French revolution, was absolutely clear that the physics and cosmology of an era form a crucial element in the way humans look at themselves.

In the Biblical account of Genesis we are told that the Creator created humankind in a definite act that was equally as distinct as the other acts by which He had created the rest of the world. According to the account in Genesis, the creation of humankind is an act entirely distinct from the creation of the rest of the world. One of the most consequential of Descartes' teachings of which we are the heirs is that humankind and other living things in the world, indeed, humankind and all the rest of the world, living or nonliving, are part of one and the same process of evolution, or coming-to-be. There was, for Descartes, no single, simple act of creation of human beings that was distinct from all other acts of creation. His theological defense of his teaching is simple: God is perfect and simple, and hence His creation is identical to conservation or preservation. Conservation of state is a *theological* postulate for Descartes, and it is his (physicist's) way of referring to Deity's provident care of His creation—both human and otherwise. Deity manifests His providential care for His creation in His preservation, i.e., *conservation,* of that creation both in its disposition and in its laws of nature.

In this part, we first examine Descartes' theory of the *gradual* evolution of the solar systems that form the heavens; then we show how the same laws of nature that Descartes uses to explain the way the heavens were generated are used by him to explain the generation of the human body; next we examine the natural processes by means of which the naturally evolved human body is endowed with consciousness, and, in particular, with the capacity to sense light; and, finally, we examine the relation between the capacity to sense light and the capacity to do analytic mathematics.

In short, we examine Descartes' claim that he can first apply his laws of nature to general physical matter in one way (deriving solar systems with luminous suns in the center and planets around them) and then, applying those same laws of nature to bodies that have evolved into organisms strictly in accord with the laws of nature, derive humans who both think (*analytically*) and perceive.

CHAPTER 3

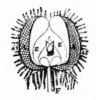

Celestial Bodies
and Civil Bodies

*Thus we have evidence of a truly wide cosmic evolution
from hydrogen atoms to* Homo . . . *We have in cosmic
evolution a fundamental principle of growth that affects
everything—atoms as well as biological species, stars,
nebulae, space-time, and matter-energy—in brief, everything that we can name, everything material and non-
material. It is around this concept that we might be able to
build revised philosophies and religions.*
—Harlow Shapley, Director, Harvard University
Observatory, *Beyond the Observatory*

THE SCIENTIFIC HEAVEN

OUR UNDERSTANDING OF what happens in heaven, in the heavens,
has long been thought to affect profoundly what happens to men on
earth. This is certainly the case in Genesis and in Job, in Hesiod's *Works
and Days* and in his *Theogony,* in Plato's *Statesman,* and in the splendid
myth at the end of the *Phaedrus.* It is, however, no less true of the so-
called physical investigators—from Anaxagoras, whose Mind begins to
move all things by instituting a (quasi-"Cartesian") whirlwind in matter
that then separates out all things, down to our contemporary cosmolo-
gists, who find the absolute origins of all things in some immense cosmic
explosion that (altogether unintentionally) echoes the Epicurean cata-
clysm. The events that take place "up there" somehow are always ultimately understood as "celestial." If those events are violent and fiery,
then men's view of the human condition tends to be pessimistic, or, at
least cynical; if those events are merciful and providential with respect to
humankind, the human condition is viewed as, at worst, only a trial
through which future celestial heroes must pass to prove their eternal
worth.

It was Democritus, it is said, who first called man a *microcosmos,* a miniature of the great world in which we live. However, man lives in two worlds: on the one hand, each of us lives in the great world, our "physical" environment, and, on the other hand, each person lives in this or that city-state or nation. Few of us will deny that we are in some essential way "re-naturalized" by our human environment to the extent that we have, as it were, two natures at once. Insofar as our human environment is profoundly reflected by our way of being a human, each of us is a microcosm of that human environment, almost by definition. Indeed, comparative anthropology could be said to be a sort of "comparative cosmology"; rituals and practices that form psychologically crucial parts of the growing-up of the cannibal societies of New Guinea would almost certainly drive a decent American businessman and his equally decent wife quite mad. A question therefore arises about the relation between the social environment as the macrocosm of which we are each a microcosm, and the physical environment as that macrocosm: to which do we look in order to discover the macrocosm with respect to which each of us is a microcosm?

Or is this the correct way of putting the question? Perhaps we would do better to ask in what way the human environment, which is certainly the immediate macrocosm for each of us, is related to that "macro-macrocosm" that is the physical environment. Once that is established, then we can expect that our relation to our physical environment will emerge via our relation to our human environment.

The relationship of the human environment to the physical environment, however, does not necessarily imply that there is some direct way in which each of us constitutes a microcosm of that physical world. A glance at Fustel de Coulanges' *The Ancient City* makes this abundantly clear.[1] Fustel says that the term 'father,' for instance, did not primarily refer to a physical progenitor; rather, the father was the priest of the family hearth. Again, in Rome, the word *mundus,* which is usually translated as "world," did not at first refer to the physical world, but to the pit at the center of the city into which were thrown clods of earth that had been brought from the lands out of which the founders of the city had come; over this pit the city altar was then built, the *focus,* on which the sacrifices for the good of the whole city were performed. Indeed, the rites of foundation of the city were such that the whole area of the city proper was a *templum* (temple), a "place cut off," in which certain prescribed rites and laws were to be scrupulously observed. (In many ancient cities, murder of a citizen was an act of treason.) Outside the walls of that temple-city was χώρα, or "space," perhaps best translated as "outer space."

In another example, among the Jalé cannibals of New Guinea the mature warrior-males wear penis-sheaths of a painted gourd that, when worn, very much resembles the *phallus erectus.* This is certainly more than sympathetic magic, and perhaps something entirely other. For, even if the gourd were chosen as being a "natural" repository for seed, the sympathetic magic that derived its use as a penis-sheath is understood by that tribe to work only because *they* use it; the rituals and taboos of one tribe are often completely senseless to members of another tribe. The "magic" thus comes from the fact that "we" use it. It was often the case in "primitive" societies that the gods of a given state were exceedingly antipathetical to other states, and that foreigners could not, without grave consequences, even look at the foreign city's cult images. In the case of the Jalé, it seems that the gourd replaces the "natural" generative member with an artifact chosen by custom and indicating the ascendancy of their custom and convention over the promptings of "nature." Many citizens and thinkers, in short, seemed to have definitively rejected larger nature as the model for their societies: their "city" was *the* macrocosm.

As far back as Anaxagoras—if not Xenophanes, who is sometimes said to have been the first of the Greek thinkers to say that "the All is one"—there have been men who looked to the larger world for that macrocosm of which individual humans are the microcosms. Whatever else Descartes might have had in mind when he chose to begin philosophy via the way of total doubt, he certainly disassociated all individuals from the lateral associations in the civil macrocosm. He thereby exposed them to the (beneficent or maleficent) influence of the "heavenly powers." That is, the way from total doubt, through knowledge of the existence of God, to any conceivable human order implies that the immediate model for the human microcosm will always be the celestial order, the great world, and that the civil order will be an enlarged reflection of the human microcosm defined within the great order. The civic order is derived from the human order. With Descartes, the civil order ceases to be in any way a macrocosm for the individual human; each of us is a microcosm of the *universal* order, and of it alone.[2] The universal order, together with its laws of nature, will provide the only authority to which any individual citizen can, by "natural right," always appeal any positive statutes of individual civil orders. Descartes, however, saw the danger of this ordering, in that he, from the beginning of the disassociation effected by doubt, envisaged essentially malevolent celestial powers to whom no human would want to look for rule. He saw, that is, the great danger of directly replacing the civil order with the great world of the heavens as the paradigm. The civil order, however imperfect, has helped human life to flourish in spite of natural cataclysms, droughts, and the like. However, for Descartes the celestial powers are ultimately good relative to men; the natural order is preordained in a way that allows humans to be happy within it—happy at least, to the degree that they succeed in discovering exactly what that preordained order is and live in harmony with it. If and when a society is founded on such a cosmological model, its governing laws will be to the participants in it what the general laws of nature of the great world are to the "parts" of that great world.

This is not to say that the rejection of the lateral association between humans (e.g., friendship, love, and the like) in favor of the vertical connection between individuals and the heavens was new with Anaxagoras, Xenophanes, or any Greek. To the contrary, the story of Abraham's willingness to sacrifice Isaac, the beloved son of his extreme old age, at God's command seems to provide a true example of this connection.[3] This story is taken by St Paul both as the figure of the supremacy of faith over law and to show that the way to "righteousness" is not necessarily through statutory law, even if it is God-given (Romans, chapter 4.)

Nor do we suggest that Descartes was significantly Pauline in his cosmology; Descartes' Deity is accessible to humans as rational beings. Rather, he seems to subscribe to a blend of Anaxagorian cosmology and a profoundly altered Christian teaching concerning providence. At any rate, according to the Platonic notice in *Phaedo* (97B–99D), although for Anaxagoras there was a first cause, Mind, that disposed things in an intelligible way (i.e., by means of a whirlwind or vortex), this cause did not also, because it was the cause that it was, dispose them in a way that was clearly the *best* way. It is precisely this point that so dismayed Socrates—the notion of an intelligible cause that does not act in the *best* way. Descartes, as we shall see, called it a crime to hold something similar to this incomplete view. Rejecting, for his own reasons, the Socratic-Platonic completion of Anaxagorian cosmology, Descartes chose in its place a part of the Judeo-Christian teaching concerning providential and beneficent disposition of creation. (Descartes quoted from Diogenes Laertes' *Lives of Eminent Philosophers,* which contains a lengthy notice of Anaxagoras' doctrines, and he almost certainly had read some of Plato.)

In the dedicatory letter to the Doctors of the Faculty of Sacred Theology at the Sorbonne with which he begins his *Meditations,* Descartes quoted from St. Paul (Romans, chapter 1, and from chapter 13 of *La Sagesse* (The Wisdom of Solomon, as it is called in the Apocrypha of the King James Version, but which is included in the Canon of the Vulgate from which Descartes quoted). The quotations both concern creation as the manifestation of God's sovereignty such that (Wisd. of Sol. 13:8–9): "Nor ought they to be ignorant of these things; for if they are able to know so much and to value so highly the things of this world [*saeculum*], how is it possible that they have not discovered its lord more easily?" From Paul he quoted the passages in Romans 1:20 where Paul says of the things of this world, "What is known of God is manifest in them." In both places, the gist of the quotation from canonical scripture is that this created world, *saeculum,* manifests the Creator to such a degree that knowledge of the world leads to a realization of God as the creator of the world. [Plato, in his *Laws* (X, 886A–E), ridiculed this point at some length; he presented it as being put forth by a very decent, albeit somewhat simple-minded old man.] That view itself points to a doctrine that seems to entail for Descartes the idea of the gradual, evolutionary manifestation of God's power and preordination in the *saeculum,* as opposed to an instantaneous, epochal revelation in the *saeculum*—what John refers to as "the word became flesh." For Descartes, the eternal will of God, at least insofar as that will concerns the *saeculum,* is not manifested to men through prophets or even through an incarnation of the creative word of God; nor is it in books of sacred scripture that one will find it clearly manifested. Rather, it is in the progressively improving books of natural history, i.e., physics, that this manifestation will be found, and, once that natural history is read in such a way that it provides the model for human things in the same way that the books of sacred history and prophecy have hitherto been read, it will entirely supercede sacred scripture, and the books of human history will then themselves become a part of the corpus of natural history. (Psychobiography and psychohistory attempt just this.)

Less than a century after his death, and only three decades before the French Revolution, French encyclopedists were identifying Descartes as the founder of a whole new political philosophy that, when fully realized in real governments, would give to men better and more just governments than they had ever had before. About the same time these men in France were calling Descartes a new Lycurgus, others were engaged in defining a cosmology. Kant in 19755 published his *General Physics and Theory of the Heavens, or, An Essay on the Constitution and the Mechanical Origin of the Whole World-System treated according to the Newtonian Axioms.* Kant went on to publish a *Critique of Pure Reason,* a *Critique of Practical Reason,* a *Critique of Judgment,* a *Foundation of the Metaphysics of Morals,* and his *Eternal Peace,* section I of which has the subtitle, "The Natural Principle of the Political Order considered in Connection with the Idea of a Universal Cosmo-Political History." Similarly, Hobbes, whose *Concerning Body* precedes both his *Concerning the Citizen* and his *Leviathan,* and Rousseau, whose *Social Contract* is also indebted to Newtonian analysis and cosmology,[4] were making their cosmogeneses.

In Chapter III of his *Constitutional Government in the United States,* President Woodrow Wilson said:

The government of the United States was constructed upon . . . a
sort of unconscious copy of the Newtonian theory of the universe. In

our own day, whenever we discuss the structure or development of anything, whether in nature or in society, we consciously or unconsciously follow Mr. Darwin; but before Mr. Darwin, they followed Newton. Some single law, like the law of gravitation, swung each system of thought and gave it its principle of unity. Every sun, every planet, every free body in the spaces of the heavens, the world itself, is kept in its place and reined to its course by the attraction of bodies that swing with equal order and precision about it, themselves governed by the nice poise and balance of forces which give the whole system of the universe its symmetry and perfect adjustment . . .[5]

In short, if indeed these authors are the founding fathers of modern political theory, as they are generally claimed to be, then the political orders that their doctrines prescribed are truly cosmo-political, and the history of the last century and a half is the history of the results of the optimism generated by these cosmo-political doctrines. No one ever had a more optimistic view of the world and all that is in it than did the cosmo-political revolutionaries after Descartes. Speaking of that optimism, the historian Norman Hampson says:

Condorcet and Chastellux wrote general histories of civilization to demonstrate that scientific rationalism had rescued man from the obscurantism and superstition of the Middle Ages and established a sure basis for continuous social development. As Cordorcet expressed it, "Just as mathematics and the physical sciences perfect the crafts that we use to satisfy our simplest needs, is it not equally inherent in the necessary natural order that the progress of the moral and political sciences should have the same effect on the motives which direct our feelings and action?"

Hampson continues:

In view of a certain tendency to dismiss the optimism of the Enlightenment as the superficial effusion of a well-heeled salon society, it is worth pointing out that Condorcet was himself fleeing from the Terror, which was to drive him to suicide, when he wrote, "No limit has been set to the perfecting of human faculties . . . the progress of this perfectibility, henceforth independent of any force that would try to stop it, will continue as long as the globe on which nature has set us."[6]

Hampson is accurate in his assessment of the root of this optimism.

Another example of this remarkable optimism of the revolutionary age is to be found in A. W. Kinglake's account of the *coup d'état* of December, 1853, in France, engineered by and in the interest of the then-president of the Republic, Prince Charles Louis Napoleon Bonaparte. The Prince was determined to overthrow the republican form of government and to reinstate the empire—with himself as Emperor. As the troops at his command ranged around Paris, a small group of deputies

> went into the Fauborg St. Antoine, and strove to raise the peo-
> ple . . . More, it would seem, by their personal energy than by the
> aid of the people, these men threw up a slight barricade at the
> corner of the Rue St. Marguerite. Against this there marched a
> battalion of the 19th Regiment; and then there occurred a scene
> which may make one smile for a moment, and may then almost force
> one to admire the touching pedantry of brave men, who imagined
> that, without policy or warlike means, they could be strong with the
> mere strength of the law. Laying aside their fire-arms, and throwing
> across their shoulders the scarves which marked them as Representa-
> tives of the People, the Deputies ranged themselves in front of the
> barricade, and one of them, Charles Baudin, held ready in his hand
> the book of the Constitution. When the head of the column was
> within a few yards of the barricade, it was halted. For some moments
> there was silence. Law and Force had met. On the one side was the
> Code democratic, which France had declared to be perpetual; on the
> other a battalion of the line. Charles Baudin, pointing to his book,
> began to show what he held to be the clear duty of the battalion; but
> the whole basis of his argument was an assumption that the law
> ought to be obeyed; and it seems that the officer in command
> refused to concede what logicians call the "major premise," for,
> instead of accepting its necessary consequence, he gave an impatient
> sign. Suddenly the muskets of the front-rank men came down, came
> up, came level; and in another instant their fire pelted straight into
> the group of scarfed Deputies. Baudin fell dead, his head being
> shattered by more than one ball. One other was killed by the volley;
> several more were wounded. The book of the constitution had fallen
> to the ground, and the defenders of the law recurred to their fire-
> arms. They shot the officer who had caused the death of their
> comrade and questioned their major premise."[7]

This account is not given with any cynical relish by its author, King-lake, nor here cited with any cynical relish; rather, it describes the actions of the deputies—adults all—whose fathers had forcibly deposed the hereditary monarch of the oldest throne in Europe and then cut off his head. On what possible grounds could the sons of such fathers feel that armed soldiers would be stopped by a mere book, the five-year-old constitution of 1848? It seems very likely that their fearlessness, that "pendantic bravery," was supported by or grew out of their faith in the manifest superiority of democracy over any other form of polity; it seems very likely that their fearlessness, in the face of their own fathers' regicide, implies an anthropological postulate of enormous moment—

that human nature is so constructed that no one who is even merely conscious of the option of living in a democratic, republican regime will, or could, reject it in favor of any other form of polity.

Part II of this work indicates in some of its details that evolutionary natural history. We end it with some remarks on Descartes' theory of man, the unique creature who evolved, for Descartes, from tbe luminous, sightless stars into the warmblooded, volitional, ingenious and, at best, analytic creature who, although he does not glow as his starry points of origin do, possesses a light of nature that, when rightly used, permits him a foresight within the realm of things disposed to be known, and hence obtained.

THE LAW OF NATURE AND THE
LAW OF THE LIVING BODY

In the Apostle Paul's Letter to the Romans (Rom. 7:21–25) we find:

> I discover this principle then: that when I want to do the right, only the wrong is within my reach. In my inmost self I delight in the law of God, but I perceive that there is in my bodily members a different law, fighting against the law that my reason approves and making me a prisoner under the law that is in my members, the law of sin. [New English Bible]

We know that Descartes knew this passage; he quoted it in the "Introductory Letter" with which he began the *Meditations* and in which he addressed a passage in which Paul says that idolaters are inexcusable, since creation itself manifests the creator, thus making the production of idols manifestly foolish. Descartes also discussed these two laws, the one active in his members, the other rational, in Article 47 of the *Passions,* whose title is, "What that battle really is which is commonly imagined to be taking place between the higher and lower parts of the soul"—a very clear echo of that passage in Paul. However, Descartes gave a very different account of the matter:

> All the battles which are commonly imagined to take place between the lower part of the soul (which is called the sensitive part) and the higher part (which is called the reasonable part)—or as they also refer to it sometimes, between our natural appetites and our will— consist in the opposition between the movements which the body (by means of the volatile, spiritous part of the blood) and the soul (by means of its will) tend to excite simultaneously in the pineal gland. For, there is only one soul in us, and that soul has no diversity of parts: the same soul which is sensitive is reasonable, and all its appetites are its volitions. An error has been committed in making it

play different roles [*divers personnages*] which are usually contrary to one another, an error which only arises because the soul's functions have not been correctly distinguished from those of the body—for it is only the body to which we should attribute all those things which can be found in us in opposition to our reason. Consequently, there is no combat in all this except that the little gland in the middle part of the head can be pushing toward one side by the action of the soul on it, and towards a different side by the action of the animal spirits (which are only bodies, as we have said before). Therefore, it sometimes happens that the two impulses are contrary, and that the stronger neutralizes the effect of the weaker.

That is, Descartes here very carefully identified Paul's "law that my reason approves" with the force of the will to move the gland; he very carefully identified Paul's "law that is in my members, the law of sin," with the force that animal spirits have to move the gland in a direction opposite to that in which the force of the will moves it. Neuroanatomical analysis becomes the sword with which the new epoch will do battle with the ethics of Christendom, and the new foundation for Descartes' own ethics will become the medical textbook of the physiology and anatomy of the nervous system. It is not too bold to identify this juncture in time as one of the, if not the, true beginnings of modernity.

This juncture, together with the modern tradition that follows it, can be characterized to a significant degree by its rejection of what can fairly be called Paul's "psychobiology" in favor of what can just as fairly be called Descartes' "medically based ethics"—and what is medically based ethics but a form of psychobiology? The medical ethics of Descartes, entirely founded in his own mechanistic psychobiology, proceeds by identifying the law in the members as the law by which the Creator of heaven and Earth both created the heavens and the Earth and subsequently rules them: that is, for Descartes, Deity both creates and rules heaven and Earth according to laws of nature. Paul's "law that is in my members, the law of sin," is, for Descartes and the tradition following him, the laws of nature, which have nothing of sin in them. Furthermore, Paul's "law that my reason approves" is nowhere better exemplified, for Descartes and the tradition that follows him, than in those very same rational laws of nature. They are simultaneously the rational guides in accordance with which we exercise our free will and the guides that rule our physical bodies. They are the laws of medicine, mechanics, and ethics.

As is seen most clearly in Article 34 of the *Passions,* the laws of physics and the free will of the human being work together in the immediate neighborhood of the pineal gland; according to Descartes, whenever we exercise our power to will, we will precisely what our sense of our own body informs us we are most immediately prepared to accomplish, namely, because appropriate organ systems of our body are most perfectly disposed and prepared to perform the action that we perceive and about which our will is concerned. Descartes calls that sense of our own body the passions of the soul. Although we can desire whatever we can imagine is good for us to possess, we only will what we are aware we can do given the state of our body (or of tools that it can use to obtain what we will). For instance, a non-mathematician only *desires* to solve a difficult mathematical problem; an accomplished mathematician *wills* to address himself to it. Thus, for Descartes, free will is the source and origin of all action that requires a precise disposition in physical matter to be effective. Desire without the means to attain its object is, at best, frustration, and, at worst, the fantasy of a slave. (As we have seen, because of the divine preordination of the universe, we can, in a fashion, will anything and everything of which we have consciousness!) Thus, mechanics, which teaches us how to dispose the parts of matter into a machine—i.e., in a manner that gives us a desired result *at a future time*— is a sort of science of the will; that is, mechanics teaches us how to dispose bits of physical matter so that we get a machine that always does what we will it to do because it is always prepared to do so. Therefore, mechanics is the science that transforms desire into will, and technology is thereby elevated to the exalted status of an artful, intentional extension of the creation that ultimately produced humans who are ingenious enough to build machines. Ingenuity is will willing the general preconditions for will: Nature is, for Descartes, above all, ingenious.

In his doctrine of the natural institution by means of which impulses in the nerves leading to the brain are transformed into sensations—some of which concern shapes, motions, etc., and others of which, the passions, concern our awareness of our organic disposition to act in relation to those perceptions—the law of sin in the members becomes translated into an essential part of the reason; to feel and to perceive, for Descartes, are, each of them, to think.

Descartes' "laws of nature" are the very same laws "that my reason approves" *and* the "law that is in my members, the law of sin"; that is to say, for Descartes there is no "law of sin" because "the law that is in my members" is the same law "that my reason approves."

Descartes first gave his laws of nature in his 1633 *Treatise on Man,* in which he introduced and developed his concept of a humanoid robot, which he refers to as "an automaton of clay." This robot is exactly like a real human except that it lacks a soul; its only law is natural law, the law of its members. He said of the robot that it is even alive. Thus "natural" men are live bodies that are entirely governed by the general laws of nature. They are real parts of the physical, nonconventional, nonreligious world. He next gave another, slightly altered—as we shall see, for the worse—version of the laws of nature in his *magnum opus, Principles of Philosophy*, which, to judge from its title, addresses directly things that, above all, are what "my reason approves."

In the Preface to the *Principles*, which has a detailed discussion of the laws of nature in Part II, Descartes wrote that the book is *incomplete* without an explanation of "each of the more particular bodies which are on the Earth . . . and principally of the nature of man" (Vol. IXB, p. 17, l. 3–6). It is only in those two treatises, in the 1633 (suppressed) *Treatise on Man* and in the 1644 *Principles of Philosophy*, that we find Descartes giving clear and exhaustive statements of the laws of nature.

Descartes' description of his proposed arrangement of the parts of the *Principles* is very interesting. He said that "the first part contains the Principles of knowledge which is what one can call first Philosophy or even Metaphysics . . ." (Vol. IXB, p. 16, l. 13–16). He then said that "the other three parts contain all that is most general in physics, that is, the explication of the first laws or Principles of Nature" (ibid., l. 18–21). The parallel between the two descriptions, then, is between "the Principles of knowledge" and "the first laws or Principles of Nature"—between *les Principes de la connoissance* and *premieres loix ou des Principes de la Nature*. Since he stated in the title of Article 49 of the *Passions* that "the force of the soul does not suffice without the knowledge [*connoissance*] of the truth," even the individual man's willful direction of his own acts and, ultimately, thoughts, depends on certain principles of knowledge that seem to govern individuals in a way strikingly parallel to the way in which the "primary laws or Principles of Nature" govern matter: that is, since willing presupposes knowledge, Descartes implied that absolute knowledge of the truth will absolutely fix the will, if the world surrounding men is understood and disposed in strict conformity to certain laws or principles of nature that apply to bodies both animate and inanimate, both natural and social.

Descartes also stated, however, that he planned in the future [*cy-apres*] to include in the *Principles* plants, minerals, and, principally, men, and then "finally, to treat exactly of Medicine, Ethics, and of Mechanics [*enfin, traitter exactement de la Medicine, de la Morale, et des Mechaniques*]" (ibid, p. 17, l. 2). Furthermore, in a letter to Chanut dated February 26, 1649, Descartes related ethics and mechanics:

> But, although I have received, as an entirely unmerited favor, the letter which that incomparable princess [Christine, Queen of Sweden] has deigned to write me, I wonder [*i'admire*] that she should have gone to such trouble about it; but, I don't wonder in the same way that she has wished to go to the trouble to read something of my *Principles*, since I am persuaded that it contains several truths that might elsewhere be found with difficulty. One could say that these truths are only of little importance, touching matters concerning

Physics, which seems to have nothing in common with what a Queen ought to know. But in so far as the mind of this Queen is capable of all things, and since these truths of Physics are part of the foundations of the highest and most perfect Ethics [*de la plus haute et plus parfaite Morale*], I dare to hope that she will take some satisfaction from knowing them. [Vol. V, p. 290, l. 15, to p. 291, l. 2].

Given such a thought, can "the laws or Principles" of medicine and ethics be distinct from the laws of mechanics? Are we to suppose that Descartes' Man is medically healthy, socially ethical, and intellectually speculative outside any interpersonal context? Outside any structured body of humans, such as Queen Christine's Sweden? If so, why send the *Principles* to the Queen?

As we have seen, in his "Preliminary Discourse" to Diderot's *Encylopedia of 1751*, d'Alembert says that:

Descartes dared at least to show intelligent minds how to throw off the yoke of scholasticism, of opinions, of authority—in a word, of prejudices and barbarism. And by that revolt whose fruits we are reaping today, he rendered a service to philosophy perhaps more difficult to perform than all those contributed thereafter by his illustrious successors. He can be thought of as a leader of conspirators who, before anyone else, had the courage to arise against a despotic and arbitrary power and who, in preparing a resounding revolution, laid the foundations of a more just and happier government, which he himself was not able to see established.

Our question then is how did Descartes accomplish this revolution in the process of giving his philosophy of the principles of knowledge, which are also the principles governing matter? The answer to this question is not simple, as is evidenced by the fact that, with the exceptions already noted, no historian of either ethics, medicine, or political philosophy would give Descartes a nod or understand what d'Alembert meant. In what follows, we begin to reconstruct what d'Alembert saw that caused him to say such a thing about the author who is nowadays primarily famous for his "cogito, ergo sum," his analytic geometry, and the "mind-body problem."

THE PRINCIPLES OF KNOWLEDGE
AND THE LAWS OR PRINCIPLES
OF NATURE

Descartes' *magnum opus*, his 1644 *Principles of Philosophy*, has four parts. The first two are Part I, "Concerning the Principles of Human Knowledge," and Part II, "Concerning the Principles of Material

Things." Parts III and IV are "Concerning the Visible World" and "Concerning the Earth." Parts I and II concern principles, and Parts III and IV concern what can be understood in light of those principles. However, if Part II has principles that are distinct from those of Part I, the principles of human knowledge would be distinct from the principles of material things, and in that case, there could be no science of material things—something Descartes would never claim.

In Part II, "Concerning the Principles of Material Things," Descartes enumerated three laws or principles of nature. He did not, however, enumerate obviously corresponding principles of knowledge, although Part I is titled "Concerning the Principles of Human Knowledge." Some of the principles of human knowledge that are discussed in Part I are: the three substances—thinking substance, extended substance, and God; the five universals—genus, species, substance, difference, and accident; and the four causes of our error—prejudices of our youth, our inability to forget those prejudices in our maturity, our liability to drowsiness when we attempt to judge attentively for a long time, and, our attachment to words used imprecisely. The enumeration of the "Principles or Laws of Nature" in Part II is, however, very precise (Vol. IXB). (I give both statements here, that of the *Treatise* and that of the *Principles,* for reasons that become clear as we proceed.)

In the *Treatise,* written in 1633, nine years before Newton's birth, Descartes said:

[I.] Each part of matter in particular always continues to be in one same state, as long as a meeting with the others does not at all constrain it to change. [Vol. XI, p. 38, l. 9–12]

[II.] When a body pushes another, it cannot give to it any movement during that same time which it does not lose itself; nor can it take from it any movement which does not augment its own by the like amount. [Vol. XI, p. 41, l. 1–5]

[III.] When a body is moved, although its movement is in fact made most often in a curved line, and although it cannot make any other which is not circular in some fashion . . . still, each of its individual parts tends to continue its own movements in a straight line. And thus their action, that is to say, the inclination which they have to be moved, is different from their movement. [Vol. XI, p. 43, l. 26, to p. 47, l. 7]

In the *Principles,* written in 1644 (at which time Newton was 2 *years old*), Descartes said:

[I.] Each thing remains in the state that it is in, as long as nothing changes it. [Vol. IXB, p. 84]

[II.] Every body which is moved, tends to continue its motion in a straight line. [Ibid., p. 85]

[III.] If a body which is moved meets with another stronger than itself [*plus forte que soy*], it loses nothing of its movement, and if it meets another weaker which it can move, it loses as much as it gives to it. [Ibid., p. 86]

Although we are not given a clearly exhaustive enumeration of the principles of knowledge in Part I that would be clearly analogous to the three laws or principles of nature of Part II, we can gather certain things concerning the principles from Part I when we consider it as an exact foreshadowing of Part II. (Its title forces us to do this.) We gather, for instance, that the reasons we do not naturally know everything, and hence why the principles of knowledge are not constantly operative in the way that the laws of matter are, seems to be parallel to the statement in Part II concerning the fact that bodies naturally move in straight lines, although their real motion is almost always in a curved line. This suggests that it is external circumstances or, at best, relative weakness of the individual with respect to the magnitude of the task of knowing, that leads to falsehood. It is noteworthy that all the causes of error listed in Part I are remediable by human effort alone, unaided by any divine grace. (We except the relative cerebral weakness of the individual scientific investigator for reasons that become clear later.) We also find discussions of the objects of true knowledge, i.e., the substances: God, *res extensa*, and *res cogitans*.[8] We find, furthermore (Part I, Article 35): "That the will is more extended than the understanding, and that our errors proceed from this cause," paralleling Laws II and III if we understand 'error' in its Latin meaning of "a swerving out of the right or direct path." In light of Article 47 of the *Passions,* moreover, the excess of "the extension" of will over understanding implies the identification of error and impotence; that is, "to be ignorant of the truth" and "to err" both seem to mean, "to be unable to achieve, and hence to fall short of, what one wants"—to lack power or force. Article 37 of Part I of the *Principles* says, "That the principal perfection of man is to have a free will, and that it is this which renders him worthy of praise and blame." ("Perfection" for Descartes means "completion.") However, Article 40 states "that we know also very certainly that God has preordained all things," and Article 41 discusses "How one can harmonize our free will with divine preordination." Since the laws enumerated in Part II are the *sole* preordinations of God concerning matter, the question of the harmony of our free will and those ordinances is the question of the harmony of Part I and Part II of the *Principles,* and not of understanding either part taken alone.

Article 40 of Part I establishes the unlimited power and extent of God's (intelligent) preordination of the physical world. It says:

But, because of what we already know of God, we are sure that His power is so great that we would be committing a crime to think that we would ever be able to do anything which had not been previously ordained; therefore, we might easily entangle ourselves in very great difficulties if we undertook to harmonize the liberty of our wills with His ordinances, and if we tried to comprehend, that is, to embrace and, as it were, limit with our understanding, the entire extension of our free will [*toute l'estendue de nostre libre arbitre*] and the order of the eternal Providence.

That crime is not a logical blunder at all. It is a mistake concerning our "faith" in the providential order preordained by God, concerning our belief in the divinely ordained disposition of the world. In other words, Descartes said that, in spite of the "natural ordinances" or "laws" enumerated in Part II, our will is free; but we would be criminal to think that "we would ever be able to do anything which had not been previously ordained," i.e., we somehow freely will what has been eternally ordained. Since we will only in light of what the disposition of things permits to take place, this is not a contradiction for Descartes; it is not even a problem. Indeed, there even exists a formal method for determining whether a problem is capable of solution, since, at least since the time of Plato, there has been a technique for investigating the possibility of particular solutions in mathematics, the so-called *diorismos* (διορισμός) of Greek mathematics. This technique is thoroughly described in the classical accounts of mathematical analysis and is "philosophically" described by Socrates in Plato's *Meno* (86E–87C). In Descartes' hands, this technique is so broadened that the very statement of the limits of possibility for the solution of problems simultaneously tells us *whether* we can, and if so, *how* to, solve them. This is Cartesian analysis, and it clearly parallels, mathematically, the relationship between will, understanding, and divine preordination. We can understand this if we consider what we do know to comprise a part of our finite understanding, and all that we do not know, but that can be known by us, to comprise a part of the divine preordination.

The realm of preordained indeterminacy is accessible to the intellectual efforts of man: it is a logical necessity if man's intelligently willful efforts are to be in the least effective. To think otherwise would involve us in a "crime" of thought, an idea that, at first sight, might be much more expected to issue from the mouth of the members of the Holy Office ("Inquisition") than from Descartes. His use of the word 'crime' is especially noteworthy, coming as it did in a time that had seen Copernicus banned, Galileo arrested, and Bruno burnt for heresy in his defense of Copernicus. Descartes would not say, as some do today, that all laws are based on convention, but that there exist inalienable human rights and freedoms. His reaction to that view would be that the appeal to inalienable rights presupposes foundations far more enduring than those of any statutes promulgated in political conventions. Indeed, it is the thesis of this part of this work that the "final degree of wisdom," the most delectable fruit of Descartes' Tree of Philosophy, concerns the concord existing between the "Principles or Laws of Matter" and human freedom. Similarly, we suppose that Descartes used the word 'crime' soberly and advisedly; therefore, since a crime entails a broken law, we feel safe in inferring that Descartes' crime of thought is a crime that transgresses the laws of nature and of nature's God. This is another instance of how Part I of the *Principles* foreshadows the laws or principles of matter that are only explicitly stated in Part II.

Creative Conservation

Again, Article 21 of Part I states "That the duration of our life alone suffices to demonstrate that God is." All we have to do is to

> take note of the nature of time or of the duration of our life. For, it being such that its parts do not all depend upon one another . . . from this, that we are now, it does not follow necessarily that we are the next moment if some cause, i.e., the same which produced us, did not continue to produce us, that is to say, conserve us.

The notion of creative conservation is therefore found both in the discussion of the laws of nature in the 1633 *Treatise* and in Part II of the 1644 *Principles*. In the *Treatise* he said of the first two laws that, "Indeed, these two rules manifestly follow from this alone, that God is immutable and that, acting always in the same way, He always produces the same effect" (Vol. XI, p. 43, l. 11–14). And, after he there stated the third law or rule, he said (ibid., p. 44, l. 23–29),

> This rule is supported [*appuyee*] on the same foundation as the other two, and only depends on this, that God conserves each thing by a continued action, and as a consequence, that He conserves nothing such as it might have been sometimes previously, but precisely such as it is at the very instant that He conserves it.[9]

Similarly, in the *Principles* the same sentiment is expressed concerning the laws or rules of matter: "This rule, as the preceding one, depends on this, that God is immutable and that He conserves the motion in matter by one simple operation" (p. 86).

From these parallels we conclude that the laws of nature that operate on inanimate matter in some essential way also operate in the sphere of thinking substance. The union of *res cogitans* and *res extensa* is somehow, and to a significant degree, included in the province of these general laws of nature. Moreover, we conclude that the peculiarly creative aspect of these conservative laws enjoins us as thinking beings not to fear great changes, since, "from this, that we are now, it does not follow necessarily that we are the next moment if some cause, i.e., the same which produced us, did not continue to produce us, that is to say, conserve us."

When we compare the Cartesian doctrine of creative growth with Edmund Burke's notion of the organic growth of the laws of England described in his *Reflections on the Revolution in France* (1790), we conclude that, if Burke is the father of English conservatism, Descartes could well be a father of modern progressive liberalism, or, at the very least, he is the father of a cosmology that gave a view of general nature that could provide a heavenly paradigm to the citizens of a progressive and liberal state.

THE AUTOMATON OF CLAY

This section examines the notion of a natural, organized body, which Descartes describes as being fully alive because it possesses all the dispositions necessary for life. It exactly obeys the laws of nature, but, because it lacks a soul, it has neither eyesight nor thoughts. This examination aids our understanding of what the addition of a soul really gives to a living body, and how the law of reason relates to the law in the members.

To begin, let us recall that Descartes stated in the *Rules:*

It should be conceived that the power through which we properly know things is purely spiritual and no less distinct from all body than blood is from bone or the hand from the eye; and, further, that it is one single thing which accepts figures from the common sense together with images [*phantasia*], or which is applied to those things which are preserved in memory, or which forms new ones by which the imagination is so occupied that often it does not suffice for ideas to be accepted by the common sense for transferring them to the motive power by means of the disposition of what is purely body [*puri corporis*]. In all of which cases the power of knowing [*vis cognoscens*] is sometimes passive and sometimes active and sometimes imitates only the stylus and sometimes only the wax tablet; however, this is to be taken only as an analogy [*per analogiam tantum*], for nothing is found in corporeal things altogether similar to this. [Rule XII; Vol. X, p. 415, l. 13–27]

We must therefore proceed with extreme caution lest we miss the soul's *dis*similarity to the corporeal things dealt with by natural law directly and thereby "materialize" human beings to a degree not intended by Descartes. That is, however extensively Descartes felt he could account for the states and movements observed in humans by means of his neuroanatomy, the complete human cannot be understood without a soul. This is especially important since it is our particular aim to clarify Descartes' view of the relation of natural law to manmade, statute law, and to make clear the details of the analogy Descartes discerned between the laws of nature as applied to bodies that have no power of perceiving and knowing and as applied to those that have such a power.

The subject of Descartes' 1633 *Treatise on Man* is, surprisingly enough, a soulless automaton (robot) that simply obeys all the laws of matter, i.e., that acts in strict and entirely predictable accord with the corporeal disposition of its body without the complication of any psychic perceptions or volitions consequent on such perceptions. The *Treatise on Man* is the second part of a very great undertaking, *The World of Rene Descartes, or, Treatise on Light [Le Monde de Rene Descartes ou, Traite de La Lumiere]*. Internal evidence makes it absolutely clear that the second part, *Treatise on Man*, is a continuation of the first part, *Treatise on Light*. The *Treatise on Man* (XI, pp. 119–202) begins: "I suppose that the body is nothing other than a statue or machine of earth which God forms altogether in order to render it as similar as possible to us. . . ." The clay machine, an incomplete man, since it lacks a soul, turns out not to need a soul, except for sensation or awareness, passion and thinking. Descartes wrote (Vol. XI, 165, l. 11ff.) that the body of the automaton he envisioned is operated very much the same way as the pneumatic organs "of our churches." He said that the heart and arteries, which "push the animal spirits into the concavities of the brain of our machine" are "like the bellows of these organs," and that exterior objects around it "depending on which nerves they activate [*remuent*]," are "like the fingers of the organist"—a splendid example of what it might mean to be a truly "natural" man!

It is the senses, and particularly eyesight (*veue*) and everything implied by its possession, that are lacking in this man-machine. For, although the "eyes" of the machine receive the impressions formed by light rays bouncing off exterior objects, and, although the rays perturb its pineal gland in such a way as to modify the motion of its body, the machine no more perceives the rays than a computer perceives the holes punched on the cards it "reads." For Descartes, ideas are the forms of sensations, and thought *is* sensation, whose forms, that is, whose *discriminating determinants*, are the ideas perceived by the thinking soul. The "fingerlike" figures impinging on the pineal gland make that gland move in one way or another, depending on the figure, but, in the soulless automaton, the figures cannot be perceived in any way, any more than an organ can hear itself playing. Rather, Descartes wrote in the *Treatise on Man:*

among those figures, it is not those which are imprinted in the
organs of the exterior senses, nor those in the inner surface of the
brain, but only those which are traced in the animal spirits on the
surface of the pineal gland. . . where is found the seat of the
imagination and of the common sense, which ought to be taken as
ideas, that is to say, for the forms or images which the rational soul
will consider immediately when, being united to that machine, it will
imagine or sense some object. [Vol. XI, p. 176, l. 26, to p. 177, l. 4]

For Descartes, machines cannot think without "thinkers," i.e., without a
rational soul; and a rational soul is a soul capable of ideas, of forms,
which in the case of thinking men are naturally supplied by eyesight
above all the other senses. This man-machine or manikin is a real living
thing that has all the properties of a true human being that can be
present without the presence of a soul. Thus, for example, it has "ideas"
because it has the same forms of thought impressed on its pineal gland
that complete humans have, but it does not have thoughts because it
does not have a soul. The "ideas" impressed on the pineal gland of the
machine are the forms of the thoughts that the manikin *could* have *if* it
had a soul.

In the definition of *idea* found in the "Responses to the Second
Objections" to his *Meditations,* Descartes refined this definition of idea
only a little. There, as we have seen, he said that he will call by the name
'idea' not merely those figures or forms insofar as they are imprinted on
the pineal gland, but "only insofar as they inform the soul itself which is
applied to that part of the brain." In his accompanying definition of
thought [*pensee*], he said that a thought is "all that is in us in such a way
that we are immediately aware of it [*en somes immediatement connoisant*]."
When we become aware of the data coming from the optic nerves, then
our idea, the form of our immediate awareness of that data, constitutes
the item in the soul's realm that is strictly analogous to the physical
boundaries that give forms to physical objects in the physical realm. And
it is our thought, i.e., what "is in us in such a way that we are immediately
aware of it" that is bounded by the "forms" constituting the ideas that
terminate thought and toward which thought tends and without which
thought is incomplete. For Descartes, then, the boundaries of extended
bodies are to the inner "space" or "volumes" contained by those boundaries as the ideas in the mind are to the forms of otherwise indeterminate perception; "ideas" give boundaries to sensations. We are not surprised, therefore, that Descartes stated that our ideas are given to us, i.e.,
"instituted by nature"; so are the boundaries of most physical bodies.
Only the shapes of the bodies that are the artifacts of men are not strictly
instituted by nature; similarly, only those ideas that are free creations of
the human mind, such as the symbolic language of algebra, are not
strictly instituted by nature. The intellectual power to devise new forms,

be they new machines, new artifacts, or new modes of representation, is very nearly what Descartes meant by the term *ingenium,* as it appears in his 1628(?) *Rules for the Direction of Ingenuity [Regulae ad Directionem Ingenii].* Ingenuity, perhaps that most characteristically human of all our psychic powers for Descartes, is concerned with our awareness and subsequent treatment of the forms given us through the "intermediation [*entremise*]" of eyesight, whether those forms be the product of our own transforming efforts or merely the natural evidence of God's creative and conservative power in the course of historical time. Without that volitional power of ingenuity, we would be "church organs," that is, instruments played upon at the direction of church organists whose score is, presumably, Holy Writ, together with the discretion of the quasipolitical church councils. Therefore, we see that ingenuity concerns the will.

Because Descartes' manikins have no powers of perception, sensation, or reason, they also have no volition, even though for Descartes much of our activity is only organic in origin and not in the least a matter of choice; men have no initial control over what they perceive or are conscious of in any given case of a perturbation of the pineal gland. (The ideational reaction of the automaton is automatic and preordained— "established by nature," and, as another example, our strong inclination to flee when the form of our awareness of something is both painful as well as significant of what "causes" the pain, is not a matter of will or volition; accordingly, it is very difficult not to pull away from a doctor who is probing a wound in order to clean it out, although we are entirely aware of what he is doing, and why.) Therefore, it comes as a surprise that Descartes insisted that it is one soul that thinks, perceives, imagines, and wills. Why must the body that is united with a soul be able to think, perceive, imagine and will, altogether or not at all? Indeed, Descartes denies the presence of *any* of these psychic powers if they are not *all* present together. Descartes would never admit of the contemporary use of the expression "higher human nervous functions" when it is used in order to disassociate voluntary action from "raw" consciousness in men.

The brutes, the irrational animals, are also automatons for Descartes because they are naturally incapable of symbolic discourse; they lack the ingenuity required to create new symbolic forms, which men institute at their discretion (*ad libitum*) to represent the future analytically to themselves. Thus the indeterminateness of divine preordination makes that preordination forever a closed book to brutes; their cries, no matter how varied in any species, are "instituted by nature" and hence are not instituted *ad libitum.* Animals are therefore without free will, since they have no inkling of the divinely arranged disposition resulting from the infinite divine providence. However, we are led to suppose that we humans are conscious, no matter how dimly, of divine providence precisely because we are able to represent to ourselves symbolically what we do not yet know. Even the most optimistic of our contemporary animal psychologists would not be likely to say that "communicative" vertebrates, such as the chimpanzee or the porpoise, concern themselves with the limits of the species' knowledge. Whereas, in Descartes' view, the general mathematical expression of the laws of nature represents to mankind symbolically the idea of all possible motions of matter throughout the infinite future, that is, the distinct, discriminating form of all future perceptions. That particular symbolic representation is a representation of all possible futures and thus is entirely indeterminate in its generality, although it is at every instant manifested in the world before our eyes (in which we live). The acme of rationality is the human symbolic expression of an absolutely general but indeterminate idea, an idea or form of all possible forms of the experience in the *saeculum* (in *this* world). (No other animal, however garrulous, achieves this.) Ideas, whether determinate or indeterminate, as in the expression "$x^2 + y^2 = r^2$," are boundary forms of awareness, and nothing else, for Descartes.

Summary

In the example of the automaton, we see something of the limits of natural law as extended to a living body: because the automaton lacks a soul, it also lacks eyesight; therefore, it lacks thought and ideas, and thus it lacks any sense of the future or of the not-yet-achieved, and, finally, of the divinely preordained disposition of the universe. Automata are ignorant *both* of God's providence in the world *and* of analytic mathematics.

As an introduction to the next section, which is concerned with light, sight, and presentiment, it should be pointed out that, of all the forms of awareness that are "instituted by nature," for Descartes the most exact and important is eyesight, because "All the conduct of our life depends on our senses; and among these, that of eyesight [*veue*] being the most universal and the most noble, there is no doubt at all that the discoveries which serve to augment its powers will be the most useful possible" (*Dioptrics*, "First Discourse," *De La Lumiere*, Vol. VI, p. 81, l. 1–3). Since "all the conduct of life" depends on eyesight as the most universal and noble sense, light in the world and eyesight in the automaton, which we now consider as ensouled, have a special rank. For it is precisely "the entire conduct of our life" in which we are interested, since the conduct of the life of even the most exceptional ensouled automaton will sooner or later concern other ensouled automata. In the next section, therefore, we consider how light and eyesight might determine the conduct of "all the life" of the ensouled automaton.

LIGHT, SIGHT, AND
PRESENTIMENT

Descartes began the first essay (or "trial") of his first published work, the *Discourse on Method,* as follows:

> All the conduct of our life [*toute de la conduite de notre vie*] depends on our senses, one of which is the sense of vision. Because it is the most universal and the most noble of our senses, there is no doubt that the inventions which help increase the power of sight are the most useful possible.

This is puzzling; the expression "conduct of our life" usually refers to good and bad conduct, that is, to the questions addressed by ethics, and certainly not to being able to get around because one has good eyes. However, that is not what Descartes meant; as the next sentence states, those "inventions which help us increase the power of sight" are not instruments of the ophthalmologists' clinic, nor even eyeglasses: "It is difficult to find any inventions which augment the power of sight further than those marvellous telescopes."

We may fairly be puzzled. The inventions that aid vision in "the conduct of life" are not, for Descartes, eyeglasses or the instruments by means of which the physician can cure diseases of the eye, and, if "the conduct of life" does after all refer to ethics, it is ethics that is aided by, of all things, the invention of the telescope! For, he continued:

> Although we have been using telescopes for only a short time, we have already discovered new stars in the sky and other new objects above the Earth in greater numbers than before. Consequently, because they have extended our vision very much beyond where our fathers usually let their imaginations roam, those telescopes seemed to us to have opened the door and permitted us to come to a knowledge of nature much more grand and perfect than they had.

Thus, the telescope enormously augments that by which we conduct our lives—presumably, that knowledge on the basis of which we decide what to do and what not to do—a knowledge much more perfect than that of our fathers. To add to our puzzlement, we remember that Descartes also claimed at the beginning of his *Treatise on Light* (Vol. XI, p. 5, l. 3–19) that our conscious perception of light does not *at all* resemble what causes us to perceive light; the conscious perception is "a natural sign" and a natural convention or "institution" that no more resembles what causes it than the French word *chat* resembles a cat.[10] Thus, according to Descartes, something upon which "all the conduct of life depends" is merely a natural "sign" of something outside us of which we have *no direct awareness:* our consciousness of light and the objects of the sense of sight is really only our response to physical events (such as our present-day "photons"), which disturb and activate the nerve endings at the back of the eyeball. Is this what all the conduct of our life depends on?

This raises several questions. For one, how does our perception of new stars, ("Nova"), of sunspots, of moon-mountains, and of the satellites of Jupiter as seen first through the telescope help us in "the conduct of our life"? To begin to answer that question, however, we must also address questions about how we relate the physical, invisible causes of vision to what we actually perceive. We can even ask what grounds we have to think that we can relate physical events to psychological events. Also, why is the very fact of vision even philosophically important in a world that is blind except for a few species of entities that possess bodies of a sufficiently high degree of organization to allow for perception and eyesight?

Let us restate the questions in more Cartesian terms.

First, Descartes said that to each and every motion in the pineal gland there is a unique psychic response; but how do we relate those motions and responses to whatever it is, far away from the skull of the thinking human, that began that chain of motions—e.g., the light of a distant star in the heavens?[11] In other words, what biological, medical, or ethical purpose is served because the pineal gland can respond to light-induced pressure originating in far-distant solar systems?

To sum up these questions, which we deal with in this section and Appendix 4:

1. How do we relate external motions, some of which began very far away, to individual states of consciousness of light and color?

2. Why should we perceive as light those physical activities that began in distant stars?

3. What is the relation between medicine and ethics, on the one hand, and Descartes' theory that ties together the physics of light production in far-distant stars with the neurology of light perception here on Earth?

We can say that, in one way, question 1 has already been answered neuroanatomically: action in matter disturbs the nerve endings at the back of the eyeball and this disturbance, through a series of nerve pathways, affects the pineal gland, which in turn gives rise to a consciousness state that is naturally predetermined, i.e., "instituted by Nature." This, however, does not address the question of how it is that we can see both a candle flame in front of us and the light from far-distant stars. How does the activity of matter in very distant stars, no less than in the nearby candle flame, come to disturb the optic nerves?

A detailed account of Descartes' theory of light production and transmission is given in Appendix 4. An excellent short summary of Descartes' theory is, however, to be found in Stanley L. Jaki's *The Paradox of Olber's Paradox:*

> According to him, one may suppose the stars to be located . . . beyond any definite distance . . . The stars, according to him, shine of their own light as the sun does. He also states that unlike flame or fire on earth, the light of stars is in no need of fuel. For, in Descartes' system, light is not a chemical process but simply the very rapid motion of particles of the first kind, or the finest parts of matter. This very rapid motion is transmitted as a pressure to our eyes through the mediation of the second type of matter, or globular particles that fill everything. This transmission is instantaneous, in the same way that a blind man feels instantaneously the contact of his stick with the pavement.
>
> From these premises one can easily conclude that one's eyes are therefore constantly reached by pencils of light pressure, in analogy to rigid sticks, from every direction at all times, as there are stars everywhere . . .
>
> Here it is important to recall that according to Descartes each sun creates around itself a spherical pressure front directed radially outward, which cannot but oppose any pressure from a light ray, however narrow, that tries to pass through it . . .
>
> Stars which are visible to the naked eye were pictured by Descartes as located in the centers of vortices adjoining more or less immediately the vortex of our sun.[12]

In short, light rays are the lines along which the luminous matter of celestial bodies *would* travel *were* they not prevented from moving in a straight line by the globular, much denser and hence "heavier" particles of the second element that surround every star in the heavens. Those light rays are the paths that the first-element particles *would* begin to follow *if* they were not thwarted by a concentration of much larger particles of the second element; but, and this is crucial, because of the disposition of the particles of second element with respect to the highly agitated particles of first element, some of that thwarted motion is, in fact, communicated as a sort of shock wave through the second element. Thus, our perception of light is simultaneously a reaction to a *real* motion of second-element particles as they excite the optic nerves at the back of the eyeball, and a perception of the *thwarted* motion of first-element particles. Therefore, the physics of light deals both with a simple linear impulse through the medium composed of second elements and with a thwarted motion—a "harnessed" motion.

The three elements that we mention here are those that Descartes used to form the human embryo. The part of matter that comprises the very high-energy, low-density first element (our gas), which forms the main body of the cerebrospinal fluid or spirits, is the same first element that forms the main part of the bodies of the luminous stars. The *intermediate* element that comprises the heavens surrounding the luminous bodies and that is formed of globular particles is also the material out of which the spongy organs, such as the lungs and liver, are formed (see the way the heart rests in a sort of pocket in the lobes of the lungs). Finally, the third, relatively dense matter of the third element is the material of the Earth and the planets, as well as of our bones, teeth, etc.

When Jaki says that "this very rapid motion is transmitted as a pressure to our eyes through the mediation of the second type of matter," he is making a crucial point: Descartes said that what we sense as light is the physical result of first-element particles pushing against balls of the second element; because those globes of second element are so much bigger than the particles of the first element that form luminous bodies, the globes move only in the course of preventing the motion of the particles of luminous bodies. This is why we can see the light coming from fire without being burned by that fire: all the fire does, unless it is in contact with our flesh, is move or push the globes that comprise the medium between it and us. Thus, we never even directly sense the cause of our sensation of light unless we are being actually burned; what we do sense is motion in the medium between our nerve endings and the luminous body.

However, Descartes said something that proved to be the bane of his contemporaries, friend and foe alike: he insisted that light was solely the effort to escape the confines of the luminous body made by the particles of the first element against the globes of second element forming the medium that surrounded the luminous body. In other words, what we are sensing when we sense light is *pressure:* "the force of light . . . does not consist in the duration of some motion, but only in this, that the little globes are pressed, and try to move towards some place although they perhaps do not actually do it" (*Principles,* Part III, Article 63). Again, "it is only in this effort that the nature of light consists" (Vol. IX, p. 131; *Principles,* Part III, Article 55). In short, what we are sensing when we sense light is a thwarted action on the part of the particles of the luminous bodies: we are actively sensing the *action* of the globes of the second element as they are in the process of *actually thwarting* the motion of the particles of the first element. In sensing physical light, we are *ultimately sensing a relationship*—namely, the relationship between the medium and the particles of the luminous body. What could this have to do with vision—i.e., with the *sensation* of light?

In the sixth part of the *Dioptrics,* Descartes presented the metaphor of a blind man making his way with the aid of a staff (stick). It is obvious that a blind man does not need his stick except to detect possible obstacles to his movement straight ahead. Descartes envisaged the staff as ending in a fork, so that the blind man can hold it with both hands; it then "tells" the blind man when he is about to run into some impediment to his motion straight ahead. By means of his staff, a blind man can, as it were, see where he can*not* go. When the stick hits something, its back-and-forth motion indicates the direction in which he *would* have moved *had* there been no impediment to his continued motion straight ahead. His true motion, following his staff, is thus determined by two considerations: his inclination to move forward, and his having to move around obstacles. His motion is essentially compound.

In this picture, the staff of the blind man takes the place of pencils of light rays; in the medium, the obstacles that the staff hits, sending the blind man a message about what is in front of him (no less than his pineal gland, which "gets the message"), correspond to illuminated objects; and, strikingly, the blind man himself, taken as a union of mind and body, can only correspond to the material of the luminous body whose forward motion is being thwarted by the relatively large globes forming the medium of the second element. In addition, the nerves up to the brain are filled with cerebrospinal fluid or spirits that correspond to the first element comprising the luminous body; the brain itself, spongy as it is with all its tubules comprising the nerves, corresponds to the globes of the second element that makes up the medium. Since we are told that human beings are generated in strict accord with the laws of nature governing matter, it comes as no surprise to us that the individual human body is a microcosm, and that the physical theory of light should image the theory of vision.[13]

To answer our first question about how the external motions that are concerned in light production are related to individual acts of consciousness, two cases must be distinguished: 1) When we look directly at a luminous body, no matter how distant, our nerve endings at the back of the eyeball are moved by the globes of the second element that form the medium; those globes are moving purely in response to the motion of the particles comprising the luminous body, a motion that is thwarted by the back-pressure of just those globes of the medium closest to the luminous body; that pressure is in turn transmitted along columns of globes that touch other "light rays" until one or more columns reach a nerve ending. When this happens, we see as a reaction to a motion that is itself a reaction to a thwarted motion. 2) When we see an object illuminated by reflected light, we are sensing a pencil of pressure reflected off an opaque object. Descartes' theory of light is a theory of the mediated motion of the particles of luminous bodies.

To answer our second question, "Why should we perceive as light the activities taking place in far-distant stars?," we might begin by taking special note of the fact that we can only perceive the original motion of the particles of luminous bodies, some of which are far-distant stars, 1) because those particles themselves are unable to move beyond the confining limits of the sea of second-element globes surrounding each star; and 2) because of the "disposition" (Vol. IXB, p. 131) of the particles of the two elements, together with that of our optic nerves. The perception of motion that not only begins very far away, but also is inaugurated by the motion of extremely small particles comprising the luminous body, presupposes a *stupendously* delicate system of interrelated parts, each of which is so finely disposed to be moved that a cause as distant and as minute as the one supplied even by the particles as small as those of the first element can trip it into motion. What we "see" is that infinitely mediated, prepared-for motion; what the pineal gland is really responding to is thus a *delicately disposed system* that can be put into motion by so small a cause. This, in turn, prepares us to view the soul of the organized human body—which is fit to receive the soul because of the disposition of its organs(Vol. XI, p. 225, l. 6–25)—as being essentially concerned with disposition, that is, with a preparedness because of which something can happen, and without which it could not happen.

As we shall see in detail in the next section of this chapter, the generation of light in a distant solar system also involves processes that often lead to the formation of earthlike "crusts" over the stars at the centers. (Descartes thought sunspots were composed of such earthlike crusts.) These encrusted stars are on their way to becoming, first, giant spherical magnets, and then planets like our own, on which living things can exist. Furthermore, Descartes' account of the genesis of first magnets, and then planets, from the luminous stars in the center of far-distant solar systems, is faithfully echoed in his account of the generation of the fetus. (Since the human is "an automaton of clay" together with a soul, this is not surprising: biophysics and astrophysics are both branches of mathematical physics.)

Descartes' later account of the transformation of stars into planets is an application of natural law to the generation of solar systems; using the same natural laws and many of the same processes, he also, still later, presented a developmental embryology. His theory of the genesis of light is a theory of the beginnings of a process that culminates in the genesis of living humans who have the physical and psychic mechanisms to grasp those beginnings both in their physical theories and in their perception of light.[14] This development of Descartes' provided a relatively safe way to present a theory that directly countered the story of the creation of both the heavens and of humans that is given in Genesis: very few priests would look in his accounts for heresy; as a protection against those who did, and who might use his account against him, he only presented the parallels. He did not make much of the parallels, except that he time and time again refers to his cosmological works in his embryology (e.g., Vol. XI, p. 254, l. 27, to p. 255, l. 13). This replacement for the account of creation in Genesis is a biophysical replacement for the account that had been hitherto also the basis for ethics; that is, Descartes' physiology replaces Genesis and thereby provides a foundation for a new ethics. This is why Descartes, who stated that his design was only (Vol. VI, p. 78, l. 7–18) to improve physics to the point where he can provide a better foundation for medical theory, spent whole volumes laying down the laws of physics and deriving (as in Deuteronomy and Leviticus), a host of discrete consequences of the laws (of nature).

Our third question was, "What is the relation between Descartes' medicine and ethics, on the one hand, and his theory that ties together the physics of light production in far-distant stars with the neurology of light perception here on Earth?" According to Descartes' "design," the demands of an experimentally verifiable mathematical physics of light phenomena must be integrated with the demands made by a verifiable neuroanatomy of vision; furthermore, he must give a philosophical justification for the fact that the two truly integrate. Descartes (who was not unqualifiedly successful) was the only modern to attempt this.

An important theoretical problem is addressed in Descartes' attempt to give a neurophysiology of human vision, since that vision is so sensitive that it can detect motions originating in extremely distant stars. According to the Aristotelian-Ptolemaic (and Roman Catholic establishment) astronomy that Descartes and his fellow Copernicans were bent on overthrowing, the visible stars in the sky need not be so very far away; however, according to the new astronomy—which, Descartes said, must be the right one, or all his system fails! (Vol. I, p. 307)—those stars must be in effect infinitely distant from the viewer on the Earth.[15] How, then, can Copernicus or Descartes be correct if the light from those stars is not only to reach Earth, but even to reveal exploding novas and the like? Descartes' theory of light claims to answer that question. For, in his system, a very small cause, even very far away, can have an effect that reaches very far. Just as serious, however, is the question why those stars are visible to us, a question fully addressed by Genesis 1:14–19, concerning the creations of the stars and planets:

> God said, "Let there be lights in the vault of heaven to separate day from night, and let them serve as signs both for festivals and for seasons, and years. Let them also shine in the vault of heaven to give light on earth." So it was; God made the two great lights, the greater to govern the day and the lesser to govern the night; and with them

he made the stars. God put these lights in the vault of heaven to give light on earth, to govern day and night, and to separate light from darkness; and God saw that it was good. Evening came, and morning came, a fourth day.[16]

Why, then, according to Descartes' new mathematical physics, are those stars there for all to see?

Descartes' physics involves no real discussion of the ultimate ends of creation; but his physics was written as a foundation for medicine, and, insofar as his account disagrees with that of Genesis, we might be led to expect that the physics that he tells Queen Christina of Sweden (Vol. V, p. 290, l. 15, to p. 291, l. 2) is the foundation of the most exalted ethics, is just the physics that replaces chapter 1 of Genesis. Descartes' non-Biblical, scientific ethics is built on his theory of how highly organized bodies relate to one another in order to preserve their health. On the other hand, the very model of a delicately structured organization of matter is found in his theory of light production, and, at the same time, that theory of light will replace "The First Book of Moses, Commonly Called Genesis," the account on which Christian Europe previously based its ethics.

Whatever else light does, it shows us the way. Descartes' description of light production [which, he told his student Burman (Vol. V, p. 172), no one will really believe for a century and a half] extensively repeats the description he gives of the organization of those bodies that are fit to receive a soul, and it follows in large part the definition Descartes gave of analysis—the method *par excellence* by which the thinking soul (related to a given organically sound body that is disposed to receive the soul) in fact proceeds to think methodically. Descartes' description of light is almost identical to his descriptions both of the way a body's organization makes it fit to receive a soul, and of the correct way, the method, according to which that received soul thinks.

About the body, Descartes stated in the *Description of the Human Body:*

the soul cannot excite any movement in the body unless all the corporeal organs which are required for that movement are disposed correctly; . . . quite to the contrary, when the body has all its organs disposed for some movement, there is no need for the soul in order to produce it; . . . and, consequently, all those movements which we experience as in no way depending on our thought ought not to be attributed to the soul but only to the disposition of the organs; . . . and even the movements which we call *voluntary* proceed principally from that disposition of the organs, although these voluntary movements cannot be excited without the soul . . . which determines them.

And, although all these movements cease in the body when it dies and the soul leaves it, one ought not to infer from this that the soul produces them; one ought only to infer that it is one and the same cause which renders the body no longer fit to produce those motions and which makes the soul absent itself from that no longer fit body. [Vol. XI, p. 225, l. 12–31]

Similarly, it is not because of any enormous commotion in stars that we can see their light; rather, it is because of the extremely delicate relationship obtaining between the particles of the luminous body and the medium that we detect that motion. Descartes referred to this delicate relationship as an action or disposition to be moved (Vol. VI, p. 88, l. 1–5) and even went so far as to say (Vol. IXB, p. 131) that light is a "placement, or a disposition to be moved." To repeat, then: what we are experiencing when we experience the perception of light is a twofold, *congruent* preparedness—on the part of light, the physical motion that comes to our eyeball from remote stars in distant heavens (galaxies) is inaugurated by the effort of extremely small particles of the first element to escape the confines of the luminous body, an effort that is thwarted by the presence of globes of the second element, which surrounds luminous bodies and thereby comprises the medium between them and us. That aspect of the cause of light production that is not merely physical (in that it involves more than simply matter in motion) is the *disposition* of the parts of matter that are in motion, which gives rise to what Descartes terms the "inclination" that matter has to move when it is poised in a certain way. (His example is the stone in the whirling sling: the stone, if it could, would fly in a straight line, but, because of the sling, it goes in a circle. The *pressure* on the cord connecting the stone to the hand that whirls it is the measure of the "inclination" the stone has to travel in a straight line rather than in a circle—see Appendix 4). In the case of the human body, which is so organized that it perceives light, the corresponding disposition is the correct disposition of "the corporeal organs which are required for . . . movement. . . ." Therefore, just as the disposition of physical particles gives rise to an inclination to move in one particular way rather than another, so the dispositions of the organs of the human body give rise to an inclination for it to move in one particular way rather than in another. That inclination is so central that, no matter how much we might will to do one thing, if our organs are not properly disposed to perform those motions, we cannot move in that way, and, if the organs are disposed so that the human body is entirely inclined to one motion rather than another, there is no need for any volition for it to occur.

If light shows us the way to proceed, then our perception of light is a perception of action for which our bodies are disposed and hence toward which they are inclined. Our consciousness of the world around us, even including the stars, is thus a consciousness both of what is possible and of what is impossible because of the degree to which we are disposed or not disposed to proceed in our actions and what is possible or impossible because of the ordered structure of creation. Spinoza's maxim that the mind is the idea of the well-disposed body is thus a precious specimen of the fruit he gathered from Descartes' Tree of Philosophy.

Descartes' whole *Treatise on Man* is a proof that almost all our motions are "involuntary," i.e., made simply because we are disposed organically to make them, and so are *inclined* to do them. What possible need is there for consciousness and mind here? There are neuroanatomists whose lifelong study is precisely the physical basis for inclination, and who say that they do not even need the concept of consciousness: consciousness, many say today, is not really necessary for health and survival.[17]

For Descartes, the techniques of mathematical analysis shed light on the solutions of problems. That method of seeking truths is a method that proceeds by relating what one knows to what one is seeking. Then, once the relation between the two is absolutely clearly determined, the unknown turns out to be precisely what can be described and obtained in terms of what is known. It is only by *disposing* all the knowns in precisely the correct way, on one side of the equation, that the unknown begins to appear on the other side of the equation. Furthermore, just as the particles of globular second element act as the medium for the transmission of extremely small impulses originating in the motion of first-element particles in luminous bodies, so, in equations, the unknowns and knowns are related to one another in a continuous proportion where all the terms but the first and last are known as mean terms. To algebraists of Descartes' time, the whole notion of an algebraic equation was inextricably tied up with the notion of mean terms and extreme terms.

This is not to claim that Descartes necessarily thought that light was in some way "thinking," or that there are no real differences between light, sight, and being alive in an organized body. What is clear, however, is that Descartes was teaching that the world in which we live and about which we think is a world that is essentially accessible by means of his mathematical physics. Moreover, it seems that Descartes was presenting a *rational* account of the creation of heaven, Earth, and all that is therein. This means that there are no unbridgeable gulfs that only an act of divine revelation can span; it also means that the primordial creative motive power that disposed matter to form stars, planets, magnets, living things, and, finally, thinking humans, itself employed a *rational* method of thinking to dispose the world as we now see and experience it. This, in turn, opens the door for a total scientific replacement for any and all revealed religion.

This development brings us a step closer to understanding what medicine and mechanics have to do with ethics, "the ultimate degree of wisdom."

GENESIS: DAYS 1, 2, 4, AND 6

This section examines some of the details of the way human biological development reflects the development of the heavens and the planets. Because of the great—even extreme—importance of the concept of disposition for Descartes' thought, no presentation of his work and its ingenuity is complete without a detailed specimen of his cunning in solving a myriad of problems by employing a small handful of suppositions: that ingenuity finds the material on which it feeds by constantly presupposing an extreme delicacy and precision in the disposition of the parts of the visible world and in the structure of the mathematical formulations required to grasp it analytically. By means of this concept of delicate, precise, and exact disposition, Descartes replaced the concept of Nature as what never does anything in vain with a new concept of Nature as what is never baffled.

Sometime between 1645 and 1648, Descartes stopped his investigations into the embryology and physiology of animals in order to begin anew. He wrote in a letter that is unaddressed as we have it and that is dated 1648 or 1649 by his editors:

> As to the description of animals, for a long time I had dropped my plan of giving it clearly, not because of negligence nor for lack of desire; rather, because I now have a better description. I had only proposed to myself to put clearly what I thought I knew most certainly concerning the functions of the animal because I had almost lost hope of finding the causes of its formation; but, in meditating [*en meditant*] upon it I have discovered so many new vistas [*paix*] that I have almost no doubt at all that I will achieve all of physics according to my desire. [Vol. V, p. 260, l. 29, to p. 261, l. 12]

This letter begins by answering an inquiry concerning the relative velocities of the moon and planets as deduced from the 1644 *Principles*, and it refers specifically to Part II, Article 153 ("why the moon goes more rapidly and is carried from its path more when it is full or new than when it is waxing or waning"). This is surely an unexpected place to find a discussion of *anatomy!*

This great breakthrough of Descartes' is also mentioned by Burman in his account of a conversation with Descartes, the manuscript record of which dates it as 16 April 1648. In an interchange dealing with a passage from the *Principles*, Part III, Article 46, which concerns Descartes' opin-

ion on his hypothesis of the circular motion of the heavens, Burman
says:

> that hypothesis of the author is assuredly quite simple if we pay
> attention to the things which he has deduced from it and which are
> in number almost infinite; the connection [*connexio*] and the deduc-
> tion prove it sufficiently. For the author subsequently remarks that
> he was able to deduce from it almost everything, and he wished to
> swear before God [*et coram Deo jurare vult*] that in laying down these
> hypotheses he did not think of what followed [*de reliquis*] such as fire,
> the lodestone, etc.; that, nevertheless, he afterwards saw the pos-
> sibility of drawing from these hypotheses, on all points, very satisfac-
> tory explanations. Even more, on the very treatise concerning the
> animal on which he had worked that winter he had been able to
> make this remark: although he only wished to explain the functions
> of the animal, he had seen that he was scarcely able to do it without
> being obliged to explain the conformation of the animal starting
> from the egg [*ab ovo*], and he remarked that this followed so well
> from his principles, that he could tell the reason why the animal had
> an eye, a nose, a brain, etc., and he clearly saw that the nature of
> things was constituted so well from his principles [*ex suis principiis*]
> that it could not be otherwise. [Vol. V., pp. 170–171]

Again, in Part IV of his 1648 *Description of the Human Body,* Descartes
wrote (Vol. XI, pp. 252–253) that he is not yet ready to give a full
description of the formation of the body from the seed, but that:

> I still cannot refuse to put down here in passing something of what is
> most general concerning it, and concerning which I hope I shall run
> the least risk hereafter of contradicting myself when certain experi-
> ments give me further information concerning light [*de lumiere*].
> [Ibid., p. 253, l. 2–6]

These two passages should not be forgotten in what follows: *Descartes'*
work on animals is profoundly dependent on his astrophysical, astronomical
thought.

Descartes did not give any complete account of the analogy he said
he detected between the development of solar systems around a central
star and the human organ systems arranged around the central heart.
He did say, in his embryological works, that the material out of which the
human embryo is formed is nearly identical to that out of which the
heavens are composed.

However, because Descartes' cosmogenesis, together with its re-
capitulation in the development of the fetus, is a replacement for the
account of creation given in Genesis, he gave a myriad of clues by means
of which we, his readers—along with Ambassador Chanut and the Prot-

estant Queen Christina of Sweden—can make the analogy that reveals in Descartes' physics the foundations for the highest of all pursuits, his ethics. Our derivation must therefore be both tentative—since it is based on clues and not given in its entirety—and bold—since those texts cry out for it.

The Genesis of the Heavens

For Descartes, the term 'heavens' is a true plural; there are, he said, at least as many distinct heavens as there are stars visible in the night skies. Many of the heavens contain not only a central, luminous star (or sun), but planets as well—some of which themselves have "satellites," thereby forming what is in effect for Descartes was merely a miniature solar system within the larger solar system (a fact not lost on Descartes, who had seen the moons of Jupiter through the new telescope). Each of these heavens, Descartes said, is entirely surrounded by adjacent heavens, which touch it; since a spherical shape can be touched by only six others of approximately the same size, he concluded that each of the heavens turns around its axis, which also provides the axis for the rotation of the whole heaven—a fact that Descartes "deduced" from Galileo's observation that the spots on our own sun travel across its face in the same direction that the planets move around it. Then, arguing on the basis of the conformation of a magnetic field with its poles and equator, he stated that there is a steady stream of the first type of element flowing into both poles of each heaven, meeting in the middle, and then exiting from both the middle and the whole heaven through the equatorial regions—a situation that can be grasped graphically by means of a magnet and a light sprinkling of iron filings. These streams of the first type of element meander from one equator to the adjacent poles of contiguous heavens, *and thereby form a sort of circulatory system in the heavens.*

For Descartes, the heavens are really fluid (*vid.* Art. 24, Part III: "That the Heavens are Liquid [*Que les Cieux sont liquides*]"). So, too, are all the parts of the human body:

> the parts of all bodies which have life . . . are continually changing; so that there is no other difference between those which are called *fluids*, such as the blood, the humours, the spirits, and those called *solids*, such as bone, flesh, nerves and the membranes; except that each particle of these latter is moved much more slowly than those of the former. [Vol. XI, p. 247, l. 3–12]

What is more, the fluid moves, in both cases, in more or less a circle—Harvey's work is important indeed, since for Descartes the concept of circulation is central. Article 206 of Part IV of the *Principles* states that

Descartes' primary cosmogenetic suppositions were his three elements and the tourbillons, or whirling heavens. It *seems certain that Descartes was meditating on the general circular motion of fluid bodies when he saw the solution to the problem of the generation of animals.*

More particularly, Descartes seems to have begun to make further progress in his physiological speculations when he began to reflect on the celestial situation that involves a central sun (or star) covered with sunspots—a sort of earth. He saw this as the first intimation of an evolution of the general case, where the central star has no or only a few spots on it, in the direction of an earth-encrusted planet on which living things could arise. In the case of the star covered with spots, the circulation of particles of the first element is modified in a way that is strikingly suggestive of the relation of pairs of blood vessels, i.e., an artery and a vein directing blood into and out of organs in the body of a living animal. The point here is not merely that we can perhaps better understand Descartes' theory of the generation of the human body by comparing it to his own description of the evolution of planets from suns and of solar systems from the remnants of celestial cataclysms, but, in addition, that Descartes' texts give very firm grounds for concluding that the generation of the human organism "fit to receive the soul" is different from the generation of a solar system *only* in the degree of organization present in the latter. For Descartes, evolution is simply a matter of an increasing amount of order.

Descartes interpreted fluidity in two allied ways: on the one hand, fluidity permitted him to postulate circulatory currents of matter, which permitted him to relate causes to distinct effects; on the other hand, fluidity implied that each of the three elements could be transformed into the other two, and serve as a mechanical basis for the interrelation of compound bodies.[18] That is, for Descartes there are no truly empty spaces in the universe, and whatever occurs in one part can influence what happens elsewhere. Furthermore, this fluidity permits coagulating and rarification, so that the finer parts can form masses of relatively heavier matter; this thickening is analogous to alimentation or nutrition of a living body, as explained in Part III of *Description of the Human Body.* In the heavens, this process causes sunspots to form on the surface of the central star. These spots are earthy, and resemble the third, earthy element (of which muscle tissue is composed), but they are sometimes burned off, causing solar flares, and thus transforming the matter of the spots into particles of the first element once again. However, sometimes the bombardment of particles of the third element so rounds off their edges that they are transformed into particles of second element, "balls," where the jagged and irregular detritus of this process comprises the minute, finely grained particles of the first element. However, when particles of the first element coagulate, so that the star on whose surface they are located becomes thickly covered, the high-energy, luminous star no longer acts with sufficient force to help the heaven preserve its integrity, and it is both darkened and subsequently absorbed into the whirling matter of an adjacent heaven, becoming a planet or a comet. It is on such a planet that living things are to be found, as on planet Earth (*Terra*). Here we pursue the analogy in detail, beginning with the heavens.

This process of generation of planets from luminous stars in the *Principles* is nearly exactly paralleled in the *Description,* where the analogue to the matter of the central sun (the first element) is the seminal fluid inside the fertilized seed. The generation of sunspots is echoed in Descartes' statement that the bloodstream carries food to the growing, developing fetus in the form of tiny threads (*petits filets*), which become entangled at those extremities of the arteries from which the solid parts of the body grow in the way that hair roots grow off the tap roots of plants (Vol. XI, pp. 248–250). When, in the course of time, the channels along which this nutrient-rich blood flows are choked up, the body dies from lack of the nourishment needed to replace what is lost through the pores of the skin and through its evacuations. Although the streams of first element in a heaven do not in any way nourish the central sun of that heaven, according to Descartes, still, when that sun is so covered with spots that those streams cannot get into it any longer, the whole heaven lacks the force borrowed from the agitation of the once-continually replaced first element to keep other heavens contiguous to it from absorbing it.

Diagrams and illustrations, many of which are modeled on plates found in Descartes' own text (Vol. IX), are helpful to our understanding of this point.

Returning for a moment to Figure A-2 (Appendix 4), AB is the axis of rotation of a spinning heaven AEBG, with the poles of the axis of its rotation at A and B, and the equatorial belt going through GgeE. Descartes stated that streams or "rays" of the first element flow into the heaven at the poles A and B and proceed toward the center defg, emptied of balls of second element by centrifugal force, and which then fills with particles of first element. These opposed streams meet in the center with a great deal of force, and, like two jets of water aimed directly at one another (see Figure 1), form a flat "disk" more or less at right angles to the streams; the "disk" has its circular lip along the equatorial belt of the heaven. Thus, entering into the whirling spherical sea composed of particles of the second element are polar streams of first-element particles, which finally meet in the central space; they leave first the center and then the whirling sphere itself along the equatorial zone of the heaven *at just those places where there happens to be the pole of a contiguous*

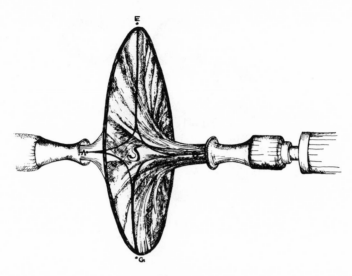

Figure 1

heaven (e.g., at E and G).[19] This situation obtains even when the sun at the center is entirely covered with sunspots, which Descartes took to be earth, and it continues to obtain until that earth becomes so thick that the streams of the first element can no longer penetrate to the interior of the central stellar mass in any great quantity.

Each of these heavens, with its central star deep inside it, is shaped like a partially deflated balloon, so that there is no space left unoccupied around any given heaven. The polar axis of rotation need *not* be along the longest axis, and no two poles of contiguous heavens touch (*Principles*, Part III, Arts. 67, 69). Thus, any arbitrarily chosen heaven can serve as the central heaven of a sixfold cluster, and it will be touched by exactly six other heavens, just as a partially deflated sphere can be touched only by six others of approximately the same size (Figure 2). Taking a central heaven with four of its six possible neighbors touching it (Figure 3), we get a group of five heavens within which there is a "circulatory" system formed by the endless streams of the first element, which circulates from heaven to heaven into the poles and out of the equators, as in Figure 4, which is designed from Descartes' *Planche IX* (Fig. ii, Vol. IX). A schematization of the circulatory system that connects the five heavens is shown in Figure 5.

Next Figures 6 and 7 show the general plan of the group of six heavens touching the central one, together with the circulation route that connects them to each other in Figures 8 and 9.

The circulatory route taken in the six heavens touching the central

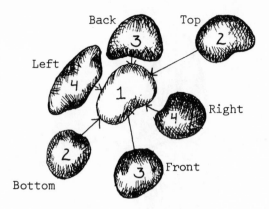

Back   Top

Left

Right

Front

Bottom

Figure 2

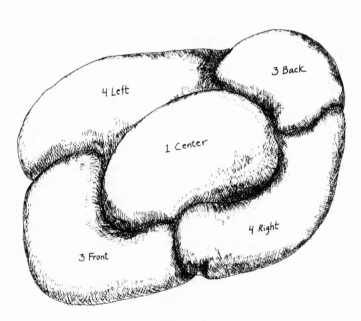

4 Left

3 Back

1 Center

4 Right

3 Front

Figure 3

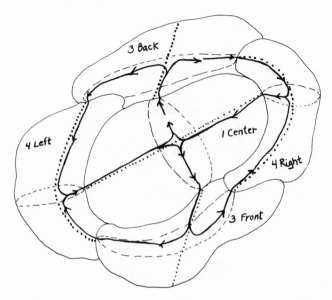

Figure 4. *This figure shows heaven 1 at the center, and touched at either pole by 4 Right and 4 Left and at two points along its equator by 3 Front and 3 Back. Streams of first element can only enter at poles and leave along the equator at points where the poles of adjacent heavens are found; therefore, 1 Center is "fed" by 4 Left and Right, and itself "feeds" 3 Front and 3 Back at their poles which touch 1 Center at its equator. Dotted lines* indicate the axes formed by the poles of each heaven; the broken lines *indicate the equators.*

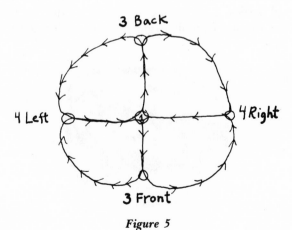

Figure 5

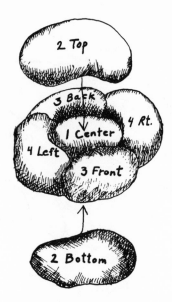

Figure 6

heaven, 1 Center, raises a problem: the first type of matter can leave heavens 2 Top and 2 Bottom only at points where a pole of another heaven touches their equators. As the illustrations to notes 19 and 20 show, this gives the cluster of six heavens a front and a back—the front being the end at which 2 Top and 2 Bottom feed 1 Center.[20] The case of 2 Top feeding 1 Center is given in Figure 8.

Figure 9 shows how 2 Bottom also feeds 1 Center at the end where 4 Right is located. This is by no means arbitrary, since we are preparing for the phenomenon of polarity, in order to permit Descartes' derivation of the celestial bodies as giant magnets that have distinct poles—and to permit the derivation of bodily organs that have distinctly directed circulatory flow.

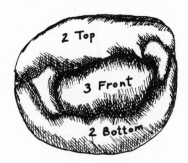

Figure 7

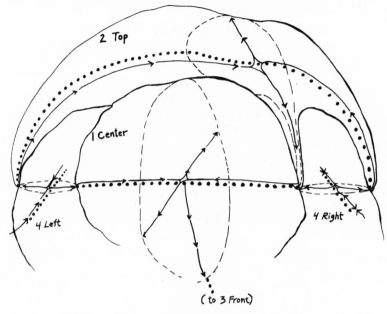

Figure 8

The Genesis of the Human Body

Descartes' great interest in circulatory loops is nourished by his insight that they concern the functioning of the human body as a total entity; that is, they concern the body as an integral entity within an outside environment. Consequently, the circulatory loops are primarily concerned with: 1) the brain as the seat of the four senses and the pineal gland; 2) the two lungs, both as the reservoir of outside air for tempering the heat of blood as well as the organ of speech; 3) the two arms as that by which we grasp; 4) the genitalia as the means of sexual reproduction, i.e., with another; 5) the two legs as the means of walking; 6) the body wall as a closure that defines the inside neighborhood within which these functions are associated with one another, and 7) the gut as the "sieve" that sorts out potential *aliment* from the masses of extraneous matter brought into the body through the mouth. If we count the lungs as two and the legs and arms together as four, and then count the brain, the genitalia, the body wall, and the gut each as one, we have a total of ten circulatory loops. We can provisionally schematize these loops as shown in Figure 10.

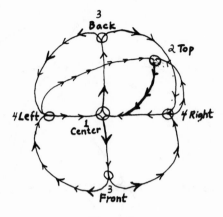

Figure 9

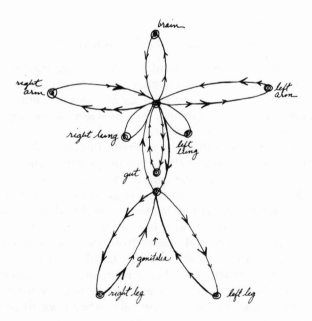

Figure 10

However, to count the two arms, lungs, and legs each as two loops is perhaps unnecessary, since: 1) the blood supply to the arms feeds off the brachiocephalic ramifications of the arch of the aorta, giving the heart-arms-heart loop; 2) similarly, both lungs feed off the pulmonary artery, giving the heart-lungs-heart loop; 3) the body walls feed off the descending aorta, giving the heart-body wall-heart loop; 4) the gut also feeds off the descending aorta, giving the heart-gut-heart loop; 5) the common iliacs supply the legs, giving the heart-legs-heart loop; and, finally, 6) the brain and head region are supplied by the common carotids (which in one case is also a ramification of the brachiocephalic artery), giving the heart-brain-heart loop. Also, the genitals could be understood as a part of the body-wall supply or even as belonging to the blood supply of the gut. If so, we then have a total of six loops feeding off the heart and hence sharing the same blood supply—one loop for each planet.[21]

How Descartes Generated Secondary Loops Within a Given Heaven

When Descartes has done the same thing in his account of the heavens, he will have generated an external circulation—analogous to the fact that humans ingest and expel matter into and out of their bodies— and a complex internal circulation, with the heart—analogous to the central star of a heaven—as its center. To do this, Descartes needed to divert the external, primary loops by means of some sort of *obstruction.* This he did by means of earthlike sunspots, which are generated on the surface of suns out of the first type of matter. The central, luminous cavity in the heaven is filled with first-element particles, which stream into the heaven at its poles, continue to the center, and then leave the heaven at one or more points situated along the equatorial belt. The material of sunspots is formed by the passage of the particles of first element through the sea of balls of second element, thus "threading" those particles of first element so that they interlace and, as it were, coagulate into hard, obstructive masses. Descartes said that one consequence of the obstructive masses is a sort of "air," which is, he says, very similar to our air on Earth. The air is generated around the sunspots near the surface of the regions of the sun that are covered with them. The air is composed of minute particles of the third element of the sunspots, which has been worn down by the action of the first element of the sun grinding away at the surfaces of the spots. We are told (*Principles,* Part III, Arts. 98–100) that this happens as follows: First, the spots become just barely submerged into the matter of the sun. Then, just as a narrow, shallow side-branch of a river flows more rapidly than the river itself, and, by its rapidity (Art. 98) elaborates the earth on its banks until it becomes very fine sand, so, prior to its breaking up into the matter of this solar air, the partially submerged spot causes an extremely rapid flow over itself, causing solar flares and "a sort of air" to be generated in the heaven just above the surface of the sun at a place where the spot is submerged. As slightly submerged spots collect over the whole surface of the sun, the air generated forms a "trough" around the sun.

When a heaven contains a sun with no spots on it, the sun is filled by means of streams of first element that enter through the poles of the heaven and flow on into the poles of the central cavity; the opposed polar streams then leave the central sun all around its equator, but they leave the heaven of that sun only at those points on its equator at which are found the poles of contiguous heavens. In the case we envision and schematically illustrated in notes 19 and 20, the central heaven, labeled 1, received streams from 2 Top and Bottom and from 4 Right and Left, but sent out streams only to 3 Front and Back. This means, then, that the equatorial belt of the central heaven, 1, had only two places on it where the poles of contiguous heavens touched it, and also that its poles provided two outlets for two pairs of contiguous heavens—i.e., for 2 Up and Down, and for 4 Right and Left. Therefore, even in this most simple organization, we may have a prototype of the "medical" distinction between arterial and venous circulation in the living human body.

In the course of long stretches of time it can happen that a sun becomes entirely covered with a thin layer of earthy spots. In this case (*vid.* Part III, Arts. 105–109), the sun is impermeable to neither the polar streams of first element that enter it nor the equatorial streams that leave it; consequently, that central sun still provides a central pressure sufficient to maintain the integrity of the heaven as a whole, and is not yet ready to be absorbed into another heaven as a planet. Such sunstars, however, are at this point in their evolution entirely surrounded by the special sort of air that is generated by the sunspots and, what is unique to this intermediate situation, the sunspots generate on the poles of the stars a sort of particle that does not coagulate into sunspots, but which continues to circulate in a peculair way. In Article 105 Descartes said that these circulating particles are threaded, and that they "are larger than the first element" (but smaller than the second). Also, they can only travel through the very pores of the spots by passing through those by which they were initially threaded, and they can move only in the same direction as they moved while they were being threaded. Consequently, once they have made a single passage through a central star covered with spots at its poles, in one pole and out the other, they can pass through no other such masses of earthy material unless it is threaded exactly right. In Article 108 Descartes said that the particles,

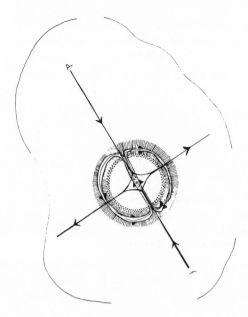

Figure 11

entering one pole, say, "f," and leaving the opposite pole, "d," begin to flow out into the heaven through the space containing the air generated by the spots; and this trough of air is, itself, surrounded by the sea of second element that comprises the body of the tourbillon (see Figure 11). This, as Descartes said (Art. 108), makes "thus a sort of vortex around the star." For, those streams of threaded particles cannot enter into the sea of second element, which thus turn them back into the trough of air, where they continue their path until they reach the solar pole through which they initially entered the sun. (This is Descartes' derivation of magnetic fields!) Here, then, is the first *internal* circulatory loop that is generated in the heavens. Whereas up to now the heaven has had two entrance points and a number of exit points, for the first time we now have a celestial body that has one pole at which the threaded particles can enter, and another at which they can exit. (We shall soon see that the very first fetal heart has, for Descartes, only two chambers, which are in a sequence with one another, rather than side-by-side, as in the adult stage.[22]

To sum up, a star that is intermediate between a fully luminous sum in a heaven and a dark planet that supports life differs from its immediate antecedent star in several striking ways:

1. The central sun here is encrusted with so many spots that much of the stream of first-element particles traversing the sunspot pores is

threaded so that the particles are "polarized" with respect to the sort of pores they can enter and pass through, and must turn either right-handedly or left-handedly;

2. The spots at the poles allow the streams of threaded particles to enter into only one pole and to exit from the other pole;

3. The covered sun is surrounded by a trough of air within which streams of threaded particles easily move;

4. The trough of air is completely surrounded by the sea of spherical particles of second element, which is impenetrable to the streams of threaded particles;

5. The stream of threaded particles is thus turned aside into the trough of air surrounding the sun until it reaches that pole of the sun by which it initially entered and which is covered by the spots in which its particles were initially threaded;

6. Streams of the finest particles of the first element still enter the heaven and its central sun—covered with spots as it is—as before, i.e., entering at the poles and leaving at the equatorial regions of both star and heaven.

We now leave the circulatory systems of the heavens in order to examine further the analogous system of a living human, beginning with the fetus.

The Human Fetus

Descartes himself stated that we can deduce from his cosmogenic hypotheses the formation of the fetus and the conformation of the developed animal, and he repeatedly referred to Part III of the *Principles* in his embryological and physiological *Description*—especially to his theory of light. His theory of light, it will be recalled, was always cardinally important for Descartes' medical theory, as we have also seen from the title of *The World,* which is subtitled "Treatise on Light." *The World* treats in great detail the soulless automaton that is operated by "natural" events in the way a church organ is operated by the fingers of the organist. These grounds alone indicate that any attempt to grasp Descartes' theory of man is seriously incomplete if it does not dwell in detail on the analogy between the formation of the heavens and the conformation of the organized body of a living man.[23]

Descartes' analogy, toward which we are working, is based on the scheme of the cluster of seven heavens, together with the internal circulatory systems or loops that one or more of those heavens develops as its central sun becomes progressively more encrusted with earthy sun-

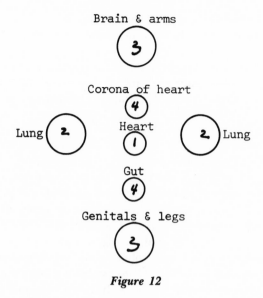

Figure 12

spots. In our first analogue (see Figure 12), we take each major circulatory loop in the body and attempt to show the analogue in the generation of *internal* circulatory loops in a heaven as its central star begins to evolve into a planet that will, at the conclusion of its evolution, revolve around the star of another adjacent planet. (The number of planets in our solar system was not viewed by Descartes as a magic or necessary number; rather, the simple fact that we have evolved six major circulatory loops, following the laws of nature, which also govern the evolution of solar systems, provides a *prima-facie* case for the possibility of a human evolution that follows the laws of nature that rule all of the parts of the universe without any appeal to divine intervention.) Descartes' own words justify the pairing of the brain and the genitalia, as well as the pairing of the kidneys to the genital circuit, since there are two renal arteries and two spermatic arteries, and there are two carotid arteries to the brain. We group the circuits of the arms with that of the brain in view of the fact that one of the great arteries to the brain, the right common carotid artery, feeds off the right subclavian artery, which also feeds the right arm, and the third great artery to the brain, the basilar artery, feeds off both the right and left subclavian arteries, and, along with the right and left internal carotid arteries, feeds into the great arterial anastomosis at the base of the brain, the circle of Willis. The circuits of blood supplying the arms and the brain together have their origin at the top of the arch of the aorta, and, with negligible exceptions, they are the only recipients of arterial blood issuing from the arch of the aorta. All the rest of the arterial blood of the body comes from the feeders of the descending aorta.

Our speculation in this direction is justified, even demanded, since Descartes said (to Burman) that his derivation of the genesis of the human embryo is derived from his study of the heavens (which in particular means the subject matter treated in Part III of the *Principles*, and, as he referred to it in Part III, his theory of light as contained in the *Dioptrics*). Therefore, whatever the difficulties in establishing an analogy between the development of the human embryo out of the fertilized egg, on the one hand, and a planet out of the centrally located space of a heaven, on the other hand, we must try to establish it. The first and last terms of the analogy are clear: in the heavens our first term is a sun, and in the embryo it is a fertilized egg. The final term, in the case of the heavenly development, is a planet, often with one or more moons around it; in the embryo, it is a mobile adult, a citizen of some country.

There are several possible ways to establish this analogy. One is for the capillary systems in the living body to correspond to the simple "earth-covered" suns with streams of first element flowing in and out. In this case, each human body as a whole corresponds to a partially covered sun. "Death" in old age is caused by clogging of the pores through which "nutrient" streams flow—streams of first element in the case of a sun, and streams of aliment in the parallel case of human nutrition. "Living" is defined as being a part of the surroundings, i.e., it is being able to temporarily utilize streams of materials entering from outside in order to maintain corporeal integrity.

However, a second, slightly modified form of the first analogy is that each capillary system—the capillaries 1) of the brain, 2) and 3) of the two lungs, 4) of the chest organs, 5) of the portal systems of the liver, and 6) of the body wall and reproductive organs—corresponds to a distinct region of a single heaven through whose poles and equator streams of first element flow in their eternal cycles. In that case, each distinct living body corresponds to a single, distinct heaven.

Finally, the analogy can be modified by considering each living human body as corresponding to a "constellation" of heavens, where each major capillary network would thus correspond to a distinct heaven with a distinct sun.[24] In this case, the whole living body, with its heart, would be analogous to a cluster of six heavens around a central heaven, *its* "heart." (To this cosmological scheme would correspond something like a body politic comprised of clusters of clusters. That body politic would thus be governed by a universal government, a truly "catholic" rule, and its laws would be "scientific.")

To recapitulate, then, the body of a living animal is generated by the formation of circulatory loops entering and leaving the heart, and the solid parts of the body are formed by the extrusion of the solid fibers from pores in the blood vessels. The pores through which the solid parts of the body are extruded are the finest pores in the body, and thus, the most-solid parts of the body are formed from the finest parts of the blood, paralleling the way in which the coarsest third element is formed from the finest first element. The spongy organs, such as the lungs and the liver, are formed primarily from the airy particles in the primordial blood, from the *particles aërienne.*

In the human body the outward half of each circulatory loop has been traversed when the arteries ramify into capillaries, which, when they have given up their nutrients from the blood, reassemble into veins, whose blood traverses the return part of the loop back to the heart.[25] (Harvey hypothesized capillaries, and Descartes thought he saw evidence for them in the venous sinuses of the head and the pampiniform plexus of arteries and veins in the scrotum.) We have tentatively identified the major circulatory loops as follows: 1) the head, 2) the two arms, 3) the two lungs, 4) the two loops that include both the coronary vessels of the heart and the vessels of the digestive organs, 5) the genitals, and 6) the two legs.[26] Since Descartes named the "principal planets" in our solar system as sun, Mercury, Venus, Earth, Mars, Jupiter, and Saturn, as well as Earth's one moon and Jupiter's six, we might look at our own solar system to establish our analogy. For, Descartes stated (Part III, Art. 146) that, before a sun can have six planets, as our sun has, six heavens around the central heaven must have collapsed into the seventh heaven as their suns became densely covered by sunspots. Indeed, it follows necessarily from the Cartesian texts that the Earth, sometime before it was in the process of being covered with a very dense layer of sunspots, must have been a sun in a heaven contiguous to which there was a heaven having a sun that later became our moon when the Earth's heaven absorbed the moon's heaven.[27]

In order to maintain our analogy, we must not go too far back in the evolution of our Earth from the sun it once was in a sevenfold cluster of heavens. The correct analogy is made, it seems, where the human body is the analogue to our own present heaven with its central sun and six planets, as in Figure 13. (The assignment of planetary names is not altogether arbitrary.[28]

In the analogy between the planetary system of our heaven and the living body, we pair the heart with the lungs, both because of Descartes' characterization of the function of the lungs in the cooling of the blood from the right heart and because at least some of those star-suns are surrounded by a trough of "air" within which the threaded and polarized particles of first element move; that is, the lungs, which more or less

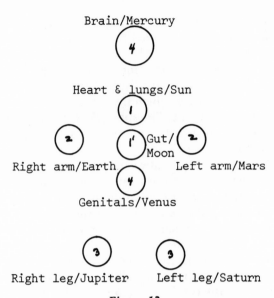

Figure 13

surround the heart, seem to provide an analogue to the trough of air surrounding the heartlike star-suns that have some sort of gaseous atmosphere. The blood entering the air-filled lungs comes from the lower right heart, and, leaving the lungs, returns to the upper left heart (Figure 14). Therefore, we have the first loop, heart-lungs-heart.

As we have mentioned, at first the embryonic heart is functionally two-chambered (Vol. X, p. 258, l. 4–15), and its circulatory system simply makes a loop out one end into the other (Figure 15). Similarly, when the central sun has a middling thick coating of spots over its surface, a miniature loop (what Descartes called "un quasi tourbillon") was formed around it so that first element entered one pole, left the other, and looped around in the trough to the first pole once again. In the embryo, the next step, for Descartes, is that the most highly agitated parts of the fetal blood force a passage through the upper arch of the loop (the brachiocephalic arteries to the arms and head), just before it begins to descend. One part of those arteries will ascend straight up to the region that will become the brain. When the blood reaches the brain region, it loses enough of its initial force to be once again turned back toward the heart. The most highly agitated remainder of the blood, which has reached the lower part of the loop, also forces its way through the base, just as it begins to ascend again, and continues until it reaches the region where the genitalia will be found. When those agitated particles there

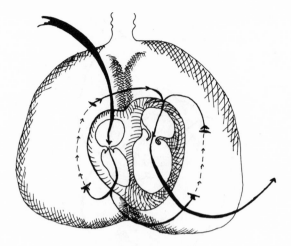

Figure 14

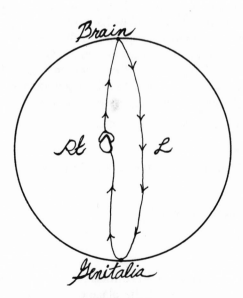

Figure 15

Figure 16

lose sufficient force, they too are turned aside and begin to travel up to the heart again, giving the third loop: heart-genitals-heart (Figure 16).

Finally, the loops supplying the arms and legs appear to be mere ramifications of the vessels formed by back-pressure—i.e., they are really ramified bubbles formed in response to the enormous pressures exerted by the formation of the brain and genitals.

Therefore, we can reconstruct Descartes' analogy as follows: Calling the heart 1, the lungs 1′, the brain 4 and the genitalia 4′, the arms 2 and 2′, and the legs 3 and 3′, we progressively get the loops:

     I.   1–1′ (in the earliest embryo), then

    II.   1–4–1, and then

   III.   1–4′–1; then, forming the arms and the legs,

   IV.   1–2–1, and

    V.   1–2′–1, together with

   VI.   1–3–1, and

  VII.   1–3′–1.

In each case, the circulatory loop connects the heart to some functional unit and returns to the heart. (The place of the gut is elusive.)

The heart, although full of very hot fluid, is never simply the analogue to a spotless luminous sun in a heaven; rather, it is the analogue to the intermediate stage occurring between a luminous sun and a "dark" planet, which is why we detailed the relationships of stars and their planets before we derived an analogy between a celestial situation and the living body. Therefore, the steps are:

1. Luminous star in its heaven

2. Partially covered star, with trough of air belonging to it, but still in its own heaven

3. Completely covered star, absorbed into another heaven containing a central sun

4. The living organism on a completely covered star.

Summary

The evidence of the spots on our own sun (discovered by Galileo using the newly devised telescope) suggests that luminous bodies constantly tend toward evolution into planets. This tendency implies that each and every star is always threatened with absorption into an adjacent heaven. [Thus, our own heaven (with its sun), absorbed six adjacent suns, along with their heavens, and two of those suns—Earth and Jupiter—themselves at one time previously had absorbed adjacent suns, becoming the Earth and its moon, and Jupiter and its Medici moons.] To repeat, planetary evolution happens when a star's earthy crust of sunspots becomes so dense and *obstructive* that the replenishing streams of first-element particles from adjacent heavens are reduced, thereby decreasing the pressure at the center of the whirling heaven so that the density at its edge no longer prevails over the countervailing forces of those adjacent heavens. Similarly, in the embryo, the blood begins to generate secondary loops *only* when the force of the retaining vessels is overcome by the force of the agitated particles of first element in the blood, and the blood begins to return to the heart *only* when the force of the vessel walls is greater than that of the first-element particles. Finally, the body dies when these vessels become clogged and the loops no longer serve to carry nutrients to the various parts of the body.

In addition, the actual conformation of the body (that is, the relative placement of its parts) also appears to have a celestial analogue, described in Part III of *Principles* in Article 119, "How a fixed star is moved when it begins to be no longer fixed," and Article 147, "Why all the planets are not equally distant from the sun." In Article 119, Descartes described the process of a star becoming so thickly covered with sunspots that it can no longer provide sufficient pressure from the center of the heaven to prevent the encroachment of adjacent heavens in its cluster. When this happens, its heaven collapses and it is absorbed into another heaven. Then, in Article 120, Descartes stated that, at the edge of a heaven, "up" from its center, the rotational motion of the heaven carries the newly absorbed planet around with it. Then in Article 147, he stated that each planet has a definite *pesanteur* ("weight")—by which Descartes meant what Newton meant by "mass" in the *Principia* (pub. 1686–87). The *ratio* of the weight of the newly absorbed planet to the density of the heaven that absorbed it determines how far from the center of the heaven it will revolve.[29]

Continuing with the conformation of the developing embryo, the (brachial) arteries going to the arms branch off either at or near the arch of the aorta, and the (iliac) arteries going to the legs branch off not far from the spermatic arteries. We can consider these loops as: 1–2–1, 1–2′–1 for the arms; 1–3–1, 1–3′–1 for the legs; 1–4–1 to the brain; and, finally, 1–4′–1 to the genitals. Each of these six loops was determined in its length of circuit from the heart by the *ratio* of the force of the agitated particles of the blood to the countervailing forces of the containing blood vessel walls. In each case, the loop began its return to the heart only when the ratio of the two forces was balanced (1:1). However, the body has the conformation it does because of the filaments of solid matter that were extruded from the nutrient-rich arteries. Therefore, the shape or conformation of the body is only an index of the primary ratios between the force of the first-element particles of blood and the restraining vessel walls.

By pursuing this analogy, we can deduce, from Descartes' theory of the heavens—by a continuous and nowhere-interrupted motion of thought reflecting the continuous and nowhere-interrupted motion of the three elements as they generate living bodies from primordial and luminous suns—the conformation of the human body.[30]

ETHICS AND THE MEAN

Whatever else it may do, our intellectual inner light illuminates for us our individual definition and integrity and concerns us as distinct entities; we are organisms that have life, but we are surrounded by more or less unorganized masses of bodies that, to the degree that they are unorganized, threaten our organic integrity, or even threaten to absorb us into their sphere of influence. Generally, to have life means, for Descartes, that a region of a heaven is filled with particles of matter that are so interconnected (*inter se componendas*) that some primary circular motion of those particles is exactly conserved and maintained, and, what is essential, this motion is *self*-conservative. This is similar to the general case of the heavens, where streams of first-element particles wander through a potentially infinite number of heavens, but, it seems, return very seldom to any given heaven once they have left it, unless the star of that heaven has a trough of "air" around it. Still, even in the general case, each heaven is a distinct whirlpool of matter, with one and only one central sun; it thus has the distinct beginnings of a real definition simply because the particles of second matter belonging to a heaven revolve around its center—although some could be broken down and perhaps later become first-element particles.

The individual, prescient living human is a "microcosm" or, because of his organ systems, a microconstellation; and, insofar as each of us is surrounded by other, potentially "absorbing" microcosms, each of us is a cosmopolitan individual. That is, out of our very ontogenesis, a human, no less than any given heaven, develops into an individual whose definition is radically incomplete without taking into consideration the existence of other, similar individuals. Descartes thus replaced Aristotle's "political animal" with an individual whose relations to any and all other individuals—alive or dead—is exhaustively governed by the general laws of nature that govern the disposition of bodies in the universe. All "interpersonal interaction" is henceforth understood as reducible to actions and reactions of bodies with one another. The human perceptive capacity interconnects individual human microconstellations by means of passions, such as love, hate, and desire, and their compounds or derivatives, such as pride, envy, recognition, and generosity. However, we must understand clearly that these "passions of the soul" have analogues in the cosmological antecedent. It appears that every passion "mirrors," as it were, a particular relational disposition to be found in the general cosmological case. Thus, for instance, we find that each heaven maintains its shape and individual integrity only because surrounding heavens push on it with a force exactly equal to its centrifugal force pushing on them. Similarly, each human maintains himself by a system in a psychological dynamic equilibrium—where love or desire corresponds to centrifugal force and, for instance, virtuous humility is the response that humans have to the "love" or "desire" of surrounding microconstellations.

In other words, to speak analytically, the passions aroused in us by our social intercourse with other humans are ultimately to be understood only as derivative psychological analogues to absolutely general conditions obtaining in the heavens from whence we evolved. Descartes' scientific ethics—founded as it is directly on medicine and mechanics—is a social mechanics or social dynamics, or even a social physics. For the heirs of Descartes, political science can only be viewed as what results from restricting general science to humans with their peculiarities.

The individuality and distinctiveness of a human microconstellation

Figure 17

are necessarily ambiguous. What is cosmopolitan is somehow universal and general; what is individual is set apart from others and somehow self-defined. We have argued that, for Descartes, the individual is cosmopolitan because the genesis and definition of that individual follow in their progress the model explicated in his scientific cosmogenesis. We particularly pointed out, within Descartes' cosmological account, the step at which the central sun is so covered with a thin layer of spots that it generates what Descartes called a kind of tourbillon, "quasi-tourbillons."

It is useful here to present some newly invented illustrations of how the fully formed and mature adult would imitate, in his vision and reaction to his vision, a spot-covered star with its miniature tourbillons: in each case, the individual conserves himself by integrating with his immediate environment by means of a miniature "tourbillon"—i.e., a sort of circulatory loop.

Figure 17 shows an adult who sees an approaching snake, which he identifies as poisonous. We imagine him to pick up a nearby spear and kill the snake. The snake is at E, and is "seen" by the eye, at A, which sends back streams of spirits to the pineal gland, at B. The stream of spirits, by continually activating muscles and nerves, finally causes the hand, at C, to move to E, where the snake is. When the spear hits the serpent, the episode is finished, and the total route (snake, light beam to eye, sight, motion in the body, thrown spear, and hit snake) gives us the "quasi-tourbillon," or loop, E–A–B–C–D–E.

In the second illustration (Figure 18), soon after leaving his (safe) home, a man sees a tree being struck by lightning, at which time he returns to his home, which he remembers to be safe. This case involves a loop only if the man *remembers* the security of his home and knows to return there during danger.

The final illustration (Figure 19) uses Descartes' own example (given in the *Dioptrics*) of a blind man with a stick walking down a road. In place of the cone of entering rays of spinning particles of second matter, we have the cone formed by the stick as the man whirls the end around. The loop here begins with the resistance to the stick that occurs at tip E and that continues until the feet are moved in a particular direction as indicated to the man by the place at which the resistance was met. However, the place at which the stick met a resistance is precisely the place to which the man would *not* move his feet. Indeed, if the tip E met resistance on its whole circuit—if, for example, the man came to a wall at the dead end of a street—the man would stop altogether. In other words, in this case, the case of a blind man, the loop is only completed when the man has in fact moved forward in a direction that the tip E has indicated has nothing to prevent motion. Where he can go is revealed to him by his knowledge of where he cannot go, just as the equatorial light of a sun in a whirling tourbillon indicates the paths by which that body would move could it move. The vision of the blind man is thus analogous to the equatorial light of the sun. Both ultimately proceed from, as a final consequence of, an opposition to motion. Whereas the central sun emits only a thin band of colorless light along its equator as a result of the thwarted impulse to motion, the blind man, as it were, "reads" the obstacle and gains from it the knowledge of where he can go. It thus seems fair to consider this power of man, be he in fact a blind man, or a man faced with decisions concerning the obscure future, or a man faced with a problem whose solution he does not know, as his "inner light."

In each case, the individual conserves himself by becoming integrated with his immediate environment by means of a miniature tourbillon or a sort of circulatory loop. These situations, however, remind us of the "mediochre" or medial stage of the evolution of a star into a dark planet. This, in turn, leads us to the development of a dark planet that

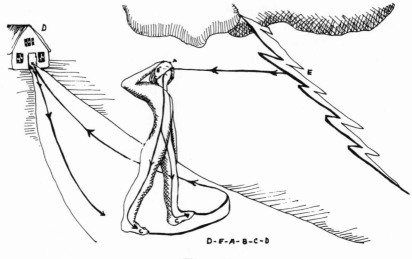

D-E-A-B-C-D

Figure 18

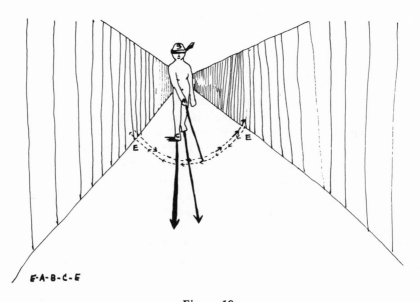

E-A-B-C-E

Figure 19

has lost its central position in its original heaven but that, by way of compensation, has a much higher degree of organization than it did as a luminous star. When on that planet there arise sentient living things with intellects, those beings capitulate the first evolutionary stage, inasmuch as they have the sense of sight and the power to see into the distant future by means of their inner "light of nature," their intellect.

The power that men have to perceive "physical" light points to the interconnectedness of each living, organized thing with other things, with other definite entities elsewhere in the universe. This "outer" light is perceived to be colored in a way that indicates to us the past history of the paths taken by the particles *en route* to the eyes. Without color, the outside would be as indistinguishable as it is to a blind man without his staff. Color gives the form, the *idea* of the seen, that is, of the visible in general. The inner light is not colored, since it most often concerns what is not present and what therefore does not have a history. Rather, the inner light of the problem-solving intellect primarily concerns the potential things have to change in a certain definite way, i.e., in a way that will result in precisely that interrelatedness of things that will confirm and strengthen the organic, self-maintaining character of our own living bodies. Thus, for example, by means of the hypotheses Descartes constructed in the *Description,* he revealed to us how an almost formless whirlwind of matter mechanically generates an ordered, living, and self-sustaining organism. As he stated in the foreword to the *Description* (Vol. XI, p. 223, l. 10, to p. 224, l. 1), from these hypotheses can be deduced both self-knowledge (*se connoistre soy-mesme*) as well as "very sure precepts, as useful for fighting sickness as for preventing it, and even, also, for retarding the course of aging." Therefore, it is through modifications of those very mechanisms by means of which light is generated in the heavens that self-sustaining, self-defining complexes of interrelated particles of matter are generated.

Descartes said in that foreword to the *Description* that the attempt at self-knowledge is the most fruitful undertaking we can embark on, and that "the utility which one can hope for from that knowledge concerns not only Ethics . . . but, particularly also Medicine." We have seen that he said at the end of the *Discourse on Method* that his ultimate goal in his great instaurations of the sciences is an improved medical science. Again, the greater part of his final meditation, Meditation VI, concerns the question of divine goodness in the face of human sickness, and ends on the note that God is good, and thus gives us no difficulties to which He does not also give us the possibility for solutions.

How does heaven, for Descartes, start us on our way to self knowledge? Certainly not by some art of gracious revelation through prophecy or extraordinary miracles. Indeed, Descartes' quotations from the

Wisdom of Solomon (chapter 13) and from St. Paul (Romans, chapter 1) in the "Letter of Dedication" to the *Meditations* are passages that concern God's creation as manifesting His sovereignty; they entirely lack any hint of the possibility for the solution to our evils, and they are certainly not prophetic—using the word 'prophetic' to apply both to a review of and a prognostication for the evils that beset man because of his foolishness and pride. It appears, therefore, that God's goodness begins with the phenomenon of sickness, which, according to Descartes, is either caused by, or remains uncured because of, a certain lack of self-knowledge. Finally, Descartes identified medicine, mechanics, and ethics as the three principal fruits of philosophy, where ethics, "presupposing an entire knowledge of the other sciences, is the final degree of Wisdom."

The ethics briefly discussed at the end of Part I of the *Passions* is a personal ethics, and concerns primarily the individual's conquest of personally harmful habits. However, the greater part of the particular passions itemized in Parts II and III of the *Passions* are by no means primarily personal, and are not definable outside a social context. For examples we need only consider some of the topics of Articles in Part II: Article 55 concerns veneration and disdain; Article 58, hope, fear, jealousy, security, despair; Article 59, irresolution, courage, boldness, emulation, cowardliness; Article 62, mockery, envy, pity; and Article 64, favor and gratitude (*reconnaissance*). Finally, Article 66, concerning glory and shame, points out that, "what is more, the good which is or has been in us, being related to the opinion that others have of it, excites in us glory, and the bad, shame." Thus, it is fair to conclude that both Descartes' personal ethics and his interpersonal ethics are based on one and the same medical theory of Part I of the *Passions*. Personal ethics is primarily based on self-interest, and interpersonal ethics on that same self-interest as affected by our relations and interconnections with others.

How then does Descartes understand the demands of self-interest in such a way that it leads to what could be recognized as ethics? Or, to put the question slightly differently, what is the relation between medicine and ethics? How does the war against disease and the course of aging entail self-knowledge and at the same time join with mechanics to provide a basis for ethics?[31]

Because ethics is the final degree of wisdom, attained only after a thorough investigation of medicine and mechanics, it appears that the true subject matter of ethics is only revealed in the course of investigations belonging to medicine and mechanics. Medicine primarily treats the interconnectedness of neighborhoods of matter, where the notion of "neighborhood" holds the place in mechanics that "organ" holds in medicine. Then the laws of nature, by means of which God conserves

His initial creation, stand to these neighborhoods of matter (e.g., a heaven) in the place of the institutions of nature in living animals, who approach what seems good to them and flee what seems harmful. That is, moving from the laws of nature as the rules operating in matter in general (in *res extensa*) to the effect that these laws produce mechanically in the myriad of distinct and interconnected heavens, and then proceeding to the natural institution operating in living organisms to the effect that each acts "by nature" for its own preservation, we finally arrive at the world of those institutions that deal with the interconnectedness of human living organisms, each of whom is immediately affected by his own realization of the institutions of nature operative in himself. These last institutions are, of course, the institutions of states and cities of men, and they are a "mean" between the universe at large and the living organism. The discovery of that "mean" is the "final degree of wisdom."

In the second section of the "General Introduction" to this work, we discuss at length a likely connection between Descartes' reflections on geometry and his reflection on his own weak constitution. For, following the laws of nature insofar as they particularly concern the celestial matter that generates light, there appears a continuous evolution from a heaven with an unblemished central sun to a planet, and we propose that Descartes thought, from there to living things as miniature "heavens"; and this path downward from the general theory of light to the formation of animals is the selfsame path by means of which we ascend upward from thoughts on disease to the most general cosmology. This descending path from the heavens to the womb of a gravid woman, and ultimately to the aches and pains of her offspring, is an example of what Descartes called "the way of synthesis, which, in examining the causes by their effects . . . shows truly clearly what is contained in the conclusions of the causes." If Descartes' interest in medical theory was occasioned by his own early pulmonary weakness, on the one hand, and by a philanthropic impulse for the betterment of man's lot on the other, then the fundamental impulse toward his universal science, which necessarily included his general cosmological investigations, was significantly bound up in his reflection of pain and sickness, both somatic and psychological.

The path from the effects, such as pain or mental distress, to their ultimate "causes," the heavens, reflects the general path from effects to their causes, which "makes clear how the effects depend on their causes." This is the path by which Descartes proceeded from his own experience of pain and the anguish of extreme and prolonged sickliness to a philosophy that bore medicine as one of its three most exalted fruits.

If we are correct in our speculations, pain and suffering themselves were, in Descartes' mind, signs of God's providential goodness, and they replace the Creation as it is viewed both by tbe author of the Wisdom of

Solomon and by St. Paul, i.e., as a sign of the true Creator. Our naturally instituted impulse to health, safety, and long life is for Descartes the fundamental sign of God's beneficence, just as much as the conservative character of His laws of nature, the search for which does not seem for Descartes to even begin until the "first law of nature," self-preservation, becomes known to us. For Descartes, then (as with the author of the Wisdom of Solomon and St. Paul), the Creator did not give the Creation in order to give men an insight into His essence and design; rather, He gave pain to purblind, lazy, and insoucient men to sting them into a closer look at His creation. For Descartes, it is neither wonder nor fear of the Lord that is the beginning of wisdom; it is fear of an early or painful death that is the beginning of philosophy.

Medical theory, the exalted fruit of Cartesian philosophy, examines why a body is fit to have life in it, and, in cases of illness, how they are direct results of the "derangement" of one or more parts of the organism. The general cosmology of Part III of *Principles* does the same thing with respect to the phenomenon of light that medical theory does with respect to life. It is striking that the less able a celestial body is to occasion light, the more nearly it approximates a state that is able to be alive or to support life. Even in the case where the central mass of a heaven is most luminous and unspotted, a definite degree of organization is present, but not one that particularly distinguishes such a heaven from any other. Luminous heavens have nothing comparable to the Ego of a thinking thing. On the other hand, insofar as a given human is thoughtless and self-satisfied, that is, insofar as each of us does not think using *sa raison*, we flow in the meandering streams of history and its accidents in a way strikingly analogous to the flight of a particle in a luminous heaven with an unspotted sun at its center. The power of thought in a living human combines the splendid luminosity of the pristine heavens of the beginning with the vitality of their end, whose only illumination is the light of nature. The sensitive vitality of the living, thoughtful human defines and sustains him, while it also effects a process of organization of circumstances toward his own goals; and that process recapitulates the genesis of his kind from primordial, splendidly luminous origins (at least insofar as his thought is provident and prudent with respect to the future). The creative-conservative action of God is thus faithfully imaged when men who are learned in true medical theory connect their beginnings with their end.

NOTES

1. Fustel de Coulanges, Numa Denis, *The Ancient City,* anon. trans. of *La Cité Antique* (Baltimore: Johns Hopkins University Press, 1980). See pp. 109, 111, 134, 136, 191, 198, and 308.

2. Descartes' doctrine of free will seems to deny this; however, in Meditation IV (Vol. IXA, p. 64), he spoke of nature as "God himself, or even the order and disposition that God has established in the created things."

3. However, cf. Daniel, chapter 4, and especially verses 17 and 22–25. In spite of the story of Abraham, and St. Paul's interpretation of that story, the Old Testament seems to view the vertical bond as essentially strengthening the horizontal one. Augustine's *City of God*, as well as his *Confessions*, establish him as the "second founder" of Christendom, i.e., of Christianity as an association where the lateral bonds between, for example, mother and son, scholar and student, and priest and congregation are confirmed in accordance with celestial archetypes. However, it is perhaps not too bold to suggest that implicit in Pauline Christianity is a certain social atomism, which is the price he paid for his designation of a congregation as being united primarily because they are "members in Christ." A bald statement of the atomicity often to be found in this view was expressed by Charles Colson, the advisor to the *quondam* president, Richard Nixon, when he said, in March, 1975: "If Christianity is true, the individual, who will live forever, is more important than governments and societies that come and go."

4. At the very least, Rousseau's "romantic" reaction to the doctrines of the cosmopolitical theorists is, as a reaction, profoundly influenced by those doctrines. It can, however, be argued that Rousseau's *volonté generale* is really a Newtonian integral. See Richard B. Carter, "Rousseau's Newtonian Body Politic," *Philosophy and Social Criticism* (1981) 7(2):144–167.

5. Woodrow Wilson, *Constitutional Government in the United States* (New York: Columbia University Press, 1908), Ch. III, "The President of the United States," pp. 54–55.

6. Norman Hampson, *The First European Revolution: 1776–1815*, (New York: Harcourt-Brace, 1969), pp. 24–25. Descartes' name occurs once on p. 161, in this revealing passage: "Alexander's main advisor was now Speranski, who, as a former lecturer on Descartes, Locke, Leibniz, Condillac and Kant, was well acquainted with the theoretical basis of the Enlightenment."

7. A. W. Kinglake, *The Invasion of the Crimea*, 5th ed., 8 vols. (Edinburgh, London: William Blackwood and Sons, 1874), Vol. I, pp. 258–259.

8. We notice here that the *"substantial"* union of physical body and thinking soul (*res extensa* and *res cogitans*), i.e., the ensouled automaton, is missing, even though Descartes said several other places that that union is an object of human science. This slight skew from the parallel suggests that the question of the lawfulness of the activities of "extendedness," *res extensa*, as modified by its union with "thinkingness," *res cogitans*, is somewhat tangential to the question of the lawfulness of the motion of *res extensa*. This could be expected, since this is a form of the question of free will and determinism. The full solution to this question, we argue later, is a part of the "last degree of wisdom," reached only when all the other fruits of the Tree of Philosophy have been cultivated. (Descartes is no simplistic mechanistic determinist.)

Genevieve Rodis-Lewis's monograph, *Descartes et le Rationalisme* (Paris: PUF, 1966), pp. 51–62, has an interesting section on body as having a soul. Her treatment is much closer to the present treatment than most.

9. Continuity of state—i.e., that there are no true discontinuities in nature—and only this axiom, guarantees that all the universe is in principle accessible to our human efforts to know. See, on this association, M. Gueroult, "Raum, Zeit, Kontinuitaet und Indiscernibilienprinzip in der leibnizschen Philosophie," in *Etudes sur Descartes*.

For a treatment of the mind-body question that is in profound agreement with this present development concerning *the questions* that Descartes addressed, see Rainer Specht, *Commercium mentis et corporis* (Stuttgart-Bad Cannstatt: Friedrich Fromann Verlag, 1966).

10. In the *Treatise on Light*, Descartes stated:

You well know that words, not having any resemblance with things which they signify, do not fail to make us conceive them—often without our even noticing the sound of the words or of their syllables; so that it often happens that, having heard a conversation very well grasped, we are not able to say in what language it had been pronounced. Now, if words which signify nothing except through the institution of men suffice to make us conceive of things to which they have no resemblance, why cannot Nature also have established a certain sign which makes us have the sensation of light, although that sign should be nothing in itself which resembles that sensation? And is it not thus that Nature has established laughter and tears in order to make us read joy and sadness on the faces of men? [Vol. XI, p. 5, l. 3–19]

However, if the physical cause of light does not resemble in the least the sensation of light that it causes in men, we must ask why Nature should have established any connection between the two. (We must add that in his dialogue, *Timaeus*, Plato presents the cosmologer-lawgiver, Timaeus, as saying that the *principal* use of eyesight is that it permits us to view the heavens! What *he* means by this, however, is not what Descartes means. Vid. *Timaeus*, 42A2–42C5.)

11. See A. I. Sabra, *Theories of Light from Descartes to Newton* (London: Oldbourne Books Co., Ltd., 1967) for very useful comments on Descartes' theory of light. Of Descartes' physics of light, Sabra says: "He had thus believed to have established a bridge between that branch of physics which studies actual motion and the other branch whose subject is light" (p. 113). As we shall see, this is somewhat misleading; however, Sabra is correct in saying that Descartes' physics treats of light, but that his biology does not. (Light loses its luminescence because it required a Natural Institution to relate what the physics of light deals with and our perception of what that physics concerns itself with.)

12. Stanley L. Jaki, *The Paradox of Olber's Paradox* (New York: Herder and Herder, 1969), pp. 42–43.

13. Ibid., p. 57.

14. Ibid., p. 55.

15. According to Copernicus's 1543 *Revolutions of the Heavenly Spheres*, the Earth, in the six months during which it travels from the point nearest the Sun (in June), to the point furthest from the Sun (in December), covered a very large distance. At both those points, Descartes could look at a star, even through a telescope, and it would still be at the same place in the heavens. Geometrically, this means that, over a six-month period, the sighting instrument is at the two ends of the very long base of a triangle whose vertex is the star and whose two sides are the lines from the eye on Earth to the star. The fact that the star did not seem to change position means, geometrically, that it must be all-but-infinitely remote; to visualize this, we need only image a triangle with an enormous base and whose sides are "parallel" to one another, or so nearly parallel that they cannot be distinguished from the parallel. It was not until 1838, when Friedrich Wilhelm Bessel (1748–1846) showed that, over six months, the position of the star 61 Cygni changed by an angle of 3″.31, that we on Earth had any experimental evidence 1) that the stars are not infinitely remote and 2) that the Earth does move. Descartes' physical theory of light and his neuroanatomy of sight were both addressing questions that were in significant measure laid upon him by his Copernicanism.

16. New English Bible (Oxford and Cambridge: Oxford University Press, Cambridge University Press, 1970).

17. For instance, Gilbert Ryle, *The Concept of Mind* (New York: Barnes and Noble, 1950). Thus, Albert Balz's *Descartes and the Modern Mind* (New Haven: Yale University Press, 1952) does not discuss the term 'soul' thematically; rather, it refers us to "substance," "thinking substance," "thinking things." As we have seen, Keeling, in his *Descartes*, replaces "soul" with "self."

18. Again, for Descartes the three elements are: 1) the first element, which is spiritous and extremely volatile, alcohol-like; 2) the second, less volatile, but still gaseous ele-

ment—resembling sooty smoke; 3) the third element, which is composed of a "coagulation" in the same way that soot forms in the chimney. Descartes the algebraist made much of the fact that the second element is "mean" (*mediochre*), with respect to the first and third types.

For a view of Descartes in which none of these issues, such as elements, their transformations, etc., even come up, see James Collins, *Descartes' Philosophy of Nature*, Ch. III, "Three Primary Meanings of Nature" and Ch. IV, "Laws of Nature." Implicit in Collins's treatment is a view of philosophy that is entirely distinct from physics. This is yet another reason why Descartes is understood in so many different ways: "trained philosophers" feel they can discourse on Descartes' physical thought without any detailed analysis of the texts dealing with physical matters.

19. Sometimes the points of exit are nearly diametrically opposed to one another, but just as often they are situated very close to one another. Each heaven will always have *at least one* exit point along its equatorial belt.

An illustration of this point follows. Taking dotted lines to represent the axis of rotation of a heaven, and the broken lines as the equator:

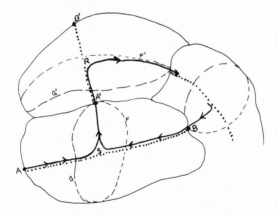

AB is the axis of rotation of the heaven with S at its center; the circle A'GF is its equator, which touches the pole A'B' of the upper heaven at A', and the equator of its right-hand neighbor at B.

20. As we here see, the case in which 2 Bottom feeds into 4 *Left* also works.

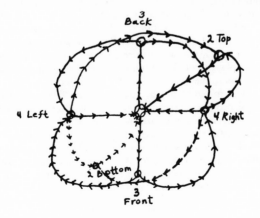

However, as we said, this case would make it much more difficult to derive the phenomenon of polarity, which William Gilbert's 1600 book, *De Magnete* showed to be a
property of the Sun, the Earth, and all the other planets. Then, Harvey's 1623 book
showing the circulation of the blood from the heart, through the organs, back to the heart,
gave, so to speak, a sort of polarity to the various organs of the body. On these grounds, we
take the more fruitful of the two possibilities—a most Cartesian procedure!

21. As we shall see, the arms are formed by back-pressure in the blood vessels that
send blood to the developing brain and pituitary gland, so that the arm-head system (fed
by the brachiocephalic vessels), forms one major system with several ramifications—in a
way analogous to that in which, for example, Jupiter with its Medici moons is a system
within a solar system. Similarly, tbe iliac arteries to the legs can be seen as part of the loop
from heart to genitals and back to the heart. The precise analogy is, perhaps, less important than the sincere attempt to form a more or less satisfactory analogy; the attempt
results in a view of the generation of the body and its circulatory systems as being in total
accord with the same general laws of nature by means of which the heavens, containing
planetary systems—making life possible—were generated. We are striving for that analogy
precisely to uncover Descartes' doctrine, which has, since then, become an axiom. [*Vid.*
Karl Jaspers, *Descartes und die Philosophie* (Berlin: Verlag Walter de Gruyter, 1956), Part III,
Ch. 5, *"Die historische Wirkung des Descartes,"* for an intimation of a process of doctrine
becoming axiom.]

22. The reader is urged to compare the Cartesian account of the early genesis of the
aortic arch with Plates 14–17 of "Development of the Major Blood Vessels" [*The Ciba
Collection of Medical Illustrations*, Frank H. Netter, M.D., 6 vols. (Ciba Pharmaceutical Co.,
1969), Vol. 5] "Heart," Section III, "Embryology," pp. 127–130.

Descartes said explicitly that the heart in the earliest embryo has only two chambers;
he knew, and said as much, that the heart of the fetus has, in effect, only two chambers—
the right auricle being largely an antechamber for blood to enter into the left auricle and
thence into the left ventricle—thus entirely bypassing the lungs. Therefore, the whole loop
to the lungs is bypassed both in the embryo and in the fetus when the blood flows directly
from the right auricle through an opening that occurs only in the fetal and embryonic
heart, the *foramen ovale*, which opens into the left auricle. Returning to the "immature"
heart through the two branches of the vena cava, the blood continues on to the right
ventricle, where only a little is required for feeding the lungs. Most of the blood in the right
ventricle, rather than going to the lungs to be oxygenated, passes directly into the pulmonary artery, and then directly into the descending aorta, via the *ductus arteriosus* (which, after
birth, becomes obliterated). Thus, for Descartes, the heart starts as two-chambered, becomes three-chambered, and then, very soon after birth, four-chambered.

Of the formation of the heart Descartes said:

But at the beginning of its formation, I believe that the first concavity, which
is tilted [*se panche*] later towards the left side, occupies the exact center of its
body, and I believe that the blood which comes from that left cavity first takes
its course to the place where the brain is formed and then towards the
opposite place, where the generative parts are formed; and that, in descending from the brain towards the generative parts, it passes first between the
heart and the place where the spine is formed; and, after that, ascending just
so high as it has descended, it returns to the heart. [Vol. XI, p. 258, l. 4–15]

(Here the lungs have not yet been formed.)

Indeed, if we take a line whose ends are the top of the skull and the groin, the heart
nearly bisects the line. Figure 20 illustrates Descartes' words, also showing how Descartes
said that the mature heart of higher mammals must both flip over as well as "tilt" (taking *se
panche* as Descartes' seventeenth-century spelling of *se penche*).

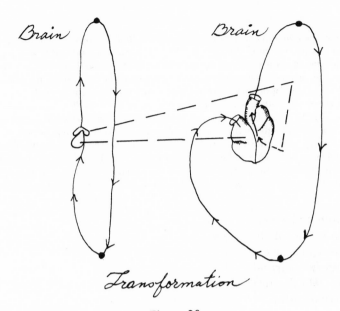

Transformation

Figure 20

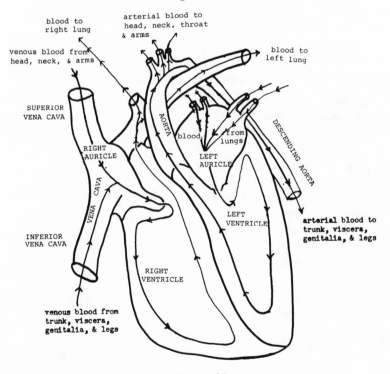

Figure 21

Since in the immature fetal heart the *foramen ovale* allows blood from the right side of the heart (*vena cava*) to enter directly into the left heart, which is tilted relative to the line that divides the bilateral symmetry of the mature body, it would appear from Descartes' words that the chamber that is at maturity at the top of the right heart, the right auricle, was originally at the bottom of the "proto-heart," and that the right ventricle of the mature adult was at the top, rather than, as in the mature adult, at the bottom of the left heart. Hence, the original heart had to flip to the left nearly 90 degrees so that the mature right heart could receive blood, from the body at large, at the top of the right auricle. (Descartes spoke as if the arms and the legs were formed by the back-pressure of the blood returning to the original two-chambered heart, thus forming two additional circulatory loops.) A reminder of the shape and function of the mature heart is given here as Figure 21.

Figure 22 is an accurate anatomical illustration of the actual blood supply, from the heart, *up:*

a. arch of aorta
b. brachiocephalic artery
b′. brachial artery
c. internal carotid
d. vertebral artery
e. basilar artery
f. posterior cerebral
g. middle cerebral
h. posterior communicatory
i. ophthalmic artery
j. anterior cerebral

Figure 23 shows the blood supply from the heart *down:*

a. heart
b. descending aorta
c. celiac artery
d. suprarenal arteries
e. superior mesenteric artery
f. renal artery
g. inferior mesenteric artery
h. common iliac
i. spermatic artery
j. vaginal tunic of testes
k. 12–13 vertebrae
l. testes

23. Again, Descartes was very clear that his physics is the foundation for his ethics, which concerns the way humans should act to achieve their ends, i.e., the preservation of life. See Wolfgang Roed, *Descartes, Die innere Genesis des cartesianischen Systems* (Munich, Basel: Ernst Reinhardt Verlag, 1964), Ch. 3, for a view of Descartes' ethics that is *not* based on his physical work; such a view of Descartes' ethics must be incomplete—*provisoire*. (However, the subject of Descartes' physics, *res extensa* or matter-prepared-to-be-known, is strikingly reminiscent of Aristotle's ὕλη of *Physics* (194a, 34–194b, 9)—a fact of which Descartes was extremely ignorant.)

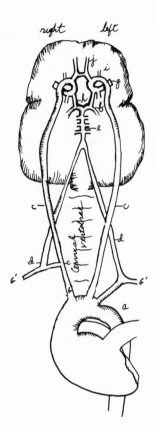

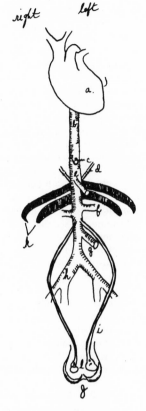

Figure 22   **Figure 23**

24. For Harvey, the existence of capillary networks from arteries to veins is a *consequence* of his assertion of the circular flow of the blood in the body. He could not see these capillaries, and no one could, until Leeuwenhoek had invented the microscope. In fact, no one saw them until 1661, when Malpighi viewed them in the membrane between the toes of a frog. To repeat: Harvey postulated the existence of capillaries as a necessary corollary to his assertion that the blood circulated through the body. The question of the existence of capillaries was a rallying point for the proponents of anti-Galenic—and hence anti-Aristotelian, anti-Scholastic, and therefore unorthodox—theory.

25. Generally nutrition is for Descartes only the continuation of that process by means of which the body was formed in its beginning, the greatest difference being that, in the beginning, the matter of the fertilized seed is composed of what later will be replenished by nutrients from outside the fetus through the umbilical cord. Hence, what in the beginning is the mechanism of the creation of the animal becomes later the mechanism of its conservation and maintenance. Descartes said:

> But in order to know in particular how each portion of aliment goes to the
> part of the body for the nourishment of which it is proper, it is necessary to
> think that the blood is nothing other than a mass of several small particles of
> food [*viandes*] which one has taken to nourish himself; so that one cannot

doubt that it is composed of parts which are very different from one another, as much in figure as in solidity and size. [Vol. XI, p. 250, l. 16–24]

Again, the growth and maintenance consequent on this assimilation of food are described by Descartes:

> Now, beside those pores by which the humours and the spirits flow, there is yet a quantity of others which are much narrower by which the matter of the two first elements (which I have described in my *Principles*) pass continually. And, as the agitation of the matter of the two first elements maintains that of the humours and the spirits, so the humours and the spirits, in flowing the length of the small threads which compose the solid parts, cause the small threads to advance continually a little, although very slowly; so that each of their parts has its course from the place where they have their roots up to the surface of the members where they terminated; and when they reach it, the meeting with air or with bodies touching that surface separates them from the trunk of the thread; and, just so much as it detached from the extremity of each thread, that much is added again to its root . . .
>
> Thus one can see that all the parts of the little threads which compose the solid members have a movement. [Ibid., p. 247, l. 29, to p. 248, l. 28]

The reader is urged to compare this account with that in Alfred Sherwood Romer, *The Vertebrate Body*, "Circulatory Vessels." Romer says, in particular:

> The vessels of the circulatory system, like the blood cells, are derived from the embryonic mesenchyme. As food-containing liquid begins to flow through the body of the early embryo, adjacent mesenchyme cells gather about such channels and surround them with a thin but continuous wall. All early formation of major blood vessels take place in this fashion . . .

With only very minor changes of vocabulary, Descartes could have written that passage, rather than an Alexander Agassiz Professor of Zoology, Museum of Comparative Zoology, at Harvard University. [*The Vertebrate Body*, 3rd ed. (Philadelphia, New York: W. B. Saunders, 1964), p. 419.

26. In each case, the blood coming from the heart travels in a stright line until it reaches an obstacle that causes most of it to deflect back toward the heart. According to Descartes, the arches at the place where deflection occurs often are the sites of critically important glands, e.g., the pituitary (which Descartes thinks is responsible for the production of cerebrospinal fluid), and the testes.

27. The following notice comes from the *International Herald Tribune*, December 8/9, 1973, under the headline, "Jupiter and its Moons Seen as a Miniature Solar System":

> Mountain View, Calif., Dec. 7 (WP): The planet Jupiter and its moons were described yesterday as looking something like a miniature solar system, with Jupiter filling the role of the sun and the moons playing the parts of the planets.
>
> "This to me is possibly the most interesting discovery of the Pioneer-10 mission so far," said Icthiaque Passool, deputy director of the planetary programs for NASA. "We are being shown Jupiter as almost starlike, and we have the moons reaching out from the planet just the way the planets of the solar system string out from the sun, with the densest closest to the sun and the lightest ones farther away."
>
> While Jupiter was described as being something less than star-like, it came across that the giant planet was close to becoming a star at the birth of the solar system. The Pioneer-10 spacecraft that flew by the planet on Monday found nothing to dispute this claim, and in fact found something that tends to give it strong support.

For Descartes, this "claim" is an absolute necessity.

28. For Copernicus and Descartes, the order of the "solar system" was: Sun, Mercury, Venus, Earth, Mars, Jupiter, and Saturn. Earth has its moon, and Jupiter has its moons, discovered through the telescope by Galileo. *This* is what Descartes and his contemporaries knew that previous ages did not!

29. Cf. the description of the so-called Cartesian devil (Cartesian diver or Cartesian imp) found in any large dictionary.

30. *Vid. Principles,* Part IV, Art. 206, where Descartes stated that his theory of the heavens is as certain as his mathematical demonstrations. This means that Descartes ends that vast work, his *magnum opus,* by claiming that he knows the heavens and the laws regulating the activity in them better than he knows what he senses going on around him here on Earth! From this it follows that he could deduce the final, missing parts of his *Principles,* concerning plants, animals, and, finally, man, from those better known principles, their celestial causes. An example of this deduction is given in the deduction of the fabric of the human body from his cosmogenic principles.

(See also Keeling, *Descartes,* Ch. V, "The Natural World and our Knowledge of Nature" for a contemporary critique of just this point.)

31. In Meditation VI, Descartes pointed out that, in the maladjusted, or even broken, clock, the individual parts all follow the laws of nature. It is only when the clock can be of use to someone—to tell time—that we can view it in a transmechanical context. Thus, fixing a clock in order to make it keep accurate time exemplifies medicine addressing mechanics to ethical ends.

CHAPTER 4

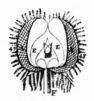

Introduction to the
Social Synthesis

THE BODY POLITIC AS A
COMPOUND BODY

So far we have dealt largely with the interconnections between bodies that affect one another only because they touch one another. The laws of nature regulating these interconnections are laws concerning motion and impact. However, in Part I we saw the soul as a link in the chain of causes, a link that performed its role via certain natural institutions. We then speculated that Descartes almost surely envisioned, in his doctrine concerning the nature of the human soul, an environment for the soul's body that would complement these natural institutions inborn in it in such a way that the conjoined soul could easily give affirmation to what it sensed around it.[1] If this situation were to be realized, then the chain of natural causation that includes the soul would not, it seems, be in effect any different than a chain of strictly mechanical causation, since the volitional faculty of the soul would, because of its own naturally instituted dispositions, affirm whatever it was aware of in its circumstances.[2]

Even under the most complementary of external circumstances, however, the soul would not cease to exercise its freedom of choice. However much its volitions might constrain it to be disposed to choose to affirm entirely complementary circumstances, that affirmation itself would be, for Descartes, the result of the soul's exercise of its freedom of choice, of its *libre arbitre*. This is exemplified by the case of a man whose awareness of hunger is his soul's naturally instituted reaction to a physiological modification of his stomach. He further is naturally disposed by that awareness of hunger to eat—which, if food is presented to him, he will freely choose to do.

The freedom of choice, which, for instance, most often results in the fact that hungry men choose to eat, is a freedom that concerns choices of things that the soul is naturally disposed to affirm or to reject. This does not in the least mean that the soul is a mere fiction, which, in light of the strict mechanism of the physical world, is really not necessary for Descartes. This view of Descartes' thought, almost coeval with the first publication of his writings, almost certainly arises from a profound misconception about Descartes' very personal evaluation of the world and all that appears in it. The soul is necessary for Descartes. Without it, men would have no presentiment, and thus progress within the providentially ordained secular world would not be possible, even though that progress is pointed exclusively in the direction of the conservation of the union of mind and body and the improvement of its lot. Descartes thought that all situations that presented true matters of choice to the soul were concerned with the preservation to which the complex of body and soul was naturally predisposed; he simply did not take seriously the possibility that there could be any other, "supra-mundane," interests for the soul. (No more would a contemporary psychoanalyst take as true the insistence of a patient that he or she had a revelation that was of divine origin.) Because Descartes was the man he was, he could not, for instance, take seriously Aquinas's remark (at I, q.1, a.6, *ad primam* of his *Summa Theologica*), a remark that Thomas got from Aristotle (*On the Parts of Animals*, 644b, 31): "But yet, the least that can be had of the knowledge of the highest things is more to be desired than the most certain knowledge which is had of the most paltry things." On his part, the young Descartes (at no more than age 24) wrote:

> I have prescribed to each and every intelligence [*ingeniis*] fixed limits which they cannot transcend. Whoever cannot find principles of discovery because of a defect of intelligence can still know the true worth of the sciences—which will suffice him for making true judgments concerning the evaluation of things.[3]

In short, for Descartes, nature has predisposed the soul of man to affirm or to reject what is presented in the mechanical order of things; but this does not in the least mean that for him the soul is unnecessary. Furthermore, we humans, whose souls are so disposed, must often depend on the good will (*bonne volonte*) of other men in order to have the disposition be operative. That is, unless men work together in a certain way, very little that is choiceworthy will be presented to the soul to choose freely. This is why we might say that *the institutions of nature in the soul are, as it were, the blueprints or plans for the institutions of society.*

Ethics, then, is to be viewed in a Cartesian light as being a twofold undertaking. On the one hand, it involves the sort of empirical psychoanalysis that reveals the inborn and natural institutions, and that involves considerations dealt with by mechanics as well as by psychology, since it deals with the relation between physiological and psychological mechanisms. On the other hand, this undertaking points outward, toward the attempt to design human institutions that are in accord with the physiological and psychological mechanisms (e.g., the use of forensic psychology in the courts, and the testimony, to legislative committees, of expert medical witnesses about laws concerning sexual conduct). The political order, with its laws governing the human sphere, is in this case no less inherent in God's creative-conservative providential order than is the mechanical order with its laws. Concerning this point, Descartes wrote (10/16/45) to Princess Elizabeth:

> I confess that it is difficult to measure exactly the extent to which reason ordains that we concern ourselves for the public—but then it is not a thing in which it is necessary to be very exact; it suffices to satisfy ones own conscience and here one can depend greatly on his inclination. For God has so established the order of things and conjoined men together into a so closely knit [*estroit*] society, that, although each man refers everything to himself and has no charity for others, he should not fail to exert himself on their behalf in all that is in his power—provided that he use prudence—especially if he lives in a century when morals [*les moeurs*] are not completely corrupted. And, besides this, since it is a more lofty and glorious thing to do good to other men than to procure it for oneself, so are they the greatest souls who are most inclined in that way and make least of the state of the good which they possess.[4] [Vol. IV, p. 316, l. 15, to p. 317, l. 10]

The term *estroit*—here translated as "closely knit"—is a term Descartes characteristically used to describe the nature of the union of body and soul. For instance,

> For it is not without some reason that I believe this body (which, by a certain particular right I call my own) belongs to me more properly and more intimately [*etroittement*] than any other.
> And although perhaps (or, rather, certainly, as I shall say soon) I have a body to which I am very intimately [*tres-etroittement*] conjoined; . . .
> Nature teaches me also by these feelings of sadness, hunger, thirst, etc., that I am not only lodged in my body as a pilot in his ship, but besides this, that I am conjoined to it *very intimately* and so mingled and mixed with it that I compose as it were a single thing with it [Meditation VI; Vol. IXA, pp. 60, 62, 64]

The passions of the soul are, it will be remembered, the reactions of the soul that specifically concern its intimate union with the body whose soul it is. The Cartesian psychoanalysis of these passions is extremely delicate, since it must perform an analysis or dissection of a union that, even under that analysis, must always be understood as a union. Indeed, that analysis leads to precisely those psychic mechanisms or dispositions whose definition entails the preservation of the union of body and soul.

Descartes' great presumption supporting his view of the importance of a synthesis or reconstitution of the components distinguished by psychoanalysis seems to be that there is possible for men an environment as fit for the primitive union of body and soul as there is a body fit to be united to the soul and a soul fit to have a body united to it. That environment is discovered and articulated through the discovery of those circumstances that alone make sense out of the passions of the soul as discovered by the Cartesian analysis of Part II of the *Passions*, that is, through defining the environment of man as what he has created as a complement to his passions in order to conserve himself. Again, corresponding to the union of the extended thing (*res extensa*) and the thinking thing (*res cogitans*), there is a public thing (*res publica*), a commonwealth of mutually interdependent "unions," i.e., living, thinking, humans. It is the passions of the soul joined intimately with a body that manifest the fitness or lack of fitness of that body and its larger environment to be the complement to that soul. Thus, the passions of the soul provide a natural measure, a "pre-rational" (not to say irrational) measure of a fitting complement for that soul.[5] Ultimately, the passions are thus the measure of the fitness of the total environment of a soul— including first its body and then its body's environment, that is, the political environment.[6] Therefore, the substantial union of body and soul, in the case of man, is not even "metaphysically" intelligible without taking the body politic into consideration. Hence, one of the three "primitive" ideas, that of the union of body and soul, is the very same idea by means of which we grasp the intelligibility of a certain kind of body politic—one very similar to Virchow's. Or, to put this in more Cartesian terms, the body politic is no more and no less a part of the divine preordination than is the human soul or the body that is disposed to receive it. Descartes' private theology is, no less than Spinoza's after him, truly 'theologico-political.'

THE IDEA OF THE PASSIONS AND THE IDEA OF THE STATE[7]

As we mentioned earlier, in the period of 1646 to 1650, Descartes wrote a series of letters to the French ambassador to Sweden, Chanut, concerning the composition and elaboration of the *Passions*. At that time, the possibility of being the philosopher in residence at the court of the Protestant Queen Christine had arisen, and Descartes certainly wrote his letters with an eye toward their being read by her. However, neither

Chanut nor Queen Christine could be supposed to be especially interested in the thoughts of the author of the *Principles*. Chanut was a man of affairs, and Queen Christine an autocratic monarch who was also a liberal dilettante of the arts and letters. This is the reason, we may suppose, that Descartes' letters to Chanut in this period were uncommonly full of assurances that the final goal of his physics was ethics (*la morale*). (It will be remembered that the Tree of Philosophy whose highest and most delectable fruit was ethics is described in the dedication of the *Principles* to Princess Elizabeth.)

In a letter to Chanut dated June 15, 1646, Descartes said:

> while I let the plants of my garden grow, from which I take experiments in order to try to continue my Physics, I also sometimes stop myself in order to think about particular questions of Ethics.[8] Thus I have this winter outlined [*tracé*] a little treatise on the Nature of the Passions of the Soul . . . [Vol. IV, p. 442, l. 8–13]

Somewhat earlier, in that same letter (ibid., p. 441, l. 25–27) Descartes assured Chanut (and through him, Queen Christine) that, "the notion of a Physics such as I have tried to acquire serves me greatly in establishing sure foundations in ethics]*la morale*]."

In letters to Chanut during 1647, Descartes was more specific about the relation between his physics and his ethics. He said, in a letter dated February 1, 1647, that he distinguished purely intellectual love from passion, saying of "purely intellectual love,"

> when a soul notices some good—present or absent—which it judges useful to it, it joins itself to that good by its will [*de volonté*], that is to say, it considers itself together with that good as comprising a whole of which one part is the soul and the other is that good. [Vol. IV, p. 601, l. 16–21]

Then, a few lines later, he wrote of the passions, saying

> I consider that from the first moment in which our soul has been joined to our body it is likely that it senses a joy and immediately afterwards, love; then, still later, perhaps also hate and sadness; . . . I judge that its first passion is joy because it is not believable that the soul would have been put into the body unless the body had been well disposed and that, when it was thus well disposed, that naturally gives us joy. I say also that love comes afterwards because, the material out of which our body is composed flows without cease, as does the water of a river, therefore, we can see the need for some new material to be always flowing in to take the place of that matter which we evacuate; it is hardly likely that the body would have been well disposed had there not been close to it some matter quite proper to serve as aliment to it and had not the soul, joining itself by means of its volition to that new matter, had some love for that matter; as

also afterwards, if it were to happen that this aliment were lacking, the soul would thereby be saddened. And, if other matter which was not proper to nourish the body came to take its place, the soul would have hate for it. [ibid., p. 604, l. 23, to p. 605, l. 16]

It is thus apparent that, for Descartes, "purely intellectual love" is hardly a love defined by the intellect's desire for a joy in something purely intellectual. It is a love *also* concerned with the union of body and soul, and it finds its fullest intellectual expression in the science of medicine. Thus, just as medicine begins with a reflection on illness and leads on to a general theory of the heavens, so, for Descartes, ethics begins with a reflection on human wretchedness and leads to a general theory of human society that can help and aid the unfortunate. In addition, the Cartesian study of ethics, of the political virtues, is a study of the passions. For Descartes, and for very many of the ethical and political thinkers after him, virtues are passions—whereas, for Plato, ἀρετή, or virtue, was a species of action.

The two "good dispositions," which Descartes saw as necessary for the soul to be joined to a body are: 1) the disposition that arises from the interconnectedness of the parts of the living organized body, and 2) the presence in the neighborhood (*proche de lui*) of matter that is proper to become part of the body in order to replace the part of it that flows out of it, which is "flowing without cease, as does the water of a river." The precondition for the soul to be joined to a body (and that precondition is the good disposition of the body), thus essentially includes the body's environment. Certain bodies in the immediate neighborhood of the organism are, so to speak, joined and united to the body to make a whole, of which one part is the well-disposed body and the other part is what it requires to keep it well disposed to be joined to a soul—to conserve the union of body and soul. (In this way, Descartes' economics, concerning conservation, implies his *theologoumenon*, his personal theology.[9])

Several years later, in a letter dated February 26, 1649, Descartes again wrote to Chanut and apologized for sending his *Principles* to a man who must be largely interested in ethics, for the instruction of the queen. He said:

> One could say that these truths are only of very little importance touching matters concerning physics which seems to have nothing in common with what a queen ought to know. But in so far as the mind [*esprit*] of this Queen is capable of all things, and since these truths of Physics are part of the foundation of the highest and most perfect Ethics, I dare to hope that she takes some satisfaction from knowing them. [Vol. V, p. 290, l. 23, to p. 291, l. 2]

In other words, Descartes spoke as if he were convinced that his own studies provide the foundation for Queen Christine's ruling art. It is the substantial union of body and soul that appears to provide the real foundation for the union of physics and political science, for the union of Descartes' studies and Queen Christine's art. We here argue that this complementary union of body and soul is, for Descartes, the paradigm or model for the union of individuals in a certain kind of society of fellow humans. From this argument it follows that the primitive notion of the union of mind and body would provide an adumbration, a foreshadowing, of yet another union of individual unions of body and mind—the "body politic." Therefore, the knowledge of this primitive notion of the union of mind and body gives a real idea of a political association that aids in man's attempt to preserve or conserve his union of body and soul, his life. In this chapter we speculate on the knowledge of the most "biologically" sound, or, as Descartes would have it, "medically" sound political association.[10]

Proceeding directly to Part III of the *Passions*, we argue for the following analogy: as the soul is related to its body, so is the union of that body and soul related to the body politic that the union "inhabits" as a citizen. When we have established the appositeness of this analogy, we can then conclude that the main task facing the citizen as a thinking being with a body is to discover his natural dispositions that arise from his being a union of mind and body and to see further that the main definition of a healthy body politic would consist in its being fit to receive and preserve the self-aware citizen. Textual evidence for this analogy is found, for instance, in his letter to Princess Elizabeth of September 15, 1645:

> After having thus recognized the goodness of God, the immortality of our souls and the greatness of the universe, there remains a truth the knowledge of which seems very useful to me: namely, although each of us should be a person separated from others, and, as a consequence, whose interests are distinct from those of the rest of the world, one ought nevertheless to think that he cannot subsist alone, and that he is, in effect,[11] one of the parts of the universe, and, still more particularly, one of the parts of that Earth, of that state, of that society, of that family to which he has been joined [*on est ioint*] by his own habitation, by his own language, by his own birth. And he ought always to prefer the interests of the whole of which he is a part to those of his own particular person—but with measure and discretion . . . [Vol. 5, p. 292, l. 30, to p. 293, l. 14]

Later in the same paragraph, he said:

> But when someone exposes himself to danger because he believes that it is his duty, or even when he suffers some other hurt in order to achieve good for others, although he does not perhaps consider reflectively that he does this because he owes more to the public of

which he is a part than to himself in his own particularity, he still does this in virtue of that consideration which is confusedly in his thought. [Vol. 5, p. 294, l. 5–14]

That "confused consideration" is a certain passion or passions. They are confused, usually, since they are usually "compounded" of several of the "primitive" passions.

In contemporary usage, the term 'passion' has a far more restricted meaning than it did for Descartes, let alone for the classical tradition to which he was so often opposed. Our present term 'reaction'—apparently stemming from the vocabulary of Newtonian physics—is the closest approximation we have to the rich term "passion" of earlier times. Even casual conversation can reveal that our contemporary use of the term, passion, largely derives from the lyrics of contemporary popular music. That is, we tend to view passion as sexual passion. A passion, for Descartes, was involved in all our conscious reception of an afferent impulse from outside. Hidden in this term, for Descartes, was the presumption that incoming impulses originating outside us did not just go through us and cause a mere physiological change that only rebalanced whatever the incoming impulse might have put out of balance; rather, hidden in his use of the term passion is the further presumption that these incoming impulses in part can be said absolutely to end somewhere in something that was to some degree modified by being affected by that impulse. The image Descartes used himself at one place (Rule XII; Vol. X, p. 414, l. 16–19, p. 415, l. 22–25) is that of a signet ring and the wax that receives the impression of the seal of the ring. Awareness of that impression is the passion caused by an incoming impulse (very nearly the impression in wax) and the soul, whose awareness it is, is the analogue to the wax.

It is, however, not so clear that for Descartes the soul ever was impressed by any experience. Rather, it seems that the *union* of body and soul alone could be modified by means of a permanent modification of the body of which its soul was consequently permanently aware. For Descartes, there cannot be any true spiritual change. The soul is a simple unit, a "monad," for him, as it was for his student Leibniz in his *Monadology*. With this teaching, Descartes rejected 2,000 years of psychology, and with it the political philosophy based on the writings of Plato's *Republic*, Xenophon's *Cyropaedia*, and Aristotle's *De Anima*, *Ethics*, and *Politics*. [12] Furthermore, psychology soon after Descartes and until now has, to an astonishing extent, been in the dark about what sense to make of *the fact of sense*.

Our intention here is to show how Descartes understood the role of the passions in the formation of civil society.

Each of the passions, Descartes said, concerns our naturally instituted awareness of some cerebral event. Insofar as they are perceived to be different passions, the character of the cerebral event in each case is different. Except for minor modifications of brain structure in the case of new afferent pathways being opened on the occasion of new experiences, however, the structure of the brain is not much modified by these events, and the principal cause of the differences of perception of passions lies in the rest of the organism. The main noncerebral causes of the difference of our perception of our passions are differences in blood pressure and the fact that upon different occasions different organs in the body send to the brain different sorts of animal spirits.[13] These changes in blood pressure and differences of animal spirits are perceived by us as differences in passions. An instructive example of how Descartes viewed the relation between a passion and its physiological basis is to be found in Article 102 of the *Passions,* "The movement of the blood and spirits in Love." Reminding ourselves that love is one of the six primitive, analytically irreducible passions, we read:

> These observations, and several others which would be too long to write down, have given me factual evidence [*sujet*] for judging that when the understanding represents to itself some object of love, the impression which that thought [*pensee*] makes in the brain conducts the animal spirits through the nerves of the six (cervical) pair, towards the muscles which are around the intestines and the stomach, in such a way as is required to bring it about that the juices of food [*suc des viandes*] which are converted there into new blood pass promptly towards the heart without being arrested in the liver, and that from there, being pushed with more force than that which is to be found in the rest of the body, it enters into the heart in very great abundance and excites in it a very strong heat because it is grosser than that blood which has already been rarified several times in passing and repassing through the heart; and this causes that it also sends spirits to the brain, and that the parts of these spirits are grosser and more agitated than usual; and these spirits, fortifying the impression that the first thought of the loveable object made in the brain, oblige the soul to arrest itself on that thought; and it is in this alone that the passion of love consists.

Having seen this *internal* source and definition of a passion, let us begin our *political* analysis of the Passions with several details out of Articles 149–161 of Part III.

Part III begins with a discussion of esteem and contempt (Article 149: *De L'esteme et du mepris*) as being the first two of the passions that are not primitive.[14] Descartes said that the six primitive passions are genera, *les genres,* "of which all the others are species." (We are thus prepared to read, several articles later, that the nonprimitive passion, generosity, is the key to the virtuous use of the particular passions.[15] All the passions are naturally instituted and, if well used, are necessarily good for humans—since God is no deceiver and nature is not malicious. Generosity is the genus of virtuous passions; it is the passion encompassing passions well used or used according to their natural institutions. This means, however, that generosity arises as the result of the knowledge of the use of all the passions, and it presupposes a complete mastery over all the passions; it presupposes an entire lack of selfishness. And, it presupposes Descartes' medically based anthropology.)

After this we find, in Article 150, that esteem and contempt are immediately deducible from admiration or wonder; for they, by nature, only concern the real worth of the thing in question with respect to reason's evaluation of them, and not their grandeur or pettiness relative to other things. Hence, esteem and contempt are, as it were, philosophically moral passions, passions, that is, on the basis of which a rational morality is to be based. They seem to be to the union of body and soul in social contexts what admiration or wonder is to the isolated individual who is to be integrated into a social context. Esteem and contempt appear to be the first *political* passions.

Articles 151–152 concern self-esteem and self-contempt along with the valid grounds for each. In Article 152 Descartes said that "one of the principle parts of wisdom [*la sagesse*] is to know how and why each man ought to esteem or condemn himself." The only just reason for self-esteem is our freedom of choice and the control (*empire*) which we have over our volitions—for we are only liable to praise or blame in those actions which depend on free choice, *libre arbitre*, "and this makes us in some way similar to God in making us masters of ourselves, provided that we do not altogether lose through cowardice the rights which He gave us." The most contemptible of men would thus seem to be he who does not insist on his God-given rights to exercise his own freedom of choice and to control his own volitions: to be a real human is to be an equal in a representative republic. It is very likely on such a passage that d'Alembert was commenting when he identified Descartes, living in 1650, as the leader of a band of conspirators.

Article 153 concerns generosity, "which makes a man esteem himself as much [*au plus haut point*] as he legitimately can." It consists first in knowing that "nothing truly belongs to him except the free dispositions of his volitions," and that he should only be praised or blamed on these grounds, together with a "firm and constant resolution to use volition well, that is, never to fail to undertake and execute all the things he judges to be best; and this is to follow virtue perfectly." In Article 154, Descartes stated that generosity gives to a man the knowledge and the sentiment that every other man can have all the virtues that he can have, because there is nothing in it which depends on anything extraneous. And this is why men who are generous disdain no one . . . all things seem to them to be very inconsiderable in comparison with a good will [*la bonne volonte*] because of which they alone esteem others, and which they suppose also to be, or at least to be able to be, in every other man [*etre ou du moins pouvoir etre en chacun des autres hommes*].

In the next article, 155, we find the psychological complement to self-esteem—virtuous humility.

Thus, the most generous are customarily the most humble; and virtuous humility only consists in the reflection on the infirmity of our nature and on the faults we have previously committed or are capable of committing—which are not less than those which can be committed by others.

This is why "we do not prefer ourselves to anyone and why we think that, others having their free choice [*libre arbitre*] as we do, can also use it as well." In Article 161, "How generosity can be acquired," we find that the virtues, "as they are commonly called," are habits in the soul and that they dispose us to certain thoughts. These habitual thoughts are "fortified by a certain movement of the spirits, and afterwards they are the actions of virtue and the passions of the soul." But, each soul "which God puts into our bodies" is not equally

noble and strong [*noble et fortes*] which is why I have named it virtue generally, following the usage of our language, rather than a largeness of soul [*magnanimite*] . . . it is certain, nevertheless, that good habituation]*la bonne institution*] is very useful for correcting the faults of birth . . .

The virtue of generosity is "as it were, the key to all the other virtues." Generosity, if supported by good habit, at one and the same time nurtures a proper self-esteem or self-assessment and leads to a proper assessment and estimation of others. This reveals that we are all only to be valued according to our present or future use of our free choice and that all other men have it no less than we. Self-esteem is the fruit of the *Je*, of the *Je qui pense*, of the Ego. It is virtuous humility, however, that is envisioned by Descartes as keeping this Ego in check and as habituating each man to a lack of ambition; this results in a willingness to entirely respect the Ego of each and every other man. Generosity, esteem, and virtuous humility lead, for Descartes, to universal toleration of socially admissible behavior. True virtue is true sociability.

Those articles, 149–161 of Part III of the *Passions* are the first thirteen articles of that part, and they form a small treatise within the larger development of the third and last part of the whole work. That small treatise deals primarily with self-esteem and humility, both based, however, on generosity. Those two passions handsomely complement one another, one correcting the excess of the other, and the other correcting the defect of the one. Self-esteem supplies vigor to humility and thus prevents it from becoming either pusillanimity or a sort of ignobility; humility restricts the extent of self-esteem and thereby prevents it from becoming overwhelming pride and arrogance. Humility thus keeps pride in check, and self-esteem gives weight and substance to humility. We are immediately reminded, in reflecting on this happy complementarity, of Descartes' figure of the stone being whirled about in a sling—a figure that he used to illustrate a balance of oppositions that results in a contained motion that does not in the least detract from the force of the moving stone. That force, in turn, is measured by the force used by the sling itself in keeping the stone in its orbit around the center. Descartes seemed to view self-esteem and virtuous humility (which is humility fulfilled by an accompanying self-esteem) as the two primitive political or social passions, as the passions that make it at all possible for men to live together obeying the same laws and still keeping their individual integrity and definition. This introductory treatise of the last part of the *Passions* concerns the psycho-physiological basis of healthy political association between men who are equal before the commonly observed laws. These laws do not in the least, if we follow the figure of the sling, take away the force of individuals, but only guide it. The strength of this association's laws is to be measured by the ability of those laws to keep men about some socially defined center. Remembering for a moment that Descartes did not at all seem to know the *astronomical* work of Kepler and that, along with Ptolemy and Copernicus, he thought that the planets traveled in circles, we can generalize on the figure of the sling, and then we get a picture of the Cartesian state that reminds us of a Copernican solar system, and with the body politic as a sort of heaven. Descartes' cosmopolitan order implies "popular" regimes.

In that the passion of generosity concerns the use of the passions in general, and since those passions are all "fortified" by the spirits of the body, generosity is concerned with the interrelation of the parts of the internal structure of the living human body in a very direct way. For, it is an imbalance obtaining between the parts of the body (relative to the balanced state that Descartes called serenity) that causes the specific passions. Furthermore, insofar as anything external to the organism can cause such passions as fear, hate, desire, love, and the like, because of our expectation with respect to them, generosity ultimately points to the total environment of the individual—to his human "ecosystem"—as an extension of his internal environment.

The real, physiological basis for the passions is the state of the internal structure of the living body together with the exterior ambience or neighborhood insofar as it is able to affect (directly) the internal structure. Hence, *the objective reality* of the passion of generosity in a man is a function of the total effective environment of the individual insofar as, and merely insofar as, he in any way consciously reacts to that total environment. The objective reality of the passion of generosity thus concerns the human being precisely insofar as he reacts to his total interior *and* exterior environment. The science that has as its object the understanding of that object is thus an amalgam of neurophysiological psychology and what we today might understand as "human ecology"— a kind of biological social science. Its model is a sort of constitutional history, where the term 'constitutional' should be taken in its medical as well as legal meaning.

In discussing how generosity can be acquired, Descartes made it clear that he was aware of differences of gifts to be found in men. However, he did not conclude that this indicates anything like the naturalness of a hierarchy of personages in the social order. We are not to expect anything like a philosopher king from Descartes, nor are we to expect anything like a theology that sanctifies the distinction between rulers and ruled. In explicitly replacing the Aristotelian notion of largeness of soul, magnanimity, with generosity, Descartes knew that he must justify the doctrine of political equality on grounds as general as those on which his general physiological doctrine of Part I of the *Passions* is based. Ethics must be based, for Descartes, on the medicine of Part I of the *Passions*, and medicine itself must be based on mechanics. From the standpoint of mechanics, nothing like the Aristotelian notion of largeness of soul can be forthcoming, since Descartes' "applied geometry" recognizes no essential differences in the strengths and forces of particles of matter, only of differing quantitative degrees of impressed force. Thus, given enough of an impulse, a very small bit of matter could have all the force of an enormous piece, since force is a product of both quantity of matter and its velocity. Thus, in a world view including Cartesian laws of nature, the notion of largeness of soul could be replaced with a notion like generosity, which, as it were, considers the soul and body together as giving a mathematical product of spiritual power and circumstance; if the soul and the body are not so well disposed initially, at birth, and the resultant human citizen is base and weak, then the habituations described in Part I of the *Passions* can produce a totality that has as much virtue as anyone has.

Descartes claimed that his ethics is based on his mechanics and his medicine. We have just seen how this implies a very great malleability in men with respect to social virtues, such as generosity and nobility. It is likely that this view of human malleability gives rise to the remarkable optimism we find in Descartes concerning the perfectibility of man.

Even the most debased man, in this view of things, is merely a product of certain natural weaknesses—i.e., a lack of physiological vigor with respect to attending to one idea at the expense of another and so to changing one's habits—together with bad environment.[16] For Descartes, the mere possibility of their possession of "the firm resolution" to use their own freedom of choice provides good grounds for esteeming all other men. Thus, one cannot esteem or disdain any man because of what he is now; rather, one always judges another within the context of his personal progress, which begins with his enjoyment of life itself at the moment of birth, and which ends with his realization of his place within the universe of heavens. That place within the universe is, in turn, determined by the doctrines taught by medicine and mechanics. When this determination is realized, it provides a terminus from which one can cast a deeply sympathetic eye on all the inane foolishness of others who have not reached this wisdom, and the wise man can have good will toward all men. Thus, good will toward all is, for Descartes, something like the passion associated with the idea whose objective reality is that of the idea of the individual united to a healthy society. It is, along with generosity, an active state characteristic of the wise man. This good will arises in us when we cease to censure men for what they are and begin to view them in light of their potential to become associates in a truly healthy body politic. Wicked and vicious men, for Descartes, are products of bad environment or the results of physiological malfunctions. Only men who are either fit to be, or really are, integrated into sound and healthy societies of men are truly natural.[17]

Not surprisingly, Part III, the last part of the *Passions*, also contains a little sermon concerning the difference between the relation of men to Heaven and the relation of man to man. It begins with Article 162, "On Veneration," which identifies the passion of veneration as the one in which the soul has "an inclination . . . not only to esteem the object that it reveres but also to submit itself to it with a certain fear. . . ." We only have veneration "for causes which are under their own control [*pour les causes libres*]," and the pagans did not worship "trees, fountains or mountains" but "only the divinities which they thought resided in them." These free causes are identified as those "which we judge to be able to do us good or bad," i.e., depending on how they are disposed towards us. In this article, the seventeenth-century Frenchman, Descartes, said that veneration is ultimately a matter of flattery, and is based on the opinion that certain free causes can do us ill or well depending on how they are disposed toward us. He continued his thoughts on these free causes in the next article, 163, "On Scorn," saying that scorn is "the inclination that the soul has to contemn a free cause" when it happens that, although that cause could be capable of either good or bad action, it is too far beneath us to affect us significantly. Then, in the next article, 164, "Concerning the usage of those two passions," Descartes discussed the relation between human veneration of God and human scorn of things human, and he made it clear, as he soon did again, that veneration is more efficacious when directed toward men than toward Heaven. He said:

> And it is generosity and weakness of spirit or baseness which determines the good or bad use of these two passions. For, in so far as one has a soul more noble and more generous, to that degree is he more inclined to render to each man what belongs to him: and so one has not only a very profound humility with respect to God but, also, one renders without distaste [*repugnance*] all the honor and respect which is due to man, to each according to his rank and authority in the world, and one scorns nothing but vice.

Toward the end of Part III, in Article 198, concerning the use of indignation, we find a similar thought propounded by Descartes. He said that:

> It is to be difficult and peevish to be much indignant concerning things of no importance; it is to be unjust [*injuste*] to be indignant concerning things which are not at all blamable, and it is to be impertinent and absurd not to restrict that passion to the actions of men, but rather to extend it up to the works of God or nature [*jusques aux oeuvres de Dieu ou de la nature*], as do those who, being never content with their condition or their fortune, dare to find blame in the conduct of the world and the secrets of providence.

Article 198 on the use of indignation is preceded by Articles 192–195, which discuss favor (192), gratitude (193), Ingratitude (194), and indignation (195). These penultimate articles, taken together, comprise an essay touching on what Descartes called, in Article 194, "On Indignation," the "principal bonds of human society."

Article 192, "On Favor," says that favor, "properly speaking," is "a desire to see some good happen to someone for whom one has good will." Descartes then continued that he would use the term in the way in which he suggested is not quite the "proper" way. He said, "but I will not here use that term to signify that good will in so far as it is excited in us by some good act on the part of him for whom we have it." The favor to which he addressed himself is not initiated by a good action on another's part toward him. It is, moreover, usually joined to "pity, because the disgraces which we see happen to the unfortunate [*malheureux*] are the reason why we are more reflective on their merits." We thus favor those men whose merits we see clearly because of unmerited misfortune and not because of good things they indeed do to us. This means that our favor or partiality will not be directed toward peers or superiors who have or could do us a good turn, but, to the contrary, to what we today call the disadvantaged of this world. Favoritism and partiality have nothing to do with friendship between equals, for Descartes, and the relations arising from favor, as Descartes interpreted that term, are always between the more and less fortunate. Precisely as in the case of medicine, a reflection on, a heightened consciousness of, misfortune and what is sorrowful permits us to care for humans from whom we can expect nothing in return, except a reminder of our own frailty.

Those who receive signs of favor from the more fortunate would be expected to be grateful, and, indeed, the next article, 193, concerns gratitude (*De La Reconnoissance*). In that article, Descartes said that gratitude is a species of love "excited in us by some action on the part of him for whom we have it." Gratitude "contains all that favor does" except that in gratitude we find added to favor the consideration of a benefit received and the desire to repay it. This article closes with the puzzling reflection that "gratitude has much more force (i.e., than favor) principally in those souls which are not very noble and generous." For Descartes, favor is more noble than gratitude.

In the next article, 194, "On Ingratitude," Descartes said that ingratitude is not a passion "but only a vice directly opposed to gratitude in so far as gratitude is always virtuous and one of the principle bonds of human society. . . ." In listing the vicious souls lost to ingratitude, Descartes distinguished:

1. "[B]rutal and foolishly arrogant men who think that all things are their due" (i.e., the men who do not understand).
2. "The stupid, who do not at all reflect on the benefits they receive" (the men who cannot understand).
3. "The weak and abject who, sensing their infirmity and their need, seek out in a base manner the aid of others and, after they have received it, because of not having the will to render their benefactors the like, or despairing of the power to do it, and imagining that all the world is as mercenary as they, and that one cannot do any good without the hope of being recompensed for it, they think they have deceived their benefactors" (the men who are selfish).

To recapitulate, favor is, in Descartes' (admittedly special) idiom, the possession of good will toward those men who cannot give any recompense for goods received; it is primarily caused by a reflection on the disparity between real merit and ill fortune. Gratitude is the same as favor, plus the addition of an awareness of goods received and the intention to recompense them. Ingratitude is not a passion, but a vice of the brutal and foolishly arrogant, of the stupid, and of the weak and the abject who either think that all things are due them, or do not realize that good has been done them, or, finally, do not even see the possibility of what Descartes called "favor." Thus, there are two political virtues here (favor and gratitude), one possessed by noble and generous souls and the other by souls not so noble and generous. The virtue of gratitude is vastly inferior to favor, it seems, and it is only a virtue in those who are inclined to ingratitude, i.e., in the somewhat arrogant, brutal, stupid, or base. Those souls capable of true nobility and generosity experience the passion of favor toward all other men—very nearly a secular form of Christian charity—by a large reflection on the pitiful condition of men, where this reflection is caused by awareness of disgraces arising from misfortune. The sight of these disgraces is not to be the occasion for any indignation against the community of man or for impugning the goodness of God or nature. It is to be the occasion for reflection on merits that are unrecognized because of ill fortune and it is to be the occasion for reflection on ways and means to ameliorate the causes of these unhappy occurrences.

Gratitude is a degeneration of favor. It begins where favor begins— with a reflection on the disparity between merit and reward—but it differs from favor primarily in that it presupposes a debt for the receipt of some good. A debt, however, implies a need. Thus, the stronger have favor toward others without any debt toward them, while the weaker have gratitude (*reconnoissance*) toward those who have helped them when they could not help themselves. The ungrateful are yet weaker in that they, too, need help, but do not recognize the implication of their need nor of the fact that it has been met. The arrogance of the ungrateful is primarily based on a *blindness* of their own weakness, just as the man who gives favors bases that giving on his full recognition of the weakness of others—although he in fact does not need others' help. Thus, favor, although a possession of the strong, does not blind its possessor to weakness. *Reconnoissance,* which also means "recognition," is thus nothing less than a consequence of "fallen" favor, i.e., the realization in oneself of the weakness of all men. Only the totally self-sufficient man could be totally capable of favor; in all others, the closest approach to it is *reconnoissance.* If, as is likely, all men would prefer to be in the position of being lenders rather than borrowers, i.e., self-sufficient, then *reconnoissance* is the passion that leads us to begin our progress toward self-sufficiency, toward favor.

It is very difficult to envision any man who is entirely self-sufficient. As a consequence, it seems highly unlikely that men can be more than grateful to benefactors; the passion of favor is hardly to be found here among weak and errant mortals. However, it is precisely our mortality, our weakness in the face of accident or disease, that will some day kill each and every one of us mortals; and just this makes true favor really possible. All we have to do is to discover some truth that will help improve the lot of mankind after we are dead. The dead receive no recompense for their gifts to their survivors and they have no weaknesses that require help in payment for their favors, and hence they will never have to be grateful to the living. The man who writes to aid a future posterity is a man possessing the passion of favor effectively. That in his work that cannot possibly be effective in his own lifetime but that will improve the lot of men after his death gives to posterity the means for a progress that he himself will not live to enjoy. As d'Alembert says of Descartes, "And by that revolt whose fruits we are reaping today, he rendered a service to philosophy . . . and . . . laid the foundations of a more just and happier government, which he himself was not able to see established." In Article 192, "On Favor," Descartes said that "favor . . . is a species of love, and not at all of desire. . . ." Favor, then, the passion of the visionary revolutionary and the "idealistic" progressive, is, in the final analysis, a form of unrequitable love.

As we have seen, the initial articles of Part III of the *Passions* formed a small treatise. These articles primarily concern esteem, contempt, virtuous humility, and, above all, generosity. We have also remarked that the articles at the end of Part III formed a little treatise. These articles primarily concern gratitude, ingratitude, veneration, and, above all, favor. What is the relation between generosity and favor?

We saw that generosity was, as it were, the passion of passions, i.e., the passion that concerns other passions. Being a passion, it is the immediate awareness of some corporeal (and, in particular, cerebral) modification; as an immediate awareness of something transpiring in the brain, it is a thought; and, as a distinct thought, it has a distinguishing form and thus an idea belonging to it. We pointed out reasons for thinking that the idea belonging to generosity was also the idea of the psychobiological unity of mind and body, of the soul merely insofar as it was "passionate" or capable of any awareness. Generosity is thus a sort of awareness, a sort of self-consciousness in general.[18]

Without generosity, and without its idea, no medically sound social psychology could be attained and hence no "healthy" union between humans. For, without such a social psychology, any attempt at a healthy political union would be defeated by a false conception concerning such things as the malleability of men, the problem of apparent excellence of some men, and, ultimately, the question of the relation of individuals to the political association of which they are members. Descartes began the

Passions by saying that in nothing else were the ancients so wrong-headed as in their theory of the passions. He said, in Article 1, at the very beginning, "There is nothing in which it appears more how very defective were the sciences we have of the ancients than in what they have written concerning the passions. . . ." *The Passions of the Soul* is thus consciously given as proof that Descartes' sciences presupposed in his discussions of the *Passions* were generally superior to those of the ancients. Pivotal to that discussion is his scientific view of the passion of generosity.

On the other hand, we argued that favor, whose stepchild is gratitude (*reconnoissance*), is the passion of visionary revolutionaries and idealistic progressives. If the idea of generosity concerns the total actual environment of an organism, then favor is the "Promethean" passion, the passion for improvement at a future date. Since it is "ordinarily joined to pity, because the disgraces we see happen to the unfortunate cause us to reflect on their merits," Descartes' Promethean philanthropy is an essential corollary to the wisdom of the generous man. That is, the effective revolutionary must be wise through his generosity and prescient through his favor. The wisdom of generosity teaches him the psychodynamics of man with respect to his total environment; the prescience of favor leads him to take whatever steps he can to ensure that sentient individuals will at some future date feel joy when they come to live in a state that is well disposed to receive them. No future will be altogether joyful to be in, because the will, for Descartes, is infinite (Meditation III), but, any given stage of progress will be the work of a man of favor. The dead Promethean benefactor will have as his only reward the recognition of being a "pioneer." *Reconnoissance,* which means both "gratitude" and "recognition" is thus also fame—the only payment due the founder of great changes that the founder will not live to enjoy himself. According to that teacher of revolutionaries, Descartes, love of fame is the highest passion among men, and it alone transcends the mediocrity's desire for immediate recompense from his debtors. It is not at all unlikely that, in Descartes' own very peculiar view of God and the human soul, immortality belongs only to the notable, recognized benefactors of mankind. If this be true of Descartes, then *reconnoissance* gives immortality—immortal fame—as the reward for favor, for *revolutionary* favor.

Ultimately, Descartes' generosity is to be defined by its insistence on the non-authoritarian character of his new sciences. Descartes' final gift to mankind is not so much a true doctrine of the world and all that therein lies, as it is in the revelation of an analytical science that grows out of his use of *sa raison* (out of Descartes' use of his own reason) and that, in that it is analytical, is presented in such a way that (Vol. IXA, p.

121): "if the reader wishes to follow it, and to cast his eyes seriously on all that it contains, he will understand the things thus demonstrated no less perfectly, and make it no less his own, than if he himself had discovered it." Descartes' science, which *analytically* examines human law no less than natural law, requires each and every one of us to use his own reason. Indeed, insofar as he taught that all thinking—be it about the subject of natural law or of human law—is for the sake of each individual thinker, he is most certainly the founder *par excellence* of our own technologically scientific, individualistically democratic age, and d'Alembert's characterization of him as "the leader of a band of revolutionaries" is the characterization most appropriate to the man.[19]

NOTES

1. In thinking of the institutions of nature inborn in the soul, we should remember that some of these concern the soul exclusively (e.g., what has once been cannot never have been), some the body exclusively (we blink our eyes, willy-nilly, even when a dear and trusted friend quickly puts his hand up toward them) but a number concern the union of body and soul that comprise a living human being (we hate, love, fear, esteem or condemn other people with whom we have effective relationships). (It is to Part II of his 1648–49 *Passions of the Soul,* written in Descartes' full maturity at age 52–53, that we shall return in our concluding investigation of these "sociological/natural" institutions.)

For an entirely different treatment of this question, see Norman Kemp Smith, *New Studies in the Philosophy of Descartes* (New York: Russel and Russel, 1966). Chapters V and VI.

2. Truly, just as Descartes foresaw, medicine, i.e., social psychology, and its constellation of ancillary disciplines such as biochemistry, have become of central importance to those advisory disciplines that modern governments employ in their search for solutions to "social ills." Anthony Kenny's "Descartes on the Will," in R. J. Butler, *Cartesian Studies,* points in this direction. Even more so does Maxime Leroy, in *"Descartes precurseur du social moderne," Revue de synthese* [Paris] (1948), 63: 9–67.

3. Descartes, and perhaps his epoch, is Stoic. See Victor Brochard, "Descartes stoicen: contribution a l'histoire de la philosophie cartesienne," in *Revue philosophique de la France et de l'etranger,* Vol. 1, 1880, pp. 548–552.

4. For Descartes, the city is by nature a reflection of man's nature.

5. *Vid.* the Stoic term *syneidesis,* misspelled by St. Jerome, in his commentary on Ezekiel, as *synderesis* and interpreted by St. Thomas as meaning *con-scientia,* or an amalgam of consciousness and conscience. The Stoic term *syneidesis* seems to have meant "a sense of well-being" and to have been applied as a sort of canon of right living.

6. As we have said, for Descartes, that political environment is synthetic and not, as with Aristotle, an element in the definition of human beings.

7. It is appropriate in this final section concerning the passions to cite La Rochefoucauld's great maxim: "Our self-love or vanity is rankled more by a condemnation of our tastes than of our opinions."

If, as experience seems to teach, popular regimes soon come to be ruled by popular tastes rather than by any considered opinions, the Enlightenment could learn much from the *Reflections Morales* of men like La Rouchefoucauld, whose thought, for all his worldliness, is surprisingly sympathetic to pre-Cartesian political philosophy.

It is also proper in this place to point out the affinities that Descartes' style and rhetoric share with the *preciosité* of the great writers of apothems and maxims. In this one respect, perhaps, Cartesian scholarship is too "academic" and not "literary" enough. See M. Legendre, "Descartes et Cervantes," *Les lettres*, June, 1924; and, above all, Maxime Leroy, *Descartes, le philosophe au masque*, 2 vols. (Paris: Rieder, 1929).

8. To move from botany to physics is an astonishing direction; that is to say, we today would find it very difficult to detect cosmological questions in the course of investigations of botany or even biology. An exception to this is the contemporary Swiss zoologist, Adolf Portmann.

9. There is thus reason to think that the Cartesian private theology is ultimately a "cosmo-economic" doctrine. Cf. Hesiod's *Works and Days* and Xenophon's *Oeconomicus* (Book VIII, Ch. 10) and *Memorabilia* (Book IV, Ch. 3, Sect. 13). See also Leo Strauss, *Xenophon's Socratic Discourse: An Interpretation of the "Oeconomicus"* (Ithaca: Cornell University Press, 1970), especially Ch. IX, "Gynaikologia"—pp. 146–152. See also Montesquieu, *The Spirit of the Laws*, Book XXI, Ch. 20, "How Commerce broke through the Barbarianism of Europe [*Comment le commerce se fit jour en Europe à travers la barbaric*]." At the very least, one could say that the eighteenth-century encyclopedia of arts and trades saw itself as a replacement for the early *Summae* of theology. (Balz, *Descartes and the Modern Mind* is interesting here.)

10. The reduction of biology to an ancilla of medicine, if not one of the happiest of the Cartesian legacies, is certainly one of the most powerful. Much of biological investigation today is essential a form of theoretical medicine. There are, however, a small handful of botanists and biologists for whom this is not true—e.g., Agnes Arber and Adolf Portmann.

11. Descartes' "in effect" is meant literally: that each individual is an effect of the universe is the theme of Part II of this book; this section draws conclusions from that Cartesian thesis.

12. The very least that one can, and must, say about the psychologies of these men was that for them all, the soul was a "form"—however difficult it is to understand clearly what they meant by that term. Still, the manifold of appearances gave them an essential strating place for their psychologies. For none of them was the soul a monad, that is, not the human soul.

13. It is not in the least attributing too much to Descartes to say that he envisaged a biochemical theory of moods and, to speak generally, what we today call "inner states." However, it is not likely that his immediate successors picked up on his thoughts here in any direct way. Rather, it seems that the tradition of mechanistic biology took several centuries to see the implications of what they did in fact take directly from his theory of the mood-changers. Because of technical details—such as the theories of definite and multiple proportions enunciated by John Dalton (1766–1844: *A New System of Chemical Philosophy*, 1808)—the tradition of medical history has given Descartes woefully inadequate praise. It has occurred to me that the nineteenth century, especially, downgraded Descartes' contributions in medicine and political thought primarily because of a sort of embarrassment over his personal theology, and not so much because of the Newtonian triumph. (See Keeling, *Descartes*, pp. 177–178, Ch. VIII, *passim*, for an argument pointing in the direction of our own treatment.)

14. The six primitive passions are, once again: admiration, love, hate, desire, joy, and sadness (or, pleasure and pain). All other passions are combinations or excesses and defects of these six, which are thus primitive or "elemental." These six alone cannot be "psychoanalytically" reduced to any others.

15. That generosity is not a primitive passion suggests that for Descartes man was not necessarily a political animal. That is, Descartes seemed to think that man evolved into his

true, political nature from a state in which only his six primitive passions operated to preserve him—or, perhaps, that in very corrupt societies, only these passions may be operative.

16. *Vid.* Descartes' psychobiological analysis of the passion of love and the role of the spirits in "fortifying" it.

17. It is to be recalled, once again, the Descartes' works were condemned by the Holy Office on the grounds that he taught the *natural* perfectibility of mankind—as opposed to the promise of an individual redemption through the gift of divine grace. His doctrine of perfectibility involved a natural, as opposed to supernatural, and social, as opposed to individual, perfectibility. The censors of the Holy Office were thus, apparently, in substantial agreement with d'Alembert's assessment of Descartes' meaning, although certainly they did not assess its worth or truth in the same way.

18. As a glance at Rousseau or at the contemporary literature of "consciousness raising" shows, this concept has had enormous influence.

19. There is a group of scholars, small but vocal, who feel that several important aspects of what I have claimed as Descartes' contribution to the tradition were clearly enumerated in Bacon's work—they even go so far as to claim that Descartes got his mathematical analysis, ethics, and scientific method from Bacon's work! (This is *not* to claim that these scholars begin to see the larger issues laid out in this book—only that several important parts of Descartes' work are claimed by them as originating in and being taken by Descartes from Bacon's work.)

My thought is that the influence of Bacon on the tradition that includes the Encyclopediasts, such as d'Alembert and Diderot—one might usefully group these men together under the general heading, "intellectual bureaucrats"—is, to be sure, substantial; Bacon's influence on Descartes, who was no intellectual bureaucrat, was marginal, and Descartes' infrequent mention of Bacon was little more than honorific name-dropping. Descartes, perhaps not altogether properly, traded on the names of the great and powerful in order to further his own profoundly subversive ends. Bacon, however, was an intellectual; Descartes was an intellect.

For a very different asessment, see A. Lalande, "Sur quelques textes de Bacon et de Descartes," *Revue de Metaphysique et de Morale,* May 1911, pp. 296–311. For a contemporary version of Lalande's thesis, see Laurence Berns, "Francis Bacon and the Conquest of Nature," *Interpretation,* vol. 7, no. 1 (1978), pp. 1–26. William Hale-While, in his excellent *Bacon, Gilbert and Harvey* [given as the "Harveian Oration delivered before the Royal College of Physicians of London, Oct. 18, 1927" (London: Bale, Sons & Danielson, 1927)], correctly points out that Bacon even got his notion of experiment, no less than his notion of scientific method, from Gilbert (p. 39). It thus appears that Bacon, whatever his relation to Shakespeare, did not act as a preceptor or teacher for Descartes and that most of what Lalande, and following him, Berns, claim as Bacon's discovery belongs to *Gilbert. Vid.* Richard B. Carter, "Gilbert and Descartes," *Zeitschrift für allgemeine Wissenschaftstheorie,* Band XIII, 1982.

APPENDIX 1

The *n*-Line Locus Problem

IN BOOK I of the *Geometry,* Descartes introduced the problem of constructing the conic sections by means of a quotation from Pappus (Book VII, Chapter III):

> The problem of the locus related to three or four lines . . . is of this nature: If three straight lines are given in position, and if straight lines be drawn from one and the same point, making given angles with the three given lines; and if there be given the ratio of the rectangle contained by two of the lines so drawn to the square of the other, the point lies on a solid locus given in position, namely, one of the three conic sections.[1]

Pappus is referring in this passage to certain theorems in Book III of *On Conic Sections* by Apollonius of Perga (fl. 230–220 B.C.).[2] In his translation and commentary to this work, R. Catesby Taliaferro gives an appendix concerning locus problems and sums it up with the remark that:

> a parabola, ellipse, circle and hyperbola are three-line loci with respect to any two tangents to them and a straight line joining the points of contact . . . The parabola, ellipse, circle and hyperbola are four-line loci with respect to any inscribed quadrilateral. . . . [Vol. II, p. 804]

Taliaferro refers to Apollonius's *Conics,* Book III, Proposition 54, where it is demonstrated that (referring to the diagram that appears on p. 254) the ratio of the "rectangle" (or, as is said algebraically, the product of the numerical lengths) FA, CG to $(AC)^2$ is constant, being equal to the ratio compounded of the constant ratios (or, algebraically, "equal to the product of the fractions whose numerators and denominators are the lengths of the lines") $(EB)^2$ to $(BD)^2$ and AD, DC to AE, EC. EB, AD, DC, AE, and EC are all given, constant magnitudes. This property, i.e., that (FA $\times$ CG)/$(AC)^2$ is equal to a constant product of ratios, $(EB)^2/(BD)^2 \times$ (AD $\times$ DC)/(AE $\times$ EC), is the heart of the matter. For the lengths of FA and CG vary—and hence are *not* constant, depending on the position of the point H, which is defined as being *any* point on the section. It cannot be stressed too strongly that the property of the curve on which all the

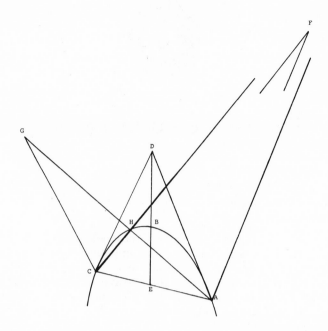

points H are located *does not* define the curve as being, essentially, an assemblage of points. In order to say that, one would have to be of the persuasion that a thing is, or exists, precisely in the way, or as that by means of which, we best grasp it. Indeed, it might appear at first that Aristotle meant exactly this when he said that the explanation or definition (λόγος) of a thing is its essence (οὐσία). However, excepting perhaps Democritus and Carneades, the classical tradition did not conclude that the concept by means of which we grasp something is itself a true part of what we grasp by means of that concept. However, Descartes postulated something like this when he considered a curve as really and truly being an assemblage of points with a certain porperty. (Nor would it be too much to suggest that this is a central modern prejudice.)

The constant magnitudes are: the two tangents AD and DC, the line AC connecting them within the section, and, finally, the line DE drawn from the apex of the triangle ADC, two sides of which are those tangents, to the midpoint of the third side, AC. AF and CG are not of constant length; AF is drawn from A parallel to the tangent DC and CG from C parallel to AD, with AF cut off by the line CF and CG by the line AG—both drawn through any point H on the section. (As different points H are chosen, the lengths of AF and CG will vary.) The "locus" property of the section is then, to quote Taliaferro (p. 799):

> Any conic section . . . can be considered as the locus of points whose distances from three given straight lines . . . are such that the square

of one of the distances is always in a constant ratio to the rectangle contained by the other two distances . . . Now, if we consider the straight lines AD, DC, and AC as fixed and given and therefore the straight line DE fixed and given as bisecting AC, then it is evident that the straight lines AC, EB, BD, AD, DC, and therefore the squares on them and the rectangles contained by them, are also fixed and given. Then although as the point H is taken at different points along the conic, the straight lines AF and CG change in magnitude, nevertheless, the magnitude of the rectangle (or, as we say algebraically, the product of) AF, CG, because of the above proportion, remains constant.[3]

Taliaferro continues:

In other words, as different points H are chosen, the rectangle contained by the distances from H to two of the given straight lines (at given angles to those straight lines) has a constant ratio to the square on the distance to the third straight line (at a given angle to that straight line). And it can be easily proved by means of similar triangles that if any other three angles are chosen for the distances, than those chosen here for the demonstration, the corresponding ratio will be constant, though not equal.

This property belongs to *each and every point* H and *not to all points* H on the curve. This property is thus the "quality" of points on the curve, and not what the curve itself essentially consists in. (Thus, when T. L. Heath translated Euclid's *Elements,* he consistently, and seriously, mistranslated such expressions as: "In each and every triangle" as "in all triangles," thereby treating Euclid as if he were post–seventeenth century.)

"The four-line locus property can be easily deduced from the three-line" (ibid., p. 800).

To sum up: the locus property of the sections involves the fact that (to quote Taliaferro again, ibid., p. 800):

as the point H changes, the rectangle [for Descartes, the product of lengths] contained by the distance from H to two of the given straight lines (at given angles to those straight lines) has a constant ratio to the square on the distance to the third straight (at a given angle to that straight line).

Interpreting Appollonius algebraically, we can express the constancy of this ratio as $(a) \times (b)/c^2 = n/m$, where n/m is a constant ratio. Cross-multiplying, we get the equation $m(a) \times (b) = n(c^2)$. Since the lines a, b, and c—the distances of the point H whose motion "generated" the curve—are each "specified" by expressions containing a single occurrence of x and y (or, sometimes, just x or y), the two products, set equal to one another in the equation, will neither of them contain any instance of either x or y that is of a higher power than (x) (x) or (y) (y), i.e., than x^2 or

y^2. Continuing, if the essential condition defining the locus property of a curve specifies that the distances of the generating point H from 5, 6, 7, or 8 lines be constant, then the algebraic expression of this condition will be (in, say, the case of 6 distances from 6 given lines), (a) (b) $(c)/(d)$ (e) (f) = r/s, so that $s(a)$ (b) (c) = $r(d)$ (e) (f)—where each of the distances a,b,c,d,e, and f is "specified" by an equation in x and/or y.

An example of this "specification" of the way the lines "for the sake of whose explication x and y are used" is here adapted from Book I of the *Geometry (vid.* Vol. VI, p. 382ff.). Consider a line, AB, given in position (but not in length) and a point C: find the distance of C, under given angles, from the line AB—i.e., find the length of BC.

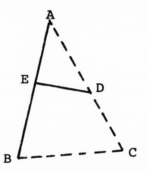

From a point D given in position along AC let a line ED be drawn meeting AB at a given angle. Let ED = x, DC = y. Then, in the triangle AED, angles DAE and DEA are given by hypothesis: and thus also angle EDA. Therefore, the ratios of the sides of triangle ABC are given. Let the ratio of side ED to DA be that of z/b, where z is an arbitrary quantity. Then, ED/DA = z/b. Further, since ED = x, then ED/DA = x/DA = z/b and DA = bx/z. Furthermore, since AC = AD + DC, and DC = y, therefore, AC = $bx/z + y$. Again, since the angles in triangle ABC are known, by hypothesis, the ratio of AC to BC is given. Let it be equal to z/d. Then, AC/BC = z/d and BC = (d) (AC)/z = $[(d)$ $(bx/z + y)]/z$. Since, then, AC = $(bx/z) + y$, BC = $[(d)$ $(bx/z)]/z$; therefore, the product of the two will not contain occurrences of either x or y of a power higher than x^2 or y^2.

NOTES

1. Smith and Latham translators, *The Geometry of René Descartes* (p. 21):
At locus ad tres, et quattuor lineas . . . est hujismodi. Si positione datis tribus rectis lineis ab uno et eodem puncto, ad tres lineas in datis angulis rectae lineae ducuntor, et data sint proportio rectanguli contenti duabus ductis ad

quadratum reliquae: punctum contingit positione datum solidum locum, hoc est unam ex tribus concis sectionibus.

2. Apollonius of Perga, "On Conic Sections, Books I–III," trans. R. Catesby Taliaferro, *Great Books of the Western World*, 54 Vols. (Chicago: Encyclopedia Brittanica, 1952), Vol. II, pp. 597–804.

3. In spite of his choice of words here, Taliaferro does *not* mean that the curve is the assemblage of points H.

The Locus Idea

IT IS, PERHAPS, within his concept of locus problems that Descartes most obviously coalesces the two species of analysis clearly distinguished by Pappus—one concerned with truth, the other with finding lines, and, by "lines," Pappus did not mean a line of an exact length, although Descartes did.

In an early letter, dated January 1632, Descartes wrote of loci as being lines (Vol. I, p. 233, l. 11) "which can be inscribed by one continuous motion [*quae describi possunt unico motu continuo*]." The title of Rule VII states:

> For the completion of knowledge, it is necessary to traverse each and every thing which pertains to our undertaking by means of a continuous and nowhere interrupted motion of thought . . . [*Ad scientiae complementum oportet omnia et singula, quae ad institutum nostrum pertinent, continuo et nullibi interrupti cogitationis motu perlustrare . . .*
> [Vol. X, p. 387]

This is his definition of all thinking—a definition of thinking as being exclusively deductive, which becomes a postulate from Hume to Hegel and thereafter.

For Descartes, the soul's power or "force" in thinking is analogous to that "forceful" motion in true body that originally caused the soul to react to that moving body, i.e., to perceive. The motive force of inanimate bodies is analogous to what Descartes called *arbitrium mentis*, the force or will of the ensouled body that thinks. The locus-generating motion of bodies exactly parallels, in its action, the "continuous and nowhere interrupted motion" of the soul when it thinks, and, in particular, when it thinks about the "one continuous motion" of true body as it generates a particular curve in front of us; *what* curve depends on the number of dimensions of the body being considered.

It thus seems that what Pappus mentions as problematic analysis's method of investigation concerning the possible and obtainable in higher geometry was transformed by Descartes into a method of investigating the *physical* possibility, i.e., using the mechanics of brain functioning, of *intellectual* solutions being obtained. His geometry being, as was Newton's after him, essentially a "rational mechanics" (Newton's phrase), even its most "abstract" speculations concerning such matters as the nature of equations are ultimately concerned with questions of physical possibility and impossibility with respect to relations obtaining between real bodies. The will, when it applies itself strictly to the representation of the soul's original reactions to motion in body, uses the imagination to set up "thought experiences" involving "images" or symbols that can be considered to relate to one another under conditions that also precisely apply to the relationships of real bodies. Those images of body, however, need not look like body; for reasons that we discuss in another section, those images often *should not* look like body. This requirement arises primarily because abstract mathematics, although its goal is to determine possibility and attainability with respect to the relations between true bodies, deals immediately with the "objective," purely intellectual reactions of the soul to bodies that are abstract to the extent that they are thought of as existing under all possible *physical* conditions of true body. The physiological foundation for using images in this way occupies the last two sections of Part I of this work.

For now, however, we illustrate the physical aspect of theoretical geometry by a simple example taken from Book I of the *Geometry*. The problem, as Descartes understood it, is to find a line of *length x*, such that $x^2 = a \cdot b$ [The length of x is a mean proportional between two given lengths, a and b—in numbers: 2, x, and 8, where 2 is to x as x is to 8 ($x = 4$). *Euclid*, VI, theorem 19, gives this same problem with no use of unknowns like x.]

Descartes considered this the problem of finding a way to solve all questions that can be algebraically represented in the equation $x^2 = a \cdot b$. Since he was looking for a way, a method, of solving a certain equation, his solution would be indeterminate in the same way that the equation is indeterminate; however, his proof that this indeterminate solution is the correct one must rely on the fact that, given the *real lengths* of the real "lines" a and b, he could find correspondingly exact *lengths* for x. This entails, in its turn, the physical fact that the length, x, is the precise correct length because it has "really," *physically*, been cut off exactly where it has been cut off. (Such a geometry is, as Newton said, "rational mechanics.")

The solution is found by seeing, first, that the sought-for length that is a mean between the two lines a and b can be related algebraically to those lines by the representation $a/x = x/b$, or, "cross-multiplying," $x^2 = a \cdot b$. We then recall from elementary geometry (*Euclid* VI, 191) that the perpendicular that divides the diameter of a semicircle into two segments at any point P is cut off by the perimeter of the semicircle so that

that perpendicular cut off is the mean between the two segments of the diameter, for example:

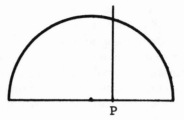

I then reflect that if I take two segments, *a* and *b*, and join them together in a straight line, I get a line *a* + *b* units in length. Bisecting that length *a* + *b*, I then describe a semicircle around that midpoint and erect a perpendicular at the point P where *a* and *b* were joined to make *a* + *b*. With the length of the perpendicular extending from the diameter to the perimeter as *x*, then *x* will have the desired property and $x^2 = (a \cdot b)$.

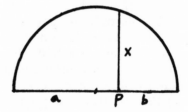

Descartes felt that he had here solved a general problem in arithmetic and geometry by means of an elementary geometrical construction. If I let *a* and *b* have determinate *numerical* values, then *x* will have a determinate length that is entirely a function of where it is physically *cut* by the semicircle having the diameter *a* + *b* units in length. Furthermore, if we consider every point on the circumference of any semicircle as being an endpoint of that perpendicular length *x* erected on every line *a* + *b* units long, then those perpendicular lengths "squared" will equal the product of the segments *a* and *b* and that circumference itself will be the real, physical trace locus of those endpoints—the real ensemble of those endpoints of the perpendiculars.[1]

In this case, the abstract semicircle as a species of mathematical figure is a representation to my consciousness of the general form of my soul's intellectual reaction to a particular true body moving in a certain complex way—namely, so that it is always the endpoint of such perpendiculars that $x^2 = (a \cdot b)$.

In this case, that semicircle is the "form" or *species* of a whole class of possible events; as such, the semicircle is an idea, a truly visible, truly intelligible, idea. However, it only becomes an idea, rather than merely a "geometrical shape" or form or figure, at the moment that the two line segments forming its diameter and the circumference cease to be mere "lines" and become lengths; they become lengths when their endpoints are *considered as known*. Before those lengths are actually measured, they are indefinite lengths that can be specified "indefinitely" by being assigned indefinite symbols of indeterminate quantity, i.e., "x^2/a" or "$a \cdot b$". When this has been done, the figure is transformed from mere figure into a species-like idea because of the constant relationships it can be considered to manifest or represent (or, as we say today, "symbolize").

For Descartes, an idea is a definite figure or shape treated as if it were a species, that is, as indeterminate with respect to all the members of a class it can figure. Such shapes are "naively" given to us as determining entities that we unquestioningly view as having distinct relationships to us as viewers; we then, for instance, take the semicircular half-moon *subjectively,* and think of love or beauty. However, considered in an indeterminate, abstract way, the shape of the half-moon can be taken as a semicircle, and therefore as the "shaping" or "figuring" for (as we say, "symbol for"), a vast number of other things. When we do this, we consider the semicircular half-moon shape as a manifestation of the limits of a class of things. Then we can relate ourselves to the figure given us by the half-moon primarily as knowers, with a rational, scientific replacement for "subjectivity" that is, ultimately, subjective to a degree never otherwise possible. Scientific objectivity, therefore, entails a subjectivity that transforms everything imaginable into means for problem-solving. As Descartes showed in the analytic geometry, we willfully dispossess the moon of its shape, and we use the "abstract" shell that remains for our own ends. We can "geometrically" view the remaining figure, the semicircle, as the indeterminate idea of all those things that can so affect our neuroanatomical perceptive apparatus that the curve forming the precise semicircular periphery precisely cuts off lengths that, as in the example at hand, permit us to find square areas equal to rectangular areas. The striking difference that we visually perceive when we look at a square and then at a rectangle is dissolved into an intellectual identity—for x^2 = the rectangle formed by multiplying a times b. These ideas are figures in which *lines cut lines;* "abstract ideas" are thus the expressions of the relationships, in position and length, between those lines. The idea-figures primarily represent to us the clarity and distinctness of an idea, as well as provide us with grounds for thinking that the idea is related to possible experiences: many such ideas are given first in experience—the half-moon, for instance. Algebraic formulae expressly represent to our perceptual apparatus the intelligible operations required to grasp fully the relationships manifested *ad occulo* in the idea-figures.

What the tradition from Locke onward came to know as "clear and distinct ideas" are forms, shapes, or figures that precisely represent the relationships obtaining between things that can be noticed by our perceptive powers; a figure considered in this way is being treated as an idea when the thinker takes a perception and "willfully" or "intentionally"— *ex arbitrium mentis,* as Descartes had it—uses it as a pure instrument for the intellectual grasp of relations between truly existing things.

The perimeter of the semicircle is, moreover, two-dimensional in Cartesian terms. That is, it is constructed in accordance with single conditions placed on each of two elements in its concept, and those two elements are precisely the lengths of *a* and *b* such that the area of a quadrilateral rectangle with sides *a* and *b* is equal to a square whose side is the length of the perpendicular beginning at the point where *a* and *b* are joined, and ending at a point on the curve. That perimeter represents to our eyes the indeterminate position of all such points. It is a "locus of all points such that $x^2 = (a \cdot b)$."

Three things of special interest to us follow from this development. The first is the fact that the locus-definition of curves, which defines them as the indeterminate position of all points with certain constant properties, seems to imply that the very intelligibility of the curve is generated along with the curve itself. The second concerns the respect in which these locus-curves are two-dimensional in Descartes' sense of that word. The third, and last, concerns the fact that Descartes' dimensional analysis of curves as loci is a causal analysis.

First, our semicircle need not be defined by reference to the ruler and compass that were used to draw it; rather, once generated, it can henceforth be defined in terms of a certain constancy of the lengths of the segments *a* and *b* to the perpendicular length, *x*, at point P. In the Cartesian analysis of this locus property of curves, we might say that the motion of the point that *generates the curves,* by its "nowhere interrupted continuous motion," also *generates the intelligible properties of the curve,* and that these intelligible properties are also arrived at by a "nowhere interrupted continuous" reaction of thought *to that motion.* In explaining the relation of perception to locomotion through the movement of the limbs in the human body and the place of ideas in that relation, Descartes said:

> And take note that the idea of that motion of the limbs only consists in the way in which the spirits (i.e., the brain fluid) travel forth from that gland (the pineal gland) and thus that *it is its idea which causes the motion* [emphasis is mine]. [*Et notez que l'ideé de ce mouvement des membres ne consiste qu'en la façon dont ces esprits sortent pour lors de cette glande, et ainse que c'est son ideé que le cause.*] [Vol. XI, p. 181, l. 10–13]

Second, near the end of Book I of the *Geometry*, Descartes stated exactly what he meant when he said that curves are "two-dimensional":

> You also see, what is more, that multiplying several of these lines by one another [producing what Pappus and Apollonius called "rectangles"] the quantities x and y which are found in the product can, neither of them, have more dimensions than there were lines which the quantities x and y served to specify. So that they will never be more than two dimensions whenever they [i.e. the "rectangles"] will be produced by the multiplication of only two lines; nor more than three whenever they are produced by the multiplication of three lines, and so forth to infinity. [*Puis vous voyés aussy que multipliant plusieurs de ces lignes l'une par l'autre, les quantités, x et y, qui se trouuent dans le produit, n'y peuuent auoir que chascune autant de dimensions, qu'il y a eu de lignes, a l'explication desquelles elles seruent, qui ont esté ainsi multiplées. Ensorte qu'elles n'auront iamais plus de deux dimensions, en ce qui ne sera produit que par la muliplication de deux lignes; ny plus de trois, en ce qui ne sera produit que par la multiplication de trois; et ainsi a l'infini.*] [Vol. V, p. 385, l. 10–19]

In the case of the semicircle and the expression "$x^2 = (a \cdot b)$," the ratio of the segment a to the perpendicular x is the same as the ratio of the perpendicular x to the segment b. In geometrical terms, those two ratios are "constant." For Descartes, the number of constant ratios determines the dimensions of the curve.[2]

The third and final point is particularly important for our understanding of Descartes' method. For, under the Cartesian dimensional analysis, a physical event can be analyzed into its distinct elementary components, that is, into its clear and distinct ideas, and there will be just so many of these as there are dimensions to the problem associated with that event. If the problem is not reduced to, i.e., analyzed into, its absolutely bare minimum possible number of dimensions, the correct number, then the intellect will take one measurable aspect of true body and consider it as two aspects of true body. When, however, we have reduced the dimensions of a problem to its barest possible minimum, then and only then is the thinker immediately conscious of the totality of the intellect's reaction to true body.[3] That is, then and only then is the living, thinking human being addressing himself to the intelligibility of the world about him and to nothing else. For Descartes, this dimensional analysis, and only it, determines for us our perception of "physical" reality.[4]

To conclude, it is through his notion of a curve as a locus of a moving point that Descartes directly bridged the gap between intellectual processes and mechanical processes. Near the beginning of the *Rules* (e.g., Vol. X, pp. 387–388, 407–409, and 423–426), he went to great lengths to make clear that the only activity of the pure intellect is discursive, and *not at all intuitive:* the only situation where we find something similar to what his predecessors considered to be intuition is his disucssion of what he calls the intuition of "simple natures." These are not directly grasped in the way in which we grasp the results of deductive reasoning through a continuous and nowhere-interrupted intellectual application, but they are indirectly indentified by our grasping the complementarity between the intellect's original reaction to the action of some body and that action of that body itself. Most of the time, however, thinking is concerned, according to Descartes, with deduction, that is, with drawing numbers of conclusions from simpler premises. When we are involved in deductive thinking—and this is very nearly always—the intellectual reflection of the nowhere-interrupted motion of true body is to be seen in the mind's carrying out its deductions by means of a nowhere-interrupted motion of thought. But, Descartes said, concerning the process of deduction:

> We say at this juncture that it is therefore useful to review in an orderly manner all the details which are presented to us in propositions, to reject all the details which do not seem to us clearly to be to the point, to retain whichever of them is necessary, and to place any doubtful ones under very close scrutiny.
>
> These very same details should be transferred to the real extension of body and set before the imagination entirely by means of unadorned figures: for, in this way they can be perceived far more distinctly by the intellect. [*Rules;* Vol. X, p. 438, l. 3–11]

When these "unadorned figures" are loci, they represent the interrelation of a number of constant relationships. Thus, there is implied here a "picture-thought," a use of perceptible curves whose inner relationships are images of the relations of proportions occurring in a proof. (The whole school of "analytic philosophy" is based on just this idea of Descartes', and owes much of its present vitality to Frege's 1879 book, *Begriffsschrift*—literally, *Concept Writing*.) This astonishing dovetailing of the powers of body with the mind's power to grasp the idea of body implies for Descartes the necessity for those theological speculations that one finds in every single one of Descartes' published works, not even excepting his 1645–1646 *Passions of the Soul.*

We have seen something of the degree to which Descartes' geometry, even his most abstract geometry, is mechanical, and thus practical— to the extent that even in that abstract geometry the true and false are transformed into the possible and the impossible, into the achievable and the non-achievable. The search for truth thus becomes the search for "Can it be done?" and "If so, how?" With this mechanization of abstract mathematics begins what can be soberly called, to borrow the phrase on the obverse of the Great Seal of the United States of America, *Novus Ordo Seclorum*—a new order of the ages, that is, of the ages of political maturity. For, the collapse of theoretical and problematic analysis produced a technique whereby we can *hypothetically* manipulate ideas as intellectual surrogates, true surrogates, for true body, to find whether what we are in need of is obtainable, and if so, how to obtain it. This, of course, is mathematical physics in its experimental aspect.

The success of the application of this abstract geometry—of applied mathematical analysis—led Descartes and his heirs to think that they had very solid grounds for supposing that now, at least, we have an intellectual technique that permits us to be at one and the same time prudent (in that our mathematical analysis permits us to take into account any and all contingencies concerning any given problem) and progressive and aggressively anticonservative (in that the single rational goal of our human institutions is to make it easy to solve human problems). With the success of the solution of locus problems, Descartes and his heirs, up to and including the visionaries at various think-tanks, can enjoy that sense of unlimited optimism that only a full knowledge of their own prudence and progressive philanthropy could give. The sense of anticonservative prudence is, perhaps, the hallmark of the Enlightenment man.

NOTES

1. In order to define that curve as the "set" of all points under any particular conditions, we would have to postulate the "axiom of choice" or a form of it. It took very nearly 300 years for mathematicians to come to terms with this!

2. The number of constant ratios must indeed be the smallest number possible, i.e., it must be impossible to "reduce" any two constant ratios to a third single ratio that also contains the unknowns. In arithmetic, this means that we must never take, for example, 2/3 and 82/123 as two distinct numbers. Similarly, in geometry, if two points are given in position, the magnitude of the line joining them must not be expressed as or considered an unknown quantity since (by Euclid's *Data*, Prop. XXVI): "If the termini of straight lines are given in position, the straight lines are given in position and in magnitude." Again, if from the extremity of a straight line given in position and in magnitude there be drawn another straight line at a given angle and having a given ratio to the given magnitude of the original straight line, then we must not express or consider the magnitude or position of the later straight line as unknown or not given. For:

   1. By *Data*, Prop. XXIX, "If to a given point in a straight line given in position another straight line be drawn by making a given angle, that latter straight line is given its position."

   2. By *Data*, Prop. II, "If a given magnitude has a given ratio to another magnitude, the other magnitude is given."

   3. By *Data*, Prop. XXVI, "If the termini of straight lines are given in position, the straight lines are given in position and in magnitude."

3. It seems that the *distinct* aspect of "clear and distinct ideas" primarily concerns the fact that, when we are performing our analysis correctly, we never 1) express knowns as unknowns, 2) express two unknowns with the same expression; 3) express two knowns as one known; or 4) express one unknown with two expressions.

4. Descartes also used this same "analytic" procedure to distinguish between even body and soul—the only difference being that after this analysis has just shown exhaustively what mathematical body is, then what remains is soul. Thus, the borderline between physics and metaphysics is the limits of geometrical analysis, and even the *"cogito, sum"* is derived as a result of Descartes' reflections on this analysis. For, "pure intellect" itself is known as a complement to mathematical body—i.e., as what knows essentially knowable body.

For Descartes, as for those after him who hold that all real knowledge is directly deducible from the results of mathematical physics—from what Descartes called "applied geometry"—to be intelligible is to be measurable, and to be measurable is to be realized as mathematical body. A direct result of this is that the intelligibility of the souls of *other* thinking human beings presented a complex problem to Descartes. Indeed, within a very short time after Descartes' death, psychology entirely dispensed with the notion of soul (for example, see La Mettrie's 1748 *L'Homme Machine*). For, unless the soul is a quantifiable aspect of a body, how can mathematical physics grasp either its possible existence or what it is?

The Objective Reality of an Idea

IN HIS 1759 *Preliminary Discourse to the Encylopedia*, d'Alembert states that Descartes was a teacher of revolutionaries and a founder of the best and most just social order that the world had ever seen. He identifies this as Descartes' major contribution to philosophy, and he says that it outweighs all the contributions of his illustrious successors. He then also immediately identifies Descartes as the discoverer of the method of "indeterminates" in science—that is, as the discoverer of the way to apply analytic mathematics to the solution of physical problems.

This section examines the relation between these two contributions. The first contribution is the foundation of a new social order that is "more just than any before it"; the other is the offering of the man who was the profound investigator both of the relation between volitional indifference and understanding (in Meditation IV) as well as of the rational grounds for philosophic optimism concerning the possibility that each man—if he will only exercise "sa raison," his *own* reason—can arrive at truth in the sciences and in the conduct of life (in Meditations III and VI). We then closely analyze Descartes' concept of "the objective reality of an idea," continuing with a consideration of the relation between that concept and the concept of the excess of the extent of will over understanding as being the principal source of human error, and then considering his arguments concerning his grounds for believing that it is not possible that we could be created so as necessarily to err, and that we must have within us means for correcting our errors—and thus for nullifying the consequences of the excess of will over understanding.

The task of comprehending what Descartes meant by the expression "the objective reality of an idea" leads the student of Descartes into a peculiarly complex thicket formed partly by the idiomatic Cartesian terminology and partly by scholarship's (usually laudable) conservatism. Concerning this notion, we find Descartes asserting (Vol. IX, pp. 62–63) that indivisible substance is of a higher order or degree of reality than divisible substance, and hence that extended body (*res extensa*)—although comprising one of two distinct substances in the universe—is of a less exalted order of being than is thinking body (*res cogitans*). We find, further, that the concept of an infinite substance has more reality (*entitas, realite*) than does the concept of finite substance. We find, as well, that by the term "the material falsity" of ideas, Descartes referred to the interrelations of ideas among themselves, whereas by the term "the formal falsity" of ideas, he referred to our judgment that an idea refers to this or that that is not an idea. Indeed, our belief is strained yet further as he speaks as if he meant to tell us that we come to know those "outside" things that are compounds of simpler elements by means of ideas that are compounds of other ideas, and that the compound ideas have more reality than do their individual component ideas; and, moreover, that, by the same token, compound things have more entity or reality than do the simpler components of which they are composed. (The only exception is God, who alone is an infinite unity.)

However, this is, in fact, how Descartes spoke about these things. He said that the original intellectual causes of our ideas (Descartes called them "patrons") have either "formal" reality or "effective" reality—by which he seems to have meant "formative" or "effecting" reality. And, what they form or effect is consequent, or caused, ideas, having *no more than* just the amount or degree of objective reality—a sort of reality that only belongs to ideas—that corresponds to the amount of formal or effective reality that belongs to their patron ideas. Similarly, in the case of, for example, a horse whose real presence outside us occasions our idea of a horse, the *idea* of the horse is no less objectively real—no less real in *its* mode of being—than the horse of which it is the idea is itself actually or formally real in *its* mode of being. The formal reality of the existent horse, insofar as that horse may be thought, measures up to the objective reality of my idea of that horse, and vice versa.

In the situation of the relation between the idea of a machine in the mind of the inventor and the machine itself, the case is only slightly different, but significantly so. There, the existing machine, which the inventor constructs in accordance with his idea of it, is caused by his idea of it in a way very similar to that in which logical consequents are caused by their intellectual antecedents; in this case, however, the antecedent is the idea in the mind of the inventor and the consequent is a really existent, working machine "out there." In this case, the "craft" or ingenuity of the inventor contains the formal reality, whose "objective artifice" or "objective perfection" (as Descartes termed it) is that of the effective, "creative" idea of the working machine when it has been built and works perfectly. Hence, that machine borrows all its actual reality as a perfectly working machine from the artifice of its inventor-craftsman, from the real power of his mind, and thus the work effected by the machine is the ultimate effect of his idea of his machine.

To determine the degree of objective reality of any idea, we must in each case determine its formal reality as well. That is to say, to grasp clearly the objective reality of any given idea, we will have to "analyze" it into its absolutely simplest components; then we will find one, and only one, existent—whether that be a patron idea or whether it be a truly existent something in front of us—that will have just the degree of entity (where the term 'degree' is crucial) that corresponds to the objective reality of our idea. The idea will be, therefore, a "synthetic" or compound idea, except in the three cases of the ideas of extended body, thinking body, and their union. Except in the cases of these three simple ideas, all our ideas are synthetic, and their objective reality is also of a higher or lower "degree" or "rank" of being depending on the number of relatively elementary ideas that compose them!

Nor must we chortle here. An example of the present-day influence of this Cartesian notion is found in our search for "neural events" that are uniquely correlative to consciousness states. This most certainly is not a causal analysis across the mind-body gap; rather, it is a search for a continuous, and hence potentially synthetic, substratum for consciousness states. Once the individual elements within that substratum have been established as being in a one-to-one functional relation to successive consciousness states, the neo-Cartesian researcher can rest assured that the composition of the neural events, their true order and number and degree of intensity, uniquely associates one member out of a causal series of "physical" causes with each and every consciousness state. The character or true content of individual states is entirely beside the point; all that matters is that a given state only occurs when a given neural event occurs. This is precisely what Descartes had in mind with respect to the objective reality of consciousness states or ideas: a given idea has the reality that it does precisely because it is the *final* member of the chain of antecedents to which it belongs.

Concerning these matters, Descartes said:

> And it follows from this that . . . what is more perfect, that is to say, what contains in itself more of reality, cannot be a consequence of and dependent on what is less perfect. Furthermore, this truth is not only clear and evident from the effects which have that reality called actual or formal by the philosophers, but it is also clear and evident in ideas, where one considers only the reality which they call objective. . . . [Vol. IX, p. 132].

He then instanced a hot stone and its idea, and continued:

> although that particular cause does not transmit into my idea any of its actual or formal reality, one should not thereby imagine that this cause must be less real. Rather, it should be known that every idea being a work of the mind, the nature of any idea is such that it

requires for itself no other formal reality than what it receives or borrows from thought or the mind—since an idea is only a mode, i.e., a manner or way, of thinking. Now, in order that an idea contain one such objective reality than another, it ought, without doubt, to have it from a cause in which there is to be found at least as much formal reality as that idea contains of objective reality . . . For, all that manner of being objectively belongs to ideas, because of their proper nature, just as, on the other hand, the manner or fashion of being formally belongs to the causes of these ideas (at least to the first and principal ones) by their proper nature. And, although it can happen that one idea gives birth to another . . . , finally, we must arrive at a first idea, whose cause must act as a patron or an original. In that patron, all the reality or perfection is contained formally and in effect which is found only objectively or by representation in the ideas stemming from it.

Thus, the objective reality of an idea is just that *in the idea* that, although it belongs to it *as an idea,* is its reality as borrowed from elsewhere. (For example, in the terms of modern set-theory, the number n is the set of the numbers less than n, so that the very "being" of that set is a dependency on its members, and not on itself, since "no set is a member of itself." The definition that denominates a cardinal number as being a set having the same multitude of elements as a uniquely distinguished "counter-set" does the same thing, inasmuch as the counter-sets are the "patron" ideas and the natural numbers then borrow their "objective reality" from them.[1])

To continue, then, Descartes wrote that each individual existent thing admits to a unique and distinct degree of reality (*vid.* Rule VIII, Vol. X, p. 392, l. 10–22). He said, for instance (Vol. IX, p. 109), "it is self-evident that it is a greater perfection in not being divisible than in being divisible. So that, if you understand only what is quite perfect in the genus of body, that is not true at all of the true God."

What can we conclude from this passage other than that soul or mind (*res cogitans*) is, in itself, of a higher degree of perfection than is extended body (*res extensa*)? Furthermore, it follows from this that mind has a sufficient degree of reality, vis-à-vis its notions or conceits, to enable it to be the formal reality from which the ideas like those we construct when we form hypotheses and conceive inventions borrow their objective reality. We have already touched upon the notion of invention. In the case of hypotheses (which are a sort of intellectual invention, concerned, in Descartes' mind, with inventing solutions to problems), something similar follows. For, if all individual existent things participate in one, and only one, degree of reality, and if the objective reality of a particular clear and distinct idea exactly corresponds, in the realm of thinking body, to the degree of reality of its object, then the rank of being of an hypothesis-idea, of an idea that concerns only the possible existence of something, takes its degree of being from the parts or elements of, or the antecedents to, the idea, i.e., from what the analysts call "the data" or the "conditions of the problem." Thus, in algebraic equations, the data, i.e., the "known," exactly equal the *quaesitum*, i.e., the sought-for or "unknown." Indeed, Descartes' doctrine of the objective reality of ideas is his own "meta-mathematical" analysis of his and Vieta's theory of algebraic equations and transformations.

"Objective reality," as we *today* use that term, is for Descartes the counterpart to the ideas we have, or may have, of things "outside." For us, *today*, the term is concerned with things; for Descartes, to the contrary, the term referred to a characteristic of ideas! More precisely, the reality or "entity" of things was, for Descartes, the counterpart to the objective reality of their ideas. The only exception, one that has been mentioned already, is the situation of a machine and the cunning or ingenuity of the craftsman who invented it; in that case, the real machine "out there" is the objective counterpart to the "objective artifice" of the idea of that machine in the mind of its inventor.

Since Descartes' time, there has been a great deal of confusion concerning the distinction between the "objective reality of an idea" and "the objective artifice of a machine." As we today understand the term, "objective reality" is what Descartes would have understood as the world of artifice, the world of technological civilization—and, it seems, the created world itself, *as* created, i.e., as a "natural" or "divine" artifact. In that Descartes was "analytic" and attempted to derive the given as the logical consequence of the more general and more intelligible, the very world about him came to be a sort of objective counterpart to the ingenious hypothesis-ideas by means of which he tried to understand that world; and those ideas are, as "analytic," characterized by their artifice. Thus, for the analytic physicist, *all* of objective reality is the counterpart to his methodically derived ideas: *all* of reality becomes, progressively, step by step (*gradatim*), the objective counterpart to his methodically achieved analytical hypotheses. Working by means of these mathematical hypotheses, he adds to his store of ideas by deriving equations step by step, gradually; correlative to this methodical procedure, the nature of physical reality will be unfolded to him step by step (*gradatim*).[2] The goal of this process is a science in which, as Spinoza, a profound scholar of Descartes' thought, had it: "The order and connection of ideas is that of the order and connection of things" (*Ethics*, Part II, Prop. IV). (Spinoza saw clearly that the question of grades, degrees, and levels of beings and ideas was a fundamental one for, of all things, *ethics*. He wrote a work connecting, even in its title, the question of the highest being, God, and the political order: his *Theological-Political Tractate.*)

Descartes was very clear about his conviction that reality is structured according to ranks or degrees of being. In the *Responses to the Second Objections* (Vol. IX, pp. 105–106), Descartes compared "lower" animals, as effects, with their causes:

> For, either it is certain that there is definitely not any more perfection in the animals which do not have any reason at all (which is the case also with inanimate bodies), or, if there is any perfection in them, it is certain that it comes to them from elsewhere and the sun, rain and earth are definitely not the total causes of these animals.

He then continued that it is irrational to doubt this, "on the sole grounds that one does not have any idea of the cause which concurs in the generation of a fly, i.e., a cause having as many degrees of perfection as there are in a fly. . . ."

Again, he said that (Vol. IX, p. 49), "God has not placed me in the rank [*au rang*] of the most noble and perfect things," and hence, that he is not to be supposed to have all the perfections that exist in the whole universe. Again, (Vol. IX, p. 63) he said that there must be some substance in which the objective reality of our ideas of corporeal things is contained formally or eminently, or that such substance may be even "God himself or some other creature more noble than body in which that very objective reality of my ideas is contained eminently." Again, in Axiom VI of his "geometrical" proof of God's existence (and what is a "geometrical" proof of God's existence if it does not explicitly reveal the interdependency of the steps or grades between things?) Descartes said (Vol. IX, p. 128) that, "there is more of objective reality in the idea of substance than in the idea of an accident and more in the idea of infinite substance than in the idea of finite substance."

In a final example that explicitly joins the concept of rank of being with his algebraic or analytic considerations, he said in Rule VIII that:

> In effect, whatever constitutes a definite and complete degree [*integrum gradum*] in the series by which it is necessary to pass from relative things to absolute things, or inversely, ought necessarily to be examined first before what follows. But if, as sometimes happens, many things belong to the same level [*ad eumdem gradum pertineat*], it is surely always useful to run through them all in order. [Vol. X, p. 392, l. 16–22]

Here Descartes addressed the methodical analysis of "natural powers" and said, concerning the search for the powers that ultimately cause the specific ratio of the angle of incidence to the refraction angle of light in different media, that:

the ratios between the angles of incidence and the angles of refraction depend on the variation of these same angles because of the difference of media; and that variation, in turn, depends on the way in which the ray of light penetrates into all the transparent body; and the knowledge of the property of penetrating into a body presupposes the nature of the action of light to be known also; and, finally, in order to understand the action of light, it is necessary to know generally what a natural power is—and that knowledge is, in that complete series, the last and most absolute term. Thus, when one has seen clearly by intuition, he should pass by the same degrees [*per eosdem gradus*] . . . and if, in arriving at the second degree [*in secundo gradu*] he does not immediately know the nature of the action of light, he should, following the 7th Rule, enumerate all the other natural powers. . . . [Vol. X, p. 394, l. 22, to p. 395, l. 9]

That "second degree" is the second power of the equation from which the whole class of "anaclastic" curves of optics is derived analytically.

From this passage it is fair to conclude that, for Descartes, the *gradual* method of reaching truth in the sciences faithfully images, intellectually, the ranks and degrees of the reality about which it is concerned; further, we can conclude that we have a truly sufficient grasp of something through its idea only if we have arrived at that idea via a path that has as many distinct steps, grades, or ranks as the thing has degrees of being.[3]

From this we are prepared to find that falsity, as well, is concerned with the question of the rank of being of ideas and their objects. Indeed, we find (Vol. IX, p. 180) that ideas are materially false only insofar as "I do not recognize that there is more of reality represented to me by one idea than by another." Take, for example, the idea of cold that we receive from the senses. Here we have two distinct ideas, one of heat and another of cold. Our ideas are materially false, Descartes said, if we take the ideas of heat and cold and "do not recognize that there is more of reality which would be represented by the one than by the other." Thus, in a sense, ideas, as such, are in themselves true or false, without reference to that of which they are ideas, when we do not recognize in an idea its own proper degree of objective reality. On the other hand, when we consider ideas formally, we consider them as representing something outside, and then we judge using these ideas. All error in judgment is, for Descartes, formal error.[4] To understand this, we can look to Meditation III, where Descartes said (Vol. IX, p. 29) that there are three forms (*formes*) of thought: 1) ideas proper, which are "as the images of things [*comme les images des choses*]; 2) volitions and affections, e.g., desire, fear, affirmation, and denial; and, 3) judgment, as when we consider something as the subject of the action of the mind, "thereby adding something to the idea [we] have of it."

It cannot be stressed too often both that judgment *adds to* the idea we have of something and that *formal* falsity concerns the association of ideas and their "objects." Volition (free will, choice) always implies the question of action in this world, but it is by no means merely a matter of action in this world, according to Descartes. That is the domain of desire. For, whereas we can desire whatever we can imagine to be good for us, we can only will what is in some degree accessible to our efforts, even if the steps to active realization are only given indeterminately. Thus, our freedom to judge that God does not exist is, for Descartes, the proof of proofs that God does exist: no knowledge whatsoever, and hence no true or false judgment, is possible, according to Descartes, unless God so ordains the interrelation of things (their disposition with respect to one another) that we are able to progress, in an orderly manner, from unknown to known. Indeed, if the unknown is not somehow implicit in the known, how could we ever even begin to realize that we do not know, let alone begin to ask questions? Descartes' "theology" contains his one and only guarantee that knowledge of the world is possible and that progress based upon that knowledge is possible. His "theology" is not that of a confused, somewhat fallen-away (but basically loyal) son of the Church; it is the ultimate foundation for his *mathesis universalis,* for his scientific method.

In judging, one takes the idea of cold, for example, *formally,* as representing something; *materially,* one takes the idea of cold and compares it with the idea of heat, in order to determine which idea has more objective reality in it. If one is materially false and concludes that the idea of cold has as much objective reality as the idea of heat, then it is likely that he will also commit an error in judgment, and assent to the proposition that cold is really contained in the ice. This power of asserting/assenting is never misused if and only if we never judge until we are absolutely sure that the degree of objective reality of the idea is exactly that of the degree of *entitas* or reality of the thing on which we pass judgment. (It is, of course, a necessary consequence of this that the inferior, more ignorant man can never pass an altogether true or accurate judgment on a superior or more knowledgeable man. Here we find a hidden, technical intimation of what d'Alembert might have meant when he called Descartes "a teacher of revolutionaries": i.e., that the traditionally chosen legislators and judges of traditional societies must be replaced by analytic physicists or their students.)

In short, we commit error, according to Descartes, when we consider an idea as being caused by something outside us (or, sometimes, even by a patron idea inside us) without asking whether or not the two are of the same rank in reality. It is this source of error to which he primarily addressed his method. All beings and all ideas of those beings are so

ranked and graded that true science consists in leading thought by definite degrees—up the ranks, grades, or steps (*gradatim*)—that exactly parallel the hierarchy of being within which we humans are placed as thinking beings. It is not too bold to speculate, first, that perhaps it is out of
this view that our contemporary fascination with historical processes and
stages takes its genesis and, second, that this fascination will endure as
long as the generally taught and received physics is "analytic." The historical analytic physics of the Enlightenment is the spring that waters
analytic history.

We judge or withold judgment as we will, and Descartes' doctrine
concerning will is essentially concerned with our rank in the hierarchy of
beings. He wrote, in Meditation IV, "Concerning the True and the
False" (Vol. IX, pp. 45–46), that we are distinctly limited in our substantial being, but that we have a will that is in no way limited. That is,
although at any given time any given understanding is strictly limited as
to what in the structured, preordained, predisposed-to-be-known universe it knows, the possessor of that understanding still has the intellectual power to assert opinions concerning anything, even though it be
above the level of his understanding—where, it must be remembered,
both will and understanding are intellectual faculties. A human's mental
faculty of willing can operate in cases where his ideas do not have the
degree of objective reality required for a clear and distinct grasp of the
situation, and, therefore, *before* those ideas have a level or degree of
objective reality commensurate with the degree of reality belonging to
what he is judging. This excess of the extent of the will over the grasp of
the mind is a precondition for the possibility of universal doubt, i.e., this
alone gives us the power to stand in a certain (i.e., analytic) sort of
anticipatory relationship with all things whatsoever, no matter on what
level our thoughts are with respect to their degree of objective reality.
Thus, although in fact the mind of any given mortal, who will live only a
finite length of time, may not be capable of grasping some particular
truth because he will never have the time to "build up" to it in the finite
time from his birth, his will is actually capable ("en effet") of choosing to
make some judgment concerning it, even when it is highest and most
beyond the degree or rank of objective reality belonging to his ideas
(since each and every particular proof has a definite rank in the universal order of creation). Consequently, those things above his present level
of understanding are nevertheless in a certain and definite relationship,
which might well be termed a relationship of "volitional anticipation."
Certainly, those things are not merely unknown, since they are objects of
his intellectual power of willing. Descartes called this tenuous relationship *indeterminacy* on the part of knowledge, and said (Vol. IX, pp.
46–48) that corresponding to it is the volitional relationship of *indif-*

ference. As Descartes stated, we are the creatures that we are, and there-fore have the power to pass judgments even on what is infinitely more real than the reality of our ideas concerning it. Also, precisely because the contents of the universe are all located within its structure, with each and every entity occupying a distinct and unique rung or degree of reality, human volition can view all things, no matter how exalted, as knowable, because each occupies a distinct rung. Just as volition, in the individual with a complex, highly organized body, is operative primarily through the dispositions and inclinations of the body to act in one way rather than another, so, because the whole universe is structured into levels or degrees, is the volition of the human predisposed toward every-thing that is accessible to mind through its place in an organization. Thus, the atheist, who judges from the extreme depth of his ignorance that his idea of God has as its ultimate patron the fiction of some con-niver, is free to pass his judgment. However, Descartes pointed out, the atheist's freedom to judge that his notion of God is ultimately a fiction of a deceiver is the lowest kind of freedom, and, relative to Descartes' own level of philosophic comprehension, the degree of objective reality that the atheist's idea of God could have—e.g., if he were to read and com-prehend Descartes' own *Meditations*—is so remote that it has no effect on his ignorant idea. Hence, the atheist has so little grounds for judging that either a negative or an affirmative judgment is equally called for, and he is thus indifferent to his choice.

However, what is a matter of indifference with respect to the will is a matter of ("analytic") indeterminateness with respect to the understand-ing, since the bare notion of the higher reality is present even if that notion does not happen to determine fully the objective reality of the idea. Thus, although the atheist is not fully aware of it, i.e., although he does not realize it in thought, the idea of God that he truly has is the unique, true patron idea from which his thinking of God must borrow its degrees of objective reality. Where else would a human being ever get the idea of something immortal, perfect, and unlimited?[5] Hence, no matter what pit of ignorance one might be in, the ultimate patron ideas are present to us. This a fundamental theme in Descartes and is the necessary precondition for his analytical mathematics as he understood it. Consequently, whatever stands between our present ignorance and the full intellectual realization of those patron ideas as being patron, is known indeterminately in the bare consciousness of the subject matter. The grades of being provide a ladder by which we can ascend out of any pit of ignorance.

In mathematics, the *quaesitum*, or solution, to the problem, is, in a determinate and definite sense of term, "anticipated" or even "indeter-minately given through anticipation." Things whose reality is of a higher degree than the present grade of objective reality of our present ideas about them are, so to speak, foreshadowed in the extension of the will over understanding; therefore, the principal source of error, according to Descartes, is also the grounds for anticipating a replacement of error with knowledge. (This is the heart of Meditation VI.) Once again, *volition is power of mind* for Descartes, no less than is methodical reasoning. Willing is an intellectual act, essentially, and the very infinitude of the extent of the will is a sign of the extent to which man can expect other powers of intellect to reach, because of the infinite extent of the order in the knowable universe. In calling volition (or choice)—where volition is *not* desire—an intellectual power, Descartes identified anything that can be chosen at any time (in or out of understanding) under any circumstance (whether drunk, sober, or ill) as a potential object of understanding, because of the graded, structured order of reality. Therefore, as an actual object of volition, everything in the universe is a sort of actual subject of intellect. We are thus led to say that, for Descartes, the very fact of willing something implies that there is some degree of something akin to objective reality even in the most wild or disordered of ideas. It is volition that supplies a sort of *pro tem* replacement for objective reality to ideas of things that are not yet grasped clearly and distinctly. Indeed, Descartes said (Vol. IX, p. 46) that once he had grasped entirely clearly and distinctly some idea, he was not at all indifferent to it, and hence it was no longer subject to volition, but rather to desire and repugnance, which are contingent on true understanding (or, upon the teaching of our complex nature). In this regard, what desire and repugnance are to understanding, so volition is to the order and disposition of things that can be known scientifically, i.e., methodically.

We can summarize this in the following analogies: as volition is to desire, so is merely being aware of the existence of something to the grasping or conceiving of an idea about it whose objective reality is of the same rank of being as the thing itself has degrees of entity or reality. Similarly, as desire and repugnance are to understanding, so is volition to the universal disposition of things. In this way, a psychic power, volition, supplies to our ideas of what is truly existent (but what is not sufficiently known), the defect in objective reality that must be made up subsequently through the methodical analytical procedure, i.e., through assuming the sought-for, *quaesitum*, as given and known, and then methodically, that is, step by step, deducing from this supposition the consequences, until we arrive at something truly given or truly known (see *Geometry*, Vol. VI, p. 372, l. 10–24).[6] The will, at any given moment, is able to concern itself with an infinity of objects beyond the present grasp of the intellect only because the general object of volition is the realm of what has absolutely definite relationships with everything else: it is the realm of the structured—whether that be the human organism or the physical world, in which distinct entities each have definite and unique realtionships to all other entities. It is a realm in which, to cite Cicero again, "each thing is so disposed that each can be referred to every other." Volition is thus ultimately concerned with dispositions.[7]

NOTES

1. This is precisely Bertrand Russell's definition of a natural number. The definitions of Peano's Postulates follow the same rationale.

2. In this development, we can see the "necessity" for Locke's history of ideas (their development from simple to complex forms), Rousseau's history of the genesis of states and citizens from pre-citizens, Hegel, Marx, and finally, Darwin. In this general context, see also Mircea Eliade, *The Forge and the Crucible*, trans. Stephen Corrin (Chicago, London: University of Chicago Press, 1978), especially Chapters 3, 4, 5, 8, 14, and 15, together with the Postscript and Appendices.

3. *Vid.* "Vieta's Introduction to the Analytical Art" (in J. Klein, *Greek Mathematics*, given as an appendix; trans. J. Winfree Smith), pp. 322, 324–325, and fn. 15, and Ch. VIII, pp. 347–353.

4. This is somewhat odd, since "judgment," whatever else it may mean, usually refers primarily to our sense of what is important or not. However, this usual meaning does not fall where we might expect. Rather, it falls under what Descartes called the question of *material* falsity, and not under formal truth and falisty, which, according to him, alone concern judgment.

Our contemporary low estimation of "value judgments" probably has its origin in this Cartesian reversal, which replaces the question of value (for Descartes, a *material* question) with that of the "objectiveness" of a state of mind (for Descartes, a *formal*, "judgmental," question). If so, this reversal of definitions is not without its momentous, not to say awful, consequences.

Finally, the characterization of error in judgment as formal error is, on the one hand, the *raison d'être* of all schools of "linguistic" and "analytic" philosophy and, on the other hand, the fundamental justification for a bureaucracy manned by "intellectuals." This relationship helps shed light on the otherwise puzzling phenomenon of political "liberals" viewing big government as good government: for Cartesian intellectuals, government is merely process within structure.

5. It is a true irony of intellectual history that Descartes gave us both a proof of God's existence (an idea of a Being so superior to human thinkers cannot have been merely made up by humans), and a closely allied theory of the progressive construction of complex, abstract ideas from simpler ideas, which has been used precisely to negate his proof. Thus, e.g., Freud's *Moses and Monotheism* shows precisely how to take simple, childhood ideas and gradually transform them into an idea of God such as Descartes said he discovers in himself.

6. *Vid.* definition IV of Descartes' proof of the existence of God, in *Responses to the Second Objections*, especially in the French version, which has important changes from the Latin version (French, Vol. IX, p. 125; Latin, Vol. VII, p. 161, l. 10–13): "The same things are said to be eminently in the objects of ideas when they are not truly such in them as in the ideas, but when they are so great [*si grande*] that they can make up for that defect by their excellence."

Gilson hardly touches upon this question of the eminent reality of ideas in Descartes' thoughts [E. Gilson, *Etudes sur le Rôle de la pensée médiévale dans la formation du système cartésien* (Paris: Libraire J. Vrin, 1967)]. When he does, it is in the entirely misleading context of discussing causality. This enters into the question, of course, but the heart of the problem with this term, as well as with the term "objective reality of an idea," lies with intelligibility, and, insofar as causality enters into the picture, it is *as the cause of knowledge.*

For a possible source for Descartes' use of the term "eminent [*eminens*]" see Cicero's *On the Nature of the Gods,* I, 27, 75: "species deorum quae nihil solidi habeat, nihil *eminentis* [that appearance of the gods which has no substance, and nothing which is *lofty*]." Descartes is almost certain to have read that work when he studied at La Fleche and, as he stated in the *Rules,* he uses Latin terms in their classical Latin meanings, and not their Scholastic Latin meanings.

7. *Vid.* Richard B. Carter, "Volitional Anticipation and Popular Wisdom in Descartes," *Interpretation* (1978) 7(2): 75–98.

APPENDIX 4

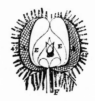

The Genesis of Light

IN THE *Treatise on Light,* Descartes said:

> You well know that words, not having any resemblance with things
> which they signify, do not fail to make us conceive them—often
> without noticing the sounds of words or their syllables; so that it
> often happens that, having heard a conversation whose sense we
> have very well grasped, we are not able to say in what language it
> had been pronounced. Now if words, which signify nothing except
> by the institution of men, suffice in order to make us conceive of
> things to which they have no resemblance, why cannot Nature also
> have established a certain sign which makes us have the sensation of
> light, although that sign should be nothing in itself which resembles
> that sensation? And is it not thus that Nature has established
> laughter and tears in order to make us read joy and sadness on the
> faces of men? [Vol. XI, p. 5, l. 3–19]

If, however, light does not resemble in the least the sensation of light
that it causes in men, why should nature have established any connection
between the two? The ability to read laughter as joy and tears as sadness
is obviously useful, but the establishment of the relation between light
and its sensation is not so clear—until we look at Descartes' metaphor of
the blind man's staff in Discourse VI of the *Dioptrics.*

In the case of the blind man, we notice, above all, that he does not
need his staff unless he is moving relative to possible obstacles. Then, if
the staff is y-shaped, as Descartes had it, he can hold it in both hands as
he walks and it will "tell" him when he is about to run into some impediment
to his forward motion. Primarily, then, the surrogate for sight, his
forked staff, which instantaneously transmits only change of forward
motion to his hands, is useful because its declination from the straight
path signifies to him impediments to his own rectilinear motion. By
means of his forked staff, he can tell where he *cannot* go. That is, whenever
the overall rectilinear motion of the staff is impeded, it indicates, by
the obstruction of rectilinear motion, *the direction in which he would have
moved* had there been no impediment to his continued rectilinear
motion.

Descartes defined light and its laws generally (e.g., Vol. VI, p. 89, l. 1–3): "For it is very easy to know that the action or inclination to be moved, which I have said ought to be taken as light, ought to follow the same laws of nature as movement." In the analogy of the blind man, when he said that light is "an action or tendency to be moved," he referred to the relation between the particular impediment to further motion and the rod that actually strikes the impediment and thereby, by its cessation of motion, makes the blind man "aware" of that impediment. Then the blind man "reads" the motion or lack of it and, therefore, the path immediately in front of him. This appendix shows how Descartes used the figure of the blind man, aided by his staff, to explain both the cause of our seeing the light from far-distant stars as well as in what sense the "blind" sight of the blind man is a sort of metaphor for human presentiment. The latter, in turn, ties together with our previous discussion of the crucial importance, for Descartes, of the so-called method of indeterminates, i.e., of analysis, and, generally, with our discussion of the place of disposition.

An image Descartes used to illustrate the idea of a thwarted tendency to movement, one in which there is no "reader," is that of a sling with a stone in it. The stone cannot leave its cradle in the sling because of the cord that connects it to the hand. If it is in very rapid motion, however, it exerts considerable force away from the center of the circle along whose circumférence it is being whirled. Then, when the sling is released, the stone flies off, but it neither drops directly away from the center of the circle nor continues whirling around in a circular path; rather, it travels off along the straight line that is tangent to the circle at the point where the stone was located at the moment of release. Descartes took this to be evidence for concluding that at every moment during which the stone is being whirled around in a circle, it has a tendency or inclination to remove itself away from the center around which it is being moved, and that the tendency is exactly opposed by the countervailing force of the cord that keeps it whirling around. The countervailing force is in effect applied at right angles to the stone at every instant—which is why it flies off at a tangent upon release. By Law I, conservation of state, the stone tends to conserve itself at each instant in the same state as it was in during the preceding instant, and its impulse is always to move in a straight line. An illustration, based on those found in Descartes' *Principles*, is of help (*vid.*, Vol. IX, *Planche* V).

If (see Figure A-1), at a certain instant, the stone is released when it is at A, and it travels along the tangent to the circle at A until it reaches C, its total translation relative to the center at E is only the distance BC directly away from E: the horizontal translation from A to C, made along the tangent GA, is real only with respect to the point A; the horizontal

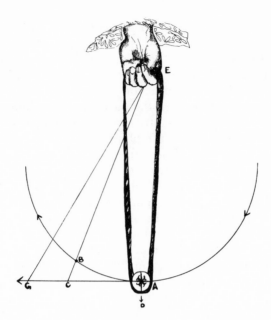

Figure A-1

translation has no "real" existence with respect to the point E except for the distance BC as the hypotenuse of triangle ABC, since all the measurable force of the stone at C could be accounted for by its drop along the distance BC directly opposite E. (We are supposing a uniform motion around E.) If the stone is not released at the point A, then by the time it reaches the point B on the circumference, it will have tended to remove itself from the center E with just that force required to make it drop the distance BC in the time it took the stone to transverse the arc AB of the circle; the faster the stone is being whirled around E, the less time it will take for the stone to traverse arc AB. Thus, if the intervals of time are considered to be equal, the length of BC will be directly proportional to the velocity around E. That centrifugal—center-fleeing—force is measured by Descartes as being equal to the pull of the cord EA against the hand whirling the sling at E.

Descartes' fullest treatment of light is detailed in the *Principles,* Part III, Articles 55–64 (Vol. IXB, pp. 130–136). We here give a rough sketch of that treatment, and then follow it with the details.

In Article 55, "What Light Is," Descartes said that light is primarily the result of the efforts that each of the three sorts of elements found in each of the many heavens surrounding ours makes to remove itself from the center of its own rapidly whirling heaven. There are at least as many heavens as there are fixed stars. The three sorts of celestial elements are: the first element, of which fire here on earth and the luminous bodies in most of the heavens are primarily composed, and whose parts are very small, round, and extremely agitated (and which is similar to the element primarily composing the thin, serous fluid in the human brain and nerves); the second element, of which the heavens themselves are composed (as are the spongy organs of living bodies on earth, e.g., liver and lungs), and whose parts are not as uniform or small as those of the first element and are much less agitated; and, finally, the third element, which is like that comprising solid bodies here on earth, and, in particular, comprising bone and muscle in our human bodies. In Article 55 of Part III of the *Principles,* Descartes' presentation is generally analogous to the example of the sling: the opposition to the stone's natural rectilinear motion away from the center provided by the length of cord, EA, is replaced in each whirling heaven by the closely compacted and compressed parts of the second element, which so surround each other in ever-widening, more or less concentric, circles formed by the primary whirling motion of each heaven around its axis that any given compression-circle presses against its neighbor away from the center.

Each circle around the center of any given *tourbillon* ("vortex" or "whirlwind") is composed of particles of the second element trying to move themselves away from that center; at the center of each heaven, consequently, there is a large evacuated space that has no particles of the second element; into and out of these empty spaces particles of the first element, very small and highly agitated, flow in and out more or less following such lines as those we see round a spherical magnet. (Descartes knew Gilbert's *De Magnete* much better than he knew most books.)

Almost all the light we on earth see coming from the sun is a direct result of the motion of the parts of the first element that fill the space in the neighborhood of the center of rotation of our heaven that has been evacuated by the matter of the heaven itself, the second element. Figure A-2 clarifies this.

In Figure A-2, the heaven whirls around center *defg*—which is empty and thus ready to receive particles of the first element. Descartes proposed that the neighborhood around center *defg* is empty because the "balls" of second element are tightly compressed and thus leave that central neighborhood vacant.

Furthermore, Descartes stated, the mere force of the rotation of a heaven would give us a thin band of light along the periphery of that central void. That belt of light, precisely across the *equator* of the central mass, is defined by the fact that it is the equator with respect to the poles—and it spins on those poles. Thus, we would see the bands because that is where the centrifugal force is greatest. The *polar* areas of

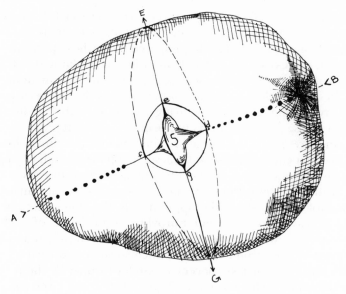

Figure A-2

the central spherical void are luminous only when there is a large quantity of first element in the central void. The extreme degree of agitation of the particles of first element is then transferred to the surrounding "sea" of particles of second element, and this, in the case of our own "heaven," causes us to see a fiery ball, the sun. As we shall see, the case is not the same for remote heavens. (Since, to my knowledge, the texts on which I argue my points are not available in English, I shall add a running paraphrase as a support for these arguments.)

In Article 56 of Part III, "How one can say of an inanimate thing that it tends to produce a certain effort," Descartes said that the small parts of the elements "make an effort, or, rather, they have a certain inclination to remove themselves from the centers around which they turn." He said that he did not intend, however, "to attribute to them any thought from which this inclination proceeds," but only that these parts would remove themselves because "they are so situated and disposed to be moved"—were they not prevented from doing so by some other cause. Light, then, is *both* the consequence of the transfer of motion from one part of the first element to parts of the second element on down to our eyes *and* the consequence of an impediment being placed in the way of bits of matter; each of the bits of matter has a disposition to move that is only realized, in a highly modified, mediated way, because of the obstacle presented by the balls of second element.

Article 57 says "How a body can tend to be moved in several different ways at once." In that article, Descartes gave his analysis of how the tendency to motion of a stone whirling around in a sling is overcome by the countering strength of the cord AE.

Article 58 discusses the stone's empirically observed tendency to remove itself (*s'eloigner*) from the center around which it moves, and it gives, as a further illustration of removal from the center, the example of a fly walking down a stick (which here replaces the cord EA) such that the fly is always on the tangent to AG and always walks directly away from the center E.

Article 59, "How much force that tension has" reveals how "tendency" is to be *quantified* into "tension" and measured by units of force! In Descartes' words, "you see also that the stone which is in the sling makes the cord stretch [*fait tendre la corde*] more and more as it turns more and more quickly; and because what makes that cord stretch is nothing other than the force with which the stone removes itself from the center around which it turns, we can know by that tension the quantity of that effort." (Stress equals strain, for Descartes.)

Article 60 connects the example of the sling to those conditions in the heavens that cause light, that is, that cause that action or tendency to motion that is perceived as light. As Descartes said in Article 52, the Whole is a plenum (i.e., having no empty places), diversified into three forms or elements; the first has parts that are round, very small, and very highly agitated; the second has less-regular parts that are bigger than those of the first element, and their motion is less great; the third element, out of which is composed the minerals and the like on earth, is yet grosser and less agitated than either of the other two. Article 60 then describes the *tourbillons*—vortices, whirlpools, or whirlwinds—of the second element, of which the heavens are composed, and which carry along with them the planets around the central "sun" of each tourbillon. The centers of the tourbillons are occupied by a mass of the first element in the space left by the whirling, which compresses the second element particles away from the center of motion of each heaven. He also said in Article 60 that,

> it is easy to apply to the parts of the second element what I have just
> said of that stone which turns in a sling around the center E . . . ,
> that is, that each of the parts of the second element exerts a force
> considerable enough to remove it from the center of the heaven
> around which it turns, but that each part is arrested by those parts
> arranged below it just as the stone is retained by the sling.

Article 64 then shows that we do not at all need any of the most subtle and highly agitated first element in order to have light coming from the center of a heaven. The relatively much grosser and less agitated second element of the heavens suffices, so that we can get light without great heat, fire, or anything approaching the concentration of the first element always present in luminous or burning bodies. All we need is a material no more subtle and agitated than the matter of the heavens, but whirling around at a center from which it cannot remove itself because of the *disposition* of parts of second element.

Continuing with his analogy of the sling in Articles 63 and 64, Descartes said that the sea of particles of the second element is very greatly compressed as we draw nearer and nearer to the outside of a given heaven or tourbillon. The particles of second element, which he calls "balls" or "globes," all tend to remove themselves from the eye of the whirlpool, and in so doing leave an empty space around that center, a space that is usually filled with a mass of the first element, which, when sufficiently condensed, composes a luminous body. Article 63 makes an assertion of great importance:

> Further, it is necessary to remark that the force of light, in order to explain which I write all this, does not consist in the duration [*la durée*] of any motion, but only in this, that the same balls of which the heavens are composed are pressed and make an effort in order to move themselves towards some place, although they should not be able to move actually.

Then, even more curiously, he said in Article 64 that, even if there were no masses of first element at the centers of the whirlpools, we would still see light emanating from the centers—only not quite so brightly as when those "stars" or "suns" made of large masses of the first element are present. (Blind men also "see" with their staffs—only not so vividly.)

The analogy between the generation of light in the whirlpools (heavens) and the tension of thw whirling sling is now complete. Returning to the figure from Descartes' *Planche* V (Figure 1), the stone is a ball of the second element, the general motion of the tourbillon is the whirling of the sling, and the relative incompressibility of the plenum is the strength of the string. A light ray, then, is the effort along ED or EC or EG that a ball carried around a tourbillon with center E makes to remove itself from E.

In the discussion of Article 63, it was pointed out that the second element, which was by far the most abundant material of any heaven, alone sufficed to produce a thin band of light, with no need for the "fiery" first element of luminous bodies to be present in the center of a tourbillon. For red-colored light, we need only small pockets of least-dense first element scattered throughout the heaven away from the center into which the highly compressed balls of second element can move. As it turns out, however, first element is very similar to the animal spirits found in the brain and spinal cord of vertebrates, and especially in men. In the unfinished *Description of the Human Body* (Vol. XI, pp. 223–256), begun about 1648, Descartes referred to passages out of Part III of the *Principles* (to which we have been directing our attention), and he used those results in a way that we shall examine in detail (especially Vol. XI, p. 247, l. 29, to p. 249, l. 14).

Before looking at the human microcosm of *The Description*, it should be pointed out (especially concerning Descartes' theory of light) that, although Descartes time and time again said that light is an effort or tendency toward motion, he also said that light is merely a motion, that is, that we perceive a motion of true body when we perceive light. In his *Meteors*, in Discourse VIII where he explains the breaking up of white light by a prism (Vol. VI, p. 334, l. 19–29), he said concerning perception of color:

> For, if it is true that the sensation which we have of light is caused by
> the movement or the inclination to be moved of some matter which
> touches our eyes . . . it is certain that the different movements of
> that matter ought to cause in us different sensations [*sentiments*] . . .
> such as that of colors.

However, just prior to this passage, which says that light is propagated by the motion of particles of the second element, he said (p. 333, l. 24–28), speaking of the spectrum A–F in his figure (our Figure A-3):

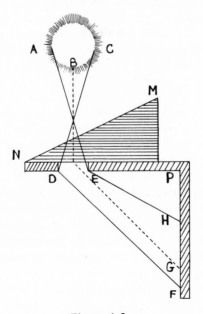

Figure A-3

"the nature of the colors which appear at F only consist in this, that the parts of subtle matter which transmit the action of light, tend to turn with more force than they are translated in a straight line."

How can an effort to move, a tendency to motion that is thwarted by an impediment, be transmitted by the real motion of spinning particles of the second element? Can a *thwarted* tendency to motion *cause* motion? This is a real problem, because it is analogous to the problem of will and that intellectual determination that concerns the future activity of humans. That is, a man's present intellectual determination, where determination ambiguously means both volition as well as clear and distinct prevision or providence, intimates now, when there is still no real action, some future action. That foresight, that intimation or presaging, is the future's presence in a "now" that, when the future is realized, will be a past to it. Only present *circum*stances thwart the instant realization of a determinate volition; but present circumstances, precisely because they are, themselves, *part of* a larger ordered, preordained universe, are not able to thwart the pre-vision of what will really and in fact be seen if and when that pre-vision is realized in the future—if that pre-vision is guided by the laws of nature, since the circumstances that presently thwart are themselves guided by those laws. The present pre-vision of the future that is given to us by our intellectual determination is, now, only a "colorless" product of our own intellectual and volitional powers.

We can summarize this analogy with light as follows: First, we remark that the term 'heavens' is for Descartes a true plural. Our solar system with its central sun is only one of many, and each sun-star is at the center of motion of each heaven. There are as many distinct heavens as there are centers around which large masses of the second element whirl (as the stone in a sling whirls around its center). Each fixed star is the center of a distinct whirling heaven and almost all the light we perceive that illuminates our immediate surroundings comes from our sun in our heaven or from some other luminous body, such as a fire or a candle, also within our heaven. We do not, for Descartes, necessarily see the central luminous body of a particular heaven other than our own, only the equatorial light of the tourbillon whirling as a whole about that central region.

Second, the matter of a heaven, like that stone of the sling, does not move relative to the (also whirling) center around which it is whirled. On the other hand, it certainly is moved away from any given circumferential point (at which, by Law II, the stone in a whirled sling naturally tends to remain or to proceed from in a straight line) and, in being moved it thereby changes its state from relative rest to motion. Concerning the change in the stone's state, Descartes said:

> I do not doubt that the movement . . . ought not to be very slow at
> the beginning and that its effort cannot seem very great if one

connects it only with that first movement; but, also, one cannot say
that it is completely nil . . . but it will advance a little more rapidly in
the second moment because, besides retaining the force that had
been communicated to it at the first instant, it will further acquire a
new one by the new effort it will make to remove itself from the
center E. . . . [Part III, Article 59]

The stone's motion around center E transmits to it an equally opposed
force to remove itself from E, and it becomes more and more disposed to
fly from E the faster it is whirled around E, although, relative to the
center E, it does not move at all. That *tendency* to remove itself from the
center around which it whirls *is realized in act* at the instant it is no longer
thwarted by the countervailing force of the cord.

According to Descartes, we do not see the luminous bodies at the
center of other tourbillons, and, indeed, may even see the tourbillons as
luminous bodies where there is no central *mass* at all. It is difficult to
understand how a tendency to motion of the parts of a tourbillon far
away can cause the balls of matter of our heaven to spin with varying
degrees of rapidity around their own axes. That is, remote heavens,
which we perceive as only pinpoints of light, are entirely luminous with
respect to us, and light comes from their entire surfaces, at which one
tourbillon is separated from its neighbors. Indeed, we often do not see
the light from their central masses, even in those cases where they *are*
present. Rather, the whole heaven "luminates" because of the tendency
of the particles of its matter of the second element to remove themselves
from the center. What motion could such a tendency cause? Descartes'
answer to this difficulty is that the tourbillons are able to send rays of
light through adjacent and interposed tourbillons. But these rays of light
are merely, once again, the paths by means of which the matter of the
tourbillons would remove itself from their centers *were there no obstacles*.
In order for this *tendency* to removal from a center around which it
whirls to be transmitted to our eyes as the *real* translation of spinning
balls of the matter of our own heavens, Descartes must suppose that
there are a great number of regions between our eye and the distant
tourbillon that are relatively free of the balls of the second element but
are filled with bits of first element, and that this tendency to motion is
realized as true motion when these regions are entered upon, i.e., these
regions do not thwart the tendency to motion of the balls, and therefore
they *can* rush into those spaces. It is as if the cord of the sling suddenly
became stretched; then the stone would remove itself a little from the
center. Descartes described the mechanics of this extremely involved
situation in Articles 77–80 of Part II of the *Principles*.

In those articles, Descartes went through a very detailed discussion
of the fact that the central sun of a heaven has two distinct light regions,

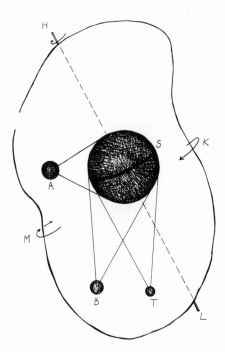

Figure A-4

that is, the "sun" of any heaven or tourbillon is lighted in different places by two different causes. On the one hand, the equatorial zone emits light because of the whirling of the heaven. However, the regions away from the equator are lighted because of a complex relation between the matter in the central space and certain pockets of that same matter found outside it in the heavens. Figure A-4 (modeled on Descartes') illustrates this. Here, S is a central sun of the heaven HKLM whirling on the axis HL. A and B are pockets of first element and T is a presumed Earth with observers on it. Descartes said that the cones from A and B with bases on S represent the regions of flow of second element into those regions A and B of lower density, and contrariwise, the flow from A and B into the sun. This violent displacement of particles of the second element causes perturbations throughout the whole heaven in which this takes place, so that, if there is an inhabited planet T in the heaven, the observers on it will perceive light as coming from the whole surface of the sun—light, that is, that is caused by the real translation of particles of second matter within the heaven. As for light from adjacent heavens, we are to suppose that, near the boundaries of the heaven in question, there are regions like A and B that are so sensitive to any motion within the sea of surrounding particles of second element that they immediately fill up with particles of second element whenever there is the least pressure from without, and thus cause a true flow of the second element into their regions. *None of Descartes' astrophysics works without a vast degree of preparation—unless everything is disposed 'just so'.*

Analogous to this case, the disposition of the organs of our bodies provides a region of relative freedom from the presence of balls of the second element. Our heads are, as it were, pockets or neighborhoods where so little of the second element and so much of the much more subtle first element are found that the tendency to motion of the balls of the second element meets with very little obstruction. We sense the *realization* of the disposition or tendency of a body to move as colored light. However, and this is crucial, were there no such pockets of first element between our eye and a very distant tourbillon, we would still see light, because our own brains and nerves would provide such a pocket.

Our idea of light is purely an idea of the totality of movements possible but not made. As such, it is an idea of indeterminacy. For, just as the degree of rotation found in the particles actually moved by luminous bodies in our own heaven provides an index of the path that the light ray took from that body to our eyes, so the very lack of color in our theory of light—and the principal thing a blind man *cannot* know about light is its colors—indicates the indeterminacy of paths that were not taken but that could have been taken had the body not been thwarted in its tendency to move. Whereas the colors of luminous bodies in the general case indicate clearly particular paths along which the force of the luminous bodies did cause motion. Color, one could say, is the index of the history of a body's motion; lack of color in our ideas of light indicates the indeterminacy and hence the futurity of the paths before the body. The perception of that colorless light is our awareness of what Descartes called "the light of nature"; it is a perception of a pure and presently indeterminate futurity and hence is a sort of indeterminate pre-vision or presentiment that is determined only subsequently by the particularities of contingencies and circumstances. The purest vision given us by the light of nature is that of the general laws of nature. The determination provided by future contingencies is, however, the giving to an indeterminate future a form or idea of how the presently thwarted body could really move (in the future). Such an idea of the future is, when considered at present, a plan or design that, if it is really possible, is the determination of foreknowledge and foresight. Articles 40 and 41 of Part I of the *Principles* state that the freedom of our will can be made to accord with God's preordinations and that God "has left the actions of men entirely free and indeterminate." We also know from the *Meditations* that God has the power to create anything that we can clearly and distinctly conceive.

Since, then, God's action in the *saeculum* is His continued conservation of His creation, and, since the *idea* we have of that conservative creation, the form in which we are most generally aware of it, is the laws of nature in the form in which Descartes exhibited them, our own human providential vision is determined in particulars only if we employ what Descartes often called the "natural light" of our intellects to form clear ideas in accord with those natural laws. Descartes did not explicitly identify "the light of nature" with the knowledge we have, before all experience, that the universe is ordained and disposed to be accessible to analytic method. This appendix is my argument for such an identification. Descartes would hardly have felt comfortable publishing such a deduction, since it directly implies a total replacement of Christian conscience with a belief in or concept of infinite progress and perfectibility of humans. It would be a crime, Descartes said, to doubt that future contingencies are not entirely determined and preordained by God. For Descartes, to be conservative and provident or prudent is to be progressive; *not* to be this is a crime of thought. The "natural light" of the intellect then, is our intellectual capacity to have presentiments of the course of things.

Indeed, for Descartes the ultimate test of the worth of a given philosophy lies in its fruitfulness, that is, not so much in the range and richness of the truths it contains as in the power of its principles to enable us constantly to discover new truths. It seems, further, that Descartes distinguished between "philosophy" and "science" precisely on the grounds that philosophy is static and science is progressive. We see that, in the preface to the French translation of his *Principles* (Vol. IXB, p. 18, l. 29, to p. 19, l. 1), Descartes dismissed Aristotle precisely on the grounds that his philosophy has made no progress since he expounded it. Descartes said, "and the falsity of the (Principles of Philosophy of Aristotle) cannot be demonstrated better than by saying that no progress has been made during the many centuries that they have been followed." Whereas, he said, the primary value of his own principles is "that, if one cultivates them, one can discover many truths that I have not at all disclosed" (Vol. IXB, p. 18, l. 18–19). We can conclude from this that any philosophy that is based on principles that do not lead to substantial progress in the course of time is based on false principles. However, if their essential lack of fruitfulness makes them false, then it is precisely their fruitfulness that makes principles true.

This implies that the criteria for the truth or falsity of the principles of his philosophy also apply to the thinking by which he achieved the thoughts comprising his philosophy. If this is true, then Descartes was of the mind that sound and good thinking is based on certain above all fruitful principles of thought. In other words, Descartes thought that the body of human thought is by nature progressive. In each good thinker, then, the biography of his thought mainly consists in a record of his ascent from certain principles of thought to a body of knowledge that Descartes calls (Vol. IXB, p. 18, l. 22) the "highest stage of wisdom [*plus haut degre de la Sagesse*]." This, for Descartes, is *la morale,* ethics. Ethics, above all, concerns progress—as is shown, for example, by the *ethical* imperative we today feel to aid "developing" countries, an imperative the early Church knew nothing of.

Name Index

Subject Index

Action. *See* Tendency
Admiration, 239
"Air," 199–204. *See also* Magnetism
Alchemy, 17, 113; and Jacob Boehme, 18; and Paracelsus, 17; and philosophers, hermetic, 18
Algebra. *See* Analysis
Analysis, 21, 34, 146 n. 4, 272, 292; abstract geometry as, 38; arithmetical operations in, 35, 36, 40, 80, 86 n. 19, 140, 255–57, 271; dimensions in, 34–35, 39, 40, 47–53, 85 n. 18; examples of, 57–58, 67–68; imagination as tool in, 132–33, 158; kinds of, 54–58, 73–78; medical science and, 116, 213; as method of problem-solving, 12, 15, 21, 37, 54–65, 189, 266; objects of geometry and, 36–54 *passim*, 83 n. 3, 84 n. 11, 152; Pappus on, 26 n. 27, 89 n. 26, 90 n. 29, 91 n. 30; passions as analogues of, 140; unknowns and knowns in, 68–69, 276–78, 281; use in mind-body distinction, 266 n. 4; use of *sa raison* in, 248–49
Analytic philosophy, 27 n. 4
Anticipation, 275–78. *See also* Presentment
Automaton, 175–79; ideas in, 176; light and, 179; soul lacking in, 176
Axiom of choice, 265 n. 1

Bible, books of: Deuteronomy, 186; Genesis, 106, 157, 159, 185, 186, 187, 190–91; Job, 159; John, 86 n. 20, 163; Leviticus, 186; Romans, 152 n. 33, 162, 166–67; Wisdom of Solomon, 162, 218
Blood, 194, 205, 208–12, 228 n. 26
Body, 31: algebraic, 34, 43, 50, 52, 94 n. 49, 263; of a man, 96–98, 145, 168, 170–211; medicine and, 50, 143; naive, 35, 48, 65, 68, 79, 266 n. 4; physical,

32–33, 43, 47, 258; political, 149 n. 13, 159–65, 247

Cartesian diver, 229 n. 29
Causes, 104–5, 262, 284; ideas as, 268, 269, 272
Christian charity, 246, 293
Circulatory systems: body in, 198–99, 205–12, 224 n. 22, 228 n. 25; double system, 203–5. *See also* Whirlpools
Compound bodies, 155–211; living, 166–67; non-living, 175–79, 238
Conic sections, 26 n. 27, 253–57, 263; as collection of points, 256
Consciousness-raising, 251 n. 18
Conservation, 158, 174, 215, 233, 281, 292. *See also* Self-preservation
Continuity, 212, 221 n. 9, 258–66
Creation, 109–10, 193

Death, 96; gratitude and, 247
Degree of reality, 266–78
Demonic possession, 130
Dessein, Descartes', 7
Determinism. *See* Natural institutions
Digestion, 26 n. 24
Dimensions, 35, 39, 40, 47–53, 85 n. 18, 258–63
Disposition, 97, 99–103, 129, 131, 142, 146 n. 34, 178, 182, 185, 187–88, 231, 235, 243, 276, 284, 286, 291. *See also* Natural institutions
DNA, 108
Doubt, 73–74. *See also* Analysis

Effort, 183, 188, 284, 286, 289
Elements, 182–83, 188, 193–212, 283–90
Embryo. *See* Genesis
Error, 274–77
Estoit (as intimate union), 232

Natural law. *See* Laws of nature
Neural events, 269
Neuroanatomy, 32, 43–46, 52–54, 59, 62, 64, 70, 85 n. 14, 91 n. 31, 102, 107–8, 113, 118–19, 121–33, 135, 146 n. 6, 152 n. 30, 167, 181–84, 228 n. 26, 238, 261–62, 286, 291
n-line locus problem, 26 n. 27, 253–57
νοῦς, 144

Objective reality, 135, 139, 153 n. 35
Organs, 97, 99–103, 109, 113, 135, 136–41, 147 n. 6, 148 n. 11, 187–88, 191, 198–99, 207–13, 218, 238, 286, 291. *See also* Heart, the; Pineal gland

Passions, 60, 80, 118–28, 133–37, 218, 241; admiration, 122–23, 134; arithmetical operations and, 80; contempt, 238–39; esteem, 238–39; generosity, 238–43, 245–46, 248, 250 n. 15; gratitude, 244–45, 247–48; humility, 240, 244; indignation, 244; ingratitude, 244, 246, 247; joy, 234–35; love and hate, 123, 126, 231–35, 245; pity, 218, 244; political, 238; primitive, definition of, 237, 238, 250 n. 24; scorn, 243; self-esteem, 240; veneration, 243, 247
Peano's postulates, 278 n. 1
Pelagian heresy, and Descartes, 15, 26 n. 27
Physics. *See* Body
Physiology, 19, 20, 53, 110, 113, 118, 212, 241, 259; psychobiology and, 20, 135–44, 149 n. 16, 213, 231–32, 247. *See also* Mind-body
Pineal gland, 44, 45, 121, 124, 125–29, 133, 151 n. 25, 152 n. 31, 167–68, 181, 185, 262
Planets, 189, 190, 207–8, 215, 228 n. 27, 285
Political philosophy, Descartes' contribution to, 8, 21, 22, 239, 247, 249, 251 n. 17, 267
Political science. *See* Ethics
Presentment (forethought), 180–89, 212, 217, 265, 281, 288, 291–93
Pressure, of light. *See* Effort; Light
Problem-solving, 33, 37–43, 50, 54–60, 61, 64, 66, 83 n. 5. 86 nn. 20, 21, 93

nn. 36, 46, 94 n. 48, 104–5, 117, 189, 249 n. 2, 258, 264, 270, 276–78
Prometean philanthropy, 248. *See also* Generosity
Pythagoreans, 24 n. 9

Reconnoissance. See Gratitude
Res, 98–99, 148 n. 8, 172, 221 n. 8, 226 n. 23, 233, 267, 270

Scholasticism and Descartes, 8–11
Science, social, 83 n. 8; mechanics and, 4–7. *See also* Ethics
Science of nature. *See* Mechanics
Secondary qualities, 103, 146 n. 6
Self-preservation, 1, 16, 31, 59, 73, 88 n. 24, 105, 108, 127, 212, 226 n. 23, 227 n. 25. *See also* Conservation
Self-sufficiency, 246–47
Sensation, 101–3, 115, 119, 135, 141, 150 n. 20, 151 n. 27, 158, 188, 264. *See also* Idea; Neuroanatomy; Vision
Set theory, 270
Shapes. *See* Idea
Solar systems, 191, 288
Soul. *See* Mind-body
Species. *See* Analysis, objects of geometry and
Specious arithmetic, 48–49
Stars, 180–88, 191, 193, 195–215, 285
Stoicism, 249 nn. 3, 5
Sun spots, 193–94, 200–205, 211. *See also* Circulatory systems
Symbols, 41, 53, 61–62, 70–73, 76–82, 91 n. 32, 99 n. 48, 117, 133–35, 178, 259, 261; Vieta's *symbolae*, 62, 64
Systems of the human body, 20, 97, 119, 143, 192, 203–4

Tendency, 285, 288–89
Threaded particles. *See* Magnetism
Tourbillons. See Whirlpools
Tree of Philosophy, 174

Virtue. *See* Ethics
Vision, 45, 179–89; blind men and, 183; telescopes and, 180–81; visionaries and, 265
Visionaries, 248. *See also* Hampson, Norman; Kinglake. Arthur W.

The Johns Hopkins University Press

DESCARTES' MEDICAL PHILOSOPHY

The Organic Solution
to the Mind-Body Problem

*This book was composed in Baskerville text and display
type by The Composing Room of Michigan, Inc., from a
design by Susan P. Fillion. It was printed on S. D.
Warren's 50-lb. Sebago Cream Offset and bound in
Holliston Roxite A by Universal Lithographers, Inc.*